Energy Science, Engineering and Technology

nova science publishers

www.novapublishers.com

Energy Science, Engineering and Technology

Integrated Energy Systems: Design, Control and Operation
Bikram Das (Editor)
Abanishwar Chakraborti (Editor)
Arvind Kumar Jain (Editor)
Subhadeep Bhattacharjee (Editor)
2023. ISBN: 979-8-89113-206-1 (Softcover)
2023. ISBN: 979-8-89113-227-6 (eBook)

Photovoltaic Systems: Advances in Research and Applications
Sudip Mandal, PhD (Editor)
Pijush Dutta, PhD (Editor)
2023. ISBN: 979-8-89113-102-6 (eBook)

Fuel Briquettes Made of Carbon-Containing Technogenic Raw Materials
Nina Buravchuk, PhD (Editor)
Olga Guryanova (Editor)
2023. ISBN: 979-8-88697-907-7 (Softcover)
2023. ISBN: 979-8-88697-944-2 (eBook)

The Fundamentals of Thermal Analysis
Mamdouh El Haj Assad, PhD (Editor)
Ali Khosravi, PhD (Editor)
Mehran Hashemian, PhD (Editor)
2023. ISBN: 979-8-88697-759-2 (Hardcover)
2023. ISBN: 979-8-88697-875-9 (eBook)

More information about this series can be found at
https://novapublishers.com/product-category/series/energy-science-engineering-and-technology/

Brian D'Andrade
Editor

Computer Engineering Applications in Electronic, Biomedical, and Automotive Systems

nova
science publishers
www.novapublishers.com

NOTICE TO THE READER

Library of Congress Cataloging-in-Publication Data

ISBN: 979-8-89113-488-1

Published by Nova Science Publishers, Inc. † New York

Contents

Preface

Computer Engineering covers a broad range of applications and overlaps with other engineering fields. This book provides insight into a few applications in electronics, medical, and the automotive fields where advances in robotics, embedded systems, and sensors are creating a bold future. The chapters are written from the perspective of scientists and engineering consultants who have highly broad experiences across multliple vendors and manufacturers of computer systems.

Chapter 1 – In this chapter, we explore the transformative impact of miniaturization, artificial intelligence, and wireless technology on consumer products, which has given rise to a diverse range of wearable electronic devices. We delve into the evolution, current status, and forthcoming trends in this field, emphasizing key features, potential pitfalls, and crucial safety considerations.

Chapter 2 – Robotics is a meeting point for many different disciplines, as robots incorporate mechanical, electrical, computational, and software aspects. This chapter focuses on electrical and computational topics in robotics, describing planning and control algorithms for achieving desired motions, as well as surveying various state-of-the-art on-board computational hardware options available to designers for achieving cutting-edge robotic performance.

Chapter 3 – Image Processing and Computer Vision are playing a transformative role in science and engineering, such as in the domains of material science and industry 4.0. In this chapter, the authors provide examples on computer vision applications that can be developed for Industry 4.0.

Chapter 4 – This chapter describes the applications of integrated circuits in the automotive electronic/electrical components as vehicles evolves toward autonomous, connected, electric and shared mobility. It lays out the stringent standard requirements for the integrated circuits to exhibit high levels of reliability in the unique automotive environment. This chapter further discusses the failure mechanisms related to semiconductor devices and the various failure analysis techniques applicable to investigate the root causes.

Chapter 5 – In this chapter, we focus on important thermal factors that are considered during the conceptual design stage of an electronic system. We present different examples of overheating effects on the detrimental lifetime of electronic devices. We detail the fundamental physics and theoretical models needed for electronic thermal design. Moreover, this chapter covers different thermal materials used for effective heat removal from an electronic chip. Finally, we discuss various emerging thermal systems that have the potential to address chip cooling challenges in future electronic systems.

Chapter 6 – This chapter describes how utilizing both Lean Manufacturing and Six Sigma can aid in implementing a robust process controls system in the manufacturing of integrated circuits. It discusses statistical process control charts and industry rules of thumb as a mechanism to quantify the impact of varying conditions on quality. The chapter further discusses Lean Manufacturing and Lean Maintenance strategies that can reduce waste in semiconductor manufacturing.

Chapter 7 – This chapter introduces the premise of quantum computing, its computational advantages in comparison to conventional computing techniques, the fundamental building blocks necessary for achieving such a computing system, the logical processes employed to perform meaningful operations, and the challenge of mapping hardware to control software. This chapter further discusses software tools and technologies designed for enabling computer scientists and engineers to explore quantum computing approaches and develop associated algorithms, while not requiring users have a detailed knowledge of quantum mechanics.

Chapter 8 – Advancements in energy storage technologies are enabling the success of modern electronic systems. Lithium-ion batteries have been adopted as the storage means of choice for most rechargeable mobile products, like laptops and cell phones, because of their relatively high storage density, voltage potential, and long lifespan. This chapter focuses on the safety of lithium battery systems.

Chapter 9 – This chapter discusses Advanced Driver Assistance Systems which have seen an increased rate of deployment on new vehicle models in the last decade. While there is no unified definition of such systems, it they generally refers to a suite of support features that provide warnings to the driver and/or some degree of vehicle control to assist the driver with the driving task.

Chapter 10 – This chapter discusses the progress in medical robotics, specifically looking at commercially successful robotic devices that have received FDA approval. It also explores the challenges this field faces and considers its future direction. The chapter emphasizes the importance of using computational modeling and simulation for designing, validating, and verifying these devices, as well as for conducting clinical trials.

Acknowledgements

I would like to acknowledge Nancy Rivera for her efforts to get all the materials ready for publication and Jessica Austin for creating graphics for this book.

Chapter 1

Wearable Electronic Devices and Technologies

M. Hossein M. Kouhani[1,*], PhD, PE
Kyle D. Murray[1], PhD
Zachary A. Lamport[2], PhD
and Surya Sharma[3], PhD
[1]Exponent, Inc., Phoenix, AZ, USA
[2]Exponent, Inc., New York, NY, USA
[3]Exponent, Inc., Menlo Park, CA, USA

Abstract

In microelectronics, artificial intelligence and wireless technology have led to the development of various form factors of wearable electronic devices, connecting human beings with their surrounding digital ecosystem with ever-increasing convenience and an accelerating adoption. In this chapter we provide a perspective on past efforts, the current state of technology, and future trends, with a close look at popular features, some of the failure modes, and important safety considerations.

Introduction

Integrating the human body with computing devices safely in small form factors and with long-lasting performance has been a central goal for twenty-first century technologists. Wearable technology encompasses any electronic device that is worn either in proximity to the skin or on it. These devices detect,

[*] Corresponding Author's Email: hosseinkouhani@gmail.com.

In: Computer Engineering Applications …
Editor: Brian D'Andrade
ISBN: 979-8-89113-488-1

analyze, and transmit signals of the ambient environment, but are typically aimed at relaying information about the wearer. Devices that enter the human body or are inserted anywhere under the skin fall outside of the family of wearable devices; these are typically called implantable devices.

Table 1. Examples of wearable electronic device categories and products

Category	Brand	Type	Need/Outcome Monitored
Smart Clothes/ Patches/ Straps/ Textiles/ Masks	Nix	Biosensor	Hydration
	Apollo	Nerve Stimulator	Stress Reducer
	QardinoCore	Electrocardiogram Sensor	Cardiac Monitoring
	Lumo BodyTech	Posture Sensor	Biomechanical Feedback
	WiemsPro	Muscle-Stimulation	Electro-muscle Stimulation
	Clottech	Heated Jacket	All-weather Clothes
	PneuHaptic	Pneumatic Band	Visuo-Haptic Interface
	BodyBeat	Clip-On Device	Audio-Haptic Interface
	Kailo	Smart Patch	Pain Relief
Head-Mounted Artificial Reality/Virtual Reality (AR/VR) Smart Glasses/ Contact Lenses	Sensimed Triggerfish	Contact Lens	Eye Pressure Sensing/Glaucoma
	Microsoft HoloLens	AR/VR Headset	Interactive Mixed Reality Interface
	Oculus Quest	AR/VR Headset	Interactive Mixed Reality Interface
	Google Glass	AR/VR Headset	Interactive Mixed Reality Interface
Smartwatch Fitness/Health Trackers	Samsung Galaxy	Smartwatch	Interactive Fitness Tracker & Watch
	Google Pixel	Smartwatch	Interactive Fitness Tracker & Watch
	Garmin	Smartwatch	Interactive Fitness Tracker & Watch
	Apple	Smartwatch	Interactive Fitness Tracker & Watch
Smart Jewelry	Oura	Smart Ring/Sensor	Fitness, Stress, Sleep & Health
	McLear	Smart Ring/Radio-frequency Identification	Contactless Payment
	Bellabeat	Smart Ring/Sensor	Women Health Tracker
	Leaf	Smart Ring/Sensor	Sleep and Fitness Tracker
	BodiMetrics	Smart Ring/Sensor	Blood Oxygen Saturation and Heart Rate Tracker
	Circular	Smart Ring/Sensor	Fitness, Stress, Sleep & Health

As a result of advancements in wireless electronics, today's wearable devices and their linked gadgets enable the capture and access of data in real time without the need to offload and upload data using memory cards or cables. This expansion of use and development of wearable devices has allowed for the growth and integration of a digital ecosystem and the anticipated Internet-of-Everything (IoE).

The promise of technology integrating seamlessly with the human body is the driving force behind wearable technology. The gadgets one wears that can sense things and talk to us, like a watch that reports our heartbeat, can also send data immediately, allowing real-time diagnostics and information. Sending information from the body to devices in our immediate surroundings, such as from our watch to our refrigerator, IoE promises meshed, integrated, and harmonized electronics and computation. Wearable devices can sense stimuli around us and about us, providing feedback through advanced processing and data integration techniques.

We are on the brink of witnessing devices that redefine our reality. Eyeglasses project holographic screens, letting us access information with a mere glance; rings not only adorn our fingers, but also monitor our health, sending real-time updates to our phones; clothing adapts to our body temperature, ensuring unparalleled comfort in any environment. The symbiotic relationship between human and machine is evolving, transforming ordinary experiences into extraordinary ones. We are moving towards a world where our devices anticipate our needs, providing insights before we even ask. Some main categories of wearable devices are summarized in Table 1.

Early Inventions

Throughout history, humans have been on a continuous quest to develop methods of observing, overseeing, and enhancing a range of bodily functions. This pursuit has evolved alongside consistent technological progress in both mechanical and electronic devices. In the fourteenth century, wearable spectacles were invented, primarily designed to address long-distance vision issues. These spectacles (called goggles) lacked side arms, were positioned on the bridge of the nose, and featured quartz lenses nestled in frames crafted from wood, bone, or metal. A replica of the first spectacles with a bone frame is depicted in an investigative article in which the author also presents other paintings illustrating men wearing these early versions of spectacles [1]. Moving forward three centuries, portable timepieces created by European innovators gained popularity and were worn by many as symbols of high social standing. At the Uffizi Gallery in Florence, a circa 1560 painting of the Duke of Florence, Cosimo I de Medici, shows him with an early pocket watch [2].

In addition to wearable spectacles and portable timepieces, another early invention in wearable devices was the abacus ring. This device is thought to have been invented during the Ming Dynasty [1368-1644] by Cheng Dawei, a famous mathematician who lived from 1533-1606 [3]. A 300-year-old example of an abacus ring features a small abacus (1.2 cm long by 0.7 cm wide), typically with beads that could be moved along the ring to perform arithmetic calculations [3]. They were worn on the fingers, allowing individuals to perform calculations without the need for external tools or writing surfaces. Abacus rings were particularly popular in cultures where mathematics and accounting were essential skills, and they served as early wearable aids for mathematical calculations. Although the above examples may seem rudimentary compared to the innovations that are commonplace today, they represent some of the earliest steps towards augmenting human capabilities through external, wearable means.

Growing Market

According to a recent study from the global technology intelligence firm ABI Research, the number of wearables shipped worldwide in 2020 increased to 259.63 million, with sports, fitness, and wellness trackers accounting for 112.15 million and smartwatches accounting for 74.30 million [4]. The upward trend is predicted to continue due to the increasing number of uses and improved features. The wearable technology market is projected to grow from USD 53.1 billion in 2023 to USD 466.5 billion by 2032—a compound annual growth rate of 31.2% during the forecast period [5].

Several factors and key trends drive the accelerating adoption of wearables including:

1. *Prioritization of Health:* Since the Coronavirus disease (COVID-19) pandemic and its long-term effects on the habits and lifestyle of billions of people, health and fitness are increasingly prioritized by individuals and government bodies. From body temperature to blood pressure, blood sugar to electrocardiograms (ECG), blood oxygen saturation (SpO2) to movement and sleep quality, consumer interest

in health and fitness monitoring devices continues to increase. Moreover, research and development in personalized medical connectivity tailored to special conditions and specific diseases continues to increase, leading to not-yet-fully-realized, but game-changing novel signals to track and monitor medical outcomes. The fitness tracker market was valued at around USD 39.5 billion in 2022 and is estimated to grow to approximately USD 187.2 billion in 2032, a compound annual growth rate of slightly over 17.3% between 2023 and 2032 [6].

2. *Convenience:* Wearable devices offer easier methods to engage with technology and obtain information without using a phone or laptop. Wearables are more convenient to use and less heavy than traditional gadgets because they can be worn on the wrist or fastened to clothing. Consider a busy professional in a meeting who receives an important notification. Instead of disrupting the flow of the meeting by reaching for a phone, the individual discreetly glances at their smartwatch, quickly assessing the urgency of the message without drawing attention away from the discussion. This unobtrusive interaction showcases the seamless integration of technology, allowing for efficient multitasking without compromising social etiquette.
3. *Technological Advances:* The inexorable trend of miniaturization, as exemplified by Moore's Law, is an inevitable force driving technological progress. This principle, articulated by Gordon Moore, asserts that the number of transistors on a microchip doubles approximately every two years, leading to exponential growth in processing power. This paradigmatic principle is not exclusive; wearables also adhere to this trajectory, benefitting from ongoing advancements in power and processing technologies. For example, Intel Corporation is working on novel materials (just three atoms thick) that are expected to enable fitting 1 trillion transistors in one package by 2030 [7].
4. *Spread of 5G Access:* Faster data transfer, increases in the number of connected nodes in a network, and the enormous amount of data generated by or fed into wearable devices leaves no other option than to integrate 5G chipsets into these devices. To further illustrate the significance of 5G integration, let us delve into the realm of augmented reality (AR). AR glasses, which overlay digital information onto the user's physical surroundings, rely heavily on real-time data processing and ultra-low latency connections. For

instance, professional technicians wearing AR glasses could receive step-by-step instructions to repair a complex machine, with digital annotations guiding their hands and ensuring precise execution. In this context, a lag or delay in data transmission could lead to errors, safety hazards, or decreased productivity.

Application Domains for Wearable Devices

Wearable devices have many applications across commercial domains including medicine and healthcare; health, fitness, and sports performance; entertainment; the clothing industry; as well as in the government domain and the military. In medical applications, wearable technology can be used for patient monitoring, disease detection, and health history. For example, common wearables applications include real-time vital sign monitoring in healthcare environments, glucose monitoring for diabetes management, and detection of sleep apnea. Several companies are working on implantable devices that can be paired with wearable technology for glucose monitoring [8]. Another real-time monitoring capability that can be paired with smartphones or smartwatches are ECGs to monitor heart rate (HR) and heart rate variability (HRV). Several types of sensors can be used to obtain ECG readings, which can be very important for patient status updates and treatment plans.

Further, wearable technology is being leveraged to include monitoring capabilities for mental health. Research groups have recently demonstrated that certain devices may be used to detect and monitor anxiety and stress, which may help to inform mental health treatment plans [9]. Finally in the medical domain, wearable technology is being incorporated in patient monitoring platforms such as open-source Integrated Clinical Environments [10] to provide clinicians and other medical staff with real-time patient health updates to effectively prioritize care across patients, while simultaneously providing patients with personal health data to keep them more informed of their own care. As open-source platforms such as this become more widely implemented throughout the healthcare industry, wearables have the potential to revolutionize patient care.

In the sports performance domain, wearable fitness and health trackers are used by millions of people to inform users of fitness progress during and after exercise activities. For professional athletes, several companies, including Nike and Under Armor, are developing smart shoes and fitness trackers specifically aimed to measuring physiological and positioning data for athletes to improve performance over time [11]. Data-driven approaches to health and fitness are becoming more mainstream and common for professional athletes, casual users, and all levels of athletes in between. For example, in the running community, runners can use smartwatches such as those from Apple, Fitbit, or Garmin, to measure HR, HRV, SpO2, the maximum rate of oxygen consumption attainable during physical exertion (VO2 max), velocity, and global positioning system (GPS) tracking over the course of a run. All these data can be viewed and analyzed after the activity to inform the runner about performance, such as how many miles were run (GPS), mile split times (velocity and GPS), exertion levels that can be classified by HR zones at each stage of the run (HR, velocity, acceleration, and GPS), and overall health over the course of the run (HR, HRV, SpO2, VO2 max, GPS, and velocity).

Other kinds of wearable devices can be used to monitor health performance, including bands, respiration belts, and rings; some prominent gyms even provide customers with access to wearable monitoring technology to help track their progress with strength training regimens over time. Additionally, machine learning (ML) algorithms are being integrated into applications on wearable devices and external devices that use wearable data to predict measures of fitness.

In the entertainment industry, wearable technology is being incorporated via smart clothing, smart glasses, and smart jewelry, for both fashion and functionality. For example, Google released Google Glass, which are smart glasses that can wirelessly communicate with other devices to display videos and data for the user. Other kinds of head-mounted devices are commonly used for VR and AR. VR headsets use wearable sensors to track head, body, and eye movement of users, which allow users to interact with virtual environments in natural and intuitive ways. AR is another form of VR that superimposes virtual content over the real-world experiences of the individual. Prominent companies that have wearable technologies for VR and AR include Google, Apple, Samsung, and Microsoft [12]. VR and AR demonstrate the application of wearables to enhance immersive experiences of users in both virtual and real-world environments.

Additionally, wearable technology is being used to provide users customized and exclusive entertainment and hospitality experiences. For example, Disney introduced Magic Bands for all park visitors, which include functionality that allows the bands to interact with sensors around the entire park, such as park entrances, restaurants, and hotel rooms. This provides each visitor a simple way to quickly experience things around the park and provides users with fast and easy ways to pay for merchandise or food by linking the Magic Bands to credit cards. Overall, wearable technology is continuing to expand into the entertainment industry to provide users with engaging and customized experiences in several areas.

The use of wearable technology in the United States military is expected to expand over the next several years [13]. Wearable sensors and trackers have introduced relevant capabilities that may be leveraged in tactical and garrison environments [14]. In garrison environments, the fitness performance and medical health monitoring applications previously described can help inform warfighters and military leaders of warfighter health, readiness, and disease status. Several government programs are investing in wearable technology to support warfighters in every domain. For example, incorporating biometric trackers and introducing wearables-derived capabilities such as chemical and biological warfare exposure and earlier disease detection can help tactical leaders make faster and more informed decisions about the readiness and status of troops and squads. Other physiological-based wearables capabilities that may be of use in the military include detection of dehydration, fatigue, hypothermia, hyperthermia, and sleep apnea, as well as disease prediction, COVID-19 detection and monitoring, and mental health monitoring, among other capabilities [15]. Sensors that provide geophysical data can help develop capabilities such as assured positioning, navigation, and timing in environments without GPS access, blue force tracking, and geofencing. With the wider inclusion of wearable devices and wearables-derived data capabilities, the safety and health of all warfighters can be more readily tracked and improved.

As can be seen, wearable devices are becoming increasingly prevalent and popular in contemporary society, with millions of devices sold each year. Wearables have increasingly complicated functionality and capabilities that can be leveraged in several domains across the commercial and government sectors. In this section, domain applications of wearable technology spanned medicine, fitness and sports performance, entertainment, and military operations. As wearables continue to improve and introduce greater technological advances in sensor and capability development, wearables are expected to increase in versality and demand in all these domains.

Form Factors for Wearable Devices

Wearable devices are available in many form factors, some more common than others. The form factor of a wearable device can greatly influence the use of the wearable in day-to-day life, for example, a study of 55 participants determined that most participants preferred a watch compared to a necklace or smart glasses [16]. Common form factors include:

1. Smart Watches
2. Head-Mounted Devices
3. Smart Rings
4. Necklaces
5. Hearables or Ear-worn Devices
6. Smart Textiles/Clothing
7. Wearable Cameras
8. Contact Lenses

Smartwatches are the most common wearable device form factor—followed by head-mounted devices used for meetings, video games, and entertainment; implantable sensors such as continuous glucose monitors (CGM); smart rings; smart textiles; and others that are less common. We discuss each form factor in detail below.

Smartwatches

Smartwatches are ubiquitous in society, partly due to widespread acceptance of wristwatches, and partly due to the wide range of capabilities that can be supported by a watch-sized computing device [17]. One of the key factors for the widespread adoption of smartwatches is the rise of fitness applications that are easy to use, as well as increased spending on consumer electronics by the population [18, 19]. The common sizes of wristwatches are large enough to allow for multiple electronic components to create a multi-functional device, such as microcontrollers with built-in memory and communication modules (Wi-Fi, Bluetooth), batteries, microphones, speakers, inertial measurement units (IMU), displays, and other sensors required for a wearable application.

Modern smartwatches such as those sold by Apple, Google, and Samsung run operating systems such as Apple's WatchOS, Google's WearOS, and

Samsung's Tizen, while those sold by Garmin or Fitbit may run proprietary operating systems to provide similar features. These operating systems allow the smartwatch to perform many functions, similar to mobile phones, by running applications to send emails or texts, show notifications, play music, or make payments using technologies such as near-field communication (NFC) radiofrequency identification (RFID) tags. Many smartwatches are equipped with virtual assistants with which one can interact using voice control to perform functions such as sending texts or make calls using the smartwatch.

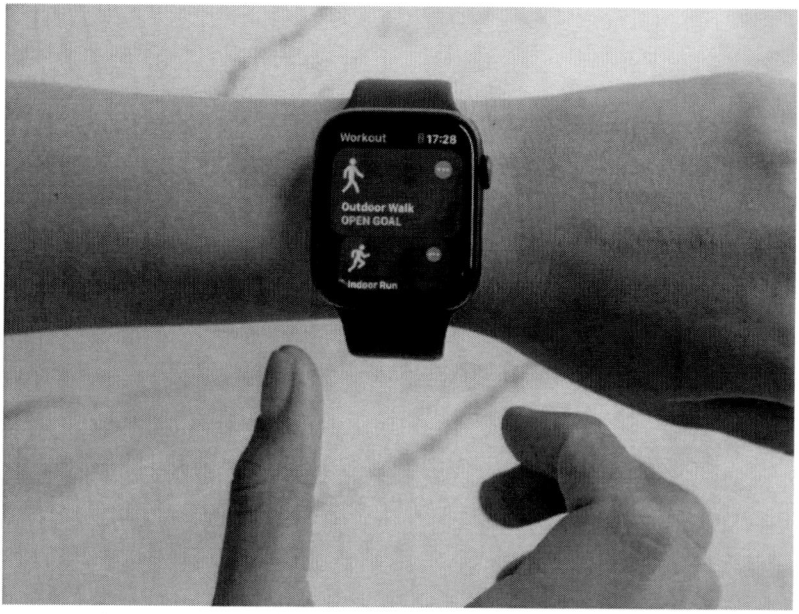

Figure 1. A user turning on activity tracking on an Apple smartwatch.

Additionally, their location on the wrist allows smartwatch developers to build in many applications that use internal sensors to detect motion and HR and obtain ECG data. Specifically, IMUs mounted on the wrist can track the direction of gravity, the rotation of the wrist, or coarse location data using magnetometers. Applications available on smartwatches can detect and log activities such as running, walking, cycling, rowing, eating, or smoking [20, 21]. Recently, Apple's smartwatch, shown in Figure 1, demonstrated the ability to detect heart attacks by tracking data from ECG sensors in the watch.

In addition, media reports indicate the potential to add CGM to future Apple smartwatch products [22].

The multiple uses of applications running on smartwatches has made this form factor very popular compared to others. Improvements in computers and electronics allow more powerful applications and systems to run on the smartwatch, making this form factor ripe for novel applications in the future.

Head-Mounted Devices

Helmets or goggles are wearables commonly known as HMDs. Like smartwatches, the size and form factor of HMDs allow these devices to run complex operating systems that can work in conjunction with other electrical components and sensors. The most well-known applications of HMDs are found in the entertainment and gaming domains, with Sony's PlayStation VR, Meta's Oculus headsets, HTC's Vive, and Valve's Index offering a VR experience by using stereoscopic displays in front of the eyes to simulate three-dimensional (3-D) environments. These devices contain built-in sensors to track the movements of the user or the user's head and adjust the images accordingly giving the user the feeling of interactivity or being present in the virtual environment.

Newer HMDs (for example those from Meta and Apple) are adding pass-through video features to their HMDs, which use cameras on the HMD to capture the point of view (POV) of a user, and then replay the video with additional overlays. This use of HMDs is commonly known as AR, mixed reality (MR), or extended reality (XR). This use of HMDs is also finding acceptance outside the entertainment industry, such as in the domain of healthcare and surgery, where researchers are using HMDs to provide remote surgery support. For example, the University of Washington has demonstrated their Virtual Interactive Presence in Augmented Reality (VIPAR) system. Their demonstration suggests use cases where a remote surgeon can provide surgical assistance to a local surgeon performing surgery inside an operating room; in this scenario, both surgeons wear HMDs [23]. Beyond the operating room, HMDs such as Microsoft's Hololens show promise in the field of education. In 2021, researchers showed how the Hololens can be used to deliver a remote access teaching experience while visiting a hospital ward. Most participants (8 out of 11) provided positive feedback of the system [24].

HMDs are also being used in industrial manufacturing plants. Smart glasses like Google Glass can provide industrial workers with reference material in their visual field. HMDs for use in the aviation industry have been tested by Boeing, General Electric, and Delta, and in the automotive industry by Toyota. In 2011, the company Daqri promoted its Smart Helmet for use in the manufacturing industry or at construction sites. Their Smart Helmet uses IMU and light detection and ranging (LIDAR) to localize itself in a work environment and provide a worker with visualized data. An HMD can guide a worker through difficult tasks using a see-through display, reducing the chance of error in the field [25]. HMDs also provide remote assistance from experts who can observe the worker's view of the environment and provide guidance and support [18].

HMDs have been used in the military for decades, first by pilots [26]. These HMDs displayed critical flight data and helped with weapon system information. Today, HMDs help enhance situational awareness, provide real-time data to warfighters, and monitor their health and performance in combat situations. These wearables provide a hands-free approach to access important information and display critical data. For example, some of the wearable devices feature AR technology that overlays digital information onto a real-world situation, helping warfighters identify potential threats and navigate complex environments [27]. These wearables are typically ruggedized to support their use in the military and can withstand harsh environmental conditions.

In summary, the wide-ranging capabilities of computing devices mounted near the head, and their ability to augment the visual field suggests a promising future for this form factor as it gains acceptance in the general population.

Smart Implants

The medical field has long made use of implantable devices since the development of cardiac pacemakers in 1958; this category now includes implantable cardiac defibrillators, cochlear implants, and other devices. As new applications become possible due to the advent of more flexible devices and substrates, along with the further miniaturization of individual components, more specialized active and diagnostic implants can be developed.

The inclusion of electronic devices into an aqueous environment such as the human body requires significant consideration to avoid causing harm to the user or the device [28]. Given the environment of the human body, any implanted device must be encapsulated such that electrolytic solutions do not intrude where sensitive components reside, but also so that any harmful materials or chemicals do not leach from the device to the body of the user.

Additional considerations are necessary for the power sources of implantable devices, where direct access to such devices could require surgery, so developments in high-density batteries, wireless charging, or other methods for charging the implanted device are critical to achieve a useful application [29].

The functionality for smart implants includes widely varied use cases in monitoring (e.g., brain sensor) or influencing the body (e.g., pacemaker) in some way, so the array of sensors that could exist in a smart implant includes a similarly wide variety of possible sensing modalities. For instance, sensors that monitor brain activity could use light or electrical signals, while devices that analyze biomarkers in blood may require chemical and electrical impedance sensors [30].

Smart Rings

Smart rings are currently a fledgling consumer application, where the form factor of the smartwatch is minimized, while retaining much of the functionality and sensor suite present in a smartwatch. The benefits of a smart ring include more consistent contact with the skin compared to a smartwatch that can separate slightly from the arm through twisting motions. Smart rings also have the ability to conduct measurements through the finger, whereas a smartwatch typically has sensors and light emitting diodes (LED) on the same side of the wrist. Commercial examples like the ŌURA ring include infrared photoplethysmography (PPG) sensors to measure HR, a temperature sensor to measure body temperature, and an accelerometer to track movement [31].

Smart Clothing/Textiles

Moving beyond form factors that more traditionally incorporate electronics, smart clothing and smart textiles are a burgeoning field that provides an untapped application space. The ability to integrate electronics into clothing offers the opportunity to collect and utilize an entirely new suite of data.

One example of smart clothing allows for a haptic response based on the movement of the wearer. Wearable X has developed a pair of yoga pants that tracks the wearer's movements and provides a haptic response to correct a yoga pose or to notify the wearer to move to the next pose [32].

Smart Glasses

Smart glasses are wearable devices equipped with computers and sensors in the eyeglasses form factor. This form factor is similar to HMDs but is less bulky and easier to use. Their size and common acceptance of eyeglasses and sunglasses enables a wide acceptance of smart glasses. The uses and applications for smart glasses are similar to those of HMDs, however their smaller size limits the electronic components that can be added to these devices. This form factor has found applications in multiple domains such as healthcare, medicine, field service, logistics, industrial worker safety, and the military.

In medicine, smart glasses have been used to improve on traditional glasses to provide assistance to people with impaired vision. A smart reader demonstrated by Punith and colleagues was designed to identify text in front of the viewer, convert the text to speech, and then read the text to the viewer through earphones [33]. Another rendition of a similar concept provides speech-to-text features for use at night—providing the ability to recognize obstacles at night [34].

Smart glasses share many other use cases with HMDs, such as assisting with surgical procedures, or helping surgeons view and interact with patient data. Google's Glass is a well-known example of commercially available smart glasses. These glasses have been used to evaluate patients for surgery, obtain patient records, photograph surgeries, display vital signs during a surgery, and communicate with other physicians [35-38].

Smart glasses are also used in the consumer electronics domain; for example, Snap's Spectacles and Ray Ban's Stories both contain cameras that can record point-of-view videos for the wearer, which can be shared on social media, while Bose's Frames are sunglasses equipped with speakers.

Sensors and Sensing Modalities in Wearable Devices

There are several categories of wearable sensors that allow for the capabilities described previously in each of the various application domains. These categories include:

- Physiological Sensors
    - Heartbeat
    - Electromyography (EMG)
    - Biometric and Bioimpedance
    - PPG
    - SpO2
- Geophysical Sensors
    - Inertial Sensors
    - GPS
- Environmental Sensors
    - Temperature
    - Chemical and Biochemical Sensors
    - Microphones

This section provides a brief overview of some of the major sensors and sensing modalities that are currently used in wearable devices.

Physiological Sensors

Bioimpedance

Bioimpedance sensors use electrical or impedance sensors to measure the electrical properties of living tissues. An example of the functionality of a bioimpedance sensor is a small electrical current applied to the body to measure resistance and reactance of the resulting electrical signal detected at the sensor. This works similarly to some types of chemical sensors described below. The resistance and reactance readings can be used to calculate impedance of the skin and body, which can provide information on several physiological metrics, such as HR, respiration rate, and hydration level.

Several wearable devices use electrical or bioimpedance sensors for health monitoring. The ŌURA ring, for example, uses bioimpedance sensors to monitor HR, HRV, body temperature, and respiration rate. Bioimpedance measurements provide real-time biofeedback that can be used in a variety of settings, including fitness and exercise regimens and therapeutic treatment responses. Bioimpedance sensors can also be incorporated into patches or straps to obtain information relating to stress, anxiety, sleep quality, and disease monitoring.

Heartbeat Sensors

ECG sensors are used in wearable devices to measure the electrical activity of the heart. An ECG sensor typically consists of at least two electrodes that are placed against the skin across the heart, with an electrolytic gel to increase the transmission of electrical signals of the heart to the sensors. This combination of electrodes detects electrical signals throughout the heartbeat cycle. The measured signals at the electrodes process the raw signals via amplification, filtering, and other signal processing techniques to produce the ECG waveform. This processed ECG waveform represents the activity of the heart and thus ECG sensors may be used to measure the heartbeat during various kinds of activities. ECG readings are commonly used to diagnose heart conditions, including arrythmias such as atrial or ventricular fibrillation, myocardial infarctions, and heart failure.

In general, an ECG is the most clinically accepted heartbeat waveform sensor. These sensors are burdensome to use, however, in daily activities and are prone to data collection errors if the user undergoes heavy motion, or is subject to other electromagnetic equipment, such as a magnetic resonance imaging (MRI) machine. For MRI applications, researchers are continuing to improve signal processing techniques to reliably incorporate noisy ECG signals in functional MRI (fMRI) studies. Since ECG sensors are not straightforward to use for daily activities, more portable kinds of sensors for daily use may be used to measure HR, HRV, or the electrical signals of the heart.

Wearable devices that can inform on HR data include pulse oximeters and smartwatches. Pulse oximeters use LED pulses to measure the transmission of different wavelengths of light through the skin to detect changes in SpO2 levels as a function of time to provide a sense of how quickly blood is pumped throughout the body, which is directly related to HR. Smartwatches, on the other hand, use different technology to estimate the ECG waveform without using typical ECG electrodes.

Electromyography

EMG is a technique used to measure the electrical activity of muscles. These sensors measure the electrical activity of contracting muscles and are typically adhered or tightly strapped to the skin at the point where muscular activity is to be measured. The electrical signals detected from muscle activity is then processed to provide information on the timing and strength of the muscle contractions.

EMG sensors in wearable devices are used for fitness tracking, sports performance monitoring, and physical therapy. The Myo armband [39] is one example on the market of EMG sensors incorporated in a wearable device, which uses several EMG sensors to measure signals from the forearms. Athos fitness apparel [40] is another example, which uses EMG sensors in compression shirts and shorts to monitor muscle activation during exercise. Applications of forearm signals include the ability to control devices with simple gestures, while apparel EMG sensors can be used to provide feedback on the forms of movement and muscular imbalances in real-time.

EMG sensors also inform on rehabilitation, robotics, and physical therapy. By monitoring the activation of muscles, EMG can analyze movement patterns, track muscular fatigue, and provide feedback on the improvement of muscular performance to prevent injury and facilitate faster recovery. Physical therapists commonly use EMG sensors to help patients recover from muscular injuries and neuromuscular disorders. In the field of robotics, EMG sensors are being integrated into prosthetic limbs to improve their overall control and functionality. Future applications of EMG sensors may include the control of assistive devices or brain-machine interfacing applications.

Photoplethysmography Sensors

PPG sensors are one of the most ubiquitous features included in wearable devices, and typically include a pulsed LED and a photodiode used to measure light reflected from the skin. The wearer's HR can then be determined by monitoring the change in reflected light as the volume of blood changes in the microvasculature near the surface of the skin. Further information can be gained from examining the signal from the photodiode, including the relative oxygen saturation because of the different light absorbance of oxygenated and deoxygenated hemoglobin, as discussed below.

SpO2

SpO2 is a measurement of oxygen saturation in the blood. SpO2 sensors are non-invasive optical sensors that emit and detect light through the skin. Like pulse oximeters, the absorption of light is dependent on the SpO2 level at any point in time. As such, for SpO2 readings, the absorption of light in response to an LED pulse can be used to determine the amount of oxygen in the blood at any given time. A typical measurement of SpO2 uses electromagnetic waves in the red and infrared wavelength ranges, by which a ratio of the two signals can be used to estimate SpO2 levels. More recent devices use a green light, since a red light is more prone to errors arising from movement because it can penetrate further into tissue. SpO2 measurements are particularly applicable to respiratory conditions and sports performance monitoring.

In addition to applications in respiratory monitoring and sports performance, SpO2 sensors gained popularity during the COVID-19 pandemic. One of the potential symptoms of the COVID-19 virus is a decrease in SpO2 levels. Several companies developed wearable devices to monitor COVID-19, such as the Whoop Strap 3.0 [41] and the ŌURA ring. These devices use a combination of SpO2 sensors and other sensors to track symptoms and predict an early onset detection method. SpO2 sensors are also used in other contexts in hospitals and clinics to monitor patients with respiratory illnesses, including pneumonia and acute respiratory distress syndrome.

Geophysical Sensors

Motion

Motion sensors, also known as inertial measurement units (IMUs), are commonly used to detect the motion of users via wearable devices. IMUs may include sensors such as accelerometers to measure linear acceleration, gyroscopes to measure rotational inertia, gravimeters to measure the local gravitational field, and magnetometers to measure local magnetic fields, and therefore the orientation of the device with respect to the earth's geomagnetic field. By combining data from these various inertial sensors, accurate positioning, device orientation, and movement can be realized.

IMUs are heavily relied upon to track physical activity and provide accurate and reliable health and fitness data. Other biometric sensors can be further incorporated, such as a sensor to detect or estimate calories burned, to provide a more wholistic understanding of the overall fitness level of users. The Apple smartwatch includes a tracking feature to automatically detect workouts and falls, which allows for automated tracking of physical exertion without the user needing to activate a tracking capability. The WHOOP strap uses IMUs to track sleep patterns, training, and recovery data for athletes [41]. Fitbit uses accelerometers to track or estimate the number of steps taken, distance traveled, and number of stairs climbed [42].

IMUs have applications that extend beyond health and fitness monitoring and tracking, including VR, AR, navigation, and medicine. IMUs are used to track user motion, which help to inform data relevant to more immersive gaming experiences and AR. In healthcare, motion sensors can be used to track the motion of patients and help to provide feedback on patient recovery and rehabilitation in response to treatment plans and protocols. In robotics, IMUs are used to track and control movements of robots. Overall, motion sensors in wearable technology are powerful techniques that can be utilized to understand the movement and behavior of humans and machines. As sensor technology continues to develop, there is an expectation that applications of motion sensors for wearable devices will also expand into even more domains and industrial areas.

Global Positioning System

GPS sensors on devices utilize the global navigation satellite system (GNSS) to determine the precise location of a device. A GPS sensor in a wearable device receives signals from several GPS satellites to determine the distance between the device and each satellite. By calculating the distances to at least three satellites, it is possible to uniquely determine the position of the device with high accuracy via triangulation. In the same manner, a GPS sensor can track the position, speed, and direction of movement of a device by continuously receiving signals from satellites.

Wearable devices that incorporate GPS sensors include sports watches, fitness trackers, and smartwatches. Garmin, Apple, and Fitbit, among others, use GPS sensors to track outdoor activities and provide real-time information on running, hiking, and cycling routes, distance traveled, speed, and elevation gains. Apple and Samsung also provide location-based services such as navigation via their respective smartwatches. Other applications of GPS sensors in wearable devices include location tracking of individuals, geofencing, and transportation logistics monitoring.

Environmental Sensors

Temperature

Temperature sensors can be used to measure the temperature of the environment or more targeted applications, such as the skin of a user. Temperature sensors detect changes in resistance or voltage across electrical components such as local or ambient temperature changes. Examples of temperature sensors incorporated in wearable devices include thermistors, resistance temperature detectors (RTD), and thermocouples. These temperature sensors can be incorporated into wearable devices in flexible strips placed directly on the skin or as part of an on-chip embedded system in a device.

Fitbit [43] uses temperature sensors in their products. For example, the Fitbit Sense contains a temperature sensor to track changes in skin temperature throughout the day and overnight, which can be used to gain insights into a user's overall health and wellbeing. Tracking skin temperature overnight can help inform users of the quality of their sleep patterns and cycles. Several manufacturers specifically included temperature sensing in devices with the express purpose of monitoring COVID-19 throughout the pandemic. For example, BioIntelliSense's BioButton [44] was designed to continuously monitor temperature for up to 90 days.

The widespread practicality of temperature as a data metric makes temperature readings particularly applicable to several applications, including monitoring of body temperature; detecting hypothermia, hyperthermia, and fevers; and monitoring ambient environmental conditions. Temperature monitoring is especially relevant in medical applications to monitor patient health. Temperature sensors on wearable devices provide a convenient and simple way to obtain a more comprehensive understanding of a user's health. Further, temperature readings may also be combined with data from other sensors to develop a more complete picture of the health.

Chemical Sensors

Chemical sensors are hardware that can detect and quantify chemical compounds or changes in environmental chemicals. For example, many wearable devices can monitor chemical biomarkers such as glucose, lactate, and cortisol in sweat. Typically, in the case of chemical detection in bodily fluids, the sensor encounters the fluid and the signals measured are processed to calculate relevant chemical information.

One example of a chemical monitoring device that makes use of chemical sensors is META's glucoWISE [45] glucose monitoring system. The glucoWISE device utilizes a non-invasive electrochemical sensor to measure glucose levels in the interstitial fluid of the skin. To measure glucose levels, the device is placed in contact with the skin where a small electric current is applied to stimulate glucose in the skin to react with the sensor. The sensor then receives the current remaining after passing through the resistance of the skin, which allows for an algorithm to calculate the glucose level in the skin.

Another example of a chemical monitoring device is the Gatorade GX sweat patch [46], which combines several sensors and calorimetric assays to quantify sweat composition, including electrolytes, glucose, and lactate. This patch can be worn directly on the skin during exercise and sweat composition can be displayed on a smartphone application (app). These two examples of glucose monitoring can also be applied to medical applications for CGM for disease management.

The BACTrack Skyn [47] is another product that uses chemical sensors. The wearable uses a transdermal alcohol sensor to measure transdermal alcohol content (TAC) [48]. These TAC measurements are converted to analog or digital signals that can be stored by a microcontroller. A supporting mobile app continuously reads TAC values from the microcontroller and uses ML algorithms to convert these values to blood alcohol content (BAC), informing wearers of their sobriety levels. Such a wearable can inform users of safe conditions for activity, and used as a tool by law enforcement.

In sports performance, chemical monitoring is used to help athletes optimize training regimens by monitoring changes in sweat composition and hydration levels. For environmental applications, chemical sensors may be used to detect and monitor pollutants or other harmful substances in the environment. This application can also be used in military tactical environments to inform on chemical and biochemical attacks and chemical warfare.

Microphones

Microphones are sensors commonly included in wearable devices to record and analyze audio signals. Microphones detect changes in the air pressure of sound waves and convert them into electrical signals. These signals can then be processed using various techniques to perform various tasks, such as noise cancellation or speech or song recognition. Microphones are also used in smartwatches to allow users to interact with the device. For example, the Apple Watch features a built-in microphone by which a user can initiate and maintain a phone conversation and interact with virtual assistants. Similarly, Google Glass uses a microphone to capture voice commands from the user for hands-free operation.

Microphones can also be used in fitness, health, and environmental monitoring. For example, breathing rates can be detected from sound waves and used to detect sleep apnea. As another example, ambient environmental noise levels can be measured, which may help inform which safety measures to include while working in loud or hazardous conditions.

The sensors and sensing modalities that are incorporated into wearable devices are a subset of the sensors available on the market today. Research is being performed to develop new sensing modalities and improvements are being made to existing sensors to increase reliability and accuracy of the data features derived from these sensors. Further, new technologies are being incorporated into future generations of wearable device sensors, such as the use of quantum technology for increased accuracy and reliability. As sensor technology develops, wearable devices will continue to gain additional capabilities beyond what is available today.

Artificial Intelligence and Machine Learning Algorithms for Wearable Devices

The previous sections discussed many types of wearable devices, their sensors, and their components. A large driver of the capabilities of modern wearable devices are the computational algorithms that process the data collected by these devices and present it back to the user. Artificial intelligence (AI) and ML are often credited for processing collected data. For example, VR devices and head mounted units can track the motion sensor and location data of the wearer, process these data along with other inputs such as camera feeds and limb locations using ML algorithms, then generate a realistic image to the user of the VR device. Similarly, the Apple Watch and Fitbit devices track wrist motion, PPG, ECG, GPS, and other sensor data, then process these data using ML algorithms and present information to the user through mobile phone applications or on-screen notifications on the device.

In the past, computer algorithms were sets of instructions executed by a computing device to perform specific, well-defined tasks. The output of such algorithms was well defined and deterministic, and often used mathematical models developed by a human to process data. Consequently, the models once developed were rarely changed. The data supplied to such computer algorithms were often structured, such as in the form of numerical or textual data. Programmers often speculated whether machines and computers powered by these algorithms could think or be "artificially intelligent" [49]. Consider the example of algorithms that can play chess. To a human player, the computer demonstrates intelligence. By modelling the game of chess using formal mathematical rules, and setting a rigid mathematical objective, a computer algorithm can demonstrate the ability to be intelligent. In this example, chess represents a problem that is difficult for a human to solve, but easy for a computer, since the problem can be described easily using computer structures and structured data.

In contrast, modern AI/ML algorithms help solve problems that are often easy for a human to solve—such as vision-based perception in which a person determines with certainty that a certain photograph depicts a picture of a dog running in a park or understanding the semantics of language to identify that a restaurant review offers praise or admonishment. These problems would be difficult to formulate and then solve using traditional computer algorithms due to the unstructured nature of the problem, and the challenge of describing the problem to a computer. AI/ML algorithms often make use of probabilities and probabilistic models—ones that consider the fuzziness of life and model probabilities instead of concrete numbers, to help solve such problems. Algorithms can further be classified by the methods they use and are generally split into two categories: ML and deep learning, though many scientists consider deep learning algorithms to be a subset of ML. This concept can be best described by the Venn diagram shown in Figure 2.

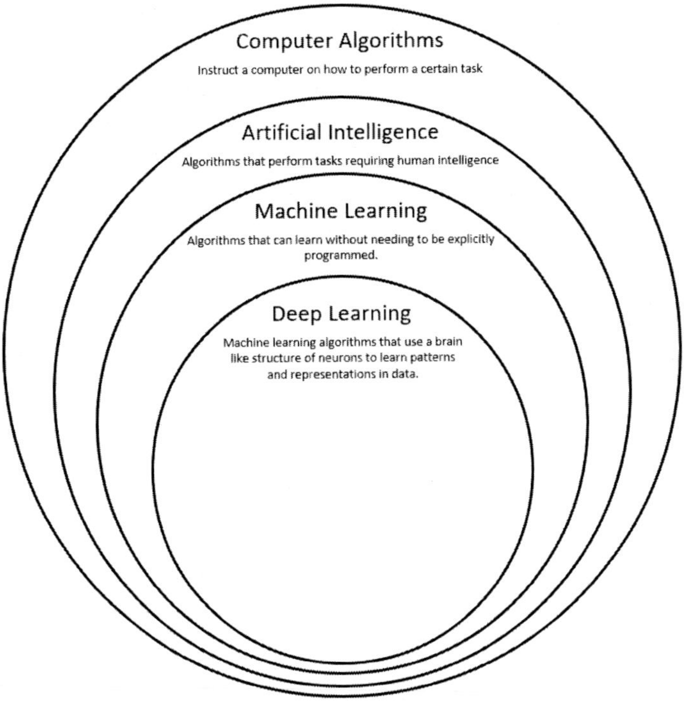

Figure 2. The various kinds of algorithms used for computation in the field of wearables.

Specifically, ML is the name given to models that require human intervention to describe or train the model. Figure 3 shows how ML models are organized based on how they solve a problem. Consider the problem of detecting steps taken from wrist motion data obtained from a smartwatch. A programmer first needs to identify which data or signals may be more important than the others, asking for example, is linear acceleration more important than rotation, HR, and SpO2 for the task of step detection? Next, the programmer may have to perform feature selection or feature engineering, where raw data are processed to calculate properties that may be more relevant to a statistical model, such as the rate of change of acceleration (jerk), velocity of wrist motion, or distance travelled by the wrist over a particular time. While IMUs may only provide acceleration, angular velocity, or magnetometer data, quantities like velocity or distance may correlate to the task of counting steps much better, resulting in better models.

Most commercial wearable devices use ML to achieve objectives using the classification approach, for example, detecting if an activity is running, jogging, walking, swimming, or weightlifting. Specifically, a wearable step counter may first capture wrist motion data (such as acceleration) and use classification to detect if the values of acceleration correspond to running or walking. Another wearable that monitors HR may use a classifier to provide notifications if the heart data are suggestive of atrial fibrillation.

Such approaches require a large amount of data to train a model, as well as careful model selection for best performance. Since the spread and behavior of sensor data or selected features often affect the accuracy by which a model may perform, the design of a wearable device is often a massive, time-consuming effort that can require contributions from multiple stakeholders such as human factors and data scientists, and electronics and computer engineers. The flowchart in Figure 4 summarizes an exemplar development process for a ML algorithm for a wearable device.

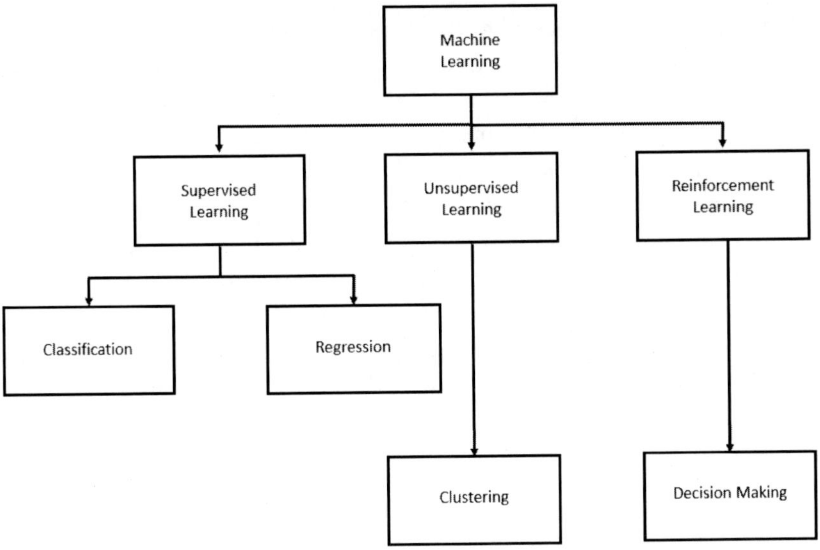

Figure 3. Organizing ML algorithms by how they solve a problem.

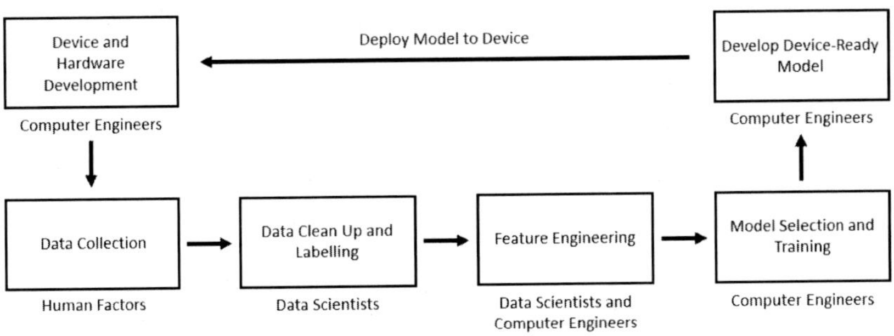

Figure 4. Development of a wearable device that uses an ML model.

Since a priori, it is unknown how a model may perform on a given set of data, an engineer may often train and test multiple models, in a process known as "model selection and training," before selecting one for their task. Some of the more common ML and deep learning algorithms used for classification are listed below:

- Logistic Regression: A linear model that predicts the probability of an outcome using a logistic function.

- Naïve Bayes: A probabilistic model that calculates the probability of a class based on Bayes' theorem, assuming independence between features.
- Support Vector Machine (SVM): A model that separates data points using a hyperplane in a high-dimensional space to maximize the margin between different classes.
- Decision Tree: A model that uses a tree-like structure to make decisions by splitting the data based on feature values.
- K-Nearest Neighbor (KNN): A model that classifies new data points based on the class of the majority of their KNNs.
- Random Forest: A model that classifies new data points based on the class of the majority of their KNNs.
- Neural Network: A model inspired by the human brain that uses interconnected layers of artificial neurons to learn complex patterns and make predictions.

A full discussion of these algorithms is beyond the scope of this chapter. In the interest of limiting scope, we discuss logistic regression and the Naïve Bayes algorithms in detail, and briefly discuss the other algorithms. The differences between these algorithms can be demonstrated using a toy example. Consider a hypothetical wearable that alerts a caretaker if the wearer has fallen down. Such a wearable may contain sensors such as a motion sensor and a glucose monitor. To design the ML algorithm for such a wearable, a team will first have to collect a large amount of data from the target population wearing the device, and then label any falls in the data. This can be done by marking time periods (i.e., samples) from the collected data as falls or not-falls. Specifically, every hour of data could be split into 5-minute samples and labelled as one of two classes as falls (class label=1) or not-falls (class label=0). Each sample of data is represented by feature values, which may be sensor data obtained directly from the sensors. For example, instead of using the instantaneous glucose level in the blood in mg/dL as a feature, an engineer may prefer a calculated value of the standard deviation in blood glucose over 5 minutes denoted as σ(Blood Glucose), expressed as σ(BG), as a feature, and instead of rotation or gyroscope data, an engineer may prefer acceleration as another feature. ML algorithms can then be trained on this combination of samples and their labels, and once trained can process a given sample of 5-minute data and output a class label indicating a fall (1) or not-fall (0).

The data set (samples and labels) can be visualized as points on a two-dimensional (2-D) plane as shown in Figure 5. Given there are two features of interest: σ(BG) and Acceleration, the σ(BG) value for a sample can be reported on the x-axis, while the y-axis reports the acceleration measured during the event. This results in the sample (i.e., time period) with low σ(BG) and low acceleration appear in the bottom left of the plot, while the results with a high σ(BG) and high acceleration appear in the top right of the plot. Colors are used to visualize events that are safe or unsafe (e.g., Figure 5 has dark dots representing unsafe behavior, and light dots representing safe behavior).

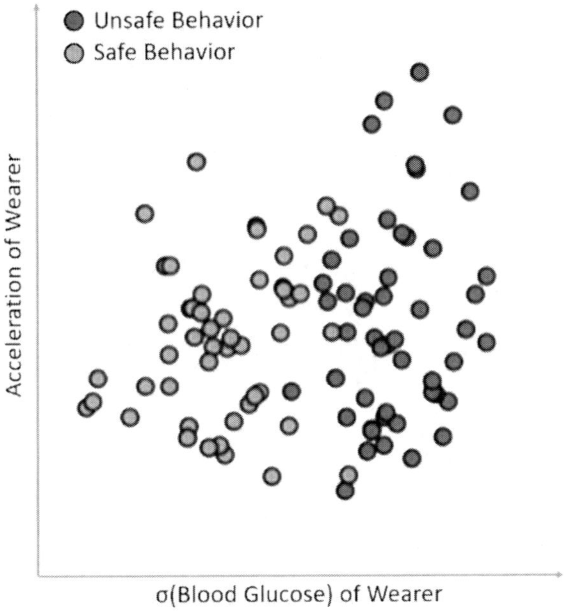

Figure 5. Safe and unsafe behavior events as a function of the acceleration of the wearer and the standard deviation of the blood glucose level of the wearer.

Once a labelled data set (such as the one described above) is prepared, ML models can be trained by providing them with many examples of incidents (Blood glucose levels, accelerations, and fall/not-fall labels). The ML models learn the relationship between the input data, σ(BG) and accelerations, and the fall/not-fall labels in different ways. The following is a detailed discussion of two common models—logistic regression and Naïve Bayes.

Logistic Regression

This model is commonly used for classification because a classification problem maps the input variables to output variables in a non-linear manner. Given two input variables x_1 and x_2 that represent the BAC and acceleration data, respectively, linear regression models the relation between x_1, θ_2, and the output y using the sigmoid function $\sigma(z)$, which maps real-valued numbers to a value between 0 and 1 as follows:

$$\sigma(z) = \frac{1}{1+e^{-z}} \qquad (1)$$

Here, z is a linear combination of the input variables and their associated coefficients (weights). The equation for z can be written as:

$$z = \theta_0 + \theta_1 x_1 + \theta_2 x_2 \qquad (2)$$

where θ_0 is the intercept or bias term, and $\theta_1$and θ_2 are the coefficients or weights associated with the input variables (x_1 and x_2), respectively. Given a resulting value of $\sigma(x)$ for an input sample, the classification label y can be obtained by applying a threshold of 0.5,

$$y = \begin{cases} 0\ (safe), \sigma(x) < 0 \\ 1\ (unsafe), \sigma(x) \geq 0.5 \end{cases} \qquad (3)$$

The model is trained by finding the optimal values of θ_0, θ_1, and θ_2 using a method such as gradient descent, which minimizes the errors between the values of y output by the model, and those from ground-truth labelling. Once the model is trained and optimal values of θ_0, θ_1, and θ_2 are obtained, the same equations can be used to obtain a classification label y. In Figure 6, we overlay the class output by the logistic regression classifier under the data samples to help visualize the boundaries obtained by the model during training, which result in the output value of y. The accuracy of the model, obtained by comparing the ground truth labels to the outputs of the model, is 95%, and reported in the bottom right of Figure 6.

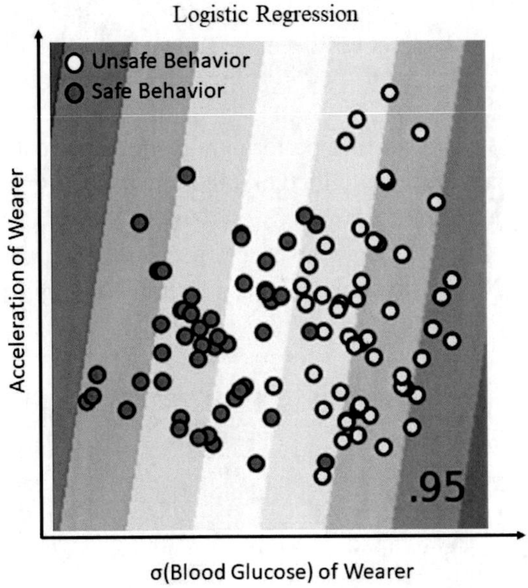

Figure 6. Classification results of a logistic regression ML model applied to the data shown in Figure 5. In this example, any data point within and to the left of the white stripe is classified as safe behavior and all other data are classified as unsafe behavior. One unsafe behavior would be classified as safe, while three safe behaviors would be classified as unsafe, resulting in a 95% accuracy across the entire dataset.

Naïve Bayes

The Naïve Bayes classifier is based on Bayes' theorem, and assigns a class to a sample given feature values x_i as shown below:

$$y_i = \arg\max_{y} P\,(y_i) \prod_{j=1}^{n} P\big(x_j \mid y_i\big)0 \qquad (4)$$

A normal distribution can be used to calculate the probability of a sample belonging to a class $P(y_j|x_i)$. By assuming a normal distribution, the mean μ and standard deviation σ can be calculated for each feature in each class of a dataset. $P(y_j|x_i)$ can be then be calculated given μ and σ for the different features in different classes as shown below:

$$P(x_j|y_i) = \frac{1}{\sqrt{2\pi\sigma_{i,j}^2}} exp\left(-\frac{(x-\mu_{i,j})^2}{2\sigma_{i,j}^2}\right) \quad (5)$$

The Naïve Bayes classifier performs well in many real-world situations, in spite of the many over-simplified assumptions made by the classifier.

For our toy example of classifying a sample as a fall (y=0) or not-a-fall (y=1) given the blood glucose level and acceleration feature values for an event, a trained Naïve Bayes classifier is illustrated in Figure 7.

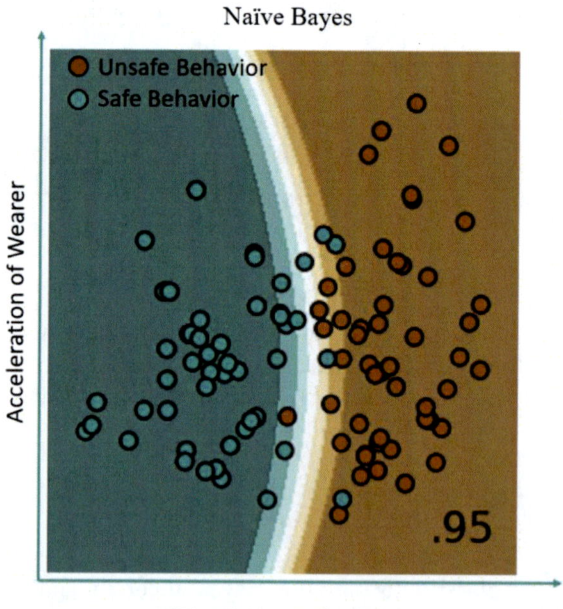

Figure 7. Classification results of a Naïve Bayes ML model applied to the data shown in Figure 6. In this example, any data point within and to the left of the white stripe is classified as safe behavior and all other data are classified as unsafe behavior. In this example, one unsafe behavior would be classified as safe, while four safe behaviors would be classified as unsafe, resulting in a 95% accuracy across the entire dataset.

As discussed previously, other ML models can also be used for classification. The classification results from our toy example and two other spreads of input data using various models are illustrated in Figure 8, which shows that the logistic regression and linear SVM classifiers almost always draw straight lines for decision boundaries, while the Naïve Bayes classifier uses ellipses. The KNN classifier seemingly draws decision boundaries at random, while the decision tree draws rectangles, and the neural net is capable of modeling straight lines or ellipses. These boundaries result in different performance accuracies on the input datasets, demonstrating that there is no one-size-fits-all solution for input data.

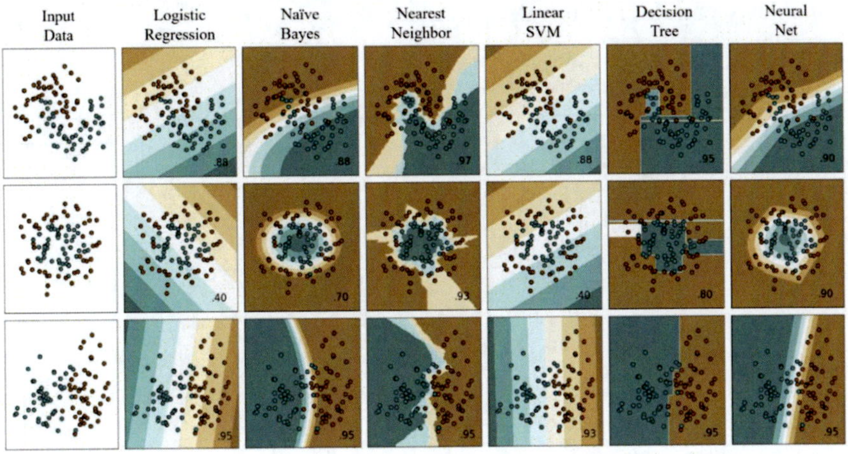

Figure 8. A comparison of ML models and their classification boundaries for different input datasets. Model accuracies are shown in the bottom right-hand corners of the plots.

It is important to note that most ML approaches require significant effort in the feature selection and model selection phases. In comparison, deep learning models require much less intervention and manipulation from an engineer. Deep learning models are complex neural networks. The term *deep* refers to the depth of these neural networks, which typically consist of multiple hidden layers between the input and output layers. The depth allows deep learning models to capture and model intricate features and abstractions, enabling them to handle highly complex tasks and learn hierarchical representations of the data. The depth of these models also facilitates automatic feature extraction, as the lower layers learn low-level features and the higher layers learn more abstract and high-level features. Continuing with our toy example, an engineer can provide deep learning models with sensor data directly from a smartwatch, such as all motion sensor data (acceleration, gyroscope, and magnetometer), and all chemical sensor data (such as blood glucose data), then let the deep learning model calculate and identify which features are important for a task. This may result in a model that performs better than the previously listed ML models. In another example, consider the task of detecting the number of steps from smartwatch data. All the sensor data captured from a smartwatch can be provided to the deep learning model, and a deep learning model can then identify which signals are important, and how to use them to identify the number of steps taken. This distinction between ML and deep learning is illustrated in Figure 9.

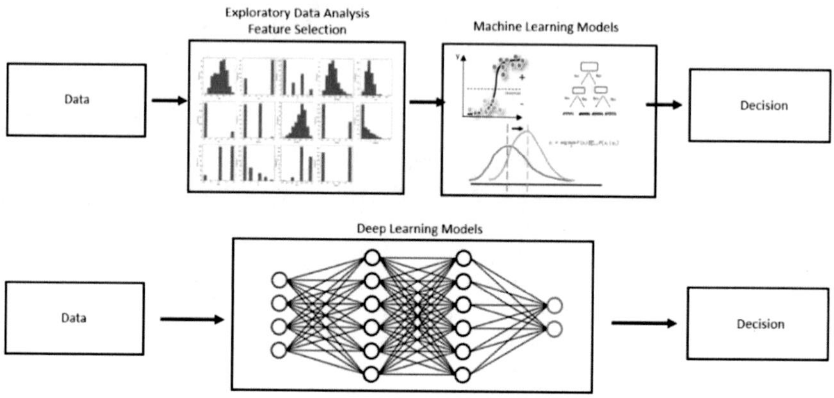

Figure 9. The difference between ML (top) and deep learning approaches (bottom).

Common deep learning approaches used by wearables are listed below.

Convolutional Neural Network

The simplest form of a deep learning model consists of multiple layers of neural networks. Convolution neural network (CNN) operations are performed between layers to automatically extract relevant features from input data, as well as provide a final classification. Convolution is a mathematical operation typically performed on matrices. Since image data are often stored as a matrix on a computer, CNNs and their variations find many applications in computer vision and image processing for wearable devices (examples shown in Figure 10), such as:

- Gesture Recognition: Wearable devices equipped with cameras and CNN-based algorithms can accurately recognize hand gestures. This technology is particularly useful in applications like VR and AR, where users can interact with the virtual world using natural gestures. This technology is often used in the domain of video games.

- Object and Scene Recognition: CNNs can identify and classify objects and scenes captured by wearable cameras. This is valuable in applications ranging from assisting visually impaired individuals to enhancing the capabilities of security personnel. This is an up-and-coming field, as evidenced by recent patent applications relating to object tracking for HMDs (e.g., U.S. Patent 11,189,059 B2, *Object tracking for head-mounted devices* [50]).
- Facial Recognition: Some wearables utilize CNNs to perform facial recognition tasks. This enables features such as personalized user experiences and improved security through facial authentication.

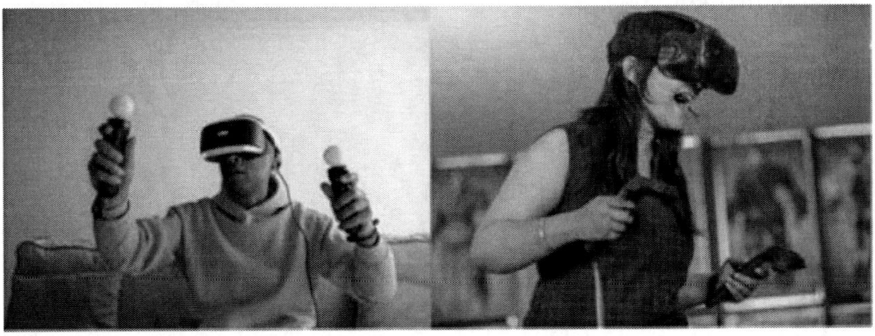

Figure 10. Examples of wearable headsets that make use of deep learning for object recognition and gesture recognition.

Recurrent Neural Network

A recurrent neural network (RNN) is a deep learning model capable of handling sequential data by utilizing recurrent connections to capture temporal dependencies and process data with varying lengths. These models are often used for time series data.

Long Short-Term Memory

Long short-term memory (LSTM) is a specialized type of RNN that improves on them by addressing the vanishing gradient problem in RNNs, and can effectively model long-term dependencies in sequential data by incorporating memory cells with gating mechanisms. These models are used in tasks such as voice recognition for wearable devices and translate text that cameras capture from the environment. Products such as the HMDs or smartwatches make use of these algorithms.

Transformers

Transformers are more complex than RNNs and LSTMs. This model architecture is widely used for natural language processing tasks and operate by effectively capturing long-range dependencies in sequential data, such as words in literature. These algorithms have become popular after the release of products such as ChatGPT and Bing Search, which generate text for users.

Generative Adversarial Networks

Generative adversarial networks (GAN) consist of two neural networks—a generator and a discriminator—that compete against each other to generate realistic data samples. These models are often used to generate training data when not enough is available for model training. These models are used in the domain of computer vision and can be used to generate stylized images and videos in real time.

It is worth emphasizing that this discussion on ML and deep learning for wearables is not complete. The domains of ML and deep learning are experiencing rapid advancements and exhibit no indications of deceleration, largely due to remarkable progress in the hardware and software that form the foundation for ML and deep learning. Ongoing advancements in computing power, including the development of specialized hardware accelerators and high-performance computing systems, have significantly enhanced the training and inference capabilities of ML and deep learning models. Simultaneously, continuous innovations in software frameworks, libraries, and algorithms improve the efficiency and accessibility of these techniques. As a result, researchers, engineers, and practitioners are consistently pushing the boundaries of what is achievable using these models.

Failure Modes and Failure Analysis of Wearable Devices

In the world of wearables, where technology meets fashion and function, a range of potential pitfalls can disrupt our experiences. While these devices are designed to provide real-time data, connectivity, and functionality, they are not without vulnerabilities. Understanding these vulnerabilities is crucial for both users and manufacturers to ensure the longevity and safety of these devices.

Design Failure Mode and Effects Analysis (DFMEA) is a systematic approach used to identify and mitigate potential failures and risks in the design of a product. When it comes to addressing safety and performance concerns in wearable devices, DFMEA can be applied to analyze and mitigate potential failure modes and their effects. DFMEA begins with identifying potential hazards and then analyzing the potential failure modes. That is followed by an assessment of severity and development of detection and prevention measures. Once the mitigation strategies are identified, risk is calculated for each failure mode and mitigation actions are taken to correct the design and manufacturing root causes. Eventually DFMEA concludes with a series of verification and validation tests to evaluate the effectiveness of mitigation actions.

Battery Failures

One common failure mode is the battery life running out, which can lead to the device shutting down unexpectedly. Battery failure can either simply cause performance issues (e.g., lowered capacity) or in more severe cases lead to safety concerns. Overheating, skin irritations, and burn hazards are some of those safety concerns. Battery thermal runaway can rapidly release energy from inside a device and harm the user. For this reason, it is not typically recommended to employ high energy batteries in wearable devices. The battery capacity of a smartwatch can range from as low as 100mAh to over 500mAh, depending on factors such as the display type, features, and intended use.

When a battery goes into thermal runaway, it can release a significant amount of energy in the form of heat, gas, and flames. The energy released during a battery thermal runaway event is typically much higher than the energy stored in the battery itself. In the event a smartwatch battery goes into thermal runaway while being worn on the body, the consequences can be serious. The heat generated could cause burns, skin damage, and discomfort to the wearer. Additionally, if the battery catches fire or explodes, it could lead to more severe injuries. Overall, while the energy stored in smartwatch batteries is relatively small, the consequences of thermal runaway can still be significant. Manufacturers prioritize safety measures to prevent such incidents, and users should exercise caution and follow best practices to reduce risks when using wearable devices.

Synchronization and Connectivity Failures

Integration and linkage issues are common culprits that can disrupt the seamless operation of wearable devices. These problems arise when a wearable device struggles to establish proper connections with other devices within their ecosystem, such as smartphones. Such failures can lead to disruptions in data transfer and communication. These issues can stem from various sources, including electronic component malfunctions related to wireless connectivity modules, as well as software glitches or compatibility conflicts. For example, a fitness tracker might encounter difficulties syncing data with a smartphone app due to a malfunctioning Bluetooth module.

Manufacturers can prevent synchronization and connectivity failures in wearable devices by conducting thorough testing of wireless components, ensuring compatibility with various devices, providing regular firmware updates, offering user-friendly troubleshooting guides, implementing secure pairing mechanisms, collaborating with app developers, establishing responsive customer support, gathering user feedback, and enforcing strict quality control procedures during manufacturing. These measures collectively enhance the reliability of connections, minimize issues, and contribute to a more seamless user experience.

Physical Failures

Physical damage jeopardizes both the functionality and appearance of wearables. Accidental drops or extreme conditions can result in cracked screens, malfunctioning buttons, or water damage. To mitigate this, users should employ protective cases and handle devices with care. Manufacturers must design wearables with durability in mind, using resilient materials and reinforced components, while also providing guidelines on proper use and care.

Inaccurate Sensors

Wearable device accuracy relies on sensors, but inaccuracies can arise from calibration issues or manufacturing defects. For example, a fitness tracker's misaligned accelerometer sensor can lead to unreliable step counts, illustrating this problem. Regular calibration checks and stringent quality control during manufacturing are crucial to ensure sensor accuracy. Manufacturers should also incorporate self-calibration mechanisms and user-friendly calibration processes.

Electromagnetic Interference

Electromagnetic interference (EMI) from external sources can disrupt the functionality of wearable devices. For instance, signal disruptions caused by a nearby microwave oven can affect smart wearables. Proper shielding and interference-resistant design methods are crucial for manufacturers to minimize the impact of EMI. Additionally, manufacturers can educate users about potential EMI sources and how to avoid them.

Signal Integrity Issues

Signal integrity issues caused by poor internal circuitry design can lead to degraded performance. To prevent this, manufacturers must adhere to best practices for circuit layout, grounding, and component shielding. Users can keep wearables away from strong electromagnetic fields to reduce signal integrity risks. Manufacturers should implement rigorous testing and simulation to ensure signal integrity and provide guidelines on proper use environments.

Unreliable Software

Software glitches can disrupt wearables, causing unexpected crashes or shutdowns. Adequate testing and software quality control are essential to prevent such malfunctions. Users can avoid software glitches by installing updates promptly and providing feedback to manufacturers when encountering software-related issues. Manufacturers should conduct comprehensive software testing, offer regular updates, and establish user-friendly error reporting mechanisms.

Liquid Intrusion

Liquid intrusion is a common issue for wearable devices, particularly those that are designed to be worn during physical activity or in dusty and wet environments. Some failure modes related to water intrusion are discussed below.

Short Circuits

Water can cause a short circuit in a device, which can damage or destroy the electrical components, or create a fault resistance that may overheat or ignite. These short circuits can be prevented if the circuit boards have conformal coating, or the power leads are covered with insulating materials. Firmware within the battery management's integrated circuits can be helpful to identify and protect against some of these short circuit events by sensing overcurrent in various parts of the main circuit board and other miscellaneous boards, such as battery management units. Battery management units themselves can also sense overcurrent and shut down power in some short-circuit scenarios. These features are developing rapidly and becoming less and less costly to add to wearable devices. In some cases, there are overcurrent sensors also integrated within USB dongles of charger cables to avoid powering a shorted terminal or a circuit within a device while it is being charged.

Corrosion

Water can cause corrosion on the electrical components of a device, which can lead to malfunctioning and eventually complete failure. Water intrusion can also cause physical damage to the miscellaneous parts and enclosure, result in cracked screens, or lead to malfunctioning buttons. Corrosion poses a significant threat to the functionality and longevity of wearable electronic devices, a topic of paramount importance within the broader discussion of such technology. The infiltration of water into these devices can trigger a cascade of detrimental effects, starting with the corrosion of electrical components. As moisture encounters sensitive circuitry, it initiates electrochemical reactions that gradually erode metal traces and connections. This corrosion not only disrupts the intended pathways for electrical signals, but can also lead to short circuits, voltage irregularities, and ultimately device malfunction. The consequences extend beyond mere inconvenience, potentially rendering a wearable device entirely inoperative.

Battery Damage

Water exposure can create conditions for short circuits to occur across the terminals of the battery. If these terminals are inadequately insulated, the presence of water can facilitate the flow of electrical current between them, resulting in a short circuit. Such short circuits can not only disrupt the battery's performance, but also pose serious safety risks. The flow of excessive current can generate heat, potentially leading to overheating, or in more severe cases, triggering a thermal runaway. This dangerous scenario involves a self-sustaining exothermic reaction within the battery, causing it to rapidly increase in temperature, potentially leading to fire or explosion.

Faulty Sensors

When water or any other conductive liquid enters a device, it can affect the accuracy and functionality of the sensors in a device, such as an HR monitor or GPS tracker.

Ingress Protection Rating

Manufacturers determine ingress protection (IP) ratings to notify consumers of the potential for water and dust intrusion. It is critical for users to follow the manufacturer's guidelines for device use in wet, humid, and dusty environments. The International Electrotechnical Commission standard, IEC 60034-5, classifies various degrees of protection against solid particles and water [51]. The rating is typically expressed as "IP" followed by two digits—the first digit indicates protection against solid particles, and the second digit indicates protection against water, as follows:

Degrees of Protection against Solid Particles

- **0** – No protection.
- **1** – Protection against solid objects larger than 50mm in diameter (e.g., a hand).
- **2** – Protection against solid objects larger than 12.5mm in diameter (e.g., fingers).
- **3** – Protection against solid objects larger than 2.5mm in diameter (e.g., tools and wires).
- **4** – Protection against solid objects larger than 1mm in diameter (e.g., small tools and wires).
- **5** – Dust-protected, limited ingress (dust should not completely penetrate, but may enter in minimal quantities).
- **6** – Dust-tight, complete protection against dust.

Protection against Water (Second Digit)

- **0** – No protection.
- **1** – Protection against vertically falling drops of water (e.g., condensation, dripping).
- **2** – Protection against water droplets at an angle of up to 15 degrees from vertical.
- **3** – Protection against spraying water at an angle of up to 60 degrees from vertical.
- **4** – Protection against splashing water from all directions.
- **5** – Protection against water jets (i.e., limited ingress permitted).
- **6** – Protection against powerful water jets and heavy seas (i.e., limited ingress permitted).
- **7** – Protection against immersion in water up to a 1m depth for a limited time (typically 30 minutes).
- **8** – Protection against continuous immersion beyond a 1m depth for a specified time.

An IP rating of IP67, for example, means the device or enclosure is dust-tight and can withstand immersion in water up to 1m for a limited time. Manufacturers use these ratings to indicate the environmental suitability of their products and help users choose the right equipment for specific conditions, like wet, humid, and dusty environments. Following the manufacturer's guidelines and understanding the IP rating of a device is crucial to ensure proper protection and longevity in varying environmental conditions.

The Future of Wearable Devices

Envisioning the future of wearable electronic devices offers a glimpse into a rapidly changing landscape that is driven by technological advancements and evolving user needs. Building upon the current landscape of wearable technology, the future promises a world where humans constantly interact with computing systems in real time, resulting in real-time assistance from wearable devices in many sectors such as healthcare and entertainment, as well as the military.

Integration and User-Centric Design

In the future, wearable devices will integrate more organically into users' lives. The boundary between digital and physical realms will blur as wearables evolve to adapt to daily routines. Smart textiles, leveraging microsensors and actuators, will enhance clothing with climate control and health monitoring capabilities, catering to personalized needs. The smart fabrics market size is expected to grow from 6.14 million units in 2023 to 10.27 million units by 2028, at a compound annual growth rate of 10.85% during the forecast period (2023–2028) [52].

Neural Interfaces and Cognitive Interactions

Beyond surface-level wearables, neural interfaces are on the horizon. Brain-computer interfaces such as those from Neuralink and other vendors will enable direct communication between the brain and computing devices, ushering in a new era of human-computer interaction. This technology will find applications in fields like healthcare, communication, and prosthetics, amplifying the potential of wearables. The global brain-computer interface market size is expected to grow from USD 1.81 billion in 2023 to USD 2.95

billion by 2028, at a compound annual growth rate of 10.29% during the forecast period (2023–2028) [53].

AI-Driven Personalization and Contextual Insights

The collaboration between wearable devices and AI will become more sophisticated. Wearables will transition from data collectors to intelligent advisors, leveraging AI algorithms to process real-time data streams. Users will benefit from personalized insights, predictive analytics, and recommendations that align with their health goals and daily activities [54].

Immersive Displays and Augmented Reality

Lightweight, immersive displays will redefine the way information is consumed. AR glasses with holographic displays will revolutionize education, navigation, and work processes. Real-time information overlays will enrich users' experiences, enhancing productivity and reducing cognitive load. As an example, the combination of Google Glass and VR offers substantial prospects for enriching user experiences and advancing technology in various sectors. This fusion capitalizes on the hands-free operation of Google Glass and real-time information display, merged with VR's immersive nature, and opens doors for sectors like education, healthcare, and entertainment. Overcoming challenges such as limited field of view and processing power is feasible with improved display technology, better interaction methods, and cloud-edge computing. The future holds AR integration, collaborative VR, and tailored industry solutions [55].

Ethical Considerations and Data Security

As wearable devices become integral to users' lives, ethical concerns regarding data privacy and security will require meticulous attention. Striking the right balance between utility and privacy will drive design choices, while robust encryption and authentication protocols will safeguard sensitive data. Utilizing personal health data without proper consent poses privacy and data misuse risks, affecting individuals and society. As these technologies grow, prioritizing privacy and ethics is essential. Stronger regulations and industry self-regulation are needed to safeguard personal health data and user autonomy. Through these measures, we can fully leverage the advantages of wearable digital health technology while upholding personal privacy and security [56].

Continuous and Personalized Healthcare

As wearables and sensors evolve, their application in healthcare will lead to a system of continuous 24/7 monitoring of human health. Wearables of the future will be equipped with advanced sensors capable of collecting a large array of health-related data. Wearable devices will not only monitor HR, steps taken, and sleep patterns, but will extend to measure vital signs, glucose levels, and even detect biomarkers indicative of various diseases. Through continuous data collection, wearables will enable large-scale data collection. The abundance of health data generated by wearables will fuel the development of sophisticated data analytics and ML models.

A 2013 report by the Centers for Disease Control and Prevention noted that at least 200,000 deaths from heart disease and stroke are preventable. A key strength of wearables is their ability to provide real-time health monitoring. With the integration of AI, wearables will become adept at detecting anomalies such as heart attacks or strokes, as well as deviations from baseline health metrics. This will enable early detection of health issues, such as arrhythmias or fluctuations in blood sugar levels, allowing for timely intervention and prevention. Wearables powered by ML and AI will predict health outcomes, assess disease risk, and recommend personalized lifestyle modifications leading to more precise diagnostics and personalized treatment plans. Patients will receive actionable insights, empowering them to make informed decisions about their health and well-being.

Conclusion

In this evolutionary phase of wearable devices, the convergence of technology and user-centric design is poised to redefine how humans interact with technology. The future of wearables holds the promise of practicality and functionality, with devices seamlessly integrating into daily routines and enhancing cognitive capabilities. As technological horizons expand, it is imperative to address ethical concerns and prioritize data security. By staying attuned to these trends and considerations, the wearable technology ecosystem will continue to evolve, empowering users with unprecedented levels of convenience and personalized experiences.

References

[1] Gari, Lutfallah. 2008. "The Invention of Spectacles between the East and the West." Muslim Heritage, Last Updated November 12, 2008, Accessed September 1, 2003. Available from https://muslimheritage.com/invention-spectacles-east-and-west/.

[2] BBC News. 2009. "Painting features 'oldest watch'." Last Updated October 19, 2009, Accessed September 1, 2023. Available from http://news.bbc.co.uk/2/hi/entertainment/arts_and_culture/8313893.stm.

[3] AncientPages.com. 2015. "Image of the Day: 300-Year-Old Chinese Abacus Ring from the Qing Dynasty." Last Updated September 12, 2015, Accessed September 1, 2023. Available from https://www.ancientpages.com/2015/09/12/image-of-the-day-300-year-old-chinese-abacus-ring-from-the-qing-dynasty/.

[4] Cision PR Newswire/ABI Research. 2022. "The Wearable Market Will See 344.9 Million Shipments in 2022 with Sports, Fitness, and Wellness Trackers Leading the Way." PR Newswire, Last Updated January 27, 2022, Accessed September 1, 2023. Available from https://www.prnewswire.com/news-releases/.

[5] Gupta, Ankit. 2023. "Wearable Technology Market Reseach Information by Prouduct, by Technology, by Application, and by Region." Market Research Future, Available from https://www.marketresearchfuture.com/reports/wearable-technology-market-2336.

[6] market.us. 2023. "Global Fitness Tracker Market By Age (Children's Fitness Tracker and Adult Fitness Tracker), By Product (Smart Clothing, Fitness Band, Smart Glasses, Activity Monitor, and Smart Watch), By Sales Channel (Retail Sales and Online Sales), By Application (Sports, Heart Rate Tracking, Running, Cycling Tracking, Glucose Measurement Tracking, and Sleep Measurement Tracking), By Region and Companies - Industry Segment Outlook, Market Assessment, Competition Scenario, Trends, and Forecast 2023-2032." New York, NY, Available from https://market.us/report/fitness-tracker-market/.

[7] Johnson, S. 2022. "Intel researchers see path to trillion-transistor chips by 2030." BusinessNews, Last Updated December 3, 2022, Accessed September 1, 2023. Available from https://biz.crast.net/intel-researchers-see-path-to-trillion-transistor-chips-by-2030/.

[8] Didyuk, O., N. Econom, A. Guardia, K. Livingston, and U. Klueh. 2021. "Continuous glucose monitoring devices: Past, present, and future focus on the history and evolution of technological innovation." *J Diabetes Sci Technol* 15(3):676-683. doi: 10.1177/1932296819899394.

[9] Tazarv, Ali, Sina Labbaf, Stephanie M. Reich, Nikil Dutt, Amir M. Rahmani, and Marco Levorato. "Personalized Stress Monitoring using Wearable Sensors in

Everyday Settings," in *Proceedings of the 2021 43rd Annual International Conference of the IEEE Engineering in Medicine & Biology Society (EMBC)*, 2021, 7332-7335.

[10] ANSI/AAMI. 2019. "Medical Devices And Medical Systems - Essential Safety And Performance Requirements For Equipment Comprising The Patient-Centric Integrated Clinical Environment (ICE) - Part 1: General Requirements And Conceptual Model. ANSI/AAMI 2700:2019."

[11] Kaul, Navneeta. 2018. "Smart shoes: Innovations revolutionizing the future of footwear." Prescouter, Accessed September 1, 2023. Available from https://www.prescouter.com/2018/10/smart-shoes-innovations-footwear/.

[12] Gossett, Stephen. 2023. "22 Virtual Reality Companies to Know." BuiltIn, Last Updated June 16, 2023, Accessed September 1, 2023. Available from https://builtin.com/media-gaming/virtual-reality-companies.

[13] Vergun, D. 2023. "DOD Investing in Wearable Technology that Could Rapidly Predict Disease." Last Updated April 28, 2023, Accessed September 1, 2023. Available from https://www.defense.gov/News/News-Stories/.

[14] U.S. Department of Defense. 2023. "Use of Fitness Wearables to Measure and Promote Readiness. Report to the Committee on Armed Service of the House of Representatives." Available from https://www.health.mil/Reference-Center/Reports/2023/07/24/Use-of-Fitness-Wearables-to-Measure-and-Promote-Readiness

[15] U.S. Army. 2022. "Wearable Technologies for Physiological Monitoring." Last Updated August 12, 2022, Accessed September 1, 2023. Available from https://www.armysbir.army.mil/topics/wearable-technologies-physiological-monitoring/.

[16] Kalantarian, H., and M. Sarrafzadeh. 2015. "Audio-based detection and evaluation of eating behavior using the smartwatch platform." *Comput Biol Med* 65:1-9. doi: 10.1016/j.compbiomed.2015.07.013.

[17] Alharbi, Rawan, Angela Pfammatter, Bonnie Spring, and Nabil Alshurafa. 2017. WillSense: Adherence Barriers for Passive Sensing Systems That Track Eating Behavior. In *Proceedings of the 2017 CHI Conference Extended Abstracts on Human Factors in Computing Systems*. Denver, Colorado, USA: Association for Computing Machinery.

[18] Adapa, Apurva, Fiona Fui-Hoon Nah, Richard H. Hall, Keng Siau, and Samuel N. Smith. 2018. "Factors influencing the adoption of smart wearable devices." *Int J Human–Comput Interact* 34(5):399-409. doi: 10.1080/10447318.2017.1357902.

[19] Mordor Intelligence Research & Advisory. 2023. "Smartwatch Market Size & Share Analysis - Growth Trends & Forecasts (2023-2028)." Mordor Intelligence, Accessed September 1, 2023. Available from https://www.mordorintelligence.com/industry-reports/smartwatch-market.

[20] Breslin, John G., Theodore A. Vickey, and Antonio S. Williams. 2013. "Fitness—there's an app for that: Review of mobile fitness apps." *Int J Sport Soc* 3(4):109-127.

[21] Mendiola, Victor, Abnob Doss, Will Adams, Jose Ramos, Matthew Bruns, Josh Cherian, Puneet Kohli, Daniel Goldberg, and Tracy Hammond. 2020. "Automatic Exercise Recognition with Machine Learning." In *Precision Health and Medicine:*

A Digital Revolution in Healthcare, edited by Arash Shaban-Nejad and Martin Michalowski, 33-44. Cham: Springer International Publishing.

[22] Gurman, Mark. 2023. "Apple makes major progress on no-prick blood glucose tracking for its watch." Bloomberg L.P., Last Updated February 23, 2023, Accessed September 1, 2023. Available from https://www.bloomberg.com/news/articles/2023-02-22/apple-watch-blood-glucose-monitor-could-revolutionize-diabetes-care-aapl#xj4y7vzkg.

[23] Shenai, Mahesh B., Marcus Dillavou, Corey Shum, Douglas Ross, Richard S. Tubbs, Alan Shih, and Barton L. Guthrie. 2011. "Virtual interactive presence and augmented reality (VIPAR) for remote surgical assistance." *Neurosurgery* 68(1 Suppl Operative):200-7; discussion 207. doi: 10.1227/NEU.0b013e3182077efd.

[24] Bala, L., J. Kinross, G. Martin, L. J. Koizia, A. S. Kooner, G. J. Shimshon, T. J. Hurkxkens, P. J. Pratt, and A. H. Sam. 2021. "A remote access mixed reality teaching ward round." *Clin Teach* 18(4):386-390. doi: 10.1111/tct.13338.

[25] Hottner, Lena, Elke Bachlmair, Mario Zeppetzauer, Christian Wirth, and Alois Ferscha. 2017. Design of a smart helmet. In *Proceedings of the Seventh International Conference on the Internet of Things*. Linz, Austria: Association for Computing Machinery.

[26] Melzer, Jim, Frederick Brozoski, Tomasz Letowski, Thomas Harding, and Clarence Rash. 2009. "Guidelines for HMD design." In *Helmet-Mounted Displays: Sensation, Perception and Cognition Issues*, edited by Clarence Rash, Michael B. Russo, Tomasz Letowski and Elmar Schmeisser, 805-848.

[27] Livingston, Mark A., Simon J. Julier, and Dennis G. Brown. "Situation awareness for teams of dismounted warfighters and unmanned vehicles," in *Society of Photo-Optical Instrumentation Engineers (SPIE) Conference Series*, 2006, 62260F.

[28] Baylakoğlu, İlknur, Aleksandra Fortier, San Kyeong, Rajan Ambat, Helene Conseil-Gudla, Michael H. Azarian, and Michael G. Pecht. 2021. "The detrimental effects of water on electronic devices." *e-Prime - Adv Electr Eng Electron Energy* 1:100016. doi: https://doi.org/10.1016/j.prime.2021.100016.

[29] Nelson, B. D., S. S. Karipott, Y. Wang, and K. G. Ong. 2020. "Wireless Technologies for Implantable Devices." *Sensors (Basel)* 20(16):4604. doi: 10.3390/s20164604.

[30] Seshadri, Dhruv R., Ryan T. Li, JJames E. Voos, James R. Rowbottom, Celeste M. Alfes, Christian A. Zorman, and Colin K. Drummond. 2019. "Wearable sensors for monitoring the physiological and biochemical profile of the athlete." *NPJ Digit Med* 2:72. doi: 10.1038/s41746-019-0150-9.

[31] ŌURA. 2023. "ŌURA - The most trusted smart ring." Accessed September 1, 2023. Available from https://ouraring.com/.

[32] Wearable, X. 2023. "The Ultimate Selfcare Is Guided Yoga Anywhere." Accessed September 1, 2023. Available from https://www.wearablex.com/.

[33] Punith, A., G. Manish, M. Sai Sumanth, A. Vinay, R. Karthik, and K. Jyothi. 2021. "Design and implementation of a smart reader for blind and visually impaired people." *AIP Conference Proceedings* 2317(1) doi: 10.1063/5.0036140.

[34] Mukhiddinov, Mukhriddin, and Jinsoo Cho. 2021. "Smart Glass System Using Deep Learning for the Blind and Visually Impaired." *Electronics* 10(22):2756.

[35] Drake-Brockman, T. F., A. Datta, and B. S. von Ungern-Sternberg. 2016. "Patient monitoring with Google Glass: a pilot study of a novel monitoring technology." *Paediatr Anaesth* 26(5):539-546. doi: 10.1111/pan.12879.

[36] Kantor, J. 2015. "Application of Google Glass to Mohs micrographic surgery: a pilot study in 120 patients." *Dermatol Surg* 41(2):288-289. doi: 10.1097/dss.0000000000000268.

[37] Vorraber, Wolfgang, Siegfried Voessner, Gerhard Stark, Dietmar Neubacher, Steven DeMello, and Aaron Bair. 2014. "Medical applications of near-eye display devices: an exploratory study." *Int J Surg* 12(12):1266-1272. doi: 10.1016/j.ijsu.2014.09.014.

[38] Moshtaghi, Omid, Kanwar S. Kelley, William B. Armstrong, Yaser Ghavami, Jeffrey Gu, and Hamid R. Djalilian. 2015. "Using Google Glass to solve communication and surgical education challenges in the operating room." *Laryngoscope* 125(10):2295-2297. doi: 10.1002/lary.25249.

[39] WearableTech. 2023. "The MYO Armband is a Gesture Control Armband for Presentations by Thalmic Labs." Accessed September 1, 2023. Available from https://wearabletech.io/myo-bracelet/.

[40] Wearables.com. 2023. "Athos." Accessed September 1, 2023. Available from https://wearables.com/collections/Athos.

[41] WHOOP. 2021. "WHOOP 4.0 vs. 3.0: What's new with the 4.0?." WHOOP, Last Updated September 19, 2021, Accessed September 1, 2023. Available from https://www.whoop.com/us/en/thelocker/whoop-4-0-vs-3-0-whats-new/.

[42] fitbit. Accessed September 1, 2023. Available from https://www.fitbit.com/global/us/home.

[43] fitbit. 2023. "fitbit sense 2." Accessed September 1, 2023. Available from https://www.fitbit.com/global/us/products/smartwatches/sense2?sku=521BKGB.

[44] BioIntelliSense. 2023. "The Award-Winning BioButton Medical Grade Wearable Device for Continuous Remote Monitoring." Accessed September 1, 2023. Available from https://www.biointellisense.com/.

[45] glucoWISE. 2023. "Meet the new non-invasive glucose monitor that helps you take control of your life." Accessed September 1, 2023. Available from https://gluco-wise.com/.

[46] Gatorade. 2023. "Buy Gatorade Gx Sweat Patches - Personalize Your Preparation." Accessed September 1, 2023. Available from https://www.gatorade.com/

[47] BACtrack. 2023. "BACtrack SKYN." Accessed September 1, 2023. Available from https://skyn.bactrack.com/.

[48] Brobbin, E., P. Deluca, S. Hemrage, and C. Drummond. 2022. "Accuracy of Wearable Transdermal Alcohol Sensors: Systematic Review." *J Med Internet Res* 24(4):e35178. doi: 10.2196/35178.

[49] Goodfellow, Ian, Yoshua Bengio, and Aaron Courville. 2016. *Deep Learning*. Cambridge, MA: MIT Press.

[50] Schmuck, D. A., M. Meursing, B. S. Lau, and J. C. Franklin. 2020. "U.S. Patent 11,189,059 B2. Object tracking for head mounted devices." Available from https://patents.google.com/patent/US11189059B2/en.

[51] International Electrotechical Commission (IEC). 2020. "IEC 60034-5. Rotating electrical machines-Part 5: Degrees of protection provided by the integral design of rotating electrical machines (IP code)-Classification."

[52] Mordor Intelligence Research & Advisory. 2023. "Smart Fabrics Market Size & Share Analysis - Growth Trends & Forecasts (2023-2028)." Mordor Intelligence, Accessed August 27, 2023. Available from https://www.mordorintelligence.com/industry-reports/smart-fabrics-market.

[53] Mordor Intelligence Research & Advisory. 2023. "Brain-Computer Interfact Market Size & Share Analysis - Growth Trends & Forecasts (2023-2028)." Mordor Intelligence, Last Updated June 2023, Accessed August 27, 2023. Available from https://www.mordorintelligence.com/industry-reports/brain-computer-interface-market.

[54] Sabry, Farida, Tamer Eltaras, Wadha Labda, Khawla Alzoubi, and Qutaibah Malluhi. 2022. "Machine learning for healthcare wearable devices: The big picture." *J Healthcare Eng* 2022:4653923. doi: 10.1155/2022/4653923.

[55] Victoire, T., M. Vasuki, and Dr A.karunamurthy. 2023. "Google Glass and Virtual Reality a Comprehensive Review of Applications Challenges and Future Directions." *Quing Int J Innov Res Sci Eng* 2:24-36. doi: 10.54368/qijirse.2.2.0004.

[56] Peres da Silva, Jason. 2023. "Privacy Data Ethics of Wearable Digital Health Technology." Brown University Warren Albert Medical School Center for Digital Health, Last Updated May 4, 2023, Accessed September 1, 2023. Available from https://digitalhealth.med.brown.edu/news/2023-05-04/ethics-wearables.

Biographical Sketches

Hossein Kouhani, Ph.D., P.E.

Dr. Hossein Kouhani, an electrical engineering consultant, boasts a wide-ranging expertise that extends from electrical systems to mechanical and biomedical fields. His proficiency in medical devices, electronic circuits, microfabrication, finite element analysis, semiconductor physics, high speed instrumentation, implantable and wearable devices, electrochemistry, and neural stimulation enables him to adeptly navigate a diverse range of hardware and software systems.

In his role as an industry consultant, Dr. Kouhani has primarily focused on projects related to wearable devices, consumer electronics, and batteries. His contributions encompass design review, validation and verification, failure/risk analysis, recall management, pre-certification testing, and root cause analysis.

Throughout his academic journey, he excelled in MEMS design, fabrication, and characterization. Notably, his accomplishments include inventing a pressure-sensing contact lens for glaucoma patients, introducing an optogenetic neural stimulation device for animal studies, and contributing to the development of the next generation of a bionic eye. He has also gained hands-on experience in nanoparticle synthesis, immune cell culture, and advanced microscopy techniques such as SEM, TEM, and MPI. Dr. Kouhani's steadfast commitment to problem-solving and innovation positions him as a valuable resource for addressing engineering challenges and connecting with experts in the field.

Surya Sharma, Ph.D.

Dr. Sharma has a decade of experience in the domain of Computer Science and Electrical Engineering. He has designed, developed, and deployed software, systems and websites based on machine learning, embedded computing, system design, data science, and computer vision, which are used by software engineers, clinicians, nutritionists, and healthcare and human factors researchers. Dr. Sharma applies his computer science and electrical engineering experience in a variety of litigation, mediation, and arbitration matters including patent, copyright, trade secret, and commercial.

Dr. Sharma received his Ph.D. in Computer Engineering from Clemson University, focusing on low-power wearables and connected devices that detect eating by tracking wrist motion using deep learning technologies and tools such as convolutional neural networks, Tensorflow and Keras. Algorithms developed by Dr. Sharma were deployed to Android and Apple wearable devices to be used by clinicians in diabetes research.

Prior to his Ph.D., Dr. Sharma received his B.E. in Electronics and Telecommunications Engineering from Mumbai University, where he developed unmanned aerial vehicles (UAVs) and drones, embedded computing based solutions, and e-commerce and marketing websites.

Chapter 2

Robotics, Computation, and Sensors

Daniel M. Palmer*
Exponent Inc., New York, NY

Abstract

The field of robotics has benefitted greatly from improvements in computer technology enabled by the steady transistor density scaling forecasted by Moore's Law. For a robot to function as a truly independent, untethered mobile platform, it must be able to carry all the hardware it needs to operate, balancing the weight of mechanical, electrical, and computational hardware. Robots must incorporate significant on-board computational resources, and for many years, this has limited the intelligence of robots. In recent years, however, hardware resources have become available that can accommodate sophisticated algorithms for path planning, sensor fusion, artificial intelligence, and general information processing. These advances have let robots enter new frontiers of functionality and tackle all-new applications. This chapter outlines some of these computational tasks underpinning robotics and surveys the state of computational platforms currently available in the robotics space.

Keywords: robotics, hardware, navigation, motion planning, computational platforms

---

* Corresponding author email: dpalmer@exponent.com.

In: Computer Engineering Applications …
Editor: Brian D'Andrade
ISBN: 979-8-89113-488-1

Introduction

Robotics is a broad field that represents the culmination of years of innovation in mechanics, materials science, electronics, computer science, and computer hardware development. Indeed, roboticists are often required by necessity to become jacks-of-all-trades even if they are nominally specialized in one subfield or another. This work will not attempt to cover every area of robotics and will instead focus on the electrical and computational aspects of robotics. These subfields are themselves quite broad and include high-level planning algorithms for both navigation and motion, low-level control algorithms for driving actuators, as well as customized computing hardware to handle the computational workloads demanded of robots. Recent years have seen several robotics development platforms come to the forefront offering high-performance integrated systems-on-chip (SoCs) tailored specifically for robotics applications. To be true enablers of cutting-edge robots, these chips must be able to process data streams from multiple sensors simultaneously, plan motions and navigational routes, update planned actions on the fly as new sensor information arrives, execute artificial intelligence (AI) algorithms efficiently, and manage communications with operators and other robots. This computational burden is significant, and handling it is made possible through a combination of the raw power afforded by transistor scaling and smart architectural design choices by chip designers. As transistors scale down further in size and as ever-improving understanding of robotic computational workloads allows better architectural optimization, robots will become more capable thinkers and increasingly present in everyday life.

Planning Algorithms for Navigation

A fundamental task in the field of robotics is navigation. For robots to be able to move from one place to another and not bump into obstacles, they must have knowledge of their environment (i.e., their workspace), and must have some method of figuring out where they need to go. To perform navigation, robots must be equipped with adequate computational hardware and path planning software. Basic algorithms can be used for low-cost robots navigating low-complexity workspaces such as a warehouse floor, whereas significantly more advanced algorithms are required for higher-complexity workspaces, such as driving on public roads or navigating through the air.

To aid in navigation, it is common for a robot to store a map of its workspace in its on-board memory. For environments that are already well-known and relatively unchanging, such as a warehouse floor, a map may be constructed externally and uploaded to the robot for use. In more dynamic, real-world environments, the robot may start with little to no mapping information and may need to build or update a map in an online fashion. A 2-D workspace map is represented computationally as a list of (x,y) coordinates that discretize the workspace of the robot. Each coordinate can be defined to be part of an object, or free space available for navigation. Higher-resolution maps may offer better performance, but will tax computational resources more heavily, and the designer generally must opt for the right level of granularity to balance navigation performance with resource cost.

To plan a route through a workspace, a robot can execute a navigation algorithm. Designers have many to choose from, ranging from general graph-search algorithms such as Dijkstra's algorithm to more complicated approaches tailored to high-complexity tasks. In general, navigation algorithms aim to efficiently move a robot from one point to another smoothly without extraneous movements.

The problem of navigation can be segmented into four general fields of study. These are perception, localization, motion control, and path planning. Path planning is "the determination of a collision-free path in a given environment" [1]. This environment, especially in uncontrolled, real-world settings, may feature all manner of clutter and obstacles. Certain path planning algorithms work well for certain environments, so it is important that an appropriate algorithm be selected for the environment at hand. Planning is generally harder for robots featuring more degrees of freedom. For instance, planning is much simpler for a two-wheeled, differential-drive robot (such as Roomba from iRobot [2] shown in Figure 1) than it is for a multi-legged walking robot (such as Spot from Boston Dynamics [3]).

The quality of a planned path depends both on the strength of the planning algorithm and on the knowledge a robot has about its workspace. Some workspaces are highly controlled, such as a factory floor, wherein a robot may know à priori the exact layout of the factory and can plan a path all the way from the initial position to a final position at the far end of the factory. In such a static environment, it is worthwhile for the robot to spend central processing unit (CPU) cycles to refine and optimize its computed path before embarking, since the workspace is unlikely to change, and in the process, ruin this optimization. Path planning is of great interest to the field of optimization since an explicit goal is to find routes that minimize objective functions, such as distance traveled, travel time, energy exerted, or another function tailored specifically to the capabilities and costs of the robot in question. This is called *global* path planning since a complete pathway from start to end has been determined.

Figure 1. A Roomba, which features two independently-actuated wheels on the underside that allow the robot to drive straight, turn left or right, or rotate in place.

Other environments are not well-suited to the rigidity of the global path planning approach. For instance, if a robot is moving through a largely unknown environment, wherein the robot is building knowledge about the environment through sensing in an online fashion, the robot should be equipped with the means to convert this new information into a new path. In such a case, owing to environmental uncertainty, it would not be worthwhile to attempt to plan a well-optimized route from start to finish, since this optimization would be based on generally inaccurate knowledge of the environment and could thus be a waste of time and computational resources. As such, the robot must be able to perform *local* path planning, which allows it to create new, shorter paths in response to newly encountered objects [1].

In general, path planning algorithms need to be able to effectively use the information available to the robot in order to produce high-quality paths without overly taxing a robot's on-board computational resources. Several canonical algorithms exist that embody these characteristics and have served as tools of first resort for roboticists for many years. Whether implemented directly or used as inspiration for more tailored algorithms, these baseline approaches are highly valued for their instructive quality. Several of these canonical algorithms will be covered here.

Dijkstra's Algorithm

Dijkstra's algorithm is a seminal path planning algorithm that was originally published in 1959 by E.W. Dijkstra [4]. This algorithm, given enough time, can find the shortest path through any weighted graph. A weighted graph is a conceptual tool built as an interconnected network of nodes, and when used in robotics each node represents a position in the robot's workspace. Each 'edge' of the graph, or connection line between nodes, is weighted with a number that represents the distance between these nodal positions.

Dijkstra's algorithm is highly valued for its conceptual simplicity and is often one of the first planning algorithms taught to new robotics students. However, while Dijkstra's algorithm is simple to understand and guaranteed to find the shortest path between two nodes on a graph, it can take a prohibitively long time to execute, especially for graphs of realistically large complexity. As such, methods have been researched to reduce execution time without overly comprising optimality.

A* Algorithm

A*, first published in 1968 [5], is a modified version of Dijkstra's algorithm that adds in a *heuristic*, which is essentially an educated guess informing the algorithm of a priority area of the graph to search. This algorithm was created as part of the Shakey project, which focused on building a mobile robot that could perform planning for its own motions [6]. Dijkstra's algorithm is a blind search, wherein every possible path between nodes is discovered in a nearest-neighbor fashion, then evaluated for optimality. By biasing this search towards potential solutions that can be predicted to be near-optimal, run time can be reduced. A heuristic used in A* is the straight-line distance from start to goal, which in a well-connected graph should be a strong indicator of the optimality of a given path under consideration. If the planner is building a path through a graph representation of a workspace and notices that this path under construction has grown to be considerably longer than the known straight-line distance of the real workspace, this is an indication that the path currently under consideration should be abandoned without completion and another path should be considered. In effect, a good heuristic gives a planning algorithm a ground reference to which the quality of any computed path can be compared, thus giving the algorithm a pre-considered sense of what a 'good' path looks like without having to compute every path possible across the graph. Good paths can then be accepted quickly, bad paths can be rejected quickly, and a high-quality solution can be found without undue exhaustive searching. While A* is not guaranteed to find the shortest path, as Dijkstra's algorithm guarantees, it will generally decide on a good path much faster than Dijkstra's algorithm can finish its exhaustive search.

Planning Algorithms for Motion

In the language of robotics, a distinction is drawn between *navigation* and *motion*. Navigation is the translation of a robot through its workspace. In an abstract sense, this is the path the centroid of the robot should take. No thought is given at this stage of planning to the specific actions required of the various actuators on the robot to make this planned navigation path happen.

Motion, by contrast, is the act of moving various limbs or appendages of the robot to accomplish specific tasks. For instance, a multi-joint arm twisting and turning to position a gripper (i.e., an end-effector) in just the right pose to allow for grasping an object is a complicated motion problem that requires highly capable planning software and hardware to run it [7].

Motion and navigation come together in various ways to enable robot locomotion. For wheeled, differential-drive robots, the translation from an abstract, planned navigation path to physical wheel turn rates is straightforward. For a legged, walking robot shown in Figure 2, however, this translation is much more complicated. Walking requires that motor rotation rates be determined to actuate joints such that acceptable gaits are produced that avoid obstacles, keep the robot standing upright, and navigate the robot to the intended goal. For workspaces with 3-D obstacles, this problem can become significantly more difficult if the robot must duck and swerve out of the way of objects.

The process of converting intended motions to actuator turn rates is called inverse kinematics. In this framework, a kinematic motion pathway is determined for one piece of the robot's body, and from this path the corresponding joint positions required to move the target piece along this pathway are determined. For instance, if an end-effector on a multi-joint arm (example shown in Figure 3) is to be moved through an arc, the joint motors must each rotate correctly throughout the motion such that the end-effector traverses the intended arc. This is a task of converting complex, rotational motion of several interconnected motors into a resultant linear motion of the end-effector.

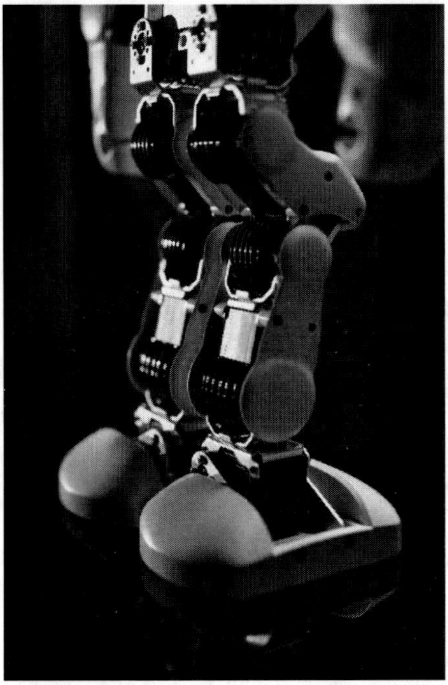

Figure 2. The legs of walking robots have multiple joints, and each must be actuated independently and correctly in order for the robot to traverse a planned path.

This planning process is then an iterative procedure wherein the starting position of the end-effector is known, the desired ending position is known, but the intermediate positions must be computed. This process may not be straightforward; for instance, a seemingly simple straight-line translation of an end-effector on a multi-joint arm may not be physically realizable, as there may be no combination of joint angles that positions the end-effector in each of the intermediate positions it must occupy as it translates from start point to end point. Thus, a capable computational platform is required to search for a sequence of end-effector positions spanning the required end-effector path that also are kinematically compatible with the joints. Many different pathways are likely possible for any given motion, therefore it is the job of the planning algorithm to choose between available routes that achieve efficiency and speed, while also respecting any additional constraints. Constraints, for example, could be the need to keep a grasped object upright, or to stay within electrical constraints such as motor current maximums.

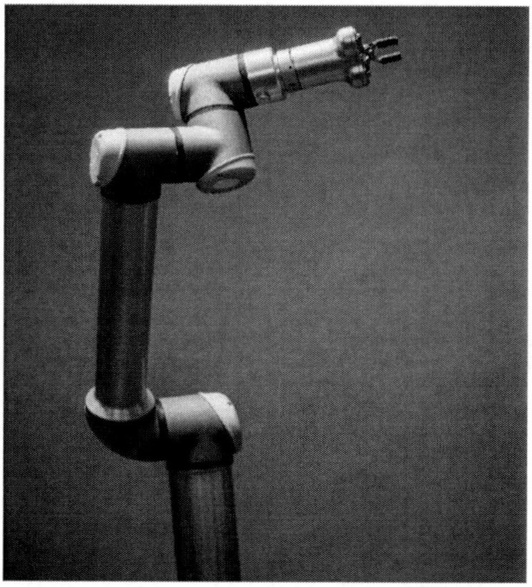

Figure 3. A multi-joint robot arm with a parallel-digit gripper serving as end-effector. The rotational position of each joint contributes to the translational position of the end-effector.

The number of joints for a given arm, leg, or other robotic limb, can be quite large. For instance, the Fetch Mobile Manipulator has seven joints in its arm leading to a parallel-digit gripper [8]. The number of possible joint positions for complex appendages can become prohibitively large for an exhaustive search, leading to the development of probabilistic methods that use educated guessing techniques to find a good motion plan quickly.

Actuator Control Algorithms

The navigation and motion planning algorithms described above operate at a high level of abstraction, deciding where a robot should try to go and how its various joints should bend to create this path. Still required are ways to ensure actuators produce the correct forces to create this motion. Low-level control algorithms are needed for this, such as the standard proportional-integral-derivative (PID) feedback control algorithm, shown in Figure 4, and its variants [9].

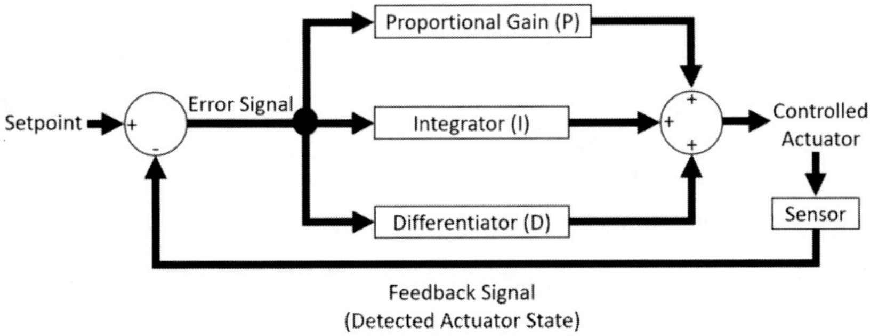

Figure 4. Block diagram depicting a PID feedback control system. The state of a controlled actuator is detected and compared to a setpoint. The difference between the setpoint value and actuator state generates an error signal, which is then input to a PID controller to generate a corrective response.

The PID paradigm is heralded for its simple effectiveness and is one of the first control methods taught in college engineering curricula. As in many feedback control systems, PID controllers measure an output variable, compute the error between its instantaneous value and the value of some predetermined setpoint, and make efforts to adjust this output value accordingly using whatever actuation means are available [10]. While the PID acronym is commonly used, PID controllers are actually a linear superposition of three independent proportional ('P'), integral ('I'), and derivative ('D') controllers, and different permutations of P, I, and D terms can be implemented to achieve different effects. For instance, in a purely proportional controller, the output is corrected in a manner proportional to the current value of the error variable. This kind of feedback is very easy to implement in hardware and is ubiquitous in operational amplifier (op amp) implementations in electronics since it can be implemented with a purely resistive network. A downside of this approach is that the error can never be driven fully to zero, since zero error necessarily produces zero corrective action. While this may seem unintuitive, this result is predicted directly by the mathematics.

An alternative approach that *can* fully cancel error and drive the output all the way to a setpoint is the *integral* controller. In an integral controller, the output variable is adjusted in a manner proportional to the integral of the error variable over time, rather than just its current value. This means that if there is a non-zero error, that error is accumulated by the integration operation and additional corrective action is provided until the error signal has been driven to zero. Once the error signal has reached zero, the integration operation sees no more error to accumulate, and no new corrective action is taken. This approach provides 100% accurate setpoint tracking, but it suffers from the drawback that pure integral controllers can be slow to respond to errors, since they depend on an integrator that must first accumulate sufficient error-time before significant corrective action can be taken. By contrast, the earlier proportional controller creates a corrective response the instant an error signal is observed, and the size of the response directly tracks fluctuations in the error signal.

The third aspect of the PID paradigm is the *derivative* controller, wherein the controller creates a corrective signal in response to the instantaneous rate of change of the error signal. This means that if the error signal is increasing quickly, the derivative controller will prescribe a larger corrective signal than for slower increases. This action is intended to prevent error signals from leaping out of control and may be considered a kind of *predictive* correction, since it is detecting a fast-ramping error signal that could become large in the very near future even if its current value is quite small. But since only the rate of change of the output signal is controlled, no long-term value of the output is prescribed, and thus this kind of controller is difficult to use in isolation.

As mentioned above, it is common, as the PID name suggests, to combine two or three of these base control paradigms into a composite, PI, PD, or full PID controller in order to realize the benefits of each kind of controller while also using each sub-controller to compensate for the faults of the others. For instance, the derivative controller prescribes large corrections for error signals with fast rates of change that can correct for the sluggish initial response of an integral controller that could allow the error signal to grow very large before prescribing any meaningful corrective action. The integral controller, however, is the means by which the error signal is eventually driven to zero, something neither the derivative nor the proportional controller can do on their own. Furthermore, the proportional controller can speed up the composite controller's response to large but slow-moving error signals, and can be used for response time improvements without the same level of susceptibility exhibited by derivative controllers to rapidly-fluctuating noise on the error signal.

The combination of these different sub-controllers into a larger controller is a demonstration of the power of linearity in control systems. By simple addition, which can be done either in analog hardware or digital processing, a complex controller with sophisticated behavior can be realized. However, when building a complex controller, a designer must be careful to ensure that the feedback system remains stable. Feedback control systems generally have the potential to destabilize. In qualitative terms, this means that the loop exhibits too much propagation delay for certain signals, and by the time its corrective signal has reached the output, the output has changed in such a manner that the corrective signal actually makes the error worse. This can occur in a self-perpetuating manner, thus causing the loop to produce oscillatory output (i.e., said to oscillate). Simpler feedback loops can also 'latch up,' wherein they can be stuck in a static, self-reinforcing state that prevents any further ability to react to measured errors.

Analysis tools exist to determine stability [9]. These tools are generally based on the response of the control loop across frequency, and in particular on the locations of frequency cutoff points (i.e., "poles and zeros") of the controller. Amplifier gains, filtering cutoff frequencies, and other parameters can be tuned to push system poles and zeros into acceptable locations. Ensuring stability while meeting performance targets, especially to achieve fast response times, can be very difficult, and oftentimes compromises must be made.

Existing Robotics Development Platforms

There are many robotics platforms in use today. Some are fully integrated, complete robots that can be programmed to perform desired behaviors, and others are modularized development platforms to be integrated by end designers into custom robotic hardware systems.

NVIDIA Suite of Robotics Products

As one example of the latter category, the NVIDIA Isaac robotics platform is a set of software tools intended to accelerate the development of robotics [11, 12]. Described by NVIDIA as an "End-to-End Robotics Platform," these tools allow the user to train neural networks, simulate robot action in a physics-based graphical simulator, then deploy the developed tools on actual hardware. The use of a simulator allows for faster, cheaper, safer, and more efficient robotic behavior development, and allows for multiple developers to work in parallel. This parallelization is critical as robots are often expensive, and a given development team may have only a single robot. Furthermore, having a simulator to work with allows for vetting of behaviors before deployment, reducing the risk that the physical robot will behave erratically or damage itself.

In terms of physical hardware to implement their software offerings, NVIDIA produces the Jetson embedded computation platform [13, 14]. This system includes Jetson modules, the NVIDIA JetPack software development kit (SDK), and what NVIDIA describes as "an ecosystem with sensors, SDKs, services, and products to speed up development." NVIDIA markets Jetson as "a complete System on Module (SOM) that includes a GPU, CPU, memory, power management, high-speed interfaces, and more." Several Jetson products are available, including the Orin, Xavier TX2, and the Nano series, all offering different combinations of price, performance, and form factor.

At the high end of this product line, the AGX Orin model is advertised to be an advanced AI computer, offering "275 trillion operations per second for multiple concurrent AI inference pipelines and high-speed inference support for multiple sensors." Described by NVIDIA as a "system on module (SOM)," the AGX Orin series is based on an Orin SoC, integrating an Arm Cortex-A78AE CPU and integrated Ampere GPU [15]. The Arm Cortex CPU replaces the older NVIDIA Carmel CPU. The GPU is critical for accelerating AI applications, and the move to the Ampere architecture allows support for sparsity operations, wherein zero-valued weights in neural networks are skipped, decreasing execution time. The Orin SoC also includes a deep learning accelerator (DLA) block, which is a "fixed-function accelerator optimized for deep learning operations … designed for offloading deep learning inferencing from the GPU, enabling the GPU to run more complex networks and dynamic tasks" [15]. The Jetson AGX Orin module focuses heavily on providing AI capabilities, as these are of ever-increasing importance in today's robotics applications.

Boston Dynamics: Spot

Boston Dynamics is a notable robotics company famous for releasing videos of their highly complex robots executing sophisticated maneuvers. One of their most prominently advertised products is the Spot robot, a large 4-legged robot with the capacity to carry high-tech sensors on its body [16]. This robot is advertised as providing site inspection and monitoring services [17]. A thermal camera can be included to allow for thermal sensing, enabling detection of hot spots within equipment on-site [18]. A pan-tilt-zoom (PTZ) camera can be included to allow visual inspection of the site [19]. Spot offers gauge-reading functionality with range augmented by zoom lenses, and on-board acoustic imaging equipment that can detect water and gas leaks. Furthermore, Spot can take laser scans of a worksite to allow creation of a 'digital twin,' that is, a digital model of the site that engineers can use to plan maintenance or future improvements [20]. Continued monitoring of the site can feed into this digital twin and keep it accurate to the current state of the site. To enhance the autonomy of the robot, a charging station that allows autonomous self-charging is also available. An operator can teleoperate the robot as well when needed, or can simply monitor the live operation of the robot to keep an eye on its activities. Boston Dynamics includes a proprietary SDK to create custom programs for the robot [21].

Qualcomm Suite of Robotics Products

Qualcomm offers a number of robotics-oriented electronics and development platforms, leveraging the company's existing foothold in the mobile technologies space. An example platform from Qualcomm is the Qualcomm Robotics RB1 Platform (Qualcomm QRB2210) [22]. The objective of this platform is to provide AI and heterogenous computational capabilities. Communications hardware is also included, and the platform aims to achieve "new levels of cost-effectiveness and accessibility for the industry." This platform targets small-scale robots and aims to minimize power consumption. The QRB2210 includes an ARM Cortex-A53 CPU and Qualcomm Adreno 702 GPU. Two cameras can be supported concurrently, and various image processing techniques can be executed on-board. A dedicated digital signal processor (DSP) is included to operate on sensor data.

Another Qualcomm platform is the "Qualcomm Flight RB5 5G Platform," which is a reference design drone featuring Qualcomm electronics hardware, purchasable from ModalAI [23]. The design claims the "world's first 5G and AI drone platform and reference design with best-in-class heterogeneous computing and Wi-Fi 6 connectivity" [24]. The design offers low power consumption, AI capabilities, and 5G and Wi-Fi 6 connectivity [25]. In terms of computational power, the platform utilizes a Qualcomm QRB5165 SoC, which is advertised as being "customized for robotics applications" [26]. This SoC features a Qualcomm AI Engine that can deliver 15 Tera operations per second (TOPS) to power "deep learning workloads and autonomous flight," which incorporates a Hexagon 698 DSP with a hexagon tensor accelerator (HTA) to support edge inferencing. In addition to these AI offerings, the SoC integrates a Kryo 585 CPU, an Adreno 650 GPU, and a Qualcomm Spectra 480 computer vision (CV) image signal processor (ISP) to support high quality video capture and up to seven concurrent cameras. The QRB5165 is advertised by ModalAI as an integrated "premium tier robotics processor," indicating formal recognition of the importance of developing specialized computer chips to handle the computational workloads facing modern robotics [23].

Texas Instruments Suite of Robotics Products

Texas Instruments (TI) has many offerings in the field of microelectronics for computation and sensing, and accordingly has developed many products marketed for use in robotics applications. These offerings run the gamut from low-level sensors, to meso-tier integrated sensor-processor combinations, to full microprocessors offering accelerators designed to execute AI algorithms. TI markets its Sitara AM57x processor as able to run AI "at the edge" [27, 28], a common marketing phrase in the industry to describe computation taking place on mobile embedded devices, an area that has grown significantly as embedded microprocessors have become more capable. TI describes a general framework for integrating AI into mobile, resource-constrained systems: (1) training neural networks takes place on desktops or the cloud in an offline fashion, wherein there are no power or real-time execution constraints, and (2) executing these pre-trained algorithms occurs on embedded processors, which ideally feature hardware optimized for executing AI algorithms. This framework is commonplace since training AI algorithms tends to be much more resource-intensive than the actual execution of these algorithms once training is complete. As such, low-power, embedded hardware can make use of AI, although this framework may place limitations on whether any meaningful online modifications of these algorithms can be made on an embedded processor in response to conditions encountered in the field. No matter the AI algorithm, embedded hardware must be able to execute these algorithms in real-time. To aid in this goal, AI accelerators can be integrated into SoCs.

For an embedded SoC to be useful as a unified robot brain, it must be able to interface to a variety of sensors. A plethora of sensing modalities are currently in use for robotics platforms, each with their own costs and benefits. These features include visible light-based sensing, such as video captured by one or more cameras, optical time-of-flight (ToF) sensors, and light detection and ranging (LIDAR). Other ranging modalities such as radar, millimeter wave (mmWave), and ultrasonic detection, as well as temperature, humidity, and vibration sensors, should be supportable by an embedded SoC.

Optical ToF detection systems comprise an active illuminator and a photodiode to detect reflected light. In ToF range detection, light is emitted and the reflection of this light off an object is detected by a photodetector. The time between emission and the instant of first detection is measured and used to calculate the distance to the object causing the reflection, operating in much the same way as radar. Advanced optical ToF, however, can go beyond basic object detection and allow for actual vision of the robot's environment. For instance, TI reports that their OPT8320 3D ToF sensor has been used to enable "robots to determine the exact angle of a screw and then fine-tune the screwdriver so that screws consistently align without human intervention" [27]. As another example, TI advertises that "a ToF-based analog front end like [TI's] OPT3101 can help identify the distance of a robotic arm to a target and help in accurate positioning" [27]. Enabling these technologies 'at the edge' can require innovation at the base electronics level, and TI offers products that utilize novel and exotic technologies, such as gallium nitride (GaN) devices and time-to-digital converters, to push the limits of optical ToF.

While sensing based on visible light has many advantages, it has the stark disadvantage of only working for materials that reflect light. This can become a problem for detecting transparent obstacles, such as glass. To overcome this issue, radar can be utilized, particularly in the mmWave regime, which operates on the principle of emitting radio-frequency radiation and measuring the return waves bouncing off objects in the environment. This is radio-echo based detection, rather than optical reflection, and objects that fail to reflect visible light may still reflect radio-frequency signals. TI offers products that can perform mmWave detection, advertising "highly integrated single-chip mmWave radar sensors [that] are small, lightweight, and enable real-time processing to occur within the sensor edge, often removing the need for additional processors" [27]. As an added benefit, mmWave sensors can be smaller than optical detection systems, as bulky external optics are not required, and they can be fully enclosed in plastic casing without compromising their functionality.

Owing to their abilities to detect differing classes of materials, robots can likely benefit from including both optical and radio-echo based object detection if area, power, and budget allow. In addition to these object-detection sensors, other sensors such as vibration, temperature, and humidity sensors can be used to monitor the health of a robot, which may be especially useful in harsh environments. Vibration sensors are already used widely in industrial automation to inform maintenance schedules, and these can be added to robots meant to operate in other settings. Temperature and humidity sensors can be used to ensure that the robot's electronics systems are not thermally overstressed, or compensate for thermal drift in other sensors [27, 29].

Academic Interest in Robotics Computing Hardware

A paper published by researchers at Stanford and the University of Illinois describes the notable absence of a CPU task scheduler available in the widely-used robotics software platform Robot Operating System (ROS) in order to optimize CPU usage for robotics workloads [30]. This complex task is left entirely up to the programmer, which can be an enormous burden. The authors debut 'Catan,' an automatic CPU scheduler that considers a user-developed custom application's 'semantic requirements,' and dynamically schedules CPU workloads in response. This can be a very complex problem, as robots are expected to continuously receive stimuli from their many sensing systems and may need to react suddenly to emergent conditions. The required reaction may be a complex physical maneuver of one of the robot's appendages and performing this action may require rapid execution of motion planning software. A CPU workload optimizer would need to be able to re-task enough of the CPU's compute power from lower-priority tasks to the immediate, high-priority task, without causing other failures.

Intuitive

Intuitive, not to be confused with Intuitive Surgical, which produces surgical robots, or Intuitive Robots, which is a Boston Dynamics distribution partner for bringing the Spot robot to Europe, has been described as a 'vision-on-chip' processors company [31], since they architect chips specifically for robotic vision. Vision is a resource-intensive mode of sensing, and these chips are designed to support high-resolution, high-capability vision applications. As robotics requires ever-increasing resolutions and channels of video capture, this strains computation pipelines tremendously. Intuitive's NU4100 is advertised as a single, mission-complete computer chip that incorporates a dual ISP that can handle two video streams at 4K resolution and 60 frames per second (FPS), a depth processing engine, an engine for performing simultaneous localization and mapping (SLAM), a convolutional neural network (CNN) processor for AI image processing, and three CPU cores [32]. The company also sells the older NU4000, as well as larger, more complete sensor modules [32]. These include the M4.5S module, which is based on the "NU4000 Robot-on-Chip (RoC)," and offers 3-D sensing and image processing with AI capabilities, to endow robots with high-quality vision [33]. Furthermore, Intuitive offers the M4.3WN, which provides long-range 3-D tracking and AI capabilities optimized for robotics, visual reality, and drones [34].

Conclusion

This chapter describes examples of certain computational tasks that robotics must perform. Motion and navigational planning, as well as low-level simultaneous control of potentially dozens of actuators, are all tasks that electrical and computing hardware embedded on a robot must be able to handle. Concurrently, robots must support multiple sensors and be able to reason appropriately about their sensor feeds. AI can assist greatly, and in recognition of this, many robotics-tailored computation platforms include both GPUs and dedicated AI accelerators. As general-purpose computing continues to improve as the result of transistor scaling, AI becomes more well-understood in edge-computing applications, and robotics SoC architecture continues to develop, robots will find ever-greater capability and applicability.

References

[1] Karur, K., N. Sharma, C. Dharmatti, and J. E. Siegel. 2021. "A survey of path planning algorithms for mobile robots." *Vehicles* 3:448-468. doi: 10.3390/vehicles3030027.

[2] iRobot. 2022. "Roomba Robot Vacuums." Accessed September 1, 2023. Available from https://www.irobot.com/en_US/roomba.html.

[3] Boston Dynamics. 2023. "Spot - The Agile Mobile Robot." Accessed August 9, 2023. Available from https://bostondynamics.com/products/spot/.

[4] Dijkstra, E. W. 1959. "A note of two problems in connexion with graphs." *Numer Math* 1:269-271. doi: https://doi.org/10.1007/BF01386390.

[5] Hart, P. E., N. J. Nilsson, and B. Raphael. 1968. "A formal basis for the heuristic determination of minimum cost paths." *IEEE Trans Syst Sci Cybern* 4(2):100-107. doi: 10.1109/TSSC.1968.300136.

[6] Nilsson, Nils J. 2010. *The Quest for Artificial Intelligence*. New York: Cambridge University Press.

[7] Tzafestas, Spyros G. 2018. "Mobile Robot Control and Navigation: A Global Overview." *J Intell Robot Syst* 91(1):35-58. doi: 10.1007/s10846-018-0805-9.

[8] Wise, Melonee, Michael Ferguson, Daniel King, Eric Diehr, and David Dymesich. "Fetch & Freight: Standard Platforms for Service Robot Applications," in, 2016.

[9] Johnson, M. A., and M. H. Moradi. 2005. "PID Control Fundamentals." In *PID Control: New Identification and Design Methods*, edited by M.A. Johnson and M.H. Moradi, 47-107. London: Springer-Verlag.

[10] Somefun, Oluwasegun Ayokunle, Kayode Akingbade, and Folasade Dahunsi. 2021. "The dilemma of PID tuning." *Ann Rev Control* 52:65-74. doi: https://doi.org/10.1016/j.arcontrol.2021.05.002.

[11] NVIDIA. 2023. "NVIDIA Isaac: The Accelerated Platform for Robotics and AI." Accessed August 10, 2023. Available from https://www.nvidia.com/en-us/deep-learning-ai/industries/robotics/.

[12] Sheshadri, Suhas H. 2023. "Build High Performance Robotic Applications with NVIDIA Isaac ROS Developer Preview 3." Last Updated April 18, 2023, Accessed August 10, 2023. Available from https://developer.nvidia.com/blog/build-high-performance-robotic-applications-with-nvidia-isaac-ros-developer-preview-3/.

[13] NVIDIA. 2023. "NVIDIA Jetson: Accelerating Next-Gen Edge AI and Robotics." Accessed August 10, 2023. Available from https://www.nvidia.com/en-us/autonomous-machines/embedded-systems/.

[14] Robot Report Staff. 2022. "NVIDIA releases robotics development tools at GTC." Accessed August 10, 2023. Available from https://www.therobotreport.com/nvidia-releases-new-robotics-development-tools-gtc/.

[15] Karumbunathan, L. 2022. "NVIDIA Jetson AGX Orin Series: A Giant Leap Forward for Robotics and Edge AI Applications, NVIDIA Jetson AGX Orin Series Technical Brief v1.2." Santa Clara, CA: NVIDIA, Available from https://www.nvidia.com/content/dam/en-zz/Solutions/gtcf21/jetson-orin/nvidia-jetson-agx-orin-technical-brief.pdf.

[16] Boston Dynamics. 2023. "Spot: Enterprise Asset Management Kit." Accessed August 9, 2023. Available from https://bostondynamics.com/wp-content/uploads/2023/07/Spot-Enterprise-Kit-23-0606-1.pdf.

[17] Boston Dynamics. 2020. "Game Changing Automation: Six Steps for Implementing Agile Mobile Robots." Accessed August 9, 2023. Available from https://bostondynamics.com/whitepaper/6-steps-for-implementing-agile-mobile-robots/.

[18] Boston Dynamics. 2023. "Thermal Sensing & Inspection Solutions." Accessed August 9, 2023. Available from https://bostondynamics.com/solutions/inspection/thermal/.

[19] Boston Dynamics. 2023. "RATP: Inspections after Dark." Accessed August 9, 2023. Available from https://bostondynamics.com/case-studies/ratp/.

[20] Boston Dynamics. 2023. "Efficiently Capture Digital Twins." Accessed August 9, 2023. Available from https://bostondynamics.com/solutions/site-management/digital-twin/.

[21] Boston Dynamics. 2023. "Spot SDK." Accessed August 9, 2023. Available from https://dev.bostondynamics.com/.

[22] Qualcomm. 2023. "Qualcomm Robotics RB1 Platform (Qualcomm QRB2210)." Accessed July 25, 2023. Available from https://docs.qualcomm.com/bundle/publicresource/87-61720-1_REV_A_QUALCOMM_ROBOTICS_RB1_PLATFORM__QUALCOMM_QRB2210__PRODUCT_BRIEF.pdf.

[23] ModalAI. 2023. "Qualcomm Flight RB5 5G Platform Drone Reference Design." Accessed August 10, 2023. Available from https://www.modalai.com/products/qualcomm-flight-rb5-5g-platform-reference-drone?variant=39517470326835.

[24] ModalAI. 2023. "Unleashing 5G with Qualcomm Flight™ RB5 5G Platform." Accessed August 10, 2023. Available from https://www.modalai.com/pages/qualcomm-flight-rb5-5g-platform.

[25] Qualcomm. 2021. "Qualcomm Flight RB5 5G Platform." Accessed August 9, 2023. Available from https://www.qualcomm.com/content/dam/qcomm-martech/dm-assets/documents/qualcomm_flight-rb5-5g-platform-product-brief_87-28734-1.pdf.

[26] Qualcomm. 2021. "QRB5165 SoC for IoT." Accessed August 29, 2023. Available from https://www.qualcomm.com/content/dam/qcomm-martech/dm-assets/documents/qrb5165-soc-product-brief_87-28730-1-b.pdf.

[27] Chevrier, Matthieu. 2019. "How Sensor Data Is Powering AI in Robotics." Dallas, TX: Texas Instruments, Available from https://www.ti.com/lit/pdf/sszy036.

[28] Texas Instruments. 2015. "Sitara AM57x processor with dual ARM Cortex-A15 cores." Texas Instruments, Accessed August 9, 2023. Available from https://www.ti.com/lit/pdf/sprt689.

[29] Texas Instruments. 2020. *An Engineer's Guide to Industrial Robot Designs: A Compendium of Technical Documentation on Robotic System Designs*. Dallas, TX: Texas Instruments.

[30] Partap, A., S. Grayson, M. Huzaifa, S. Adve, B. Godfrey, S. Gupta, K. Hauser, and R. Mittal. "On-Device CPU Scheduling for Robot Systems," in *2022 IEEE/RSJ International Conference on Intelligent Robots and Systems (IROS)*, 2022, 11296-11303.

[31] Wessling, B. 2022. "Intuitive announces NU4100 IC robotics processor." Last Updated September 26, 2022, Accessed August 10, 2023. Available from https://www.therobotreport.com/inuitive-announces-nu4100-ic-robotics-processor/.

[32] Intuitive. 2016. "NU4100." Accessed August 10, 2023. Available from https://www.inuitive-tech.com/product/nu4100/.

[33] Intuitive. 2023. "M4.5S." Accessed August 10, 2023. Available from https://www.inuitive-tech.com/product/m4-5s.

[34] Intuitive. 2023. "M4.3WN." Accessed August 10, 2023. Available from https://www.inuitive-tech.com/product/m4-3wn/

Biographical Sketch

Daniel M. Palmer, Ph.D.

Dr. Palmer has extensive experience in the design of integrated circuits that are highly specialized for robotics applications, which was the focus of his Ph.D. work at Cornell University. Dr. Palmer has formal education in both robotics and electronics and takes great interest in exploring the intersection of the two fields. In addition to his experience designing and testing integrated circuits, Dr. Palmer has developed and published novel, formal theory analyzing how the low-level sensing performance of his chips translates to their high-level effectiveness at tracking the position of mobile platforms on which they are mounted. Before pursuing his Ph.D. in Electrical & Computer Engineering at Cornell, Dr. Palmer received the B.S. degree in Engineering from Swarthmore College. He now lives near New York City.

Chapter 3

Applied Image Processing and Computer Vision for Materials Science and Engineering

Surya Sharma[1,*], PhD
Janille Maragh[1], PhD
Susan Han[2], PhD
Chongyue Yi[1], PhD
and Cathy Chen[3], PhD, PE
[1]Exponent, Inc., Menlo Park, CA, USA
[2]Exponent, Inc., Natick, MA, USA
[3]Exponent, Inc., New York, NY, USA

Abstract

Image processing and computer vision is playing a transformative role in science and engineering, such as in the domains of material science and the fourth industrial revolution referred to as Industry 4.0. We shed light on cutting-edge applications that have the potential to reshape these fields. We also explore the integral connection between computer vision and Industry 4.0, underscoring the significance of computer vision in the industrial manufacturing processes. Throughout this chapter, we demonstrate how computer vision applications can be developed for Industry 4.0.

Keywords: image processing, computer vision, materials science, particle size analysis, edge detection

---

* Corresponding Author's Email: ssharma@exponent.com.

In: Computer Engineering Applications …
Editor: Brian D'Andrade
ISBN: 979-8-89113-488-1

Introduction

Computer vision is a field of computer engineering that focuses on enabling computers to interpret and understand visual information provided as images, videos, or other visual data such as point clouds or matrices. Computer vision often relies on the subfield of image processing, which uses mathematical operations on the pixel data of images to enhance images so the resulting data are easier for computer algorithms to process. Examples of image processing operations are ones that make the images sharper or extract edges to highlight information that may be more relevant to the problem being solved by computer vision.

Some of the most popular applications of computer vision include:

- Autonomous Vehicles: Computer vision has found a booming use in self-driving cars to detect and recognize objects, such as other vehicles, pedestrians, and road signs; enabling autonomous driving in vehicles.
- Healthcare: Software using computer vision is being rapidly developed that can be used to detect diseases such as cancer by analyzing medical images in the form of X-rays, magnetic resonance imaging (MRI), and computed tomography (CT) scan data.
- Optical Character Recognition: Image processing and computer vision is used to recognize text in images and convert it into machine-readable text, for example, to import handwritten forms or printed text into computer software.
- Biometric Systems: Facial detection, fingerprint scanning, and iris detection are commonly used to identify persons. This information can be used for identity verification in commerce, law enforcement, and personnel tracking.
- Robotics: Computer vision is used in robotics for object recognition, tracking, and navigation.
- Security: Computer vision can be used for surveillance and security purposes, such as detecting intruders or suspicious behavior.

In this chapter, we discuss novel applications of image processing and computer vision within the domains of materials science and engineering. We first provide a tutorial on classical image processing techniques and computer vision applications. We then discuss lesser-known applications of these techniques as applied to real world problems and data sources, such as using computer vision in industrial manufacturing processes [1], often cited as the fourth industrial revolution, or Industry 4.0 [2]. We discuss this computer vision-based inspection using concrete examples of computer vision deployed in industry, for example defect inspection techniques used in manufacturing plants. We also discuss the application of computer vision in the retail industry where it is used to estimate mounted gemstone weight. In the latter half of this chapter, we explore another lesser-known application of computer vision—material science. We discuss the application of computer vision to problems such as particle size distribution analysis for quality control, as well as estimating properties of matter using computer vision such as the reflectivity and hardness of particles found in situ.

A Tutorial on Image Processing and Computer Vision

While image processing and computer vision are related, and computer vision relies on image processing to function, they have distinct focuses and objectives. These differences are presented in Table 1.

Table 1. A comparison of image processing and computer vision

Aspect	Image Processing	Computer Vision
Definition	The manipulation and enhancement of image data to extract information or improve their quality without understanding the content.	Algorithms and systems that enable machines to interpret and understand visual information from the world, similar to human vision.
Primary Goal	Modify or extract features from images for subsequent analysis or to reduce noise.	Enable a machine to understand and interpret the contents of an image, such as object recognition, tracking, and scene understanding.
Key Techniques	Filtering, transformation, noise reduction, and image enhancement.	Object detection, segmentation, recognition, and three-dimensional (3-D) reconstruction.
Example of a Use Case	Enhancing a photograph by adjusting contrast, brightness, and color balance.	Detecting and tracking pedestrians in a video feed for autonomous driving.

A typical application of computer vision typically involves many steps, such as data collection to generate a dataset, which includes representing images digitally on a computer, image processing to reduce noise or improve the quality of the image, and then computer vision algorithms to perform an artificial intelligence (AI) task. Figure 1 shows a flowchart on how image data is processed in a computer vision application.

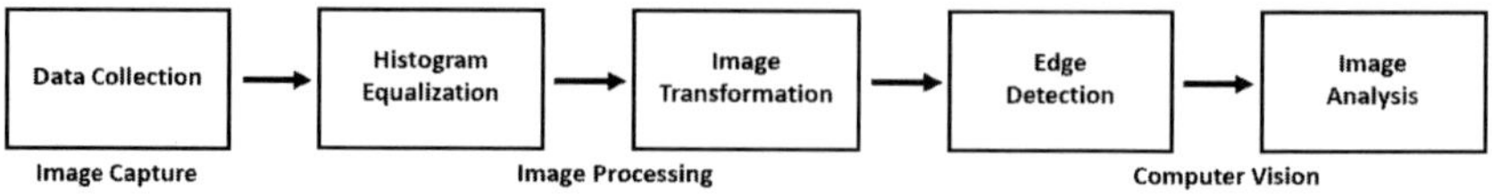

Figure 1. Flowchart showing how image processing and computer vision are combined to provide a computer with the ability to process image data.

Representing Images Digitally

Before discussing image processing or computer vision in detail, it is helpful to understand how images are represented and stored in computer systems, since the method of storing images will greatly impact how images are processed by a computer. Images are often represented digitally as matrices containing numbers. Each matrix element (i.e., cell) is a picture element (i.e., pixel [px]). Images may be monochrome (such as black and white), grayscale, or colored. Colored images are represented by multiple matrices, one for each of the primary colors—red, green, blue (RGB). The figures below show how images can be represented using matrices in an example image that is 9px wide x 9px high.

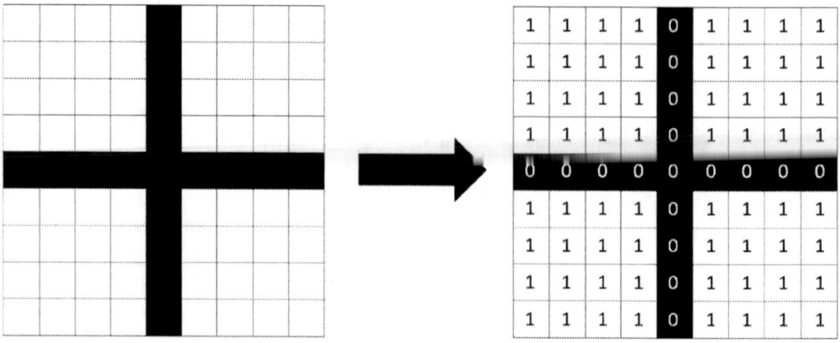

Figure 2. An example of how 0 and 1 values may be used to represent a monochrome image digitally. White pixels are represented by 1, while black pixels are represented by 0.

First consider a monochrome image. Visually, a monochrome image may be represented as a black and white image, also known as a binary image. Since there are only two possible values for a pixel, each cell can be represented as 0 (for white) and 1 (for black), or vice-versa. In Figure 2, we show how the image on the left may be represented on a computer (right).

A grayscale image, in comparison, can visually appear to have gradients, such as in black and white photographs. Such images can be represented digitally using values between 0 (for white) and 1 (for black), or vice versa. For example, in a system where 5 values are possible, matrix values may be 0, 0.25, 0.5, 0.75, and 1. Modern computers often use bytes to represent values, which allows values between 0 and 255 (the maximum value that can be stored by a byte). When using one byte to store data for every pixel in an image, the grayscale image shown on the left in Figure 3 may be represented using the values on the right.

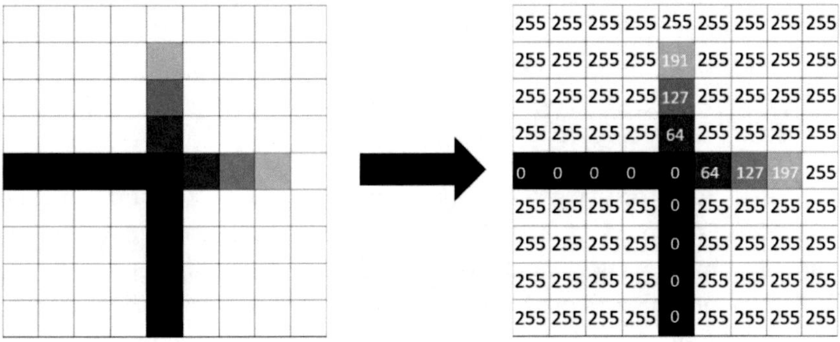

Figure 3. An example of how the values 0 – 255 may be used to represent a grayscale image digitally. White pixels are represented by 255, while black pixels are represented by 0.

Finally, for a color image to be represented digitally, a system will often use multiple matrices, one for each primary color that can be displayed by a computer system. Modern displays that use light emitting diodes (LED) are manufactured using individual RGB pixels in the hardware because these colors are considered the primary colors for displaying image data. Figure 4 shows a 9px by 9px color image, and how such an image is stored digitally as three individual matrices, one for each color.

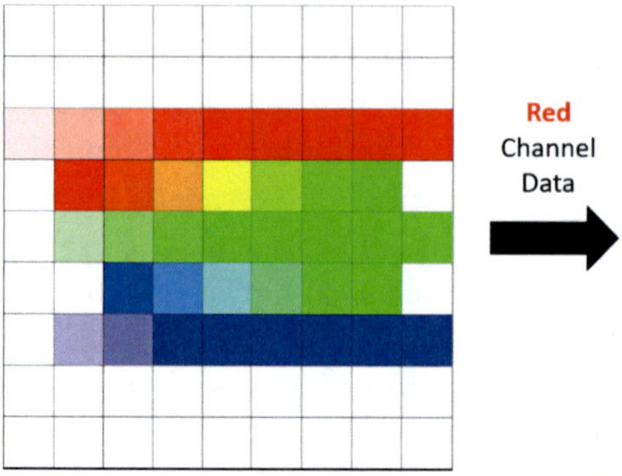

255	255	255	255	255	255	255	255	255
255	255	255	255	255	255	255	255	255
255	255	255	255	255	255	255	255	255
255	255	255	255	255	195	68	17	255
255	255	255	255	255	255	255	255	255
255	255	255	255	255	255	255	255	255
255	255	255	255	255	255	255	255	255
255	255	255	255	255	255	255	255	255
255	255	255	255	255	255	255	255	255

Figure 4. An example showing the digital representation of the red channel in a color image. As the pixel becomes greener, there is less red in the pixel, and thus the red channel values are lower. The color image also contains data from green and blue channels, which are separate and independent. The green and blue channels behave similarly to the red channel shown here. A white pixel in a color image is represented by assigning the value of 255 to all three channels.

Digital Image Processing

Digital image processing is deeply intertwined and built on the knowledge learned in the field of digital signal processing (DSP), a discipline that harnesses mathematical methods to manipulate and analyze signals, often stored as one dimensional (1-D) matrices or arrays on a computer. The transition from 1-D signals to two dimensional (2-D) images creates a fundamental shift in the operations applied to them. In image processing, many operations revolve around matrix transformations, allowing us to manipulate the content of an image with mathematical precision. Cross-correlation (often called convolution) is the most common of these transformations and form the basis of many digital signal processing techniques [3]. Convolution involves sliding a small matrix, called a kernel or a filter, over a signal. At each position, element-wise multiplications are performed, and the results are summed to produce a new signal value. In digital image processing, convolutions are performed on 2-D image data using 2-D kernels. This operation, akin to a stencil being applied to a canvas, as shown in Figure 5, enables a wide range of results, such as edge detection, blurring, or sharpening.

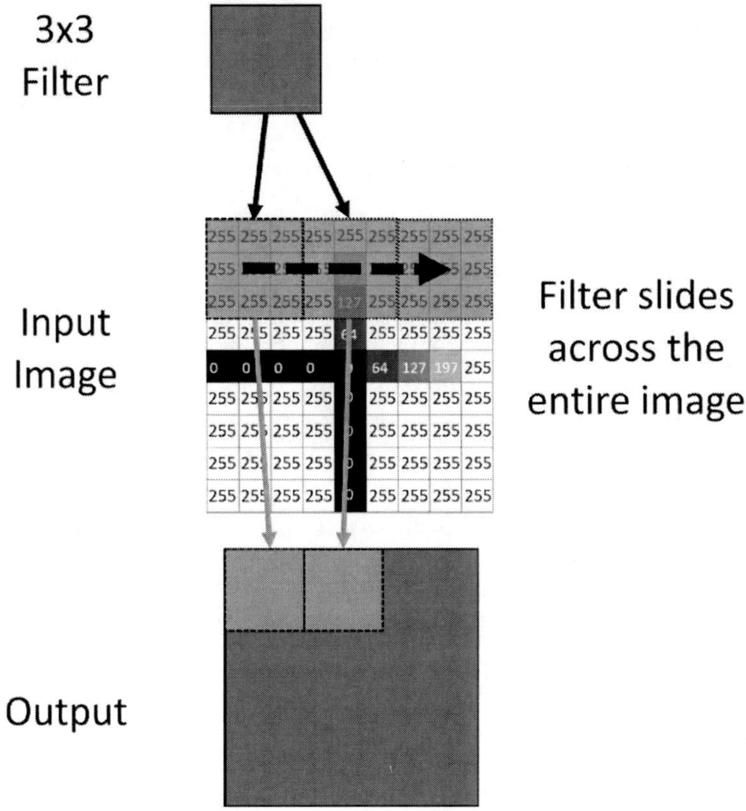

Figure 5. The cross-correlation (i.e., convolution) operation of image processing. A filter slides across an input image and mathematical operations are performed at each step of the slide.

In the domain of digital image processing, this process is often called applying a filter—a callback to the days of traditional photography where physical filters were applied to camera lenses to achieve similar effects. These processes help a computer clean raw image data obtained from a camera so that other algorithms can process the image easily. For example, raw images from a camera may contain noise that makes it difficult to see interesting shapes in an image. The blurring operation using a kernel that averages local sections of the image can remove this noise from an image. Kernels such as the mean or median kernel help achieve this noise removal goal. Alternatively, an image that is too blurry may also be difficult to process because it may be difficult to identify important shapes in an image. In such a case, simpler kernels, such as a sharpening kernel, may be used, although, often specialized filters, such as an edge detection filter, are used for this task. An exhaustive discussion of these operations is beyond the scope of this chapter, so we discuss many of these operations in brief, and focus on the small subset of operations that are relevant to the themes of this chapter—applied image processing and computer vision for material science and engineering.

Image Filtering

Image filtering is used to filter images using processes that remove noise or enhance certain features in an image. Filtering is performed using a structuring element (kernel or filter) that is passed over an image in a window-like manner, which, as noted above, is called convolution. This element is typically a square or a disk-shaped set of pixels [4]. Operations performed between the pixels of the kernel and the pixels of the image as aligned with the center or origin of the kernel are defined by the values of other pixels that are covered by the kernel [5]. The determination of the value of this pixel at the origin of the kernel is what distinguishes different morphological transformations.

Image filtering can be performed using various filters such as a median, Gaussian, or a Laplacian filter. Image filtering is commonly used in applications such as edge detection, noise reduction, and image sharpening.

Image Transformation

Image transformation operations are used to change the geometric properties of an image, such as its size, orientation, or perspective. Common image transformations include scaling, rotation, and perspective correction. Image transformation is commonly used in applications such as image resizing and image registration.

These operations are crucial techniques in the field of computer vision. They are used modify the geometric properties of images, rectify distortions, and enhance the quality of visual information. Perspective correction specifically addresses issues related to the perspective projection of 3-D scenes onto a 2-D image plane, which is common when using camera data. For example, in the domain of augmented reality (AR), virtual objects need to be rendered realistically in a real-world environment captured using a camera. Image transformations ensure that virtual objects align correctly with the real-world scene, even as the camera moves or changes orientation. These transformations are also useful for image data obtained from techniques other than cameras such as X-ray, MRI, or CT scan data, and ensure accurate measurements and analysis can be conducted for diagnostics.

In the domain of object detection, often used for technologies like autonomous driving, perspective distortion can lead to inaccuracies in identifying objects. Correcting the perspective distortion enhances the accuracy of object localization and classification. For autonomous vehicles, this helps in navigation, obstacle detection, and lane detection. Additionally, image transformations can also be used for camera calibration, which involves determining parameters of a camera such as the focal length or lens distortion coefficients.

Image transformations are also useful for document scanning and optical character recognition (OCR). Pages are often scanned at an angle or with perspective distortion. Image transformation processes scanned documents to make them appear flat and rectangular, making it easier for OCR algorithms to accurately extract text.

By rectifying perspective distortions or changing the geometric properties of images, these operations improve the reliability and overall quality of visual data such that other computer algorithms can better interpret and analyze images, making them an important component of image processing.

Image Morphology

These operations are used to analyze the shape and structure of objects in an image. Common morphological operations are erosion, dilation, opening, and closing.

Dilation and Erosion

Dilation and erosion are the two fundamental techniques on which all other morphological image processing techniques are based [4]. Morphological image processing involves the alteration of shapes in images through the modification of pixels based on the values of pixels in their vicinity. This modification leads to shape reduction in the case of erosion and shape expansion in the case of dilation; the consequent changes in these shapes are dictated by the structuring elements used to carry out these processes.

A structural element is often a kernel or filter, and typically a square or disk-shaped set of pixels [4]. As the kernel is passed over an image, the value of the image's pixel that is aligned with the center or origin of the kernel is defined by the values of other pixels that are covered by the kernel [4]. The determination of the value of this pixel at the origin of the kernel is what distinguishes different morphological transformations.

In the case of dilation, the maximum value of all the pixels covered by the kernel is assigned to the pixel at the origin of the kernel. Conversely, in the case of erosion, the minimum value of all of the pixels covered by the kernel is assigned to the pixel of the image located at the kernel's origin [4]. Both dilation and erosion tend to lead to smoothing borders of a closed object within the image [6].

Table 2 shows examples of kernel shapes used for dilation and erosion, such as the square, cross, diagonal, and disc kernels. All kernels are 5px x 5px to emphasize the shape of the kernel.

Table 2. Example kernel shapes used in image processing

Square	$\begin{bmatrix} 1 & 1 & 1 & 1 & 1 \\ 1 & 1 & 1 & 1 & 1 \\ 1 & 1 & 1 & 1 & 1 \\ 1 & 1 & 1 & 1 & 1 \\ 1 & 1 & 1 & 1 & 1 \end{bmatrix}$
Cross	$\begin{bmatrix} 0 & 0 & 1 & 0 & 0 \\ 0 & 0 & 1 & 0 & 0 \\ 1 & 1 & 1 & 1 & 1 \\ 0 & 0 & 1 & 0 & 0 \\ 0 & 0 & 1 & 0 & 0 \end{bmatrix}$
Diagonal	$\begin{bmatrix} 1 & 0 & 0 & 0 & 0 \\ 0 & 1 & 0 & 0 & 0 \\ 0 & 0 & 1 & 0 & 0 \\ 0 & 0 & 0 & 1 & 0 \\ 0 & 0 & 0 & 0 & 1 \end{bmatrix}$
Disc	$\begin{bmatrix} 0 & 0 & 1 & 0 & 0 \\ 0 & 1 & 1 & 1 & 0 \\ 1 & 1 & 1 & 1 & 1 \\ 0 & 1 & 1 & 1 & 0 \\ 0 & 0 & 1 & 0 & 0 \end{bmatrix}$

The result of performing the erosion operation on an input image results in the painted regions of an image becoming smaller. This is demonstrated in Figure 6 which shows an input image that is 9px x 8px. The input image represents an image containing a white disc that is 7px at its widest section, surrounded by a border of 1px around the white disc.

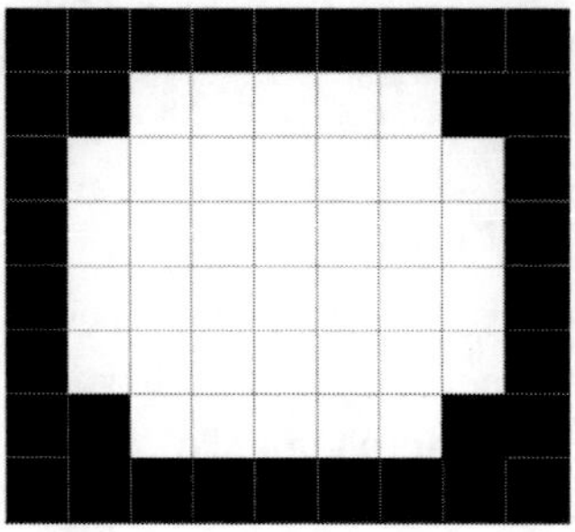

$$\rightarrow \begin{bmatrix} 0 & 0 & 0 & 0 & 0 & 0 & 0 & 0 & 0 \\ 0 & 0 & 1 & 1 & 1 & 1 & 1 & 0 & 0 \\ 0 & 1 & 1 & 1 & 1 & 1 & 1 & 1 & 0 \\ 0 & 1 & 1 & 1 & 1 & 1 & 1 & 1 & 0 \\ 0 & 1 & 1 & 1 & 1 & 1 & 1 & 1 & 0 \\ 0 & 1 & 1 & 1 & 1 & 1 & 1 & 1 & 0 \\ 0 & 0 & 1 & 1 & 1 & 1 & 1 & 0 & 0 \\ 0 & 0 & 0 & 0 & 0 & 0 & 0 & 0 & 0 \end{bmatrix}$$

Figure 6. An example 9px x 8px input image shown graphically on the left and as a matrix on the right.

A square kernel of 3 x 3, as shown in Figure 7, is used for the erosion operation.

$$\begin{bmatrix} 1 & 1 & 1 \\ 1 & 1 & 1 \\ 1 & 1 & 1 \end{bmatrix}$$

Figure 7. An example 3 x 3 square kernel.

When the erosion operation using the 3 x 3 square kernel is performed on the input image, the resulting image, shown in Figure 8, contains a square that is 5px wide, showing how the erosion operation "erodes" parts of the image.

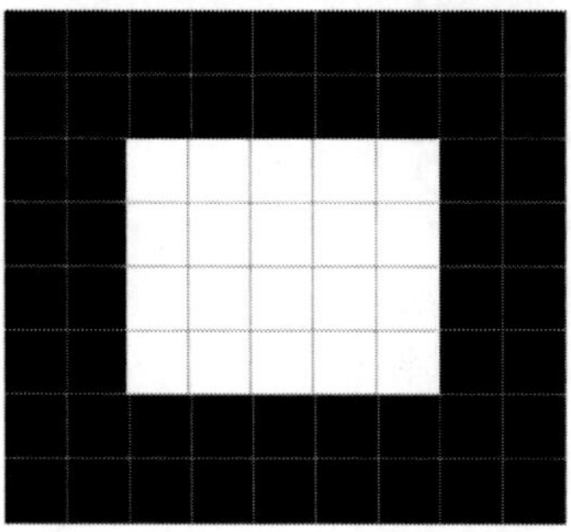

$$\rightarrow \begin{bmatrix} 0 & 0 & 0 & 0 & 0 & 0 & 0 & 0 & 0 \\ 0 & 0 & 0 & 0 & 0 & 0 & 0 & 0 & 0 \\ 0 & 0 & 1 & 1 & 1 & 1 & 1 & 0 & 0 \\ 0 & 0 & 1 & 1 & 1 & 1 & 1 & 0 & 0 \\ 0 & 0 & 1 & 1 & 1 & 1 & 1 & 0 & 0 \\ 0 & 0 & 1 & 1 & 1 & 1 & 1 & 0 & 0 \\ 0 & 0 & 0 & 0 & 0 & 0 & 0 & 0 & 0 \\ 0 & 0 & 0 & 0 & 0 & 0 & 0 & 0 & 0 \end{bmatrix}$$

Figure 8. The output image (or the result of applying the 3 x 3 kernel to the input image).

Dilation and erosion both smooth objects by removing noise, filling small holes, separating joined objects, or joining separated objects. Dilation leads to growing filled objects, thickening lines, and the filling of small holes, whereas erosion leads to the shrinking of the object, thinning of thicker lines, and the removal of stray thin lines and pixels [7].

Opening and Closing

When erosion and dilation are carried out in series, the total process is referred to as opening or closing. In morphological opening, erosion is performed first, after which dilation is performed. The effects of morphological opening are the removal of noise around objects and smoothing their boundaries. Conversely, in morphological closing, dilation is followed by erosion. The effects of morphological closing are the removal of noise within an object and filling small holes within objects [7].

The effect of the erosion, dilation, opening, and closing operations can be understood graphically. Using the computer vision tool OpenCV, in Figure 9 and Figure 10, we show examples of performing these operations on a fixed input image using two different sized filters. Figure 10 illustrates that a larger filter size results in a more drastic change on the input image. OpenCV code used to generate these examples is provided in the appendix.

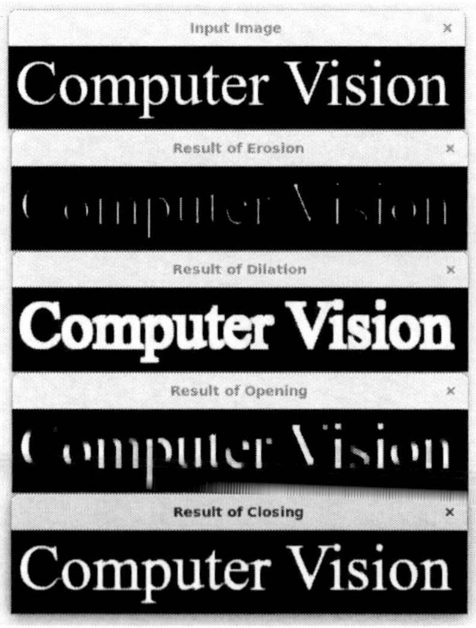

Figure 9. Screenshot from an OpenCV window showing the effect of using a 5 x 5 filter for erosion, dilation, opening, and closing.

Figure 10. Screenshot from an OpenCV window showing the effect of using a 10 x 10 filter for erosion, dilation, opening and closing. The effect of using a larger filter size is more dramatic.

Image Arithmetic

An image arithmetic operation is used to perform arithmetic operations on the pixel values of an image. Common image arithmetic operations include addition, subtraction, multiplication, and division. Image arithmetic is commonly used in applications such as image blending and image contrast adjustment.

Image Histogram Analysis

An image histogram analysis operation is used to analyze the distribution of pixel values in an image. It can be done by creating a histogram of the pixel values and analyzing its shape and characteristics. Image histogram analysis is commonly used in applications such as image thresholding and color correction.

Edge Detection

Edges within an image characterize boundaries between different textures or separation of features. Edges can correspond to changes in depth or surface orientation, a difference in material, and changes in scene illumination. Edge detection techniques can filter out noise and useless data while preserving the important structural information in an image. In early work, edges were drawn by human participants and compared to those generated by a computer. An example of edges generated by a human are illustrated in Figure 11, in which different participants were asked to visually assess where boundaries were in different images [8].

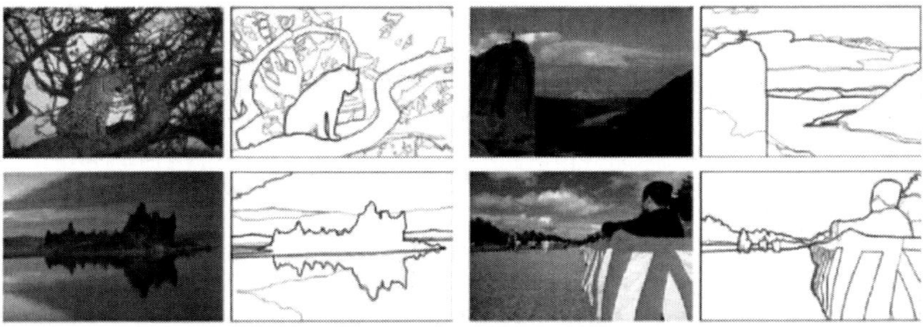

Figure 11. Example of edge detection by humans, where the darkness of the edges corresponds to how many human subjects marked an object boundary at that location (Source: Martin et al., 2004 [8]).

Edges are found by comparing pixels in an image and determining where there is a sharp change in brightness. Comparing pixels that are horizontally adjacent will detect vertical changes in intensity, and vice versa. Note that a horizontal edge detector will not show horizontal changes in intensity since the difference is zero. Generally speaking, edge detection can be grouped into two sub-categories that use different methods: the first order derivative (i.e., the gradient method) and the second-order derivative (i.e., Laplacian-based edge detection, also called zero-crossing) [9].

The gradient method, a search-based approach, searches for local maxima of the gradient magnitude using the gradient direction. The local gradient points in the direction of steepest ascent in the intensity function. The magnitude is the strength of the variation, and the orientation of the gradient is the perpendicular to the local contour [10]. In practice, edges are obtained by using kernels that are convolved on input images. There are many well-known operations that result in edge images. Here we discuss two common ones: The Sobel operator and the Canny edge detector.

Sobel Operator

The Sobel operator (also known as the Sobel-Feldman operator) was first presented in 1968 in a talk titled "An Isotropic 3 x 3 Image Gradient Operator" given at the Stanford Artificial Intelligence Project [11]. Applying the Sobel operator on an input image results in an output binary image that contains images. The Sobel operator searches for local maxima across the horizontal and vertical directions of an image.

If we consider the arrangement of pixels about a point (x,y) in a clockwise manner, the pixels can be labelled as $a_{0,}a_{1,...}a_7$, as shown below. Consider the 3 by 3 segment of an image containing the pixels labelled below:

$$\begin{bmatrix} a_0 & a_1 & a_2 \\ a_7 & (x,y) & a_3 \\ a_6 & a_5 & a_4 \end{bmatrix}$$

The Sobel operator computes the magnitude of a 3 x 3 window at each pixel of an input image using the equation below:

$$|M| = \sqrt{s_x^2 + s_y^2}$$

Where the partial derivatives S_x and S_y are computed by:

$$S_x = (a_2 + ca_3 + a_4) - (a_0 + ca_7 + a_6)$$
$$S_y = (a_0 + ca_1 + a_2) - (a_6 + ca_5 + a_4),$$

with a constant c=2. S_x is horizontal convolution matrix and $S_x$is vertical convolution matrix [12, 13].

The result of applying this operator is that edges are highlighted as they result in larger values of $|M|$. The gradient operators S_x and S_y can be implemented in software as kernels for convolution:

$$S_x = \begin{bmatrix} -1 & 0 & 1 \\ -2 & 0 & 2 \\ -1 & 0 & 1 \end{bmatrix}$$

$$S_y = \begin{bmatrix} 1 & 2 & 1 \\ 0 & 0 & 0 \\ -1 & -2 & -1 \end{bmatrix}$$

And the gradient direction can be calculated by:

$$\theta = arctan(S_y/S_x)$$

Sobel operators can be expanded to larger kernels, such as 5 x 5, 7 x 7, or larger, however as the kernel size increases, more pixels are processed and result in averaging of the result, causing blurry edges. Thus, the 3 x 3, 5 x 5, and 7 x 7 kernels are most common.

Canny Edge Detector

The Canny edge detection algorithm is a multi-step algorithm proposed by John Canny in 1986 [14]. The steps it employs are:

1. Noise reduction with a Gaussian filter.
2. Finding the intensities of the gradients in the image.
3. Determining gradient magnitude and direction with a kernel filter (common implementations use the 3 x 3 Sobel operator, but other operators or multiple operators can be used).
4. Non-maxima suppression.
5. Tracking the edge by hysteresis by finding edges that are weak and not connected to strong edges, and then suppressing them.

The output of the Canny edge detector is a binary edge map where pixels are classified as either edge pixels or non-edge pixels. Strong edges represent the most prominent and continuous edges in the image, while weak edges often correspond to faint or discontinuous edges. The Canny edge detector is generally preferred when high-quality edge detection and precise edge localization are required, while the Sobel operator is a simpler and faster option suitable for tasks where real-time processing or computational efficiency is prioritized over edge detection accuracy. The choice between the two depends on the specific needs of the application.

Computer Vision

Computer vision is the field of AI that enables machines to interpret, understand, and extract high-level insights from images and videos. The overreaching goal of computer vision is to mimic and exceed human visual perception and provide input for intelligent decision-making processes with fast, consistent, unrested, and multimodal data analysis. Computer vision was traditionally achieved using machine learning algorithms which were explicitly programmed by engineers. Today, many applications use deep learning, which requires less input from an engineer or a programmer, and provides better performance compared to traditional machine learning approaches, however deep learning methods are often computationally intensive.

Deep learning has seen an increased use in the field of computer vision after the advent of convolutional neural networks (CNN), a class of deep neural networks that can extract hierarchical features at higher level instead of considering pixel level data. CNNs have proven to be highly effective on classification, recognition, and segmentation. A typical CNN (shown in Figure 12) contains convolutional layers, which are used to generate convolved feature maps and keep only important parts of images; pooling layers, which are used for spatial dimension reduction; fully connected layers, which are used to reconfigure the features to a whole image context; activation functions, which add non-linearity to the network, and determine which features are important for the machine to understand the insight; and backpropagation, which adjusts the weights of each parameter in the network and optimizes the output. In summary, a CNN breaks down input images into features, identifies important features, and pieces them together to produce a result.

Dividing an image into distinct regions or segments based on similar characteristics is the key task for computer vision, especially when the goal is scene understanding for applications such as autonomous vehicles, medical image analysis, and manufacturing inspections. Today, CNNs have evolved into more complicated architectures, such as U-Net, fully convolutional networks (FCN), and mask region-based CNN (Mask R-CNN). These architectures are designed for specific tasks such as semantic and instance segmentation on images. To better handle the nuances and requirements of segmentation tasks, these models make use of architecture changes such as expansive paths, skipped connections, and multi-step training [15-17].

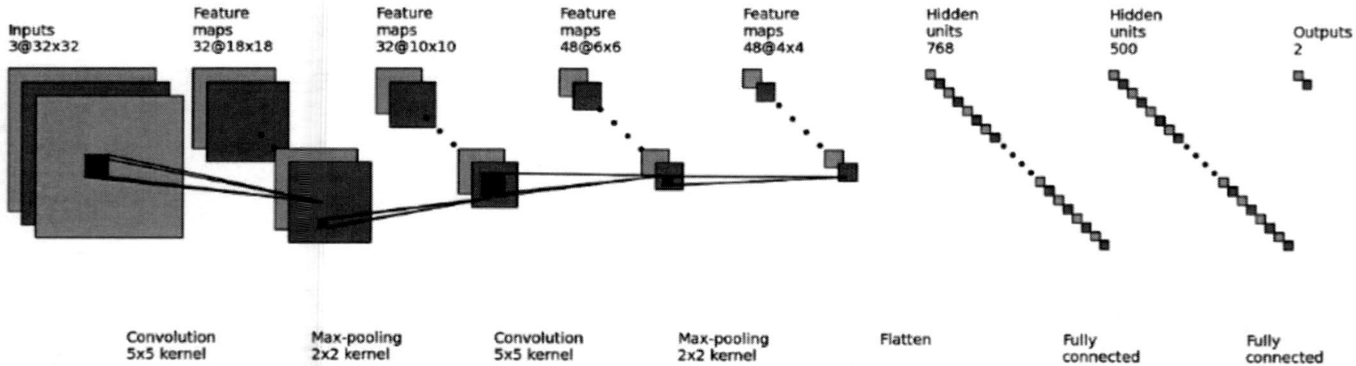

Figure 12. Example of an architecture of a CNN for classification tasks.[1] This CNN takes an RGB image as input and provides two variables as output.

[1] This figure is generated by adapting the code available at https://github.com/gwding/draw_convnet.

The choice of segmentation method should take into account the complexity of the task, available data, computational resources, and the desired level of accuracy.

The workflow of using deep learning to solve computer vision problems can be generalized as follows:

1. Mask the images to create ground truth.
2. Divide the dataset into splits, such as training split, and a testing split. Sometimes a third split known as validation split is also used.
3. Image augmentation of the training dataset to increase the number of images.
4. Train the deep learning algorithm with data and hyperparameter tuning.
5. Terminate the training when the defined performance metrics do not vary significantly as the number of epochs increases.
6. Use the trained model to predict or segment features in a new image.

Prior to any machine learning process, it is necessary to understand the critical role that data annotation plays in determining the model's performance. For segmentation, annotation typically means creating binary mask images that distinctly highlight the features to be extracted, also known as regions of interest. These annotated binary images are also called ground truth. These masks are then paired with their corresponding raw images and input into the model for training. Ensuring consistency and quality in annotations is important. This necessitates the establishment of clear, well-defined annotation standards to which all annotators adhere. Deep learning often requires a large dataset. One method of adding more input samples without requiring additional annotation is image augmentation, which is using image cropping, rotation, horizontal or vertical flipping, scaling, and adding noise. These operations change an image, however the ground truth of the input data remains the same and does not require a human to annotate or label data. After annotation, the datasets are split into at least two groups: train and test. Usually, a larger portion of data is prepared to train the model, while the rest of the test group is used to validate the model results. It is important to randomly assign samples to the train and test splits as well as splitting before any preprocessing is conducted. Otherwise, the trained model might be biased towards specific samples. Once trained, segmentation models create masks that identify specific parts of images. These masks can be then used to extract the desired objects when multiplied with the original images.

Pre-defined parameters called hyperparameters affect the performance and accuracy of the model prediction. Some common hyperparameters are learning rate, which defines how fast the model learns from the data; the batch size, which defines the smallest size of the datasets feeding to the model before it is updated; the number of epochs, where an epoch is one training step on the entire training dataset; loss function, where the model output is evaluated against the ground truth label and a resulting error is calculated; and optimizer, a gradient-descent like algorithm used to minimize the loss function. The above hyperparameters affect the speed at which the training process converges and the accuracy of the model prediction.

Additionally, it is important to choose the evaluation metrics (e.g., accuracy, precision, recall, F1-score, mean intersection over union [IoU], dice score) that are relevant to your task [18]. These metrics serve as critical benchmarks to evaluate the model's performance. The testing split is processed by the deep learning network after every epoch. Both loss function and evaluation metrics on both training and test splits should be continuously monitored. As the model trains repeating its iterative process, the model fits better to the training split and the loss function value drops as it approaches its minimum value, while the model performance improves. As the iterations are repeated, the model may overfit to a training dataset. In this state, the model performs very well on samples in the training split (i.e., samples the model has observed before) and not be able to generalize to samples from the test split. Choosing appropriate metrics and hyperparameters for computer vision tasks is important to ensure that deep learning models generalize well to unseen data.

Post Processing

Although a deep learning model can be employed to extract specific features from images, outputs of deep learning models, such as predictions are not always clean or ready to use. Additional image processing is required to eliminate noise or to separate segmented features. This post processing involves traditional image analysis such as thresholding, watershed, smoothing, and denoising, as well as the techniques elaborated above in the Digital Image Processing section.

Watershed image analysis, for example, serves as an invaluable post-processing step to refine and split connected objects into distinct parts. Segmentations generated by a deep learning model can often overlap, posing challenges when the goal is to quantify the properties of an individual object or segment. In such a scenario, watershed image analysis or the flood fill process are often employed to separate overlapping objects [19]. Open-source software, such as OpenCV and ImageJ, can be used to implement this watershed analysis.

In the realm of computer vision and image analysis, deep learning is capable of extracting high-level features and patterns from complex images. On the other hand, traditional image processing methods are adept at handling image manipulations and extracting fundamental features with datasets that exhibit similar object arrangements. Hybrid models, which bridge the gap between data-driven deep learning and domain-driven image processing, lead to more robust, interpretable, and adaptable solutions for real-world computer vision questions.

Validation of Results Using Manual Intervention

Validation of results through manual review serves as a critical quality control mechanism, ensuring that the results align with real-world expectations and domain-specific requirements. Manual intervention allows experts to independently validate, refine, or correct the outcomes of automated processes. If there is a signification offset between ground truth and prediction, such as if a certain image category does not exist or does not make sufficient presence in the training dataset, one could add such data to the dataset and re-train the model. Therefore, a continuous improvement in model performance can be achieved. This process is sometimes called hard example mining [20].

Applications of Image Processing and Computer Vision: Industry 4.0

Industry 4.0 is the idea of integrating digital technologies, automation, data exchange, and smart manufacturing in various industries. Computer vision plays a significant role in Industry 4.0 by enabling machines and computers to understand visual information (such as that from cameras), leading to enhanced automation in manufacturing and quality control. Some ways in which computer vision is being used in the industry are:

1. *Quality Control and Inspection:* Camera-based systems can be used for quality assessment and defect inspection during the manufacturing process. Computer vision-based algorithms assist by identifying defects, deviations, and inconsistencies, often in real-time, increasing production speeds. Cognex Corporation and Zebra Technologies are two organizations well known in the field for defect inspection.
2. *Object Recognition and Tracking:* Computer vision can identify and track materials, parts, components, and finished products. This tracking can be used to manage inventory and optimize logistics.
3. *Safety:* Computer vision can be used to detect the presence of personnel and ensure that safety protocols are followed, such as detecting if a worker enters a hazardous zone.
4. *Supply Chain and Logistics:* Computer vision is used for tracking and optimizing the movement of goods within a supply chain. It can identify products, the quality of products, packages, and vehicles, helping streamline logistics operations.
5. *Data Analytics:* Computer vision generates vast amounts of visual data, which can be analyzed to gain insights into production processes, quality trends, and operational efficiency, further enhancing decision-making in manufacturing.

In this section we discuss two innovative ways of applying computer vision to Industry 4.0. First, we discuss defect inspection systems commonly used in industry that depend on computer vision. We then discuss an innovative method to estimate the weight of a mounted gemstone for faster quality control and improved supply chain management that was recently patented by two authors of this chapter [21].

Defect Inspection Using Computer Vision

Defect inspection has been a long-standing application of computer vision [1]. Manufacturing plants employ humans to inspect the assembly of parts; however, worker fatigue results in many misses and defects not being identified. Inspection using camera-based systems promises to assist in defect inspections. The use of a camera and computer-based system reduces the time required for inspection, as well as the number of missed defects.

Figure 13. An example showing the identification of defects by using template matching.

Most defect inspection systems make use of template matching to identify defects for a region of interest (ROI). Here, a small section of the camera image from a "good" or "OK" product is used as a template to compare against. Every product that passes on the manufacturing line is compared against the template, and products that do not match the template with a high degree of confidence are marked as defects (fails or not OKs [NOK]) by the computer system.

This can be explained using an example of a manufacturing plant that produces reusable water bottles. Consider a scenario where the bottle and the bottle cap are manufactured separately, and then assembled into a final product. Sometimes the assembly of the water bottle fails, and water bottles are packed and shipped without a water bottle cap. A computer vision and camera-based system can be developed to inspect these defects. To use template matching, a template is first selected from camera images. Since our goal is to detect missing caps, we can select the region where the water bottle and the cap mate as the template. This template is then processed by a computer vision algorithm, which searches parts of the camera image for a match, and if a match is found, the water bottle being observed by the camera is marked as OK. If no match is found to the template, the water bottle being observed by the camera is marked as a defect. Figure 13 visualizes this process of defect inspection.

Figure 14. Using edge images for template matching instead of the original camera image results in faster inspection times and less false positives.

Template matching is well known to be computationally intensive, and results in many false alarms when using colored images due to minor variations in camera images or noise from the imaging process [22, 23]. Here, image processing plays an important role. Engineers can process camera images using the techniques listed in the Image Processing section above, such as noise removal, image filtering, and feature generation. For example, edge images can be generated from the images captured by a camera as shown in Figure 14, and used for the template and subject image during the template matching process. Since edge images are often represented on a computer as binary or grayscale images, the computation power required for template matching is lower, and results in faster matching times. At the same time, edge images contain less noise and subject to subject variation, thus resulting in higher confidence when template matching.

Mounted Gemstone Weight Estimation

Another example of computer vision in Industry 4.0 is in the domain of jewelry manufacturing. When a diamond gemstone is mounted and enclosed by other materials, not all dimensions of the gemstone are readily available for measurement. Invasively evaluating a large number of mounted gemstones can be labor intensive and unreproducible, thus costly. Also, small errors in dimension measurements might be propagated in a subsequent volume calculation and result in wrongful prediction of the gemstone value, leading to potential financial loss for either the retailer or the customer. The machine learning work described here is part of a patent currently under review [21].

The gemstone weight estimation process can be automated to achieve better accuracy and efficiency using the deep learning approach described in the Computer Vision section. Top-down gemstone images can be obtained to segment the gemstone from different jewelry settings for weight estimation. These datasets are manually labeled to create the ground truth of the pixels that belong to a gemstone. Using a deep learning algorithm (i.e., semantic segmentation), the system is properly trained to predict all the pixels that belong to the gemstone on any new image obtained in a similar manner. The extracted pixels are fitted to the predefined shape description for a gemstone, such as round, rectangle, oval, etc., to account for any occluded part. The fitted pixels are then properly scaled based on pixel size. Finally, the empirical database of the overhead gemstone size and weight are used to obtain its estimated weight.

The complexity of mounted gemstone image analysis arises due to multiple factors, including partial visibility of gemstones caused by prongs, the presence of shadows and reflections, varying lighting conditions, the demand for meticulous assessments, and the necessity for fast processing. As a result, data-driven assessment by deep learning-based segmentation can offer a more accurate and consistent approach to binarization and boundary characterizations. Fast post-processing techniques are ideal here to extract the shape parameter from irregular boundary data. This combination of deep learning-based computer vision and knowledge domain-driven image analysis algorithms, referred to as hybrid model, can ultimately benefit both consumers and retailers.

U-Net, a deep learning algorithm, is particularly well-suited for such an image segmentation task. The design is characterized by a U-shaped topology that consists of a contracting path (encoder) and an expansive path (decoder) [24]. U-Net stands out from the other algorithms due to its efficiency; it requires a limited number of training images to achieve high accuracy. The number of images in a training dataset for this task are limited to a few hundred due to the limited access to high-valued gemstones, the limited number of gemological expert labors, and the custom-built microscope that is used to capture the overhead gemstone image. A U-Net approach is also computationally faster compared to other algorithms that require two-stage segmentation techniques, such as Mask R-CNN.

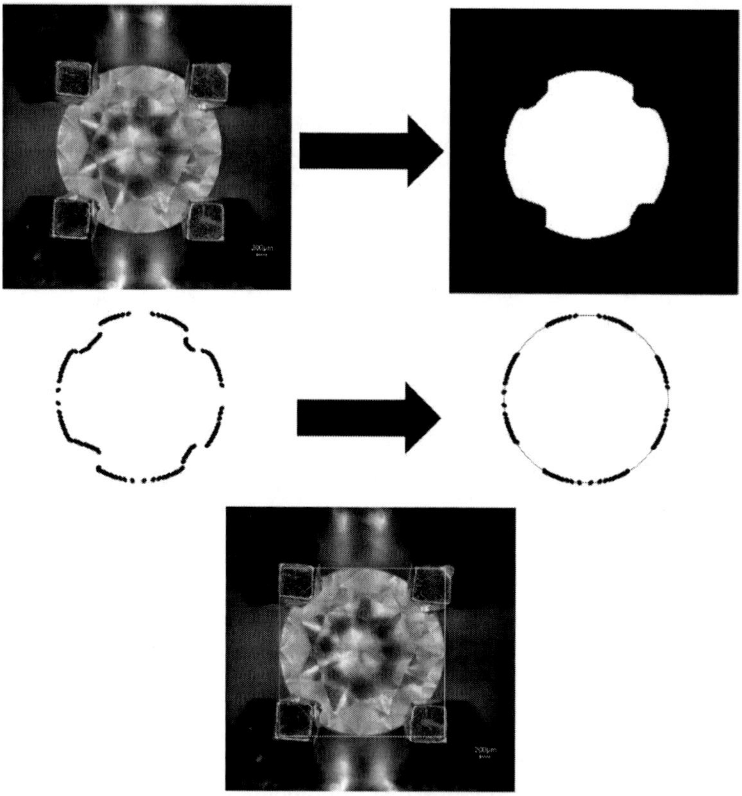

Figure 15. (a) An overhead image of a gemstone collected by optical microscope; (b) the binary mask predicted by a pre-trained U-Net model; (c) and (d) circle detection and outlier removal by the random sample consensus (RANSAC) algorithm on the contour of a mask; (e) overlay of raw images and predicted circle (red) with a bounding box (yellow) around the identified area.

The RANSAC algorithm is a powerful tool for robustly predicting shapes from the contours of a binary mask [25]. In the presence of noise, irregularities, and partial data, direct estimation of shape parameters like the center and radius of circle can be heavily biased by outliers. RANSAC first initializes a candidate circle by randomly selecting three data points on contour. Data points that sufficiently conform to the circle model (inliers) are identified, while outliers that deviate significantly from the model are removed. The mean absolute error was tracked for consensus assessment purposes. Iteratively refining the model and removing outliers continues until both the percentage of inliers among the remaining data points and the smallest mean absolute error meet or exceed the specified threshold, as illustrated in

Figure 15. In gemstone estimation consistent underestimation of values can lead to financial losses. Fine tuning on the threshold of error and RANSAC iterations are required to eliminate underestimation bias. By harnessing the power of RANSAC, we can enhance our ability to identify the shapes of objects (e.g., circle, oval, square, rectangle, triangle).

Particle Size and Mechanical Property Analysis

Many fields employ particle analysis to solve both quality control and analytical problems. This analysis is crucial for many applications in materials science and engineering because the shapes and size distribution of particles can affect material properties, such as the packing density of powders [26], the optical properties of nanoparticles [27], and the water retention properties of soils [28]. Particle analysis, therefore, has numerous industrial applications, from cosmetics to pharmaceuticals to building materials.

Particle analysis is also frequently used in academic and research applications. In cell biology, for example, particle size distributions are calculated for cells, since cell size distributions can be indicators of cell behavior. Cell sizes may be evaluated to study the material exchange interactions of cancerous cells with their environments, which may offer insights into their drug uptake behavior [29]. In geotechnical engineering, particle analysis may be applied to the study of the origins and behavior of soils, since the shapes and size distributions of soil particles may be related to their properties [30].

Manual particle analysis tends to require the evaluation of particle qualities on a particle-by-particle basis. As a result, this inevitably leads to a larger number of human-hours and a greater susceptibility to human error and bias. In addition, the amount of effort required to perform the task scales with the number of images analyzed. The automation of these processes can lead to significant time and cost savings in addition to improved accuracy and repeatability of results.

In the following sections, we describe the use of image processing and computer vision to obtain particle size information. We then show how this information can be used to obtain optical and mechanical properties, such as density or hardness. Although the following examples utilize optical microscopy images, it must be noted that particle size analysis can be done using various types of input images, including but not limited to atomic force microscopy (AFM) images and scanning electron microscopy (SEM) images.

Particle Size Analysis Using K-Means Clustering

Isolation of Dust Particles

The following describes the process for isolating dust particles in an optical microscopy image and measuring their sizes. To analyze the sizes of the dust particles in an image, they must first be isolated from the rest of the image. Since the quantity of interest is the size of a given particle, the textures and appearances of the particles are unimportant. Therefore, the image can be divided into two parts: (1) regions occupied by dust particles, and (2) regions not occupied by dust particles in a binary image (i.e., an image consisting of only black and white pixels).

The original optical microscopy image in Figure 16 shows that each pixel can be assigned to one of three categories: (1) dust particles, (2) fibers, or (3) empty space. The pixels of an image may be separated into similar groups using clustering techniques that group pixels based on their similarities to each other, or other image segmentation techniques that also take the spatial distribution of pixels into account [6]. A vast number of approaches are available to perform image segmentation [31], from clustering-based techniques [32, 33], which may be divisive or agglomerative [34], to more recently developed deep-learning-based techniques [35].

In this example, k-means clustering-based image segmentation is used to divide the image into *k* components, where the number *k* is defined be the operator. K-means clustering [36] is a commonly used data clustering technique that groups similar datapoints into clusters by maximizing both how similar the datapoints are to each other within a given cluster and how different the clusters are from each other. This is ultimately accomplished by minimizing the distance between each datapoint and its cluster's mean. In k-means clustering, *k* datapoints are randomly chosen from the dataset to be the centers of each cluster. All the other datapoints are then assigned to the cluster with the center that is nearest in value to itself, after which the center is recalculated for each cluster. This is repeated iteratively until the cluster centers are stable and the clustering result no longer changes. There are numerous approaches available to increase the optimality of clustering results and choose the best value for *k*, but these approaches are not covered in this chapter.

An example optical microscopy image used for the analysis of dust particle sizes is shown in Figure 16. The number of clusters (i.e., *k*) was chosen to be 4, and after the application of the k-means algorithm, each pixel in the image was assigned to one of four clusters. The four clusters identified in Figure 16 are shown in the cluster map in Figure 17, in which each cluster is shown in a different color.

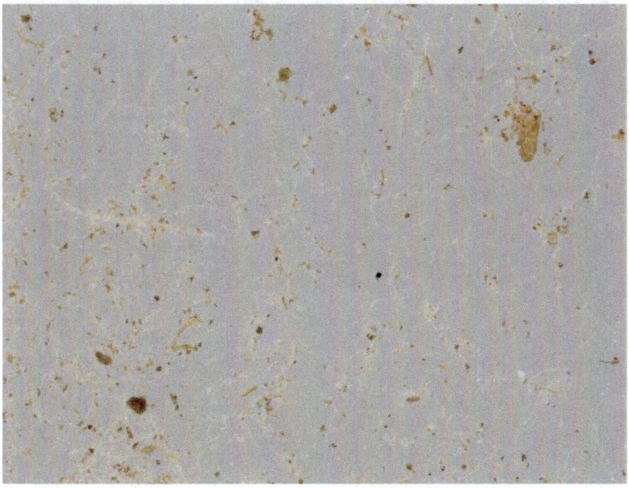

Figure 16. Optical microscopy image of dust particles and fibers.

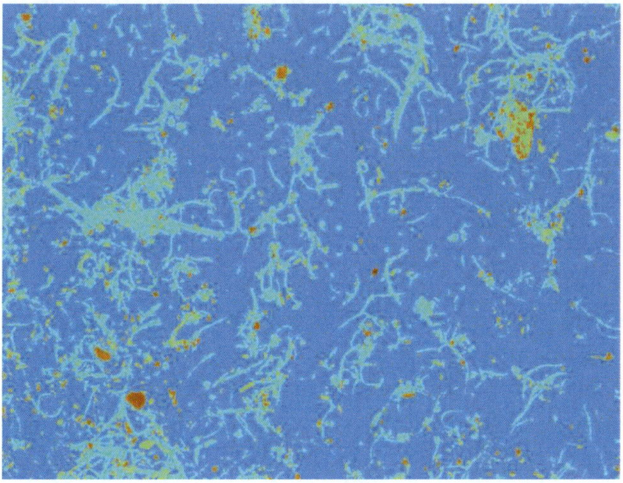

Figure 17. Visualization showing the spatial distribution of the four clusters identified using K-means-based image clustering.

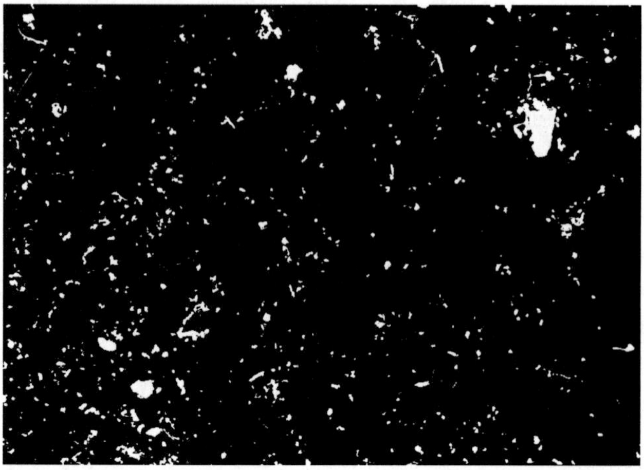

Figure 18. Binarized image showing dust particles isolated through the combination of clusters identified through k-means-based image clustering.

In Figure 17, the cyan regions correspond to the fibers and the blue regions correspond to empty space. The orange and green regions correspond to the dust particles; the darker-colored regions of the dust particles are shown in orange and the lighter-colored regions are shown in green. The green and orange clusters shown in Figure 17 were combined to form the white dust particles in the binarized image shown in Figure 18 where the black regions correspond to the blue (empty space) and cyan (fibers) clusters.

Post-Processing of Binarized Images

Hole Filling

While the k-means-based image segmentation algorithm was able to isolate the dust particles with reasonable success, holes and other artificial flaws in the white dust particles in the binarized image can still be observed in Figure 18. This could be the result of variations in lighting and consequent localized bright regions, which may cause some pixels contained within dust particles to be assigned to the fiber and "empty" space clusters. Whereas morphological operations like dilation may handle the filling of small holes in image objects, it is possible for dust particles with gaps or holes to remain. Hole filling can be used to address this issue. While there are advanced image processing techniques for hole filling [37], a simple approach is sufficient for this application. In this case, the MATLAB function *imfill* [38] looks for regions of black pixels that are surrounded by white pixels and converts them to white pixels.

Removal of Partially Visible Particles

The border of the image will likely obstruct several particles in the image. If the key feature of interest for the particles is dimension, is it crucial to eliminate all particles that are partially obscured by the image border prior to analysis to reduce the risk of underestimating the sizes of the particles.

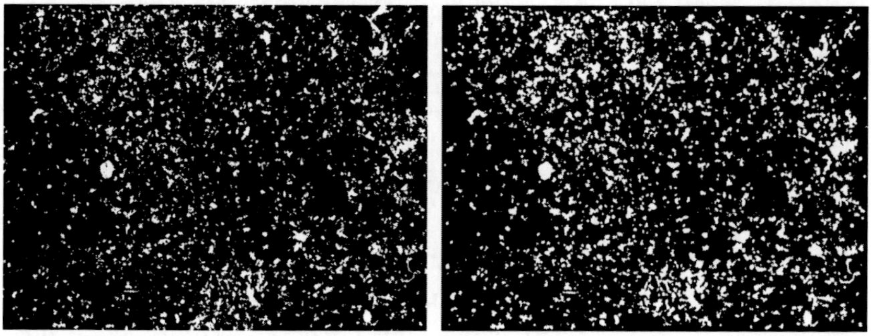

Figure 19. Left: Example binarized image of dust particles (white) and the remainder of the image (black). Right: Processed binarized image after applying erosion, dilation, hole filling, and elimination of particles partially obscured by the image border.

Particle Size Measurement

Choosing an Appropriate Dimension

Before particle sizes can be measured, their shapes should be considered and the appropriate dimension to be measured should be identified. For example, for a sphere, a radius can be an appropriate measurement, while for a cube, the edge length is the appropriate measurements. An appropriate dimension for an irregularly shaped particle can be assigned based on the property of interest for the domain. For example, in the domain of designing tea bag filters, one may choose the shortest dimension to determine whether a tea particle will be able to pass through a sieve, or one may choose the longest dimension to determine whether it is possible for a particle to block a pathway. Since the objective of the dust particle analysis is to find the particle size distribution of particles that are highly variable in their geometries, it is necessary to take a representative measure of particle size, rather than the longest or shortest dimension. The particles in this analysis were considered to be similar to spheres, and as such, the equivalent diameter was chosen to be an appropriate metric for quantifying the particle size, where the equivalent diameter of each dust particle is the diameter of a circle that has the same area as that dust particle.

Converting Pixels to Real-World Measurements

The calculated equivalent diameters are computed in pixels, and therefore must be converted to real-world measurements (e.g., μm) to be meaningful. It is recommended that this conversion be performed using a scale bar, which is usually optionally included in optical microscopy, SEM, and AFM images. More rudimentary tools, however, such as a ruler imaged using the same settings under which the particles were imaged, may also be used. Through these techniques, a conversion factor between physical units and pixels may be obtained and used to convert particles to true measurements.

In the dust particle image analysis example, the pixel sizes were converted to microns using scale bars in optical microscopy images obtained using the same parameters as the dust particle images. The equivalent diameters in pixels were then multiplied by the pixel size in microns to obtain the equivalent diameters of the dust particles in microns.

Calculating Representative Particle Sizes

The histogram in Figure 20 shows the distribution of particle sizes in the image shown in Figure 19; however, the process described can be repeatedly applied to multiple images obtained from multiple samples to reduce bias in the calculated result.

To validate the results of the automated particle size analysis procedure, the distribution obtained from our automated analysis was compared to a manually obtained distribution analysis sampled from the same region. The lengths of 300 dust particles were measured in arbitrary directions to account for the irregular geometries of the dust particles. The particle sizes were measured using ImageJ software that is freely available from the National Institutes of Health [39] that enables allows the user to edit, modify, convert, process, and analyze images [5]. The manual measurements are summarized in the histogram in Figure 21.

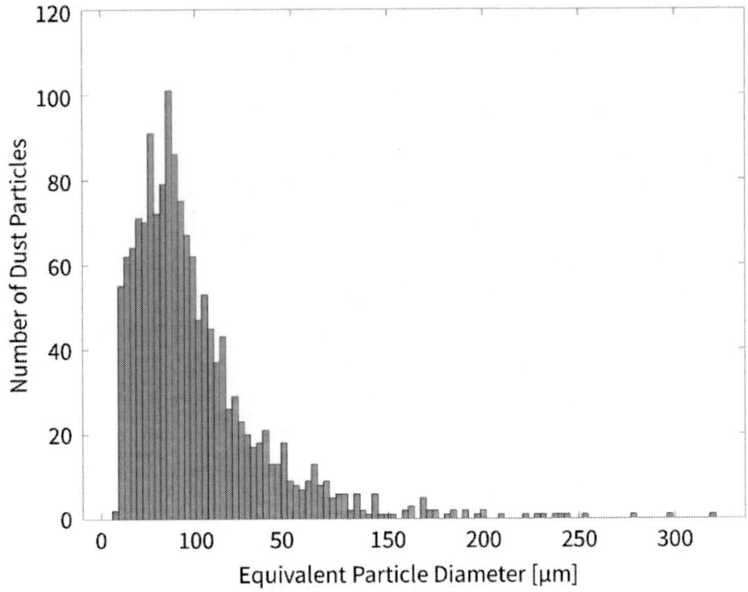

Figure 20. Histogram showing particle size distribution. The particles were measured automatically.

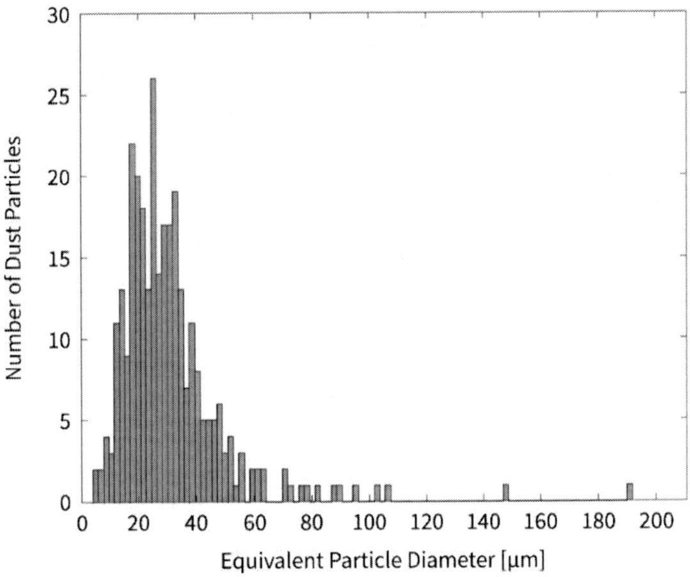

Figure 21. Histogram showing particle size distribution. The particles were measured manually using ImageJ.

The results show that while both the manual and automated measurements captured a right-skewed distribution of particle sizes, the automated process yielded a much greater number of measurements, and was able to capture the smallest particle sizes more effectively in the distribution. The reason for the latter observation is likely a result of human bias. Although the intent was to randomly sample particles of different sizes, larger particles are more obvious and would be preferentially measured. In a similar manner, darker particles that have greater contrast with the surrounding regions are also more likely to be preferentially selected for measurement. For the manual results to be more accurately representative of the population of dust particles, it would be necessary to measure every particle in a representative image instead of a random sampling of particles, which would be even more time intensive. Furthermore, it would be difficult to manually obtain an appropriately representative particle size measurement due to the irregularity in the particle shapes.

When performing automated particle size analysis, in addition to measuring the all the particles in one image, it is possible to do this with several images. This process allows for the analysis of a much larger population of dust particles than would be reasonable for a human to perform manually. The number of particles analyzed therefore becomes limited by the total dataset (all images of dust particles collected) instead of other resources, such as time and labor costs.

Particle Optical and Mechanical Properties from the Image Processing Approach

In addition to drawing information on particle size, an image can also provide insights on optical and mechanical properties. In the tutorial above, we discussed representing a color image as an RGB image. Image can be represented and interpreted in other color spaces, such as hue, saturation, value (HSV, also known as hue, saturation, brightness [HSB]); and the CIELAB color space (also referred to as LAB, where channel L represents lightness or brightness, channel A represent the color coordinate from green to red, and channel B represent the color coordinate from blue to yellow). The RGB space resembles a human's perception [21] and is one of the most commonly used color spaces. In this space, each color channel, red, green, and blue, also contains a brightness/intensity value. It can become difficult to process the image due to color and brightness entangling since adjusting each color channel also affects the brightness of the image. Some other color spaces, such as HSV [22] and CIELAB [23], can resolve this issue. In both HSV and CIELAB, lightness is also a separate channel. The other two channels in CIELAB cover the spectrum from red to green and yellow to blue.

Interpreting an image in color space could provide insights on the optical properties of a particle. The left image in Figure 22 is an image of a mixture of particles made of pencil shavings, sand, and potato chips, items found in daily life. Using a similar image processing methodology as described in the previous sections, these particles are segmented and extracted to obtain particle size. The right image in Figure 22 is the binary image of these extracted particles. Particle 1 is the graphite material from the pencil shavings and Particle 2 is the pencil's wood material. The color pixels of these two particles are extracted by multiplying the binary image of each particle with the original image. The left image in Figure 23 is a graphite particle and the right image in Figure 23 is a wood particle. Both are from the pencil shaving. Each particle's color pixels are then separated into different channels in HSB color space. The corresponding HSB distribution is plotted in Figure 24. The wooden particle hue values are narrowly distributed and the profile is smooth. In contrast, the graphite particle hue values distribute in a wider range and the profile is jagged. Both the hue distributions could indicate that the graphite is multifaceted or reflective so it distorts light in different directions and therefore broadens the hue spectrum. For saturation distribution, the mean values are distinct for these two particles. The graphite particle saturation is distributed in narrower ranges while the wood particle saturation is broader. The brightness mean values follow a similar pattern while the distributions are relatively broad for both particles.

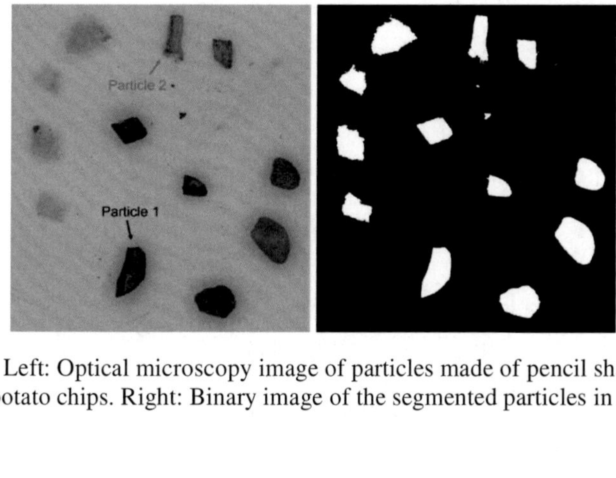

Figure 22. Left: Optical microscopy image of particles made of pencil shavings, sand, and potato chips. Right: Binary image of the segmented particles in the image on the left.

Figure 23. Left: Extracted graphite particle from the pencil shavings. Right: Extracted wood particle from the pencil shavings.

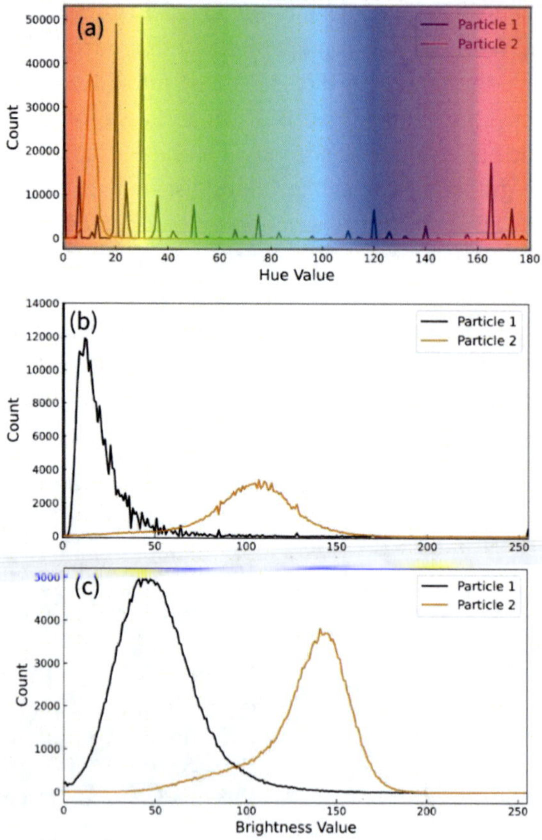

Figure 24. HSB color space interpretation of two particles: (a) hue distribution; (b) saturation distribution; (c) brightness distribution.

Image analysis of particles can also provide insights on their mechanical properties. These properties could be extracted and quantified from the binary image of the particles. Some of the relevant mechanical property metrics are defined below:

$$\text{solidity} = \frac{particle\ area}{area\ of\ convex\ hull} \quad (1)$$

where the convex hull is the smallest convex set that contains a particle

$$\text{convexity} = \frac{convex\ perimeter}{particle\ permeter} \quad (2)$$

where convex perimeter is the perimeter of a particle's convex hull

$$\text{circularity} = \frac{4\pi * particle\ area}{particle\ perimeter^2} \quad (3)$$

$$\text{roundness} = \frac{4 * particle\ area}{\pi * major\_axis^2} \quad (4)$$

which can also be calculated by the inverse of the aspect ratio. Major_axis is the primary axis of the best fitting ellipse of the particle.

$$\text{sphericity} = \frac{sphere\ surface\ area}{particle\ surface\ area} \in (0,1), s = \frac{4\pi(\sqrt[3]{\frac{3V}{4\pi}})^2}{A_p} \quad (5)$$

These equations 1-5 can be found in References [40-42]. These parameters provide insights on particle hardness. E.J. Liu et al. [43] used a list of metrics, including those noted above, to describe volcanic ash morphology and infer particle properties such as volcanic ash particle pre-fragmentation condition and density. The particles are clustered into different classes based on their solidty and convexity (Figure 25). Dense fragments (blue) exhibit the highest convexity and solidity. Microlite-rich particles (orange) exhibit the lowest convexity, but high solidity while glassy shards (dark red) exhibit lowest solidity but a relatively high convexity.

Using a similar concept, some of the parameters defined in equations 1–5 are plotted with respect to another for the particles in Figure 25 to explore as well as to validate the effectiveness of the metrics in interpreting the hardness. Figure 26(a) shows the scattered plot of the solidity-circularity of different particles. The chip and wood particles clustered in a similar range while the graphite and sand clustered in a separate range. The circularity-aspect ratio plot in Figure 26(b) exhibits a similar clustering of the properties between the chip/wood particles and graphite/sand particles. Both these two distributions likely indicate that the chip and wood particles are of similar hardness while graphite and sand particles hardness are close to each other. In addition, the hardness of graphite and sand particles are higher than chip and wood particles due to their higher values of solidity and circularity, which agree with our experience with these materials.

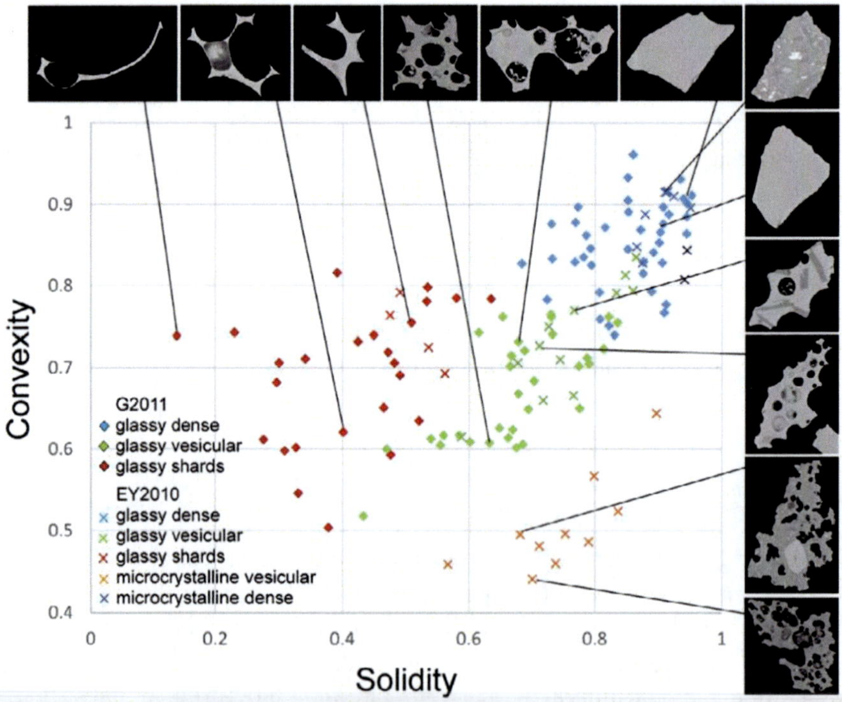

Figure 25. Solidity-convexity diagram for particles with various eruption style [43].

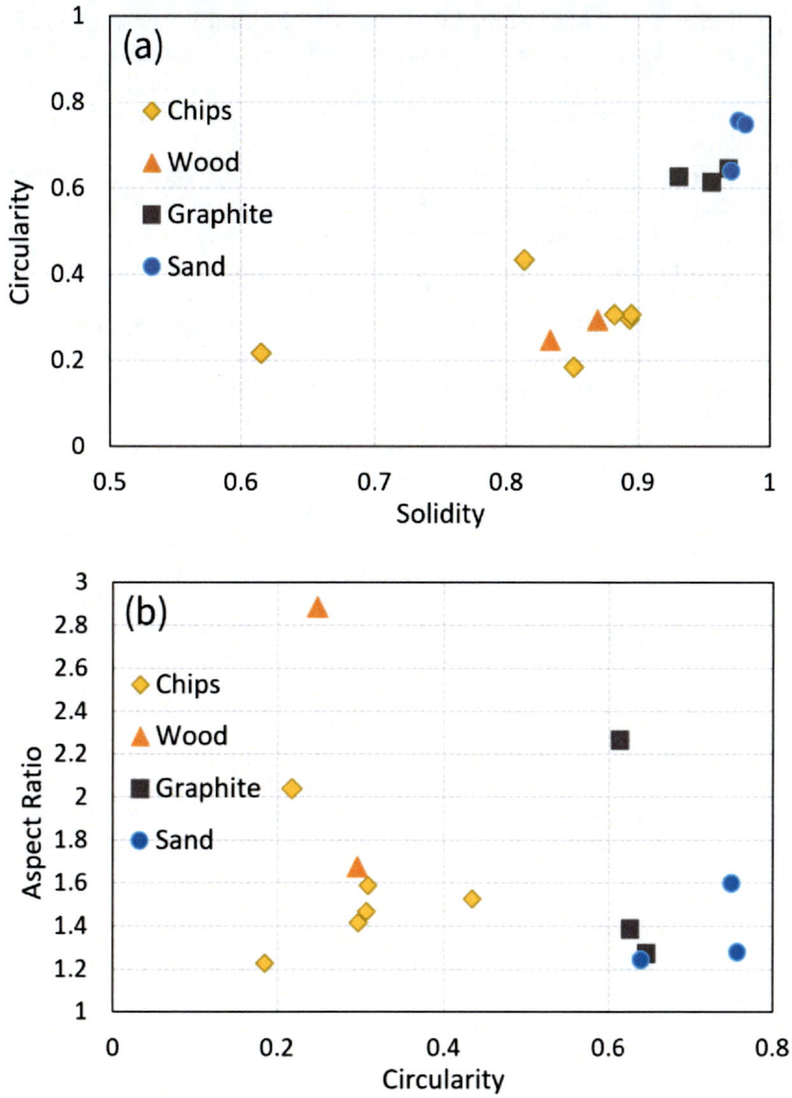

Figure 26. (a) Solidity-circularity diagram and (b) circularity-aspect ratio diagram.

References

[1] Pau, L. F. 2012. *Computer Vision for Electronics Manufacturing*. Online resource. DOI: 10.1007/978-1-4613-0507-1. Boston, MA: Springer US.

[2] Javaid, Mohd, Abid Haleem, Ravi Pratap Singh, Shanay Rab, and Rajiv Suman. 2022. "Exploring impact and features of machine vision for progressive industry 4.0 culture." *Sensors International* 3:100132. doi: https://doi.org/10.1016/j.sintl.2021.100132.

[3] Brownlee, Jason. 2019. *Deep Learning For Computer Vision: Image Classification, Object Detection, And Face Recognition In Python:* Machine Learning Mastery.

[4] Kaehler, Adrian, and Gary Bradski. 2017. Learning OpenCV3. Computer Vision in C++ with the OpenCV Library. Sevastopol, CA: O'Reilly Media, Inc.

[5] Burger, Wilhelm, and Mark J. Burge. 2016. Digital Image Processing. An Algorithmic Introduction Using Java. London: Springer London.

[6] Szeliski, R. 2022. Computer Vision: Algorithms and Applications. Cham, Switzerland: Springer.

[7] Gonzalez, Rafael C, and Richard E Woods. 2018. Digital Image Processing. 4th ed. New York: Pearson.

[8] Martin, D. R., C. C. Fowlkes, and J. Malik. 2004. "Learning to detect natural image boundaries using local brightness, color, and texture cues." *IEEE Trans Pattern Anal Mach Intell* 26(5):530-549. doi: 10.1109/TPAMI.2004.1273918.

[9] Shrivakshan, GT, and C. Chandrasekar. 2012. "A comparison of various edge detection techniques used in image processing." *Int J Comput Sci Issues* 9(5):269-276.

[10] Szeliski, Richard. 2022. *Computer Vision: Algorithms and Applications*. Cham, Switzerland: Springer.

[11] Sobel, Irwin, and Gary Feldman. 2015. "An Isotropic 3x3 Image Gradient Operator." Researchgate, https://www.researchgate.net/publication/281104656_An_Isotropic_3x3_Image_Gradient_Operator?channel=doi&linkId=55d5876408ae43dd17de57a4&showFulltext=true (accessed June 14).

[12] Fisher, R., S. Perkins, A. Walker, and E Wolfart. 2003. "Sobel Edge Detector." Accessed September 1, 2023. Available from https://homepages.inf.ed.ac.uk/rbf/HIPR2/sobel.htm.

[13] Jain, Ramesh, Rangachar Kasturi, and Brian G Schunck. 1995. Machine Vision. Vol. 5. New York: McGraw-Hill.

[14] Canny, John. 1986. "A Computational Approach to Edge Detection." *IEEE Transactions on Pattern Analysis and Machine Intelligence*:679-698.

[15] He, K., G. Gkioxari, P. Dollár, and R. Girshick. "Mask R-CNN," in *2017 IEEE International Conference on Computer Vision* (ICCV), 2017, 2980-2988.

[16] Long, Jonathan, Evan Shelhamer, and Trevor Darrell. "Fully convolutional networks for semantic segmentation," in *Proceedings of the IEEE conference on computer vision and pattern recognition,* 2015, 3431-3440.

[17] Ronneberger, Olaf, Philipp Fischer, and Thomas Brox. "U-net: Convolutional networks for biomedical image segmentation," in *Medical Image Computing and Computer-Assisted Intervention–MICCAI 2015: 18th International Conference,* Munich, Germany, October 5-9, 2015, Proceedings, Part III 18, 2015, 234-241.

[18] Sharma, S., and A. Hoover. "The Challenge of Metrics in Automated Dietary Monitoring as Analysis Transitions from Small Data to Big Data," in *2020 IEEE*

International Conference on Bioinformatics and Biomedicine (BIBM), 2020, 2647-2653.

[19] Bleau, Andrè, and L. Joshua Leon. 2000. "Watershed-Based Segmentation and Region Merging." *Comput Vis Image Understanding* 77(3):317-370. doi: https://doi.org/10.1006/cviu.1999.0822.

[20] Shrivastava, Abhinav, Abhinav Gupta, and Ross Girshick. "Training Region-Based Object Detectors with Online Hard Example Mining," in *2016 IEEE Conference on Computer Vision and Pattern Recognition (CVPR),* 2016, 761-769.

[21] Page, Christian David, Boris Michael Spokoyny, Xu Han, Gabriel Seth Ganot, Chongyue Yi, and John Paul Dombrowski. Optical Weight Estimation System. US Patent Application No. 17/888,452, issued August 15, 2022.

[22] Khare, Vihang Yashodhan. "Training a Camera-based Inspection System for Appearance Variability," Master of Science, Computer Engineering, Clemson University, 2020.

[23] Torras, Carme. 1992. Computer Vision: Theory and Industrial Applications. Heidelberg: Springer Berlin.

[24] Ronneberger, Olaf, Philipp Fischer, and Thomas Brox. "U-Net: Convolutional Networks for Biomedical Image Segmentation," in, 2015, 234-241.

[25] Fischler, Martin A., and Robert C. Bolles. 1981. "Random sample consensus: a paradigm for model fitting with applications to image analysis and automated cartography." *Commun. ACM* 24(6):381–395. doi: 10.1145/358669.358692.

[26] Bai, Yun, Grady Wagner, and Christopher B. Williams. 2017. "Effect of Particle Size Distribution on Powder Packing and Sintering in Binder Jetting Additive Manufacturing of Metals." *Journal of Manufacturing Science and Engineering* 139(8) doi: 10.1115/1.4036640.

[27] Nehl, C.L., and J.H. Hafner. 2008. "Shape-dependent plasmon resonances of gold nanoparticles." *J Mater Chem* 18:2415-2419.

[28] Zhuang, Jie, Yan Jin, and Tsuyoshi Miyazaki. 2001. "Estimating Water Retention Characteristic from Soil Particle-Size Distribution Using a Non-Similar Media Concept." *Soil Science* 166(5):308-321.

[29] Khetan, J., M. Shahinuzzaman, S. Barua, and D. Barua. 2019. "Quantitative analysis of the correlation between cell size and cellular uptake of particles." *Biophys J* 116(2):347-359. doi: 10.1016/j.bpj.2018.11.3134.

[30] Dipova, Nihat. "Determining the Grain Size Distribution of Granular Soils Using Image Analysis," in, 2017.

[31] Kaur, A. 2014. "A review paper on image segmentation and its various techniques in image processing." *Int J Sci Res* 3(12):12-14.

[32] Zou, Y., and B. Liu. "Survey on clustering-based image segmentation techniques," in *2016 IEEE 20th International Conference on Computer Supported Cooperative Work in Design (CSCWD),* 2016, 106-110.

[33] Kaur, Dilpreet, and Yadwinder Kaur. 2014. "Various Image Segmentation Techniques: A Review." *Int J Comput Sci Mobile Comput* 3(1):809-814.

[34] Minaee, S., Y. Boykov, F. Porikli, A. Plaza, N. Kehtarnavaz, and D. Terzopoulos. 2022. "Image Segmentation Using Deep Learning: A Survey." *IEEE Transactions*

on Pattern Analysis and Machine Intelligence 44(7):3523-3542. doi: 10.1109/TPAMI.2021.3059968.

[35] Lamrous, Sid, and Mounira Taileb. "Divisive Hierarchical K-Means," in *2006 International Conference on Computational Inteligence for Modelling Control and Automation and International Conference on Intelligent Agents Web Technologies and International Commerce (CIMCA'06),* 2006.

[36] MacQueen, J. "Some methods for classification and analysis of multivariate observations," in, 1967.

[37] Criminisi, A., P. Perez, and K. Toyama. 2004. "Region filling and object removal by exemplar-based image inpainting." *IEEE Transactions on Image Processing* 13(9):1200-1212. doi: 10.1109/TIP.2004.833105.

[38] MathWorks. 2023. "Documentation - imfill." Accessed September 1, 2023. Available from https://www.mathworks.com/help/images/ref/imfill.html.

[39] ImageJ. 2023. "Image Processing and Analysis in Java." National Institutes of Health, Accessed September 1, 2023. Available from https://imagej.nih.gov/ij/docs/intro.html.

[40] ImageJ. 2023. "ParticleSizer." National Institutes of Health, Accessed September 1, 2023. Available from https://imagej.net/imagej-wiki-static/ParticleSizer.

[41] Sheets, Kris. 20911. "3D Convex Hul." Accessed September 1, 2023. Available from https://imagej.net/imagej-wiki-static/ParticleSizer.

[42] ImageJ. 2023. "Analyze." National Institutes of Health, Accessed October 30, 2023. Available from https://imagej.net/ij/docs/guide/146-30.html#sec:Analyze-Menu.

[43] Liu, E. J., K. V. Cashman, and A. C. Rust. 2015. "Optimising shape analysis to quantify volcanic ash morphology." *GeoResJ* 8:14-30. doi: 10.1016/j.grj.2015.09.001.

Appendix

```
# This is example code to demonstrate how erosion and dilation affect images.
# Surya Sharma, Ph.D., Janille Maragh, Ph.D.,
# Cathy Chen, Ph.D., P.E., Susan Han, Ph.D. and Chongyue Yi, Ph.D.

import cv2
import numpy as np

# Reading the input image
img = cv2.imread('CompVisTextInverted.JPG')

# Taking a matrix of size 5 as the kernel
# This is the same as the Square 5x5 element
kernel = np.ones((10, 10), np.uint8)

# The first parameter is the original image,
# kernel is the matrix with which image is
# convolved and third parameter is the number
# of iterations, which will determine how much
# you want to erode/dilate a given image.
result_img_erosion = cv2.erode(img, kernel)
result_img_dilation = cv2.dilate(img, kernel)
result_img_opening = cv2.morphologyEx(img, cv2.MORPH_OPEN, kernel)
result_img_closing = cv2.morphologyEx(img, cv2.MORPH_CLOSE, kernel)

cv2.imshow('Input Image', img)
cv2.imshow('Result of Erosion', result_img_erosion)
cv2.imshow('Result of Dilation', result_img_dilation)
cv2.imshow('Result of Opening', result_img_opening)
cv2.imshow('Result of Closing', result_img_closing)

cv2.waitKey(0) # This is required to hold the images on screen
```

Citation 1. Code to demonstrate the effect of erosion, dilation, opening and closing.

Biographical Sketches

Surya Sharma, Ph.D.

Dr. Sharma has a decade of experience in the domain of Computer Science and Electrical Engineering. He has designed, developed, and deployed software, systems and websites based on machine learning, embedded computing, system design, data science, and computer vision, which are used by software engineers, clinicians, nutritionists, and healthcare and human factors researchers. Dr. Sharma applies his computer science and electrical engineering experience in a variety of litigation, mediation, and arbitration matters including patent, copyright, trade secret, and commercial.

Dr. Sharma received his Ph.D. in Computer Engineering from Clemson University, focusing on low-power wearables and connected devices that detect eating by tracking wrist motion using deep learning technologies and tools such as convolutional neural networks, Tensorflow and Keras. Algorithms developed by Dr. Sharma were deployed to Android and Apple wearable devices to be used by clinicians in diabetes research.

Prior to his Ph.D., Dr. Sharma received his B.E. in Electronics and Telecommunications Engineering from Mumbai University, where he developed unmanned aerial vehicles (UAVs) and drones, embedded computing based solutions, and e-commerce and marketing websites.

Janille Maragh, Ph.D.

Dr. Maragh is a researcher and engineering consultant with training and experience in materials science and engineering, mechanical engineering, and civil engineering. Dr. Maragh applies her broad engineering experience to support clients in matters regarding the failure analysis of batteries and consumer electronics, intellectual property disputes, facilities integrity management, and engineering critical assessment. Her research focus prior to joining Exponent was the application of cutting edge chemomechanical analysis and visualization techniques to the study of ancient materials, including ancient Roman concrete and the Dead Sea Scrolls.

Susan (Xu) Han, Ph.D.

Dr. Han has experience in matters pertaining to machine learning and image analysis for consumer products, retail industry, and medical device applications. She additionally has experience in data acquisition via various systems including high speed video camera, optical profilometer, and light detection and ranging (LiDAR) sensor. She employs design of experiments (DOE) to collect representative and comprehensive datasets with minimal bias. She interprets the visual world and predicts future behavior via color space theory, image analysis of 2D and 3D data, deep learning, regression, and signal processing. Dr. Han has worked in projects involving from the design of imaging systems, data acquisition, software-hardware integration, to image processing algorithms development and data interpretation. Dr. Han also has experience in electronic systems failure analysis, design review, and safety evaluation for a broad range of products including battery management systems, medical devices, power systems, and consumer electronics. Previously, Dr. Han worked as a statistical process control engineer in Intel Corporation where she developed models for feedforward and feedback control for 3D NAND memory production. Dr. Han completed her Ph.D. at the University of Massachusetts Amherst. Her research focused on numerical modeling and simulation of electron and hole transport in innovative semiconducting materials, including organic nanoparticle assemblies and hybrid perovskites, for photovoltaic devices. She also has extensive experience in numerical modeling of species transport in ternary semiconductor quantum dots (QDs).

Chongyue Yi, Ph.D.

Dr. Yi is a Senior Scientist at Exponent, Inc., where he specializes in artificial intelligence, computer vision, semiconductor manufacturing, and laser technology. With a comprehensive understanding of various machine learning (ML) frameworks, tools, and techniques, he extensively applies these skills to solve real-world problems. Dr. Yi is an expert in computer vision, specializing in creating advanced models for real-time object detection, segmentation, and generative AI projects. His collaborative work with hardware and cross-functional teams has led to the integration of computer vision solutions into custom imaging systems, resulting in co-published patents with clients. Dr. Yi has created machine learning and computer vision solutions in a wide variety of sectors, including utilities, retail, and consumer electronics.

Prior to joining Exponent, Dr. Yi served as a Technology Development Engineer in Intel's lithography module. He contributed to AI automation, Design of Experiments (DOE), New Product Introduction (NPI), and Statistical Process Control (SPC) within advanced chip manufacturing and development processes. As a postdoctoral researcher at Rice University, Dr. Yi's worked on optical modelling and spectroscopic analysis on highly congested microscopic data. Dr. Yi received his Ph.D. degree at Florida State University in 2015. His Ph.D. thesis represents a compelling intersection of high-precision technology fields, including laser technology, optical sensor systems, spectroscopy, fabrication, and advanced modeling. Dr. Yi has a portfolio that includes 18 published papers in renowned journals. Additionally, Dr. Yi's has been served as independent peer reviewer for 10 different journals over the course of 8 years.

Cathy Chen, Ph.D., P.E.

Dr. Chen has a background in electrical and computer engineering, with a focus on computer architecture, embedded systems, consumer electronics, and optical networks. Dr. Chen assists technology clients manage global-scale projects that are aimed at bringing next-generation products to market. Dr. Chen has helped design, manage, and execute human participant studies for wearables, advanced imaging, artificial intelligence, and biometrics in global environments, often involving large teams to fulfill client needs across the US, Africa, the Middle East, and Asia. Her experience helps clients build products that perform for a wide variety of participants while preventing data bias, collecting personal data with consideration for privacy, while managing the risks associated with global data collection. Her expertise includes: multicore systems, photonic interconnects, memory systems, artificial intelligence, usability studies, human computer interaction, machine learning, user study design, and the development of network interfaces on field programmable gate arrays (FPGAs). Dr. Chen completed her Ph.D. in Electrical Engineering at Columbia University in the Lightwave Research Laboratory. Her research focused on the development of FPGA-based test-beds for analyzing photonic networks for applications including: telecommunications, data centers, and heterogeneous utility computing systems. This involved routing and switching in photonic networks, particularly transparent interfaces to electronic communications and designing switching nodes with minimal optical-electronic-optical conversions (OEO). Prior to her Ph.D. studies, Dr. Chen received her B.S. in Electrical and Computer Engineering from Cornell University with a focus on cache coherence in computer architecture and embedded systems. Dr. Chen was also a project management intern at the Microsoft Corporation where she developed diagnostic tools and ran usability studies for operating systems. During this time she also assisted in drafting technical documentation for use by outside software and hardware manufacturers in diagnosing issues when interfacing to computer operating systems.

Chapter 4

Integrated Circuits Application in the Automotive Environment

Yike Hu[*]**, PhD**
and Xiang Wang, PhD
Exponent, Inc., Shanghai, China

Abstract

As the automotive market evolves towards an autonomous, connected, electric, and shared mobility future, advanced automotive functions require ever increasing electronic/electric components. The various applications of semiconductors in the automotive environment present unique requirements different than traditional consumer markets. Automotive integrated circuits (ICs) are expected to exhibit high levels of reliability and remain operational in more extreme environments for longer periods. Ensuring that ICs meet the stringent standards of the automotive industry helps mitigate risks and build safe vehicles. Various failure analysis techniques also play a critical role to identify root causes in the event of failures and take appropriate corrective action to address the issues.

Keywords: integrated circuit, functional safety, reliability, electromagnetic compatibility, failure analysis

[*] Corresponding Author's Email: yhu@exponent.com.

In: Computer Engineering Applications …
Editor: Brian D'Andrade
ISBN: 979-8-89113-488-1

Introduction

Automotive integrated circuits (ICs) are electronic semiconductors used in automotive applications, serving functions such as engine management, transmission control, safety systems, infotainment, powertrain, and body electronics, among others. The demand for ICs increases as the automotive industry develops towards electrification and artificial intelligence. On average, the number of chips used in an internal combustion engine vehicle is around 1,000, which is doubled in an electric vehicle (EV) [1]. At the same time, EV markets are experiencing exponential growth. The share of EVs in total sales has more than tripled in three years, from around 4% in 2020 to 14% in 2022 [2], as shown in Figure 1.

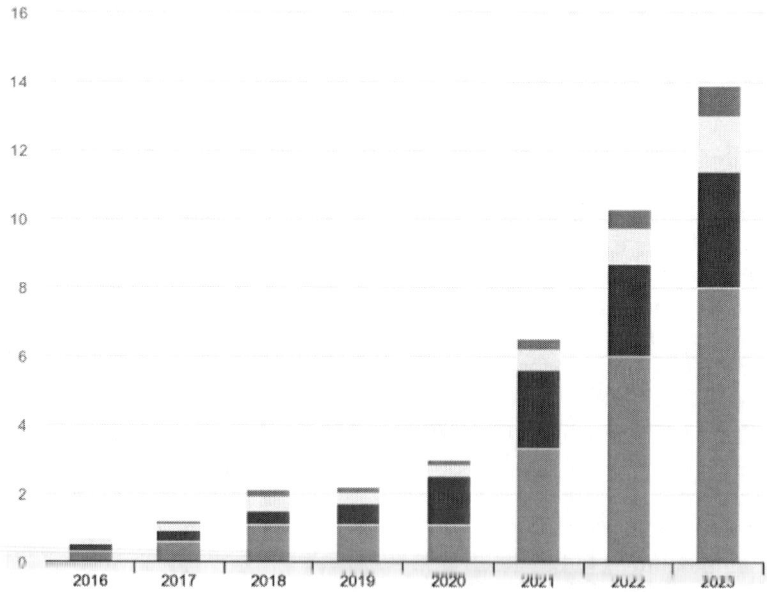

Figure 1. Electric car sales, 2016–2023. From the bottom to the top are different regions: China, Europe, the United States, and other regions [2].

ICs contribute to enhanced vehicle safety and reduce the risk of accidents, with features such as collision avoidance, lane departure warning, and automatic emergency braking in advanced driver assistance systems (ADAS). Automotive ICs can also improve energy efficiency by managing overall energy consumption. ICs with increasing computing power also enable communication features. The ability of automotive ICs to process data, control critical functions, and provide real-time responses makes them indispensable to ensure a smooth and efficient driving experience.

The application of ICs faces challenges from different areas due to the unique requirements of the automotive environment. One of the challenges is theharsh operating conditions [3]. Automotive ICs can experience wide temperature variations due to external weather situations. Various road conditions bring about vibrations and mechanical stress. Heavy rain or flooding can expose ICs to humidity, moisture, or even liquid ingress. In addition, ICs designed for automobile systems need to have the goal of zero defects to ensure the highest safety standards. Even a 1 part-per-million (ppm) component failure rate translates into a 1.5% (i.e., a 15,000 ppm) failure rate at the vehicle level [3]. Considering that vehicles have a long product lifecycle, automotive ICs must remain functional throughout this period, requiring manufacturers to maintain production and support for extended periods. Rigorous testing and redundant designs are required to adhere to strict quality standards.

Power Management Integrated Circuits

Various drivetrain architectures are applied in internal combustion engine vehicles, hybrid EVs, and EVs [4]. Power management ICs (PMICs) are considered essential components in a vehicle since they control and execute functions related to energy storage, power conversion, and power consumption. EVs generally require more PMICs than internal combustion engine vehicles due to the involvement of large battery packs, electric motors, high-voltage components, and complex power electronics.

Battery Management Integrated Circuits

The battery is one of the most important parts of an EV; it is the primary energy storage and power source. The performance of the battery directly impacts various aspects of an EV, including its range, efficiency, acceleration, and charging time. The cost of the battery also plays a major part in EV pricing since the average cost of an EV battery is between 30% and 57% of the vehicle's total value [5].

The architecture of an EV usually consists of a number of functional blocks. The accelerator pedal receives input from the driver. The electronic control unit processes the position input and calculates the actions to take. The power converters are connected between the battery and the electronic control units to distribute battery energy for motion, and in some cases, to recharge the battery. The motor driven wheels receive energy from the power converter to drive the vehicle. Bi-directionally connected between the battery and the electronic control unit, the battery management system (BMS) performs functions to ensure the proper and safe operation of the battery. Some of the functions commonly observed are cell balancing, state of charge (SOC) estimation, state of health (SOH) estimation, communication, pack authentication, and diagnostics. Those technologies together determine the overall performance of a battery. For example, slow charging has a negative impact on the availability of EV usage, but charging too fast might lead to a temperature rise with adverse effects. Large temperature variation further leads to rapid battery aging or even overheating, which will eventually shorten the battery service life or cause a thermal hazard [6]. Battery management ICs monitor individual battery cells, manage charging and discharging, ensure cell balancing, and provide real-time data to the vehicle's control systems to achieve efficient and safe operation.

Motor Control Integrated Circuits

Motor control ICs convert electrical energy from the battery into mechanical motion. Based on driver input or system requirements, motor control ICs regulate the speed and the torque output of the electric motors, allowing smooth acceleration, deceleration, and varying power outputs. Meanwhile, feedback from the various sensors equipped in a vehicle, such as accelerator or Hall effect sensors, is used by the motor control ICs to monitor the motor's position, speed, and direction. The driving experience is improved using the accurate control and the fast response of motor control ICs.

Power Conversion Integrated Circuits

Power conversion ICs manage electrical energy conversion between the battery, electric motor, and auxiliary systems. These ICs play a critical role in optimizing energy flow, managing voltage levels, and ensuring reliable power distribution. Figure 2 presents the general electrical structure of power conversion inside EVs [7].

Direct current-direct current (DC-DC) converters are used to convert voltage levels between different components in the EV to supply the correct voltage to various subsystems. Alternating current-direct current (AC-DC) converters serve as the connection between AC power and DC power, determining the performance of the charging process, regenerative braking, and other AC-related conversion. Voltage regulators are used to maintain a stable output voltage despite fluctuations in input voltage or load conditions, ensuring that critical components receive a consistent voltage level for reliable operation. Gate driver ICs generate control signals that drive the switching devices in power converters, such as insulated-gate bipolar transistors (IGBTs) or metal-oxide-semiconductor field effect transistors (MOSFETs) in power conversion circuits.

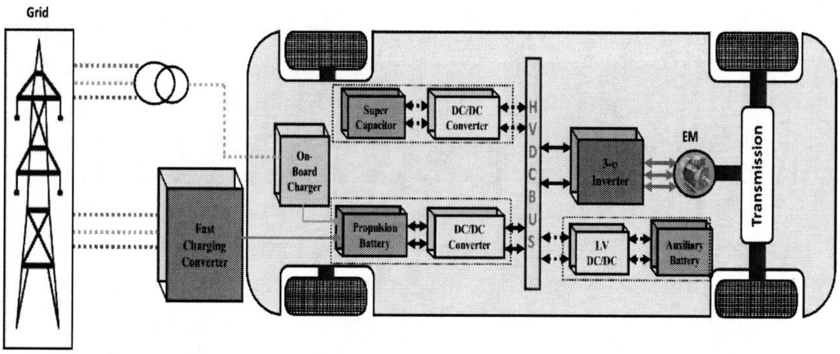

Figure 2. Schematic diagram of an EV powertrain with fast-charging stations [7].

Integrated Circuit Failure

Semiconductor Device Failure Mechanisms

Harsh environments can degrade the reliability of ICs due to the wear-out effect. Extreme temperature, thermal cycling, and thermal shock could cause gradual degradation of IC components and materials. High humidity levels or condensation may corrode metal contacts and cause electrical leakage. Mechanical stress might lead to solder joint fractures or wire bond failures within the IC. Automotive ICs may also be exposed to radiation from natural sources (e.g., cosmic rays) or human-made sources (e.g., x-rays) resulting in soft errors or latch-ups. The failure mechanism is different for each stress condition and needs to be understood fully in order to investigate its root cause. Some of the IC failure mechanisms that are typically observed in semiconductor devices are discussed below.

Hot carrier injection (HCI) is one mechanism contributing to device aging in ICs. HCI occurs when high-energy carriers gain enough energy to overcome the energy barrier of the gate oxide, tunnel through the gate oxide, and be injected into it. The gate oxide layer becomes damaged, leading to oxide breakdown and increased leakage current. HCI can further modify the charge distribution in the gate oxide, leading to a shift in the transistor's threshold voltage. This shift affects the transistor's operating characteristics, including its speed and power consumption. There are four commonly encountered HCI mechanisms [8], as illustrated in Figure 3.

a) Drain avalanche hot carrier (DAHC) injection. This occurs when high voltage applied at the drain under non-saturated conditions (i.e., $V_D > V_G$) results in very high electric fields near the drain, which accelerate channel carriers into the drain's depletion region.
b) Channel hot electron (CHE) injection. This occurs when both the gate voltage and the drain voltage are significantly higher than the source voltage (i.e., $V_G \approx V_D$). Channel carriers that travel from the source to the drain are sometimes driven towards the gate oxide even before they reach the drain because of the high gate voltage.
c) Secondary generated hot electron (SGHE) injection. This involves the generation of hot carriers from impact ionization involving a secondary carrier that was likewise created by an earlier incident of impact ionization. Photons are generated in the high field region near the drain and induce a generation process for electron-hole pairs. The avalanche multiplication near the drain region leads to the injection of both electrons and holes into the dielectric. The injection process is supported by the substrate bias, which is additionally driving carriers to the interface.
d) Substrate hot electron (SHE) injection. This occurs when the substrate's back bias is very positive or very negative (i.e., $|V_B| >> 0$). Under this condition, carriers of one type in the substrate are driven by the substrate field toward the silicon-silicon dioxide ($Si\text{-}SiO_2$) interface. As they move toward the substrate-oxide interface, they further gain kinetic energy from the high field in the surface depletion region. They eventually overcome the surface energy barrier and are injected into the gate oxide, where some of them are trapped.

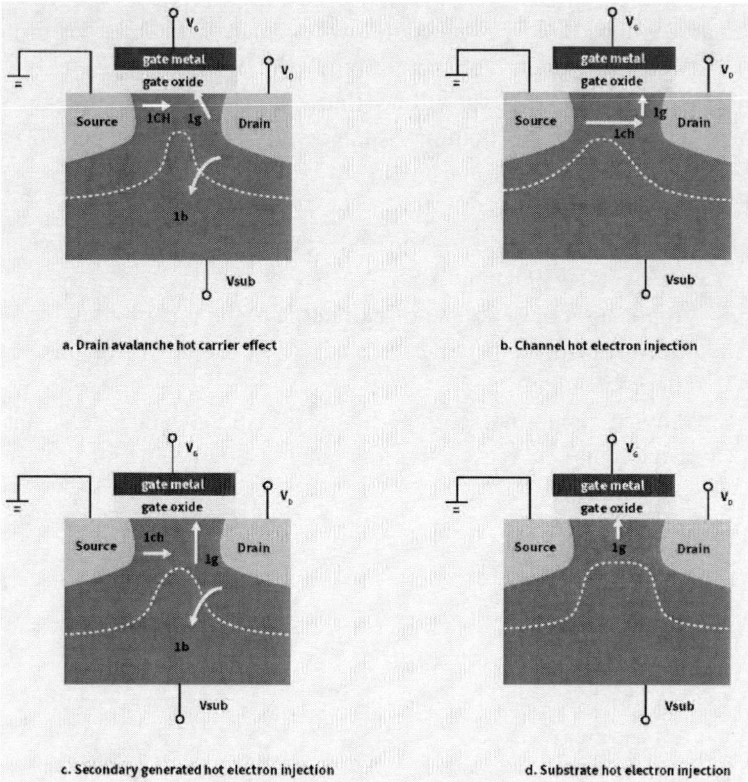

Figure 3. Hot carrier injection mechanisms.

The latch-up event is associated with turning on a thyristor-like structure in the complementary metal-oxide semiconductor (CMOS). A bipolar-type parasitic transistor circuit is constructed in the CMOS IC, which has the same structure as the thyristor. When an external surge triggers the thyristor, a large current will continuously flow, and lead to abnormal operation of the device or even thermal damage of the IC.

Figure 4 shows a cross section of a CMOS inverter consisting of parasitic bipolar transistors. As explained in a semiconductor reliability handbook, *Failure Mechanism of Semiconductor Devices* [9], the equivalent circuit using such parasitic transistors (i.e., lateral positive-negative-positive [PNP] transistors and vertical negative-positive-negative [NPN] transistors) is the same circuit as that of the positive-negative-positive-negative (PNPN) structure thyristor. If the CMOS circuit is operating properly, this thyristor is in a high impedance status. If the thyristor is triggered by a factor, however, impedance will be rapidly reduced to low impedance, and a large current will flow between the drain voltage terminal (VDD) and the source voltage terminal (VSS). This current will continuously flow until the power supply voltage drops below the holding voltage (i.e., the holding current) of the thyristor. The factors that can trigger the thyristor are as follows:

1. Breakdown caused by an extremely large reverse bias applied between the VDD and VSS.
2. Application of external noise or surge to the input/output terminal.
3. Flow of displacement current caused by a rapid change in the power supply voltage.
4. Flow of abnormal current in the substrate, well, etc., caused by irradiation of a radioactive ray, such as heavy ions or protons from cosmic rays.

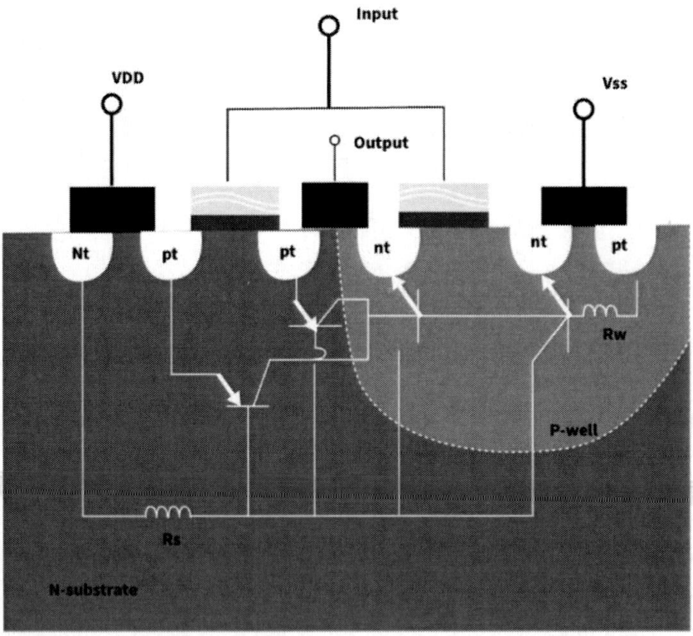

Figure 4. Structure of a CMOS inverter.

Among these factors, application of external noise or surge to the input/output terminal (factor 2) causes most of the problems in practical use [9].

Additional failure mechanisms commonly seen include electromigration, negative bias temperature instability (NBTI), time dependent dielectric breakdown (TDDB), soft error, stress migration, aluminum (Al) corrosion, passivation cracking, growth of a gold (Au)/Al compound, secondary breakdown, thermal fatigue, ion migration, tin (Sn) whisker, package cracking, and electrostatic discharge. Understanding the mechanism of how a certain failure develops can help identify the root cause and design mitigation measures against its occurrence.

Automotive Electrical Overstress

Electrical overstress (EOS) is typically associated with semiconductor damage or failures related to electrical events. The terms *melted metal, dissolved metal, melt-through,* and *burnt metal* were used by Lee [10] and May [11] when reporting EOS damage from power circuits to power transistors. The global leader in developing open standards for the microelectronics industry, the Joint Electron Devices Engineering Council (JEDEC), in their JEP174 White Paper, proposed a definition of EOS in terms of its impact inside applications with a focus on exceeding specifications.

> An electrical device suffers an electrical overstress event when a maximum limit for either the voltage across, the current through, or power dissipated in the device is exceeded and causes immediate damage or malfunction, or latent damage resulting in an unpredictable reduction of its lifetime [12].

Electrical events such as power surges, electrostatic discharge (ESD), or electromagnetic interference (EMI) can damage an IC. The relevant events could be incorrect power supply sequencing, an uncontrolled power surge on the power supply, or voltage spikes due to internal switching or external connection or disconnection. Events could also be caused by ESD due to lack of grounding or poor grounding, latch-up, an external charged source discharging into the device, or the charged device discharging into the environment. The sources of electrical energy can be attributed to a wide variety of causes. Three basic categories where EOS damage can occur are identified in JEP174 [12], as follows:

1. Powered handling: hot plugging, overshoot/overvoltage, power surge, and misorientation.

2. Unpowered handling: charged-person discharge or charged-device discharge.
3. Switching/AC applications: coupled radiofrequency (RF) or EMI interference.

Different causes of EOS damage result in different damage patterns in ICs. The electrical failure symptoms [13] from the application end could manifest themselves as:

- Excessive supply current draw.
- Low resistance between the supply voltage and ground.
- Shorted input or output pins to either the supply voltage or ground.
- Open connections to one or multiple pins.
- Functional failure due to a device's internal damage.

As a result of excessive energy dissipation during EOS events, thermal damage associated with elevated temperatures are often observed in damage to ICs. Some of the failure characteristics were identified as cracked IC packages, burnt mold compounds, melted metal, electromigration in multiple locations, metal trace damage, die surface burn marks, open bond wires, delamination, substrate cracking, and oxide layer breakage. These signatures are terms used in failure analysis to guide the investigation of root cause.

Automotive Integrated Circuit Requirements

Manufacturers of automotive ICs implement different quality controls to ensure the reliability of ICs and prevent against failures. Screening, testing, and qualifications under various conditions are the typical measures to implement quality controls. These conditions have specific requirements based on the conditions within which the automotive components operate. A set of international standards and industry best practices have been developed to cope with the challenges.

Automotive Quality Management System

The International Automotive Task Force (IATF) standard IATF 16949 represents the global manufacturing quality management system (QMS) standard for the automotive industry. IATF created the first edition of International Organization for Standardization/Technical Specification (ISO/TS) 16949 to harmonize the different worldwide assessment and certification systems for the automotive sector supply chain. IATF 16949 was released in 2016 as an automotive QMS standard based on feedback from certification bodies, auditors, suppliers, and original equipment manufacturers. Developed under the concept of a process-oriented QMS that focuses on continual improvement, defect prevention, and reduction of variation and waste in the supply chain, IATF 16949:2016 incorporates the structure and requirements of the ISO 9001:2015 QMS standard with additional automotive requirements. Some of the key areas of focus for IATF 16949:2016 are:

- Continuous improvement
- Defect prevention
- Reducing waste
- Product safety
- Risk management
- Contingency planning
- Requirements for embedded software
- Change and warranty management
- Management of sub-tier suppliers

With the rapid growth of semiconductor use in automotive applications, the semiconductor supply chain is a key part of a manufacturer's product planning. The IATF 16949:2016 standard requires IC manufacturers to perform and record all processes and activities in a standarized format. In addition, IATF 16949:2016 certification is commonly seen as an indication of improvement toward a quality production process and product quality.

Automotive Functional Safety

The increasing functionalities of modern vehicles rely on properly operational electric/electronic (E/E) systems. The technological complexity involving software and mechatronic implementation exposes the vehicle to risks of systematic failure and random hardware failure. The functional safety standard, ISO 26262, was developed to addresses the possible hazards caused by malfunctioning behaviors of safety-related E/E systems, including the interaction of these systems. Adapted from the functional safety standard, International Electrotechnical Commission (IEC) 61508, ISO 26262 covers the E/E systems of automotive products and ensures the design and build of functionally safe vehicles. This standard intends to establish a framework to integrate functional safety activities into a company-specific development framework.

In ISO 26262, functional safety is defined as the absence of unreasonable risk due to hazards caused by malfunctioning behavior of an E/E system. To achieve functional safety, the ISO 26262 series of standards [14].

1. Provides a reference for the automotive safety lifecycle and supports tailoring of activities to be performed during the lifecycle phases (i.e., development, production, operation, service, and decommissioning).
2. Provides an automotive-specific, risk-based approach to determine integrity levels (i.e., Automotive Safety Integrity Levels [ASILs]).
3. Uses ASILs to specify which of the requirements of ISO 26262 are applicable to avoid unreasonable residual risk.
4. Provides requirements for functional safety management, design, implementation, verification, validation, and confirmation.
5. Provides requirements for relations between customers and suppliers.

Some requirements focus on implementing functional safety on a product using technical specifications, while some requirements emphasize the development process and showcase an organization's capability to adhere to the functional safety concept. Functional safety is achieved throughout the development process (requirements specification, design, implementation, integration, verification, validation, and configuration), the production and service processes, and the management processes.

Functional safety requirements for semiconductors refer to the specific criteria and measures implemented to ensure the safe operation of semiconductor devices within safety-critical systems. ISO 26262, Part 11, contains possible interpretations of other parts of ISO 26262 with respect to semiconductor development [15].

Automotive Integrated Circuit Qualification Requirements

While non-automotive devices are qualified with test methodologies performed primarily to the intent of the JEDEC, the Automotive Electronics Council's (AEC) *Q100-Failure Mechanism Based Stress Test Qualification for Integrated Circuits*, as created by the AEC's Component Technical Committee, is often referred as the automotive industry standard specification that outlines the detailed qualification and requalification requirements for packaged ICs. AEC was originally founded in the 1990s by a group of automotive manufacturers and their suppliers to define common electrical component qualification requirements. Over the years, a series of stress test qualification specifications based on failure mechanisms for different parts categories were developed by the AEC Component Technical Committee. Particularly AEC-Q100 establishes a set of documents that describe the stress tests capable of stimulating and precipitating semiconductor device and package failures comparable to use conditions in an accelerated fashion.

Compared to general commercial products, which are tested at room temperature after reliability stress, an AEC-Q100-certified product is qualified based on temperature grade. Four operating temperature grades, listed in Table 1, are defined for automotive parts in AEC-Q100. The temperatures for a particular grade specify the endpoint test temperatures for hot and cold tests and the qualification requirements. The grade is generally determined by where the product is used in the vehicle. For example, if the application is under the hood, Grade 0 will be used to withstand the very high temperature environment. The temperature range also extends for a certain grade depending on the testing type and packaging material of a part. For example, for a temperature cycling test, the testing condition for Grade 1 is -55°C to + 150°C for 1,000 cycles, where the large temperature range introduces high thermomechanical stresses. Care should be taken when selecting the suitable temperature ranges to test for a certain type of ICs.

Table 1. Part operating temperature grades

AEC Grade	Ambient Operating Temperature Range
0	-40°C to + 150°C
1	-40°C to + 125°C
2	-40°C to + 105°C
3	-40°C to + 85°C

Table 2. Qualification test methods for BGA devices

Stress	Sample size/lot	Number of lots	Test methods
Test group A: Accelerated Environment Stress Tests			
Preconditioning	77	3	JEDEC J-STD-020 JESD22-A113
Temperature-Humidity Bias or Biased HAST	77	3	JEDEC JESD22-A101 or A110
Autoclave or Unbiased HAST or Temperature- Humidity (without Bias)	77	3	JEDEC JESD22-A102, A118, or A101
Temperature Cycling	77	3	JEDEC JESD22-A104 and Appendix 3
Power Temperature Cycling	45	1	JEDEC JESD22-A105
High Temperature Storage Life	45	1	JEDEC JESD22-A103
Test Group B: Accelerated Lifetime Simulation Tests			
High Temperature Operating Life	77	3	JEDEC JESD22-A108
Early Life Failure Rate	800	3	AEC Q100-008
Non-volatile Memory (NVM) Endurance, Data Retention, and Operational Life	77	3	AEC Q100-005
Test Group C: Package Assembly Integrity Tests			
Solder Ball Shear	5 balls from a minimum of 10 devices	3	AEC Q100-010 AEC Q003
Test Group E: Electrical Verification Tests			
Pre-and Post-Stress Function/Parameter	All	All	Test to specification
Electrostatic Discharge Human Body Model	See test method	1	AEC Q100-002
Electrostatic Discharge Charged Device Model	See test method	1	AEC Q100-011
Latch-Up	6	1	AEC Q100-004
Electrical Distribution	30	3	AEC Q100-009 AEC Q003

The qualification tests in AEC-Q100 include a general test, device specific tests, and wear out reliability tests. Under the category of general tests, there are accelerated environment stress tests, accelerated lifetime simulation tests, package assembly integrity tests, die fabrication reliability tests, electrical verification tests, defect screening tests, and cavity package integrity tests. Not the entire list of testing is applicable to a particular device type. The exact suite of testing depends on the packaging type (hermetic, plastic, ball grid array [BGA]), the surface mount, and whether it is lead-free. For example, Table 2 lists the required tests for devices with a solder ball surface mount package (i.e., a BGA), of which many test methods are defined in JEDEC publications. The complexity of a testing program depends on the end application, wafer technology, and package structure. IC manufacturers should carefully select the adequate testing that is most suitable for its end application to assess IC reliability. An example is the Semiconductor Reliability report published by RENESAS Electronics Corporation on their website, which includes the Q-100 Qualification Test Results for their R7F702300EBBB-C semiconductor [16].

When a new technology or material relevant to a certain wear out failure mechanism is to be qualified, it is required to test the IC for the identified failure mechanism. The list of testing required for the die fabrication stage is as follows:

- An electromigration assessment is performed according to JESD61 [17]. The test method monitors the microelectronic metallization lines at the wafer level to evaluate process options in process development. It also monitors metallization reliability in manufacturing and evaluates process equipment.
- A time-dependent dielectric breakdown assessment (i.e., the gate oxide integrity test) is to be performed according to JESD35 [18]. Three test procedures including the voltage-ramp (V-Ramp), the current-ramp (J-Ramp), and the new constant current (Bounded J-Ramp) test are designed to estimate the overall integrity and reliability of thin gate oxides.
- An HCI assessment is to be performed according to JESD60 [19] and JESD28 [20]. The tests measure the P-channel and N-channel MOSFET hot-carrier induced degradation under DC stress.
- An NBTI assessment is performed according to JESD90 [21]. The procedure investigates NBTI stress in a symmetric voltage condition with the channel inverted and no channel conduction.
- A stress migration assessment is performed according to JESD61 [17], JESD87 [22], and JESD202 [23]. The procedures will assess the reliability of Al-copper, refractory metal barrier interconnect systems. It will also characterize the electromigration failure-time distribution of equivalent metal lines subjected to a constant current-density and temperature stress.

Electromagnetic Compatibility Requirements

EMI is an unintended disturbance of the expected operation of an electronic system. The electrical system is required to function properly within its electromagnetic environment and not cause EMI for other devices in the same environment. Vehicles with advanced driving assistant features are typically associated with the addition of electronic components with increasing electromagnetic compatibility (EMC) challenges. EMC testing has provided benefits to verify the performance and reliability of electronic devices and systems, and ensures that the devices meet the relevant regulations and safety standards. Zhang and colleagues summarized the standards for EMC testing at the automotive system level [24], as listed in Table 3.

Table 3. Automotive system-level standards [24]

System-level	Standard	Name
Overall	ISO 60050:1990	EMC terms summary of Summary of electromagnetic compatibility Application and interpretation of basic EMC terms and definitions
Electronic components	International Special Committee on Radio Interference (CISPR) 25	Limits and measurement methods for protecting radio disturbance characteristics of vehicle-mounted receivers
	ISO 7637	Road vehicles Electrical harassment caused by conduction and coupling
	ISO 11452	Road vehicles. Test methods for immunity of electrical / electronic components to narrow-band radiated electromagnetic energy
	ISO 10605	Road vehicles Test method for electrical disturbance caused by electrostatic discharge
Whole vehicle	CISPR 12	Vehicles, boats, and internal combustion engines - Radio disturbance characteristics - Limits and methods of measurement for the protection of on-board receivers
	ISO 11451	Road vehicles Vehicle immunity to narrow band radiated electromagnetic energy
	ISO 7637	Road vehicles Electrical harassment caused by conduction and coupling
	ISO 10605	Road vehicles Test method for electrical disturbance caused by electrostatic discharge

EMC and the immunity of individual ICs affects the EMC of the entire system. For designs without electrically-conductive shielding, electromagnetic emissions generated from IC devices could couple to EMI in the environment. It is important to consider and evaluate the EMC properties at the IC level during the development process. A collection of standards were published for this purpose. Testing electromagnetic emissions is specified in IEC 61967 [25] and testing electromagnetic immunity is specified in IEC 62132 [26]. The immunity to transients is considered separately in IEC 62215 [27].

IEC 61967 [25] provides guidance on the measurement of conducted and radiated electromagnetic disturbances from ICs under controlled conditions. There are seven parts currently under this standard.

1. IEC 61967-1, provides general information and definitions on the measurement of conducted and radiated electromagnetic disturbances from ICs. It also provides a description of measurement conditions, test equipment and set-up, as well as the test procedures and content of the test reports. The object of this document is to describe general conditions to establish a uniform testing environment and to obtain a quantitative measure of RF disturbances from ICs.
2. IEC 61967-2, defines the method to measure electromagnetic radiation using a transverse electromagnetic (TEM) or wideband gigahertz TEM (GTEM) cell. The IC being evaluated is mounted on an IC test printed circuit board (PCB) that is clamped to a mating port (referred to as a wall port). Unlike conventional usage where the test board is inside the cell, the wall port is cut on the top or bottom of the TEM/GTEM cell and becomes part of the cell wall. This method is applicable to any TEM or GTEM cell modified to incorporate the wall port.
3. IEC 61967-3, defines an evaluation method for the near electric, magnetic, or electromagnetic field components at or near the surface of an IC. This measurement method provides a map of the near electric- or magnetic-field emissions over the IC up to 6 Gigahertz (GHz).
4. IEC 61967-4 specifies a method to measure the conducted electromagnetic emission of ICs by direct RF current measurement with a 1 Ohm (Ω) resistive probe and RF voltage measurement using a 150 Ω coupling network.
5. IEC 61967-5 describes a method to measure the conducted electromagnetic emission of ICs applied either on a standardized test board or on a final PCB.
6. IEC 61967-6 specifies a method to evaluate RF currents on the pins of an IC by means of a non-contact current measurement using a

miniature magnetic probe. This method can measure the RF currents generated by the IC over a frequency range of 0.15 Hertz to 1,000 Megahertz.

7. IEC 61967-8 defines a method to measure the electromagnetic radiated emission from an IC using an IC stripline. The IC being evaluated is mounted on an EMC test PCB between the active conductor and the ground plane of the IC stripline arrangement.

IEC 62132 [26] provides guidance on the measurement of electromagnetic immunity of ICs to conducted and radiated disturbances. There are six parts currently under this standard.

1. IEC 62132-1 provides general information and definitions about the measurement of electromagnetic immunity of ICs to conducted and radiated disturbances. It also defines general test conditions, test equipment and setup, as well as the test procedures and content of the test reports for all parts of the IEC 62132 series.
2. IEC 62132-2 specifies a method to measure the immunity of an IC to RF-radiated electromagnetic disturbances.
3. IEC 62132-4 describes a method to measure the immunity of an IC in the presence of conducted RF disturbances (e.g., resulting from RF-radiated disturbances).
4. IEC 62132-5 describes a measurement method to quantify RF immunity of ICs mounted on a standardized test board, or on their final application board, to electromagnetic conductive disturbances.
5. IEC 62132-8 specifies a method to measure the immunity of an IC to RF-radiated electromagnetic disturbances over the frequency range of 150 Kilohertz (kHz) to 3 GHz.
6. IEC/TS 62132-9 defines a method to evaluate the effect of near electric-field, magnetic-field, or electromagnetic-field components on an IC.

Transient immunity tests are covered under IEC 62215 (IE62215 2007). There are two parts currently under this standard.

1. IEC/TS 62215-2 defines the test method to evaluate the immunity of ICs against fast-conducted, synchronous transient disturbances. This synchronous transient immunity measurement method uses short

impulses with fast rise times of different amplitude, duration, and polarity in a conductive mode to the IC.

2. IEC 62215-3 specifies a method to measure the immunity of an IC to standardized conducted electrical transient disturbances. This method intends to classify interaction between conducted transient disturbances and performance degradation induced in ICs regardless of transients within or beyond the specified operating voltage range.

Given the number of testing standards at different automotive levels for various applications, it is challenging to obtain comparable EMC test results for ICs from different suppliers. Efforts were made by a cross-company working group to develop a test specification that could obtain relevant quantitative IC-level EMC measurement results with the necessary minimum number of tests. A generic IC EMC Test specification was published by ZVEI (the German Electrical and Electronic Manufacturers Association) referencing international standards. According to the latest edition published in 2017:

> This document defines common tests characterizing the EMC behavior of integrated circuits (ICs) in terms of RF emission and RF immunity in the frequency range from 150 kHz up to 3 GHz as well as pulse immunity and system level ESD), based on international standards for integrated circuits and related standards for IC applications. It contains all information to evaluate any kind of ICs in the same way. In this document general information and definitions of IC types, pin types, test and measurement networks, pin selection, operation modes and limit classes are given. This allows the user to create an EMC specification for a dedicated IC as well as to provide comparable results for comparable ICs [28].

The specification classifies IC functions into four modules: the port module, the supply module, the core module, and the oscillator module [29]. The port module contains at least one output driver or one input stage, including line drivers and line receivers, the symmetrical line drivers and line receivers, regional inputs and drivers, high side and low side drivers, and an RF antenna driver and receiver. The supply module provides current to at least one IC function module. A core module is an IC function module without any connection to the outside of the IC via pins, including central processing units, digital logic fixed-functional units like watchdog timers, analog fixed-function units like analog-to-digital-converters (ADC), and sensor elements like accelerometers. An oscillator module generates a periodic signal internally as a charge pump or clock generator. It is defined as a separate module because of the special EMC characteristics.

Using these definitions, any IC can be categorized into different blocks by function modules. Based on the operating functions of the IC application, the pin selection and testing network can be further determined by the function modules for emission, immunity, and ESD tests.

Integrated Circuit Failure Analysis Technique

IC failures could manifest themselves at the system level as parameter drifting, performance degradation, or function loss. The electronic component might have one or more parameters shifted out of range. Degradation is typically associated with characteristic changes. Function loss could be complete, partial, or intermittent. Identifying the root cause of failures is critical in the IC manufacturing and application process. Many advanced analytical skills are available for IC failure analysis. Some of the typical methods are discussed in this section.

Electrical Measurement

Electrical measurement is widely used in IC failure analysis for fault isolation at the device level. Resistance measurements can identify changes in resistance indicating open- or short-circuit faults. Voltage measurements at specific nodes can help identify circuits with improper voltage levels, leakage, or incorrect biasing conditions.

A more complicated method in electrical measurement is curve tracing. Current-voltage (I-V) measurements and capacitance-voltage (C-V) measurements are commonly used to characterize the electrical behavior of the devices. For example, measuring the I-V characteristics of a semiconductor structure helps determine if its threshold voltage has changed, which can be used to understand the device's operating conditions and compare with specifications. C-V measurements are commonly used to assess the quality and thickness of insulating oxide layers (e.g., gate oxide) in metal-oxide semiconductor (MOS) devices, which can be interpreted for the presence of interface traps and charges at the semiconductor-insulator interface.

Time-Domain Reflectometry

Time-domain reflectometry (TDR) is often used to identify cracks or defects in a trace. TDR works on the principle of sending short pulses of electrical signals down a transmission line and measuring the reflections that occur at impedance mismatches or faults within the line. An example of the use of TDR is to locate the crack in flex resulting in an open circuit. TDR is particularly useful to detect fault inside a package where miniaturization and high-density interconnections increase the risk of failures. TDR can also measure the signal propagation delay along the transmission lines, which can be used to understand the timing issues and identify the location of defects along the transmission line. An example of the use of TDR in open-failure analysis is illustrated in Figure 5.

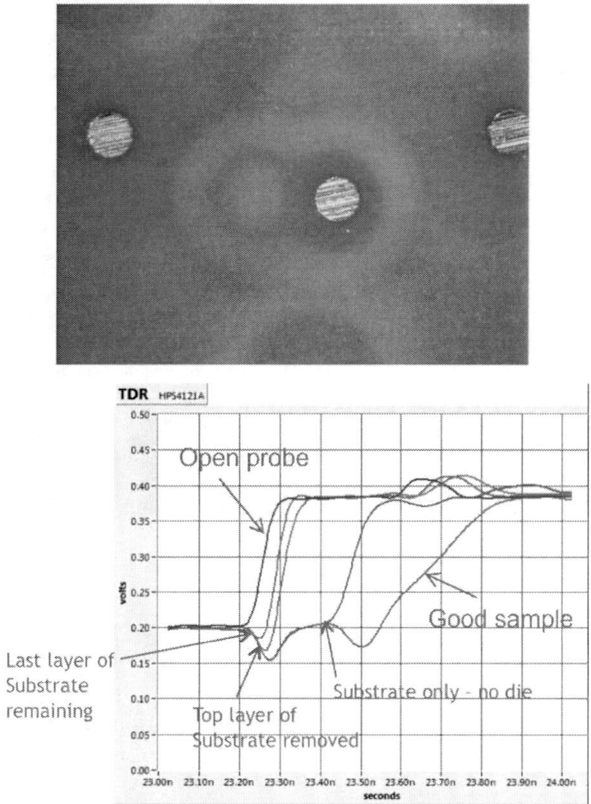

Figure 5. TDR used to identify the location of failure to a substrate, interconnect, or die [30].

Computed Tomography and X-ray Imaging

Computed tomography (CT) and X-ray imaging are normally used to inspect ICs without a destructive disassembly process. For example, X-ray imaging can locate bond wire failures in microchips by revealing disconnections or inconsistencies. Since CT is capable of constructing three-dimensional (3-D) images, it is employed to examine solder joints and identify issues like poor wetting, solder voids, and incomplete connections at the PCB assembly level. With enhanced resolution from nano-CT, features like micro-voids or fine metal lines formed by electromigration can be readily inspected to identify the region of interest.

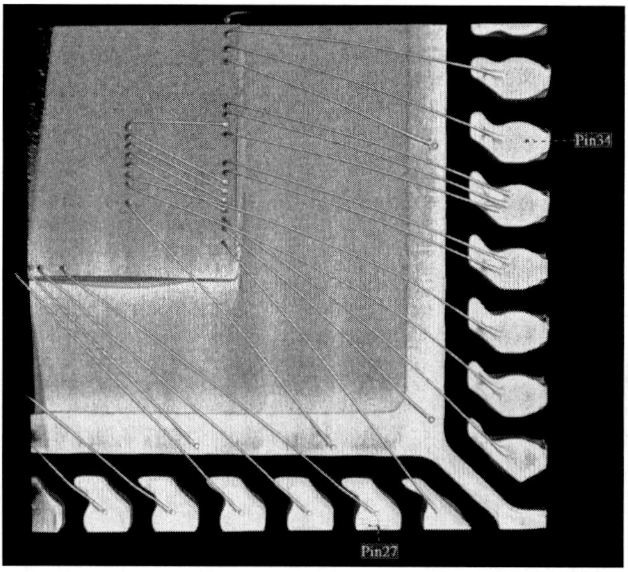

Figure 6. CT image of a typical fingerprint of solder joint cracking [31].

Although CT is often considered non-destructive, it might lead to unintended damage to the IC due to radiation exposure or an ionizing effect. To mitigate these potential risks, precautions like limiting the duration and intensity of exposure to X-rays should be taken. Figure 6 shows the typical fingerprint of solder joint cracking in a CT image.

Scanning Acoustic Microscopy

Scanning Acoustic Microscopy (SAM) is another imaging tool to inspect the internal structures of various materials. SAM operates by sending ultrasonic waves into the sample being analyzed and then measuring the reflections of these waves. Water is commonly used as the coupling medium in SAM applications. For certain types of samples, other coupling fluids or gels with specific properties may be used to optimize the acoustic coupling. For IC failure analysis, SAM provides information about density, thickness, and acoustic impedance variations within ICs. This enables the identification of internal defects such as delamination, voids, and cracks. Additionally, SAM can be used to examine the packaging quality of ICs, including the inspection of bonding interfaces and package encapsulation integrity. An example of a SAM reconstruction image of an IC is presented in Figure 7.

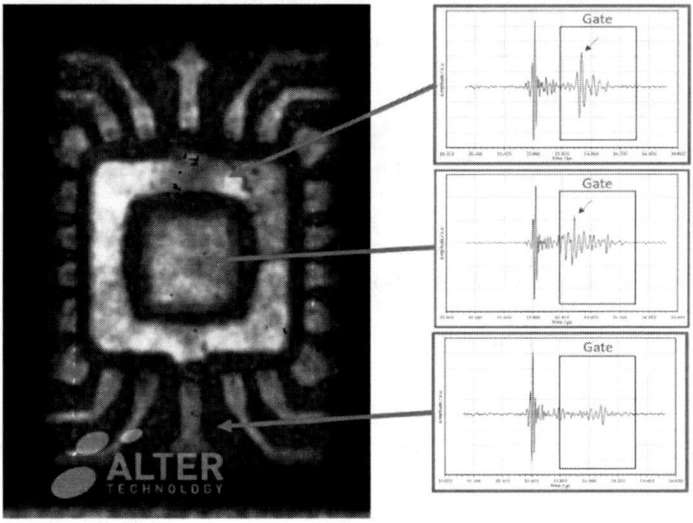

Figure 7. SAM reconstruction image [32].

Infrared Thermography

Infrared thermography serves as a powerful tool to identify IC anomalies based on thermal information. Operating on the principle of capturing infrared radiation emitted by objects, infrared thermography can detect temperature variations within ICs. For instance, malfunctioning transistors or resistors within an IC might generate localized heat, which can be visualized using infrared thermography. Infrared thermography can be used to locate defects by visualizing temperature distribution across ICs.

Furthermore, lock-in thermography (LIT) works by applying a periodic electrical signal to the sample and then detecting the resulting thermal response under infrared thermography. By using a lock-in amplifier, the thermal signal that corresponds to the modulation frequency is extracted from the background noise. This allows for the identification of cracks in semiconductor materials, voids in packages, or other thermal irregularities, as shown in Figure 8. The technique enhances sensitivity to small temperature differences and anomalies.

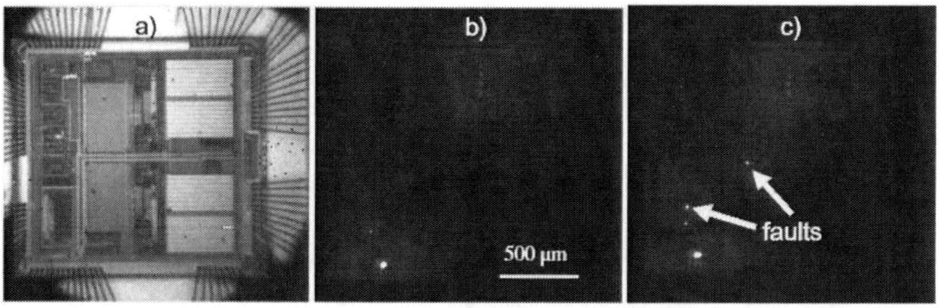

Figure 8. Topography image (a); a LIT amplitude image of an intact IC (b); and an LIT amplitude image of a faulty IC (c). The arrows point to the fault locations [33].

Optical beam-induced resistance change (OBIRCH) is another thermographic technology. The principle of OBIRCH revolves around the concept that when a laser beam illuminates a small portion of an IC device, it generates localized heating. This heating induces changes in the resistance of the device's components, such as transistors and interconnects. By analyzing these changes in resistance, defects or weak spots within the device can be identified.

Scanning Electron Microscopy

Scanning electron microscopy (SEM) provides high-resolution imaging of the surface morphology of IC components. SEM can be coupled with energy dispersive spectroscopy (EDS) to perform elemental analysis of materials. When a sample is bombarded with high-energy electrons in SEM, the interaction leads to the emission of characteristic X-rays from the sample's atoms. EDS detectors measure the energies and intensities of these emitted X-rays, allowing for the identification and quantification of the elements present. For example, when investigating a defective IC, EDS can detect the presence of foreign particles or materials that might be causing the malfunction.

SEM can also be used in conjunction with focused ion beam (FIB) technology to create precise cross sections, revealing the composition and layering of materials within the IC. FIB uses a finely focused beam of ions, typically gallium ions, to perform precise milling and etching at nanoscale. FIB is used for sample preparation, cross-sectional, and even circuit editing. Combined with SEM/EDS, FIB can reveal the internal structure of ICs and uncover defects. The cross sections created by FIB are shown in Figure 9.

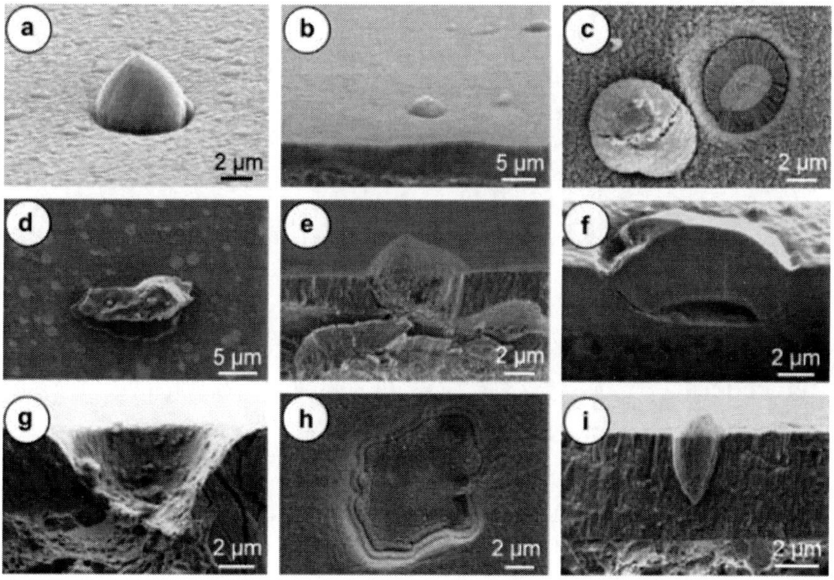

Figure 9. FIB-SEM characterization of defects [30].

Looking Forward

The development of autonomous vehicles has been driven by advancements in automotive ICs and related technologies. High performance ICs with increased processing power will be in growing demand as autonomous vehicles require sophisticated algorithms and real-time, decision-making capabilities. It also facilitates the integration and synchronization of sensor data collected from cameras, radar, lidar, and ultrasonic sensors to perceive surroundings. Automotive ICs also need to incorporate robust security features to protect the vehicle's systems from cyber threats, ensure data privacy, and secure proper communication between various components and external entities. ICs are expected to support over-the-air software updates to allow remote deployment of a software fix and feature enhancements. The advanced autonomy raises challenges for the vehicle to ensure safe operation under all conditions.

Another aspect of automotive safety, the safety of intended functionality, as described in ISO/PAS 21448, refers to the absence of unreasonable risk due to hazards resulting from functional insufficiencies of the intended functionality or by reasonably foreseeable misuse by persons. Features like self-tests, error detection, and fault tolerance mechanisms need redundant processing units or sensors to ensure system reliability and mitigate risks associated with potential failures. These trends and requirements highlight the need for automotive ICs that can provide powerful processing, sensor integration, functional safety, energy efficiency, security, and support for technologies based on artificial intelligence. As autonomous vehicle development progresses, automotive ICs will continue to advance to meet the demanding requirements of autonomous driving systems.

References

[1] Palwe, Swapnil. 2022. "Automotive Semiconductor Market Research Report Information." Market Research Future, Last Updated July 2022. Available from https://www.marketresearchfuture.com/reports/automotive-semiconductor-market-10444.

[2] International Energy Association (IEA). 2023. "Electric car sales break new records with momentum expected to continue through 2023." IEA, Accessed September 1, 2023. Available from https://www.iea.org/energy-system/transport/electric-vehicles.

[3] Dhond, P. 2015. "Packaging ICs to survive the automotive environment." Accessed September 1, 2023. Available from https://13b5a0af191f0d6f4eb2-bfbf198c248718c4e4d3ad858e5de63a.ssl.cf2.rackcdn.com/2018/01/10_15-Packaging_ICs_to_Survive_the_Automotive_Environment.pdf. Reprint from Chip Scale Review.

[4] Tie, Siang F., and Chee W. Tan. 2013. "A review of energy sources and energy management system in electric vehicles." *Renew Sust Energ Rev* 20:82-102.

[5] Jones, Peter. 2022. "How Much Do Electric Car Batteries Cost." *Motor and Wheels,* Last Updated August 25, 2022, Accessed September 1, 2023. Available from https://motorandwheels.com/how-much-do-electric-car-batteries-cost/.

[6] Liu, K., K. Li, Q. Peng, and C. Zhang. 2019. "A brief review on key technologies in the battery management system of electric vehicles." *Front Mech Eng* 14:47-64.

[7] Maroti, P. K., Padmanaban, S., Bhaskar, M. S., Ramachandaramurthy, V. K. and Blaabjerg, F. 2022. "The state-of-the-art of power electronics converters configurations in electric vehicle technologies." *Power Electronic Devices and Components* 1.

[8] Entner, Robert. 2007. *Modeling and Simulation of Negative Bias Temperature Instability*, Technische Universit, Wien, Germany.

[9] Panasonic Corporation. 2009. "Failure Mechanism of Semiconductor Devices."

[10] Lee, T. W. 1983. "The Interpretation of EOS Damage in Power Transistors." *ISTFA*:157.

[11] May, J. T. "The interpretation of EOS damage in power circuits," in *ISTFA 1985 International Symposium for Testing and Failure Analysis Proceedings*, 1985, 92.

[12] JEDEC Solid State Technology Association (JEDEC). 2016. "JEP174 Understanding Electrical Overstress."

[13] Infineon Technologies AG (Infineon). 2018. "Electrical Over-Stress (EOS) Review and FAQ - KBA225846." Infineon Developer Community, Last Updated December 16, 2022, Accessed September 1, 2023. Available from https://community.infineon.com/t5/Knowledge-Base-Articles/Electrical-Over-Stress-EOS-Review-and-FAQ-KBA225846/ta-p/260181.

[14] International Organization for Standardization (ISO). 2018. "ISO26262-1 Road vehicles - Functional safety- Part 1: Vocabulary." Geneva, Switzerland: ISO.

[15] International Organization for Standardization (ISO). 2018. "ISO 26262-11:2018 Road vehicles–Functional safety–Part 11: Guidelines on application of ISO 26262 to semiconductors." Geneva, Switzerland: ISO.

[16] Renesas Electronics. 2021. "Renesas Semiconductor Reliability Report." Tokyo, Japan: Renesas Electronics, Available from https://www.renesas.com/us/en/document/prr/r7f702300ebbb-c-reliability-report-aec-q100.

[17] JEDEC Solid State Technology Association (JEDEC). 2007. "JESD61, Isothermal Electromigration Test Procedure."

[18] JEDEC Solid State Technology Association (JEDEC). 2001. "JESD35, Procedure for Wafer-Level-Testing of Thin Dielectrics."

[19] JEDEC Solid State Technology Association (JEDEC). 2004. "JESD60, A Procedure for Measuring P-Channel MOSFET Hot-Carrier-Induced Degradation Under DC Stress."

[20] JEDEC Solid State Technology Association (JEDEC). 2001. "JESD28, A Procedure for Measuring N-channel MOSFET Hot-Carrier-Induced Degradation Under DC Stress."

[21] JEDEC Solid State Technology Association (JEDEC). 2004. "JESD90, A Procedure for Measuring P-channel MOSFET Negative Bias Temperature Instabilities."

[22] JEDEC Solid State Technology Association (JEDEC). 2023. "JESD87 Standard Test Structure for Reliability Assessment of AlCu Mettalizations with Barrier Mterials."
[23] JEDEC Solid State Technology Association (JEDEC). 2006. "JESD202, Method for Characterizing the Electromigration Failure Time Distribution of Interconnects Under Constant-Current and Temperature Stress."
[24] Zhang, J. 2020. "Overview of Electromagnetic Compatibility in Automotive Integrated Circuits." *J Phys Conf Ser* 1607:012034.
[25] International Electrotechical Commission (IEC). 2018. "IEC61967 Integrated Circuits - Measurement of electromagnetic emissions."
[26] International Electrotechical Commission (IEC). 2015. "IEC62132 Integrated Circuits - Measurement of electromagnetic immunity."
[27] International Electrotechical Commission (IEC). 2007. "IEC/TS62215 Integrated circuits - Measurement of impulse immunity."
[28] German Electro and Digital Industry Association (ZVEI). 2017. Generic IC EMC Test Specification Version 2.1. Frankfurt, Germany: ZVEI.
[29] Klotz, Frank. "EMC Test Specification for Integrated Circuits," in *18th International Zurich Symposium on Electromagnetic Compatibility*, 2007.
[30] EAG Laboratories (EAG). 2023. "Time Domain Reflectometry (TDR)." Accessed September 1, 2023. Available from https://www.eag.com/app-note/time-domain-reflectometry-tdr/.
[31] IC Failure Analysis Labs. 2023. "IC X-Ray Inspection." Accessed September 1, 2023. Available from https://icfailureanalysis.com/ic-x-ray-services/
[32] Rebollo, Francisco J.A. 2023. "How it works Scanning Acoustic Microscopy (C-SAM)." Alter Technology, Accessed September 1, 2023. Available from https://wpo-altertechnology.com/how-it-works-scanning-acoustic-microscopy-c-sam/.
[33] Breitenstein, Otwin, and Steffen Sturm. 2019. "Lock-in thermography for analyzing solar cells and failure analysis in other electronic components." *Quant Infrared Thermog J* 16(3-4):203-217.

Biographical Sketches

Yike Hu, PhD

Dr. Yike Hu's area of expertise is in product safety evaluation and failure analysis of electrical and electronic systems. She has worked extensively on technical investigations at hardware level and system level evaluation in automotive electronic systems, circuit design reviews and prototype validation testing for consumer products, and risk assessment and design failure modes analysis for energy storage systems. Dr. Hu has also assisted clients with technology landscaping review regarding technical standards, regulatory requirements and pre-certification preparation for the North America, China and Europe market. Dr. Hu received her Ph.D. in Physics from Georgia Institute of Technology, where she worked on understanding the growth mechanism and improved the growth process to achieve high quality graphene thin film obtained through thermal sublimation of silicon carbide. Her work focused on advancing the understanding of graphene physics and its application toward high-speed electronics.

Xiang Wang, PhD

Dr. Xiang Wang's area of expertise is in electrical and electronic system design and its safety evaluation. He has worked extensively on electrical test design for consumer products safety evaluation, circuit board design review and testing, failure analysis of consumer products and automatic data processing. Dr. Wang has also assisted clients with technical review on electrical related data, standards, requirements and documents. Dr. Wang received his Ph.D. in Power Electronic from Newcastle University, where he worked on understanding and measuring the threshold voltage shift of silicon carbide power MOSFET. His work focused on the evaluation of oxide reliability. Before joining Exponent, Dr. Wang worked as a research engineer in Toshiba Bristol Inventory and Research Laboratory, where he worked on the design and testing of optimized gate driving method for power MOSFET.

Chapter 5

Electronics Thermal Design for Optimum Chip Cooling

Qiming Zhang*, PhD
and Farooq Siddiqui, PhD
Exponent, Inc., Hong Kong

Abstract

In this chapter, we focus on important thermal factors that are considered during the conceptual design stage of an electronic system. We present different examples of overheating effects that are detrimental to the lifetime of electronic devices. We detail the fundamental physics and theoretical models needed for electronic thermal design. Moreover, this chapter covers different thermal materials used for effective heat removal from an electronic chip. Finally, we discuss various emerging thermal systems that can potentially address chip cooling challenges in future electronic systems.

Keywords: chip cooling, thermal design, thermal materials, thermal stresses, future trends

---

* Corresponding Author's Email: qzhang@exponent.com.

In: Computer Engineering Applications …
Editor: Brian D'Andrade
ISBN: 979-8-89113-488-1

Introduction

For modern computing systems, a large portion of performance, safety, and reliability problems is related to thermal degradation or overheating. Thus, a good thermal design plays an important role during the planning and prototype stage. Most modern central processing units (CPU) and other power chips, such as graphics processing units (GPU), microcontroller units (MCU), and power-supply chips already include an overheating prevention mechanism to reduce heat generation and stop the operation under overheating conditions. The insufficient cooling capacity of a computing system affects its performance, which may result in system failures. Moreover, long-term overheating can cause material degradation or permanent damage to components, which leads to reliability problems and safety hazards.

The thermal factors in modern computer systems involve multiple dimensions of design considerations. At the chip and package level, the most critical consideration is power generation density from the heat source and how rapidly and uniformly the heat source (i.e., the silicon die) transfers heat to the surrounding package materials (e.g., the lead frame, chip carriers, epoxy molding compound, or metal lid). The low thermal resistance from the heat source to the package material is an important factor in preventing the accumulated heat inside the package. The design of heat transfer mechanisms from the printed circuit board (PCB) and the additional heat sink should be highly efficient in transferring heat from the package to other parts of the device and the environment to keep the system operating in a reasonable temperature range.

The design guidelines of the cooling system in modern computers are still based on the physics of thermal dissipation, involving conduction and convection. A conduction method with passive convection may be used for a relatively low-power heat source, such as a thicker thermal conductive material or a metal heat sink. Conduction and positive convection, such as air fans or a liquid cooling system are required for a relatively high-power heat source.

Examples of Acute Effects of Overheating

Physical Factors

Materials can expand under heat due to their physical properties. Computing system components and chips are made of different materials that generally have different coefficients of thermal expansion (CTE), which can lead to distortion stresses between different materials under heating. Excessive heating will introduce excessive distortion stresses to the entire system and cause thermo-mechanical damage to the components.

Figure 1 is a typical example of a silicon-die fracture of a chip caused by a thermal effect [1]. This is a typical, cyclic, stress-induced thermal crack caused by the fatigue bending moment between the silicon die and the substrate. Even if the heat is not sufficient to cause direct failure, the long-term application with repeated temperature cycling can still induce structural damage. Thus, keeping the operating temperature under a certain limit is quite important.

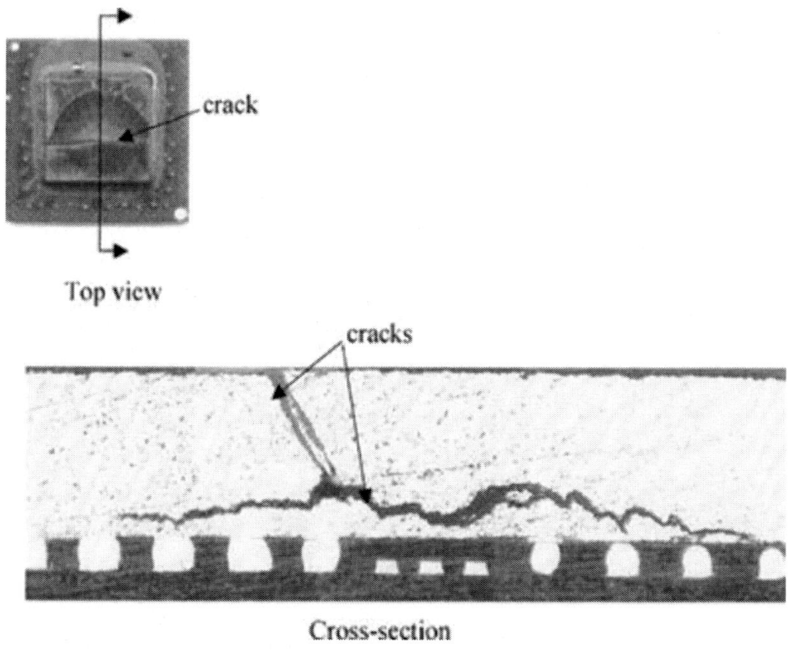

Figure 1. Silicon-die fracture caused by thermal cycling effect [1]. (Reprinted with permission from *IEEE Transactions on Components and Packaging Technologies*).

Chemical Factors

Overheating can trigger material degradation effects due to material chemical factors. For typical polymers and organics, the molecular chain can be damaged causing the material to lose its original strength or other critical factors such as dielectric resistance. High temperatures can also accelerate the oxidation effect or boost other chemical reactions within the mixture of organics and further trigger material degradation. For metals used in chip packaging or that serve as electrical conductors, overheating will accelerate the metal's oxidization, induce a larger electrical resistance, cause corrosion by reaction with other chemicals, or even trigger an electrochemical migration effect. The yellowing effect indicates the chemical change of the PCB material, which had already lost its original dialectical resistance. Under these conditions, the area will be more vulnerable under extreme conditions, and may burn if there is a leakage current or short circuit from component leads.

Physics for Thermal Design

Understanding the physics of thermal design is crucial to develop efficient thermal systems for electronic chip cooling. The reliability and safety of an electronic device strongly depends on its thermal design. A good thermal design limits a device's temperature to safe levels at the worst operating conditions. Thermal design activity usually starts in the early stages of product design. As the product design moves through different stages from concept to final prototype, thermal design also follows through from simple heat transfer calculations to more complex thermal simulations, detailed designs, and finally a thermal system. For this reason, it is vital to understand the fundamental physics of thermal design, which is discussed in the following section.

Fundamental Physics of Thermal Design

Thermal design involves managing heat transfer to operate a device at safe temperature levels. Heat transfer occurs due to the thermal gradient from a high temperature region to a low temperature region. There can be different modes, however, through which heat transfer can occur in any thermal system.

When a thermal gradient exists in a non-moving (solid or fluid) medium, heat transfer occurs through conduction. Conversely, when a thermal gradient exists between a moving fluid and a surface, heat transfer occurs through convection. In electronic devices, heat transfer between a chip and a heat spreader occurs through conduction, while heat flow from a heat spreader to the surrounding moving fluid (such as liquid or air) occurs through convection. For this reason, in this section, we mainly focus on these two modes of heat transfer since they commonly occur in electronic devices.

Thermal Conduction

Thermal conduction is governed by Fourier's law, which is based on temperature distribution within a medium. Fourier's law is not derived from first principles, rather it is based on observation, and therefore is phenomenological. Because the heat transfer rate is directly proportional to the material cross section area (A) and temperature difference (ΔT) while inversely proportional to its length (Δx), Fourier's law of thermal conduction is mathematically written as:

$$q_x \propto \frac{A\Delta T}{\Delta x} \qquad (1)$$

Where q_x is the heat rate.

The proportionality in the above equation remains valid for different materials. For instance, for fixed values of ΔT, A, and Δx, q_x increases as the material is replaced from low conducting material to high conducting material. Therefore, a proportionality constant can be introduced in Equation 1 that is a function of material properties. The heat rate is given as:

$$q_x = kA\frac{\Delta T}{\Delta x} \quad (2)$$

where k is a material property called thermal conductivity (W/m.K).

The thermal conductivity of various materials is shown in Figure 2. As limit Δx approaches zero, Equation 2 can be modified as:

$$q_x = -kA\frac{dT}{dx} \qquad (3)$$

where the minus sign indicates the direction of the heat flow from the higher temperature region to the lower temperature region.

Fourier's law states that heat flow is directional and is perpendicular to the cross-sectional area (A). Dividing the heat rate by the cross-sectional area gives the heat flux, determined as:

$$q_x'' = \frac{q_x}{A} = -k\frac{dT}{dx} \quad (4)$$

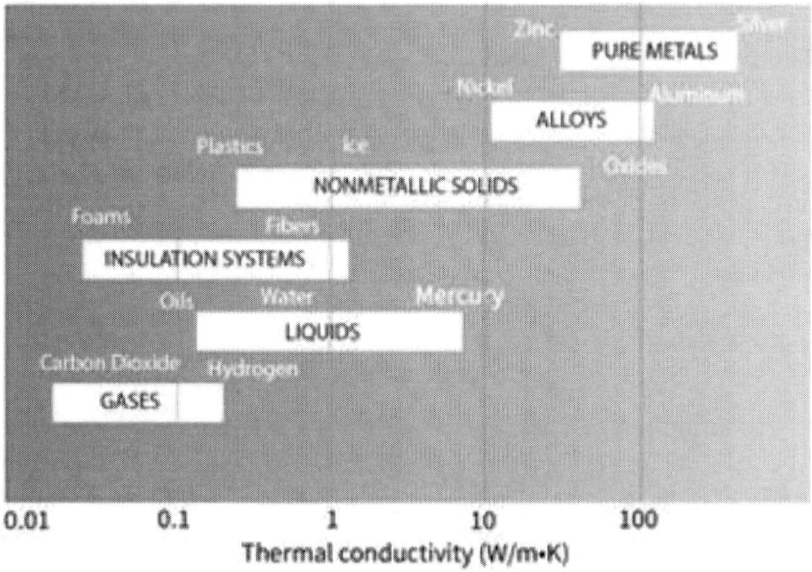

Figure 2. Thermal conductivity for various materials.

It must be noted that Fourier's law is applied to all states of matter (i.e., solid, liquid, and gas). Solids are composed of tightly packed atoms (called lattice) and free electrons, so thermal transport in solids can be explained due to two phenomena: the mobility of free electrons and lattice vibrational waves. Like a photon, which is the fundamental quantum (particle) of light, the lattice vibrational quantum is called a phonon. Free electrons dominate the contribution to heat transfer in pure metals, while phonons dominate the contribution to heat transfer in insulators and semiconductors. Therefore, the thermal conductivity in solids is the sum of thermal conductivity due to phonons and thermal conductivity due to electrons (i.e., $k = k_e + k_{ph}$). The thermal conductivity from kinetic theory is expressed as:

$$k = \frac{1}{3} C\bar{c}\lambda_{mfp} \qquad (5)$$

where C is the specific heat for phonons in nonconductive materials and the specific heat for electrons in conductive materials, $\bar{c}$ is the speed of sound in nonconductive materials and the mean electron velocity in conductive materials, while λ_{mfp} is the mean free path velocity of an electron or phonon.

Thermal Conduction in Microelectronics

In the previous section, we discussed the concept of bulk thermal conductivity applicable for macroscale dimensions. The characteristic dimensions in modern electronic chips are usually in the microscale or nanoscale magnitudes, so a modified form of thermal conductivity is used due to their small physical dimensions. The electron and phonon (energy carriers) trajectories in a microelectronic system with micro/nano scale thickness h is demonstrated in Figure 3. The scattering and redirection of these energy carriers are affected by the characteristic dimension h of a microelectronic chip. For large values of h/λ_{mfp}, physical boundaries have a small effect on reducing the mean free path of energy carriers, and therefore, thermal conductivity is the same as in bulk materials. For small values of h/λ_{mfp}, such as in modern microchips, the physical boundaries may considerably affect the mean free path of energy carriers. As a result, the energy carriers moving along the y-axis are affected more than those moving along the x-direction. Therefore, $k > k_x > k_y$, where k_x and k_y are thermal conductivities along x and y directions, respectively, while k is the bulk thermal conductivity of a microelectronic chip. There is no available literature to date on thermal conductivity estimation for $h/\lambda_{mfp} < 1$. For $h/\lambda_{mfp} > 1$, thermal conductivity can be estimated within 20% approximation using the following equations:

$$k_x = k\left(1 - 2\lambda_{mfp}/3\pi h\right) \qquad (6)$$

$$k_y = k\left(1 - \lambda_{mfp}/3h\right) \qquad (7)$$

There is a critical thickness (h_c) below which the microscale effects must be considered for heat conduction. At a temperature of 300 K, the critical thickness for silicon and silicon dioxide is 290 nm and 4 nm in the y-direction, and 180 nm and 3 nm in the x-direction, respectively [2]. Moreover, the energy carriers may also be scattered from grain boundaries and different dopants within a material.

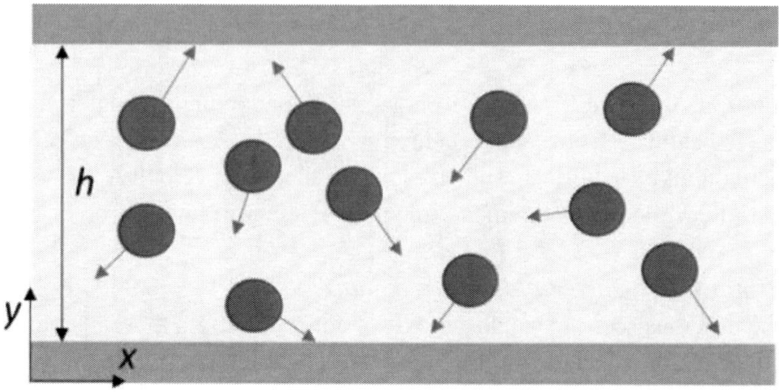

Figure 3. Energy carrier (electron or phonon) trajectories in microelectronics.

Thermal Resistance Model

Heat flow can be modeled using thermal resistance concepts in a similar way as current flow is modeled using electric circuits. Since temperature varies linearly for steady state conduction in a one-dimensional plane wall without any heat generation (as illustrated in Figure 4), the conduction heat transfer rate is given by the following equation:

$$q_x = -kA\frac{dT}{dx} = -kA\frac{T_{S1}-T_{S2}}{L} \quad (8)$$

where $T_{s1} - T_{s2}$ is the main driving potential that brings about the heat flux across the plane wall.

Using a similar principle to electrical resistance, thermal resistance (R_t) can be defined as the ratio of the driving force ($T_{s1} - T_{s2}$) to heat transfer rate (q_x) and can be written as:

$$R_t = \frac{T_{S1}-T_{S2}}{q_x} = \frac{L}{kA} \quad (9)$$

Equation 9 suggests that thermal resistance is proportional to the length of the plane wall and inversely proportional to the normal area and thermal conductivity of the plane wall. The thermal resistance may also be considered for convection heat transfer. The convection heat transfer on a wall surface based on Newton's law of cooling is given as:

$$q_{conv} = hA(T_s - T_a) \quad (10)$$

The thermal resistance to convection heat transfer can be written as:

$$R_{t,conv} = \frac{T_s - T_a}{q_{conv}} = \frac{1}{hA} \quad (11)$$

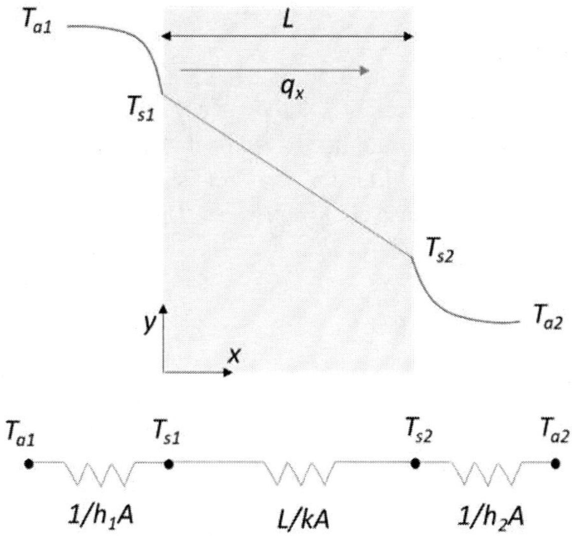

Figure 4. Thermal resistance model in a one-dimensional plane wall with no heat generation.

The thermal resistance circuit for conduction and convection heat transfer illustrated in Figure 4 shows that overall thermal resistance is considered for both conduction and convection heat transfer due to different air temperatures on each side of the wall. Therefore, the total thermal resistance will be the sum of individual thermal resistances connected in series in the thermal resistance circuit (as demonstrated in Figure 4) and can be expressed as:

$$R_{total} = \frac{T_{a1} - T_{a2}}{q_x} = \frac{1}{h_1 A} + \frac{L}{kA} + \frac{1}{h_2 A} \qquad (12)$$

Thermal Convection

Unlike conduction, thermal convection involves bulk motion of fluid particles carrying heat energy from one place to another. The convection heat transfer is governed by Newton's law of cooling shown in Equation 10. In many cases, the heat absorbed or released by the bulk motion of fluid particles does not involve any phase change process (such as air cooling). In such cases, the sensible heat transfer rate is given by the following equation:

$$q_{sen} = \dot{m}C_p\Delta T \qquad (13)$$

where $\dot{m}$ is the mass flow rate, C_p is the specific heat capacity, and ΔT is the temperature change in the fluid due to the heat transfer process.

The convection heat transfer may cause high kinetic energy fluid molecules to undergo a phase change process. The latent heat transfer rate can be expressed as:

$$q_{lat} = \dot{m}h_{fg} \qquad (14)$$

where h_{fg} is the latent heat of vaporization.

The latent heat transfer involves higher rates of heat transfer compared to the sensible heat transfer process. Latent heat transfer processes can be observed in various thermal applications, such as pool boiling, evaporative cooling, spray cooling, and flow boiling. Convection cooling in high performance microelectronics is performed using microfluidic devices. These microfluidic devices have hydraulic diameters at microscale levels ($D_h < 100$ μm) resulting in high heat transfer rates. This is because the convection heat transfer coefficient increases with decreasing hydraulic diameters leading to a significant increase in heat transfer rates. The bulk motion of fluid particles is highly restricted by physical boundaries in microfluidic devices, so convection heat transfer equations and correlations developed for macroscopic systems may not be valid for micro/nanoscale flows. The convective heat transfer for micro/nanoscale flows has been a subject of attention for the research community in recent years.

Effective Medium Theory

In previous sections, we discussed different heat transfer modes involved in a chip cooling process. In this section, we focus on the composite material properties at macroscopic levels using the effective medium theory (EMT). EMT is based on a bottom-up approach where component values at microscopic levels are averaged with suitable approximations to describe material properties at macroscopic scales.

These approximations are used to account for inhomogeneities that exist at the microscopic level. EMT can be used to predict many important material parameters, such as effective permittivity and permeability. EMTs cannot well estimate multiphase medium properties near the percolation threshold due to the missing long-range correlations. The long-range connectivity in stochastic systems can be described by the percolation threshold. A giant component only exists above the percolation threshold, and therefore, the percolation threshold represents a critical surface for studied parameters.

Percolation Model

Among various percolation models, the most common is a regular lattice of random networks with statistically independent probability. The long-range connectivity and clusters initially appear at a critical threshold, called the percolation threshold. The site percolation threshold can be distinguished from the bond percolation threshold based on a methodology adopted to obtain a random network. There are various probabilities in more generic systems, where a critical surface is used to characterize their transition. The concept of percolation threshold can be understood from the probability of a continuous path within a single cluster along occupied sites from one boundary to another (i.e., a sigmoidal plot for probability p as one goes from one boundary to another of the system). The sigmoidal plot transforms into a step function at a threshold probability p_t, as the system size reaches infinity. The threshold probability for a square lattice is $p_t = 0.5$ due to its symmetrical shape.

A system with random occupation sites or bonds is known as Bernoulli percolation. Different methods are used for bond or site occupation within a lattice. For instance, the Poisson process is used for random bond occupancy in a continuum system. Moreover, the Fortuin-Kasteleyn method is used for correlated percolation systems.

Series and Parallel Resistor Model

Direction-dependent conductivity can be estimated using series and parallel resistor models. Let us consider a lattice with a homogeneous and random distribution of fiber-like particles. The transport of heat transfer particles (electrons and phonons) in a material follows a sequence of traveling along the fiber direction and jumps from one rod to another at the point of contact between the two rods [3]. The thermal conductance linked to each jump step can be estimated by considering it equal to the critical surface-to-surface separation distance, thus enforcing the percolation threshold for the remaining variables. This modeling approach combines the percolation theory framework with that of the series and parallel resistor to estimate anisotropic conductivities. Moreover, percolation thresholds for isotropic conductivity of elongated fiber-like particles can be determined using an integral equation-based approach.

Thermal Materials

In the modern computational platform, any material may serve a thermal purpose. Thus, a thermal engineer may need to understand the thermal properties of all materials integrated into the system. The following sections discuss the thermal properties of various materials that are used in modern computing systems.

Semiconductor Materials

Semiconductor materials are critical factors that influence the thermal dissipation performance of cooling. The majority of conventional semiconductor material for the die is silicon-based, which usually has an approximate 145 W/m·K thermal conductivity. This thermal conductivity is better than organic packaging material, such as epoxy molding compound, or polymer chip-carriers such as Bismaleimide Triazine (BT) resin, but not as good as the thermal conductivity of metal material used in chip packaging, such as a copper or aluminum lead frame. In the modern semiconductor industry, other semiconductor materials such as gallium nitride (GaN), gallium arsenide (GaAs), and silicon carbide (SiC) may also be used; these materials have a similar order of magnitude thermal conductivity to conventional silicon-based semiconductor materials (see Table 1) [4].

Table 1. Typical physical properties of semiconductor materials

Material	E_g (eV)	ε	μ_n (cm^2/V.s)	Ec (MV/cm)	Vsat (10^7cm/s)	Total Dislocation (cm^2)	Thermal Conductivity (W/m.K)
Si	1.12	11.8	1350	0.3	1	-	145
GaAs	1.42	13.1	8500	0.4	2	-	50
4H-SiC	3.26	10	750	2.0	2	$>10^2$	370
GaN	3.44	9	1250	3.3	2.5	$>10^5$	253
Diamond	5.5	5.7	2000	13.0	1.5	$>10^4$	2290

Silicon-based material (or other semiconductor material) is usually the major source of heat generation, which also has the problem of non-uniform temperature distribution. Since the CTE of the silicon is generally small, the distortion problem caused by non-uniform heating is insignificant if the silicon die is an isolated and standalone device. Most silicon dies, however, are usually mounted with other semiconductor packaging materials such as the chip carriers and molding materials. If the adjacent materials are not low-CTE types of materials such as ceramic or glass, the CTE mismatch effect between them will be significant and cause the thermal bending behavior of the entire component, since the CTE between silicon and other polymers is generally in 1–2 orders of magnitude. This effect will be significant even in large-scale, silicon-die design, since the surface area of large-scale chips is getting bigger and bigger, such as in modern CPUs and GPUs. Thus, good thermal dissipation for semiconductor material is still quite important.

Thermal Interface Materials

To enhance the thermal dissipation of semiconductor materials, thermal interface material (TIM) between the semiconductor materials (i.e., silicon-based die or other ceramic materials) is generally used. The TIM has three major functions for thermal dissipation: 1) it serves as a high-effect, thermally-conductive path between the heat source and other materials or between the materials in the heat path; 2) it serves as a heat spreader to distribute the temperature uniformly across the entire thermal dissipation interface; and 3) it fills the unsmooth gaps between two materials in the thermal dissipation path and transfers the point contact to the surface contact. A schematic diagram is shown in Figure 5.

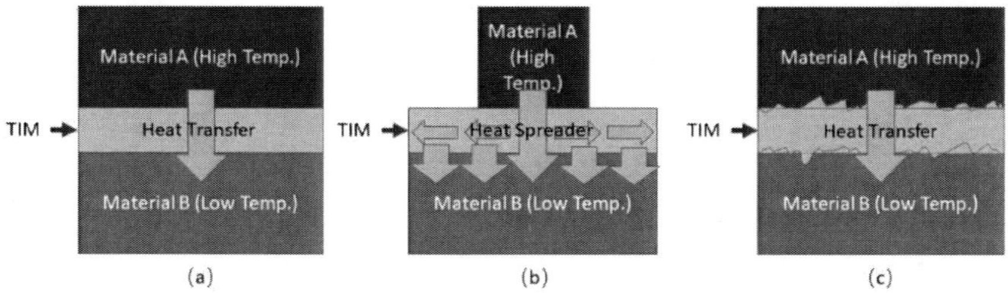

Figure 5. Major functions of TIM between different materials: (a) serves as the conductive path; (b) serves as the heat spreader; (c) serves as the gap filler between unsmooth surfaces.

Most of the TIM may also serve other functions involving mechanical and electrical connections, protection, or even insulation. For example, encapsulation[1] material for chip packaging such as an epoxy molding compound has multiple functions in addition to serving as TIM; it also provides insulation and protection of the silicon die of the chip. The lead frame of chip packaging can also serve as a chip carrier and provide electrical and thermal conduction. The metal lid of high-power chips can function as a heat distributor, protection, and structure support to prevent excessive bending of the component after the entire system is heated up.

Die Attach Material

Die attach material (also called die attach adhesive) is a typical example of the TIM that supports multiple functions in the chip structure and packaging. From the process perspective of chip packaging, the die-attach process[2] is essential before interconnection build-up such as the wire bonding process. Thus, the die attach material has a process function to fix the silicon die to the chip carrier. For the application stage, the die attach also serves as the thermal interface between the silicon die and chip carrier, so it requires good thermal conductivity for the die attach material. Moreover, the die attach material should be as thin as possible between the silicon die and chip carrier and the die attach material should also fill the air gaps with unflattened surfaces between the chip and carriers, so heat resistance between the chip and carrier can be at a minimum. This also requires certain process properties involving fluidity before curing.

Underfill and Encapsulants

Underfill (*see* Figure 6 (a)) and encapsulants are other examples of multi-function TIMs. Underfill was invented to support the structural weakness of the flip-chip.[3] It requires a decent structure stiffness under the room-temperature stage and becomes softer under a high-temperature range to prevent excessive thermal expansion-induced damage to the micro bump between the flip-chip and chip carrier. In addition, the underfill should have a

---

[1] For more about encapsulation material and process, please refer to https://advpackaging.co.uk/encapsulation.

[2] For more about the die-attach process, please refer to: https://oricus-semicon.com/what-is-the-die-attach-process/.

[3] For more about the underfill, please refer to: https://www.vtolabs.com/post/what-is-underfill.

reasonable thermal conductivity to enhance the heat dissipation between the flip-chip and chip carrier. The typical underfill dispensing process is demonstrated in Figure 6 (b). Other encapsulants such as the epoxy mold compound, glob top, and even potting material may also serve as TIMs for the high-power chips.

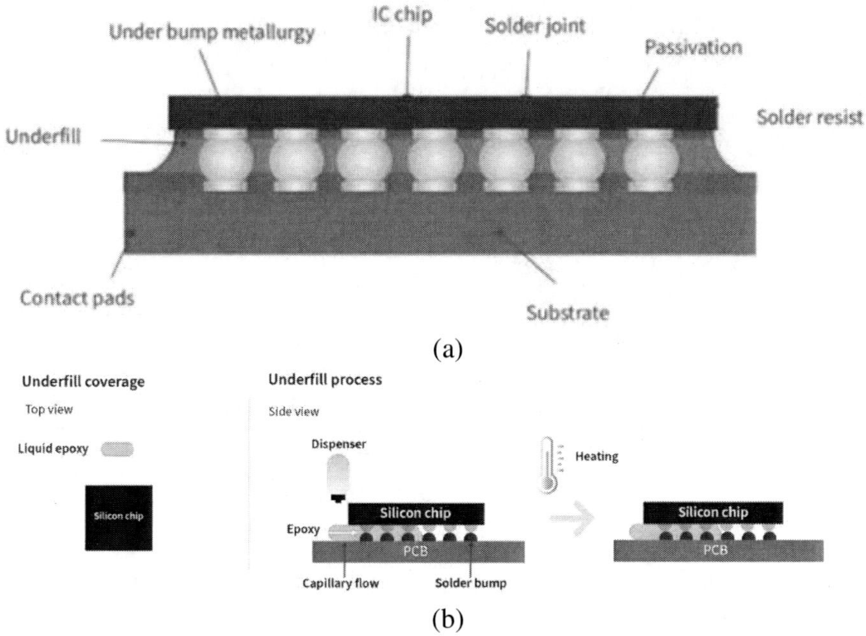

Figure 6. Underfill (a); underfill dispensing process (b).

Solder, PCB Trace, and Baseboard Materials

When the heat is transferred to the PCB assembly (PCBA) level from the chip package, the thermal conductivity of the PCBA level plays an important role in system-level thermal performance. The typical matrix material of PCB is a fire-retardant level 4 (FR4); the level indicates the thermal property of the epoxy resin material used in PCB baseboard manufacturing. Thermal properties for FR4 are not as good as metal and other TIM packaging materials (*see* Table 2). Thus, extra thermal structure design or borrowing from the electrically conductive path for thermal dissipation purposes is required. From component packing to the PCB, the connection between the component terminals and traces is solder joint [5], which is a metal alloy for electrical and thermal conductivity [6]. A solder joint is also appropriate between the thermal pad components and the PCB for the heat transfer. In the PCB, the thermal vias can be designed and manufactured to enhance thermal conductivity between layers of PCB in the vertical direction. In addition, the normal thickness (such as 0.5 or 1 OZ)[4] of PCB copper wire routing may also be insufficient for thermal dissipation in the in-plane direction. So, a thicker copper foil design (such as 2 OZ or 4 OZ) in the PCB wire routing may also be used to enhance thermal conductivity (i.e., so it can also pass even higher current and generate less current-induced heating).

Table 2. Typical thermal properties of FR4

FR4 Thermal Property	Value
Thermal conductivity (x and y axes)	~0.9 W/(m·K)
Thermal conductivity (z axis)	~0.3 W/(m·K)
Coefficient of thermal expansion (x and y axes)	~13 ppm/K
Coefficient of thermal expansion (z axis)	~70 ppm/K
Glass transition temperature (*Tg*)	From ~135 °C to ~170 °C
Specific heat capacity	~1100 J/(kg·°C)

For modern, high-power density PCBA design, other baseboard materials with higher thermal conductivities are also applied. The metal core PCB (MCPCB) is frequently used in high-temperature concentrated components such as illuminations of light-emitting diode packages. MCPCB uses thermal conductive metal (commonly aluminum) as the core material of the PCB and is insulated with copper foil with a polymer dielectric layer.

Thermal Systems

Heat Sinks

Heat sinks are components usually comprised of a conductive finned metal plate used to remove heat from heat generation devices, such as CPUs, GPUs, and microchips. The heat sink is attached to the chip surface using a TIM to reduce thermal contact resistance between the two surfaces. Heat sink helps regulate chip temperature and prevents device overheating, thus increasing its

[4] One OZ of copper thickness = 35 micrometers.

operational lifetime. The fin structure in a heat sink increases the effective heat exchange area, which increases the heat removal capacity from the chip surface. Fans are used to dissipate heat from fins to surrounding air through forced convection. Fan-cooled heat sinks are generally used in desktop computers to regulate chip temperatures. With reduced chip size and increased performance in modern computers, however, heat sinks are generally used in conjunction with heat pipes, which are discussed in the next subsection.

Heat Pipes

Recent advancement in the electronic chip industry necessitates promising cooling methods that can remove large amounts of heat in modern computers. One such cooling method is heat pipe technology with high heat transfer rates due to the phase change process. The phase change process in heat pipes involves latent heat transfer that can dissipate immense thermal energy with minimal temperature drop. The thermal conductivity of heat pipes can reach up to 100 times that of copper metal [7]. The heat pipe is considered a viable and promising cooling technology due to its design simplicity, high efficiency, and low cost.

A heat pipe essentially comprises three main sections—an evaporator section, an adiabatic section, and a condenser section. In the evaporator section, the fluid inside the heat pipe evaporates by absorbing heat from the heat source. The evaporated vapor flows through the adiabatic section and is condensed in the condenser section. The condensed fluid is wicked back to the evaporator section due to capillary action from the porous structure on the heat pipe's internal side walls. Wick structure plays a crucial role in the effective operation of a heat pipe. Moreover, the wick structure increases an effective heat exchange area resulting in high heat transfer rates in the evaporator and condenser sections. The most common wick structures are sintered wick, grooved wick, and mesh wick. Each wick type has its advantages and limitations depending on a range of applications.

Heat sink-heat pipe cooling systems are typically used in laptops. The fluid in the evaporator section of the heat pipe absorbs heat from the surface of the chips. As a result, the fluid undergoes a phase change process, and the evaporated fluid reaches the condenser section. The heat sink (comprising a fan and metal fins) attached to the condenser section further removes heat away to the surrounding air. In this way, heat sink-heat pipe systems can remove heat at a much larger scale than air-cooled heat sink systems.

Hydro-cooling Systems

In most computers with basic graphics performance, fan-cooled heat sinks can effectively thermally manage microchips. The microchip transfers heat into the air through a heat sink and the fan removes hot air through the personal computer's (PC) vents. The main source of heat generation in microchips is a transistor that switches between ON and OFF states. A higher the number of transistors in a microchip, will result in higher ON/OFF switching, and therefore a higher heat dissipation rate.

High-end microchips with a large number of transistors cannot be effectively cooled with fan-cooled heat sink systems. These microchips need hydro-cooling systems since water can remove a larger amount of heat compared to air due to its better thermophysical properties. Hydro-cooling systems for PCs are based on a similar principle to car engine cooling systems. In a hydro-cooling system, water is pumped through flexible tubing that removes heat from microchips and dissipates it in the radiator. Since water cannot make direct contact with the chip's surface due to short-circuiting issues, microchips are cooled using water blocks. Water blocks are thermally conductive metal blocks with hollow or channel-based interiors and a flat external surface. The flat surface of the water block sits directly on the chip's surface. Thermal paste applied between the chip and water block surfaces fills small air gaps which improves the heat transfer rate between the two surfaces. The microchip heat absorbed by the water block is transferred to water flowing inside the tubes which is eventually released in the radiator. The heat from the radiator is removed by a cooling fan and the cooled water from the radiator is pumped back for microchip cooling. The water pump also plays a crucial role in determining the cooling efficiency of computer chips. It is the pump's flow rate that determines how quickly or slowly water moves through different components. Therefore, the water flow rate is optimized to maximize the cooling efficiency of hydro-cooling systems.

Spray Cooling

Spray cooling is a promising technology in which fluid is atomized into numerous small droplets impacting a heated surface. A thin liquid film is formed that cools the heated surface through a convective heat transfer process. For superheated surfaces, bubbles are formed in the thin liquid film region that further improves the spray cooling mechanism through a latent heat transfer process. These atomized droplets offer a high surface area to volume ratio and low thermal contact resistance resulting in high heat transfer rates. Spray cooling is used in various high heat flux device cooling, including electronic chips used in supercomputers and data centers. Spray cooling has several benefits compared to other cooling technologies, such as uniform surface cooling, no localized hotspots, low liquid inventory, low flow rates, and a simple cooling setup. The spray cooling performance depends on several factors, such as the fluid type, nozzle type and orientation, nozzle height from the heated surface, spray droplet size, mean droplet velocity, and spray volumetric flux [8]. Heat flux up to 75 W/cm^2 was reported on a simulated electronic chip using liquid nitrogen spray cooling [9]. Spray cooling has been successfully implemented in the Cray X1 supercomputer [10].

Spray cooling can be implemented for direct or indirect electronic cooling. In direct cooling, the spray is directly impacted on a chip's surface. Direct spray cooling has been used in server electronic cooling [11]. Cheng et al. [12] achieved heat flux above 100 W/cm^2 for multi-nozzle direct spray cooling on a 3 cm x 3 cm compact heated surface. Zhang et al. [6] developed a direct spray cooling setup of 12 linearly arranged nozzles for cooling six PCBAs and reported a maximum critical heat flux (CHF) of 81.6 W/cm^2 and a corresponding heat transfer coefficient of 2.7 W/cm^2.K. Despite exhibiting reduced thermal properties, only dielectric fluids can be used for direct spray cooling to avoid short-circuiting due to direct contact between the fluid and electrical components. On the other hand, in indirect spray cooling, the spray fluid is impacted on a cold plate attached to a chip surface instead of directly impacting the chip surface. In this way, heat is transferred from the chip to the cold plate through conduction, and the heat absorbed by the cold plate is further removed by the spraying fluid. Indirect cold plate spray cooling was proposed for the thermal management of the Dawning 5000A supercomputer in China [13]. The Dawning 5000A system integrated spray cooling with an absorption chiller based on spray cooling waste heat recovery. The integrated spray-chiller system achieved energy saving efficiency of up to 49%. In another study, an energy saving of up to 60.7% was achieved using a hybrid cooling system (spray cooling and an absorption chiller) for a data center [14].

Jet Impingement

In jet impingement cooling, a liquid stream at high velocity impacts a heated surface through a high-speed jet nozzle. The liquid jet impinging a small, targeted area generates a thin liquid film with high heat transfer rates. However, as liquid flows radially outward from the targeted area, the film thickness grows with deteriorating heat transfer rates [15]. For this reason, jet impingement is an excellent candidate for localized hotspot cooling. However, unlike spray cooling, uniform surface cooling is not generally achieved using jet impingement cooling. To tackle this issue, an array of multiple jet nozzles can be used for electronic chip cooling. In a multiple jet nozzle arrangement, the interaction of jets becomes crucial to the overall cooling efficiency of an electronic chip [16]. The maximum heat transfer coefficient with jet impingement for CPU cooling has been reported as three times more than that achieved using a cooling fan [17]. A temperature drop of 40-60 °C was achieved using water jet cooling of integrated circuit chips. Heat flux removal of 310 W/cm^2 was reported using deionized water and FC40 coolants for jet cooling of 1.27 cm x 1.27 cm microelectronic chips. Moreover, heat flux removal up to 1,000 W/cm^2 was obtained for jet cooling of very large-scale integration (VLSI) chips using water and FC77 coolants [18].

Microchannel Cooling

Microchannel cooling has been an active area of research in recent years for chip cooling applications. The microchannel heat sink comprises several fluid channels with hydraulic diameter typically in a range of 10 to 200 μm [16]. Microchannel cooling offers high heat transfer rates due to its high heat exchange area and enhanced heat transfer coefficient. The high heat transfer coefficient in microchannel cooling is attributed to its small characteristic length. Microchannel water cooling was first introduced in 1981; it demonstrated a high cooling rate of 790 W/cm^2 for a VLSI chip [19]. The cooling capacity of a microchannel heat sink is further improved using structured surfaces, such as ribs, pillars, and grooves. These structured surfaces create an agitated flow with re-circulations that increase the heat transfer rate [20]. Moreover, for a given pressure drop, channels with a high depth-to-width ratio exhibit high heat transfer performance [21]. The geometrical design of microchannels also have a significant effect on the heat removal rate of electronic chips. Among four different designs of microchannels investigated by Tan et al. [22], spider-web-shaped microchannels demonstrated better chip cooling than other designs considered. In another study, rhombus fractal-like microchannels considerably improved chip cooling rates compared to conventional parallel microchannel heat sink [23].

Future Trends and Outlook

Continuous growth in the chip industry (such as miniaturization, dense packaging, and high computing performance) needs novel thermal materials and cooling systems that can address the challenges of high heat dissipation in integrated circuit chip devices. Heat dissipation in future electronic chips will exceed levels that may not be addressed with current cooling technologies. Therefore, dedicated research is needed for effective thermal management of electronic chips to address high heat dissipation in these devices.

Emerging Thermal Materials

Novel Polymers

In recent years, novel polymer-based, thermally conductive composite materials have been extensively investigated to address thermal challenges in the chip industry. Some key factors affecting the thermal conductivity of polymer materials are their crystal form, chain structure, and polymer chain orientation. Moreover, the thermal conductivity of polymer-based composites also depends on filler thermal properties, material, loading, and morphology. Recent advances in emerging thermally conductive materials involved novel approaches to manipulate the microstructure of polymer composites, such as controlling filler orientation, designing filler clusters, deploying a self-assembly phenomenon to develop filler networks, and using double percolation methods [24]. Moreover, thermal conductive paths in polymer composites can be maximized through efficient packing of fillers based on different particle sizes [25]. Most polymers have low thermal conductivity because the mean free path of phonons is extremely small due to structure defects (such as grain boundaries) and scattering with other phonons. Polymers have several advantages, however, such as their light weight, high electrical resistance, low water ingress, anti-corrosion properties, and low cost. Therefore, polymer-based composites are desirable as advanced thermally conductive materials for chip cooling applications.

Heat dissipation in next generation high performance chips is projected to exceed 1,000 W/cm^2 [26]. One major bottleneck to achieving a high heat flow path in chip cooling is thermal resistance offered by TIMs. TIMs usually have low thermal conductivities in the range of 3 to 5 W/mK. TIMs are needed to provide high thermal conductivity and excellent adhesion to fill air gaps between chip and heat sink surfaces. New emerging materials, such as graphene nanoplatelets and carbon nanotubes are potential candidates to increase the thermal conductivity of TIMs [27]. Moreover, three-dimensional (3-D) chip stack cooling is even more complex and offers greater challenges compared to single-chip cooling. Single-chip cooling can be achieved on the back side of the chip die. In a 3-D chip stack, however, the back side of the chip is not directly accessible for cooling. Moreover, high power density and low thermal conductive materials used in a 3-D chip stack offer magnified cooling challenges. A way forward to 3-D chip stack cooling is to increase thermal conductivity at chip-to-chip interfaces [28]. Highly conductive underfills with appropriate filler loading may address heat dissipation issues in 3-D chip stack packaging. High filler loading, however, may result in poor flowability of underfill materials that may affect their wetting and curing properties. Therefore, achieving high thermal conductivity without much affecting the processability of underfilled materials is still a challenge.

Porous Materials

Porous metal technology has been an area of interest recently for improving heat transfer rates in thermal systems. It is a passive technique to achieve high thermal efficiency without depending on active energy sources. The key advantages of porous materials are their large surface area to volume ratio, reduced weight, and low cost. The large surface area of porous metals increases the heat exchange area which is vital for effective heat removal on electronic chips. Porous heat sinks have been investigated recently for electronic chip cooling. A high heat transfer rate of up to 810 W/cm^2 has been reported for electronic chip cooling using porous heat sinks. The porous heat sink placed on the chip's surface removes heat by fluid evaporation flowing through it [29]. In another study, improved chip cooling efficiency was achieved using a bi-disperse porous heat sink (porosity of 0.85) compared to an ordinary porous heat sink (porosity of 0.68). Also, a mass reduction of 25.8% was reported for a bi-disperse porous heat sink compared to an ordinary heat sink [30].

The effect of a porous pin fin on chip cooling performance was also investigated. It was noted that pin fin performance reduces with an increasing Darcy number [31]. Also, better heat transfer performance and temperature uniformity was achieved by using porous copper foam as a wick structure in a heat pipe application for electronic chip cooling [32]. The effect of porous foam copper was also studied in a spray cooling application. Critical heat flux enhancement of 125.3% was obtained for a heating surface with semi-covered porous foam copper (S2) compared to a heating surface with fully covered porous foam copper (S3). Moreover, the critical heat flux enhancement was 24.58% for an S2 surface as compared to a flat heating surface [33]. The effect of porous metals filled in a channel was also investigated in a jet impingement application for electronic chip cooling. It was observed that the porous channel provided an enhanced chip cooling effect, however, the temperature profile was non-uniform with peak temperature obtained at the center of the porous channel [34].

Heat Spreaders

A heat spreader is a thermally conductive device that dissipates heat from a concentrated heat source to a heat exchanger with a large heat exchange area. Heat spreaders can be solid devices with high thermal conductivity (such as copper or aluminum) or phase change devices (such as vapor chambers or heat pipes). Heat spreaders usually act as primary heat exchangers transferring heat from a heat source to the secondary heat exchanger. Secondary heat exchangers are usually larger in a cross-section area compared to primary heat exchangers. The effect of a monolayer graphene-based heat spreader was investigated for chip cooling using a flip-chip technology. For a given heat flux of 640 W/cm^2, the chip hotspot temperature with graphene film used as a heat spreader was reduced by 12°C compared to the chip without graphene heat spreader [35]. In another study, a diamond heat spreader was used between the chip and microchannel heat sink surfaces. The maximum chip temperature was reduced up to 22.9% when the diamond heat spreader was used at the chip-microchannel interface [36]. Jaworski [37] investigated a new heat spreader design with the pin fins filled in phase change material (PCM) for electronic chip cooling. He concluded that thermal resistance for a PCM-based pin fin heat spreader was much lower compared to a simple PCM-based heat sink.

Emerging Thermal Systems

Rapid advancement in electronic chip technology has challenged the research community to develop efficient and cost-effective thermal systems. Some emerging thermal systems with the potential to address thermal management issues in current and future electronic devices is discussed in this sub-section.

Embedded Liquid Cooling

Embedded liquid cooling is a promising technology to address high heat dissipation issues in future electronic chips. In this technology, by integrating the microfluidics and chip within the same substrate, liquid cooling can be performed directly inside the chip thus bypassing several layers of interfacial thermal resistance offered by conventional heat sinks. Heat flux up to 1,700 W/cm^2 with a low pumping power of 0.57 W/cm^2 has been achieved using this technology making it a potential technology for future chip cooling [38]. This cooling technology will push Moore's law beyond current limits and will enable the electronics industry to achieve further miniaturization of electronic chips. Furthermore, this technology can still be used in densely packed chips by its state-of-the-art compact cooling design within the chip.

Immersion Cooling

Immersion cooling is another emerging technology that makes use of liquid directly contacting the electronic device to achieve high cooling efficiency. In immersion cooling, the electronic device is immersed in a dielectric thermally conductive fluid. In this way, an immense amount of heat can be effectively removed from hot areas of the device since the fluid is in direct contact with the device. Because there is no heat sink involved, this technology is preferred over current cooling technologies due to its low thermal contact resistance.

There are two main types of immersion cooling, single-phase immersion cooling and two-phase immersion cooling. In single-phase immersion cooling, sensible heat transfer occurs through direct contact between the fluid and the electronic device [39]. The fluid is cooled in a heat exchanger after absorbing heat from the electronic device. On the other hand, two-phase immersion cooling involves a phase change process and offers much higher heat transfer rates compared to single-phase immersion cooling. In two-phase immersion cooling, electronic devices are immersed in a low temperature boiling fluid. The heat dissipated from electronic devices boils the dielectric fluid that removes large amounts of heat from these devices. This enables these devices to operate below their failure temperatures, which may increase product lifetime. In a two-phase immersion cooling tank, the rising vapors from boiling fluid are condensed back into the tank from a condenser attached to the tank lid. Such an integrated cooling setup offers compactness with the ability to cool densely packed electronic devices. Immersion cooling can be the future of electronic cooling and has the potential to ensure low device failure rates. With low maintenance rates achieved using immersion cooling, Microsoft may be able to deploy its servers in remote areas in the future [40]. Moreover, in the future, immersion cooling systems can be deployed under a 5G cellular tower for advanced applications, such as self-driving vehicles.

Solid-State Air Jet Cooling

Solid-state air jet cooling is an emerging technology that has the potential to overcome thermal bottlenecks in future high-performance chips. This technology involves acoustic membranes operated at ultrasonic frequencies to generate powerful airflow. The airflow enters through inlet air vents into the air jet manifold and transforms into high-speed pulsating jets. These pulsating jets absorb heat from the heat spreader underneath the air jet manifold. The heat flows from the electronic chip into the air jet manifold via the heat spreader. The hot air jet exits from the side of the air jet manifold. Air jet cooling offers several advantages, such as compactness, low noise, and fast device operation; it is also lightweight and dustproof. Notebook processor performance was reported to increase by 1.5 times with 31% reduction in noise levels using air jet cooling compared to conventional fan cooling.

What Can We Look Forward to?

Nano PCM is an emerging cooling technology that involves the dispersion of nanoparticles in a PCM. PCMs can remove large amounts of heat due to a phase change process through latent heat transfer and therefore are desirable for chip-level cooling. Despite latent heat transfer, the low thermal conductivity of PCMs is a concern that limits their cooling capacity. Dispersing thermally conductive nanoparticles, however, increases heat transfer rates in PCMs, which makes nano PCM a potential cooling technology for future electronic devices. The performance of nano PCMs depends on the nanoparticle type, size, shape, and volume fraction. Moreover, it also depends on the thermophysical properties of the PCM used in a nano PCM cooling system.

From the rapid development of 3-D printing technology, metal printing or other high-thermal conductivity printing technology will become feasible in the future. The 3D-printed heat sink will be applicable for future thermal dissipation requirements since it can optimize the airflow and convection as requested. More finely developed 3-D printing technology will allow even high-efficiency airflow heat sinks.

References

[1] Ming-Yi, Tsai, C. H. J. Hsu, and C. T. O. Wang. 2004. "Investigation of thermomechanical behaviors of flip chip BGA packages during manufacturing process and thermal cycling." *IEEE Trans Compon Packag Technol* 27 (3):568-576. doi: 10.1109/TCAPT.2004.831817.

[2] Bergman, Theodore L. 2011. *Fundamentals of Heat and Mass Transfer*. 7th ed. Hoboken, NJ: Wiley.

[3] Chatterjee, Avik P. 2018. "Percolation-based model for tunneling conductivity in systems of partially aligned cylinders." *Physical Rev E* 98 (6):062102. doi: 10.1103/PhysRevE.98.062102.

[4] Sun, Yue, Xuanwu Kang, Yingkui Zheng, Jiang Lu, Xiaoli Tian, Ke Wei, Hao Wu, Wenbo Wang, Xinyu Liu, and Guoqi Zhang. 2019. "Review of the recent progress on GaN-bsed vrtical power Schottky barrier diodes (SBDs)." *Electronics* 8 (5):575.

[5] Lam, C. C., Cha Chan, Kong Chet Hung, and Neissner Martin Richard. "TCoB reliability for Epad LQFP 176 in automotive application," in *36th International Electronics Manufacturing Technology Conference Proceedings*, 2014, 1-5.

[6] Zhang, Wei-Wei, Wen-Long Cheng, Shi-Dong Shao, Li-Jia Jiang, and Da-Liang Hong. 2016. "Integrated thermal control and system assessment in plug-chip spray cooling enclosure." *Appl Therm Eng* 108:104-114. doi: https://doi.org/10.1016/j.applthermaleng.2016.07.097.

[7] Atay, Atakan, Büşra Sarıarslan, Yiğit F. Kuşcu, Samet Saygan, Yigit Akkus, Aysan Gürer, Barbaros Çetin, and Zafer Dursunkaya. 2019. "Performance Assessment of Commercial Heat Pipes with Sintered and Grooved Wicks under Natural Convection." *J Therm Sci Tech* 39:101-110.

[8] Liang, Gangtao, and Issam Mudawar. 2017. "Review of spray cooling – Part 1: Single-phase and nucleate boiling regimes, and critical heat flux." *Int J Heat Mass Transf* 115:1174-1205. doi: 10.1016/j.ijheatmasstransfer.2017.06.029.

[9] Tilton, Donald E., Donald A. Kearns, and Charles L. Tilton. 1994. "Liquid Nitrogen Spray Cooling of a Simulated Electronic Chip." In *Advances in Cryogenic Engineering*, edited by Peter Kittel, 1779-1786. Boston, MA: Springer US.

[10] Shedd, Timothy A. 2007. "Next Generation Spray Cooling: High Heat Flux Management in Compact Spaces." *Heat Transf Eng* 28 (2):87-92. doi: 10.1080/01457630601023245.

[11] Kheirabadi, Ali C., and Dominic Groulx. 2016. "Cooling of server electronics: A design review of existing technology." *Appl Therm Eng* 105:622-638. doi: 10.1016/j.applthermaleng.2016.03.056.

[12] Cheng, Wen-Long, Wei-Wei Zhang, Li-Jia Jiang, Shuang-Long Yang, Lei Hu, and Hua Chen. 2015. "Experimental investigation of large area spray cooling with compact chamber in the non-boiling regime." *Appl Therm Eng* 80:160-167. doi: https://doi.org/10.1016/j.applthermaleng.2015.01.055.

[13] Chen, Hua, Wen-long Cheng, Wei-wei Zhang, Yu-hang Peng, and Li-jia Jiang. 2017. "Energy saving evaluation of a novel energy system based on spray cooling for supercomputer center." *Energy* 141:304-315. doi: https://doi.org/10.1016/j.energy.2017.09.089.

[14] Chen, Hua, Yu-hang Peng, and Yan-ling Wang. 2019. "Thermodynamic analysis of hybrid cooling system integrated with waste heat reusing and peak load shifting for data center." *Energy Convers Manag* 183:427-439. doi: https://doi.org/10.1016/j.enconman.2018.12.117.

[15] Lasance, Clemens J. M. 2005. "Advances in High-Performance Cooling for Electronics." Electronics Cooling, Accessed September 1, 2023. Available from https://www.electronics-cooling.com/2005/11/advances-in-high-performance-cooling-for-electronics/.

[16] Kandlikar, Satish G., and Akhilesh V. Bapat. 2007. "Evaluation of jet impingement, spray and microchannel chip cooling options for high heat flux removal." *Heat Transf Eng* 28 (11):911-923. doi: 10.1080/01457630701421703.

[17] Shaikh, K. A., S. S. Kale, and A. S. Kashid. 2016. "Performance evaluation of synthetic jet cooling for CPU." *Int Res J Eng Tech* 3 (1):728-731.

[18] Patil, Naveen, and Tapano Hotta. 2018. "Cooling of discrete heated modules using liquid jet impingement – A critical review." *Front Heat Mass Transf* 11 (16):1-13. doi: 10.5098/hmt.11.16.

[19] Tuckerman, D. B., and R. F. W. Pease. 1981. "High-performance heat sinking for VLSI." *IEEE Electron Device Letters* 2 (5):126-129. doi: 10.1109/EDL.1981.25367.

[20] Wang, Guilian, Di Niu, Fuqiang Xie, Yan Wang, Xiaolin Zhao, and Guifu Ding. 2015. "Experimental and numerical investigation of a microchannel heat sink (MCHS) with micro-scale ribs and grooves for chip cooling." *Appl Therm Eng* 85:61-70. doi: https://doi.org/10.1016/j.applthermaleng.2015.04.009.

[21] Upadhye, Harshal R., and Satish G. Kandlikar. "Optimization of Microchannel Geometry for Direct Chip Cooling Using Single Phase Heat Transfer," in *Proceedings of the ASME 2004 2nd International Conference on Microchannels and Minichannels*, 2004, 679-685.

[22] Tan, Hui, Longwen Wu, Mingyang Wang, Zihao Yang, and Pingan Du. 2019. "Heat transfer improvement in microchannel heat sink by topology design and optimization for high heat flux chip cooling." *Int J Heat Mass Transf* 129:681-689. doi: https://doi.org/10.1016/j.ijheatmasstransfer.2018.09.092.

[23] Zhuang, Dawei, Yifei Yang, Guoliang Ding, Xinyuan Du, and Zuntao Hu. 2020. "Optimization of Microchannel Heat Sink with Rhombus Fractal-like Units for

Electronic Chip Cooling." *Int J Refrig* 116:108-118. doi: https://doi.org/10.1016/j.ijrefrig.2020.03.026.

[24] Chen, Hongyu, Valeriy V. Ginzburg, Jian Yang, Yunfeng Yang, Wei Liu, Yan Huang, Libo Du, and Bin Chen. 2016. "Thermal conductivity of polymer-based composites: Fundamentals and applications." *Prog Polymer Sci* 59:41-85. doi: https://doi.org/10.1016/j.progpolymsci.2016.03.001.

[25] Choi, Seran, and Jooheon Kim. 2013. "Thermal conductivity of epoxy composites with a binary-particle system of aluminum oxide and aluminum nitride fillers." *Composites Part B: Eng* 51:140-147. doi: https://doi.org/10.1016/j.compositesb.2013.03.002.

[26] Mudawar, I. 2001. "Assessment of high-heat-flux thermal management schemes." *IEEE Trans Compon Packag Technol* 24 (2):122-141. doi: 10.1109/6144.926375.

[27] Xu, Jun, and Timothy S. Fisher. 2006. "Enhancement of thermal interface materials with carbon nanotube arrays." *Int J Heat Mass Transf* 49 (9):1658-1666. doi: https://doi.org/10.1016/j.ijheatmasstransfer.2005.09.039.

[28] Lee, W. S., I. Y. Han, Yu Jin, S. J. Kim, and T. Y. Lee. "Thermal characterization of thermally conductive underfill for a flip-chip package using novel temperature sensing technique," in *Proceedings of 6th Electronics Packaging Technology Conference (EPTC 2004) (IEEE Cat. No.04EX971)*, 2004, 47-52.

[29] Yuki, Kazuhisa, and Koichi Suzuki. 2012. "Development of Functional Porous Heat Sink for Cooling High-Power Electronic Devices." *Trans Japan Inst Electron Packag* 5 (1):69-74. doi: 10.5104/jiepeng.5.69.

[30] Kumar, Ajay, Giran Chandran, and Pradeep Kamath. "Heat transfer enhancement of electronic chip cooling using pourous medium," in *Proceedings of the 22nd National and 11th International ASHMT-ASME Heat and Mass Transfer Conference*, 2013.

[31] Bhanja, Dipankar, Balaram Kundu, and Pabitra Kumar Mandal. 2013. "Thermal Analysis of Porous Pin Fin used for Electronic Cooling." *Procedia Eng* 64:956-965. doi: https://doi.org/10.1016/j.proeng.2013.09.172.

[32] Ji, Xianbing, Hongchuan Li, Jinliang Xu, and Yanping Huang. 2017. "Integrated flat heat pipe with a porous network wick for high-heat-flux electronic devices." *Exper Therm Fluid Sci* 85:119-131. doi: https://doi.org/10.1016/j.expthermflusci.2017.03.008.

[33] Wang, Ji-Xiang, Yun-Ze Li, Yu-Feng Mao, En-Hui Li, Xianwen Ning, and Xin-Yan Ji. 2018. "Comparative study of the heating surface impact on porous-material-involved spray system for electronic cooling – an experimental approach." *Appl Therm Eng* 135:537-548. doi: https://doi.org/10.1016/j.applthermaleng.2018.02.055.

[34] Zing, Carlos, and Shadi Mahjoob. 2019. "Thermal Analysis of Multijet Impingement Through Porous Media to Design a Confined Heat Management System." *J Heat Transf* 141 (8) doi: 10.1115/1.4044008.

[35] Huang, Shirong, Yong Zhang, Shuangxi Sun, Xiaogang Fan, Ling Wang, Yifeng Fu, Yan Zhang, and Johan Liu. "Graphene based heat spreader for high power chip cooling using flip-chip technology," in *2013 IEEE 15th Electronics Packaging Technology Conference (EPTC 2013)*, 2013, 347-352.

[36] Han, Yong, Boon Long Lau, Xiaowu Zhang, Yoke Choy Leong, and Kok Fah Choo. 2014. "Enhancement of Hotspot Cooling With Diamond Heat Spreader on Cu Microchannel Heat Sink for GaN-on-Si Device." *IEEE Trans Compon Packag Manuf Technol* 4 (6):983-990. doi: 10.1109/TCPMT.2014.2315234.

[37] Jaworski, Maciej. 2012. "Thermal performance of heat spreader for electronics cooling with incorporated phase change material." *Appl Therm Eng* 35:212-219. doi: https://doi.org/10.1016/j.applthermaleng.2011.10.036.

[38] van Erp, Remco, Reza Soleimanzadeh, Luca Nela, Georgios Kampitsis, and Elison Matioli. 2020. "Co-designing electronics with microfluidics for more sustainable cooling." *Nature* 585 (7824):211-216. doi: 10.1038/s41586-020-2666-1.

[39] Pol. 2020. "What is Immersion Cooling? The new frontier of liquid cooling." Submer, Last Updated March 16, 2020, Accessed September 1, 2023. Available from https://submer.com/blog/what-is-immersion-cooling/.

[40] Microsoft. 2023. "To cool datacenter servers, Microsoft turns to boiling liquid." Microsoft, Accessed September 1, 2023. Available from https://news.microsoft.com/source/features/innovation/datacenter-liquid-cooling/.

Biographical Sketches

Qiming Zhang, PhD

Dr. Zhang has comprehensive experience in the development cycles and field-service cycles of consumer electronic products. On the macroscopic level, he is proficient in product safety and reliability regulation and compliance, involving regional requirements of North America, European Union, Britain, Asia, and China. His expertise includes Design for Safety, Manufacturability, and Reliability (DFX) consulting on electronic products, including design and structure optimization and material selection, life-prediction of field service, harsh environmental assessment, durability testing, high-power safety involving high-power electrics and power adapters, reliability and quality control systems, process optimization and cost reduction, incident investigation, and reverse engineering. Dr. Zhang is also proficient with mechanical and thermal finite element analysis (FEA) analysis, laboratory testing techniques including standard and customized mechanical and thermal testing, material characterization involving DMA/TMA/DSC/TGA, surface analytical techniques involving SEM/FIB/AFM/Optical Profiler, harsh environmental testing, and electrical testing. He received his Ph.D. in Mechanical Engineering from The Hong Kong University of Science and Technology.

Farooq Siddiqui, PhD

Dr. Siddiqui has diverse experiences in the failure and root cause analysis, safety design reviews engineering design and prototyping. Dr. Farooq has expertise in thermal management, spray/dropwise cooling, advanced thermal fluids, high heat flux device cooling, droplet evaporation and boiling, surface wetting and wicking, phase change dynamics, colloidal dispersions, porous residues, rheology, dispersion stability, surfactants, humidification-dehumidification and HVAC systems. He worked on various research projects, such as solar-powered absorption chillers, solar desalination systems, earth-air pipe heat exchangers and thermal management of high-power electronics. Prior to joining Exponent, Dr. Farooq worked as a research assistant at the Center of Research Excellence-Renewable Energy at King Fahd University of Petroleum and Minerals, Saudi Arabia. There he designed storage systems to address intermittency issues in solar absorption chillers. Dr. Farooq also worked as a design engineer for a start-up company and later held a lecturer position at the University in Madina. He received his Ph.D. in Mechanical Engineering from The Hong Kong University of Science and Technology.

Chapter 6

Process Controls and Lean Manufacturing for Integrated Circuits Manufacturing

Catrice M. Kees[1], PhD
Melissa L. Mendias[2], PhD
and Rebecca Routson[3,*], PhD
[1]Exponent, Inc., Bowie, MD, USA
[2]Exponent, Inc., Phoenix, AZ, USA
[3]Exponent, Inc., Denver, CO, USA

Abstract

The manufacture of integrated circuits entails a complex process that can involve hundreds of intricate fabrication steps. Sophisticated process control mechanisms and quality monitoring must be in place to reliably fabricate microprocessors and other electronic components that meet customer needs and technology specification requirements. During manufacturing, quality and output goals must work cohesively for optimal results. In this chapter we discuss statistical process control charts and industry rules of thumb as a mechanism to quantify the impact of varying conditions on quality. The authors explore how utilizing both lean manufacturing and Six Sigma can aid in implementing a robust process controls system in the manufacturing of integrated circuits.

Keywords: six sigma, lean manufacturing, semiconductor, integrated circuit

[*] Corresponding Author's Email: rroutson@exponent.com.

In: Computer Engineering Applications …
Editor: Brian D'Andrade
ISBN: 979-8-89113-488-1

Introduction

The integrated circuit is essentially an electronic system whose miniaturized components are fabricated in tandem on a single substrate, typically a silicon or germanium wafer. The integrated circuit was invented during the late 1950s and early 1960s through a series of innovations, though credit is generally given to Americans Jack Kilby of Texas Instruments and Robert Noyce of Fairchild Semiconductor [1]. The resulting changes to the field of electronics have caused a paradigm shift in nearly every market and industry, including consumer products, transportation, agriculture, and health care, as well as to the associated manufacturing equipment and processes. At the heart of this revolution is the microprocessor or computer chip, which provides the *brains* through which data and logic are combined to automate and expedite actions and decisions. Other types of integrated circuits include memory chips, amplifiers, signal processors, and sensors, some of which may even have micro- or nano-scale moving features (e.g., micro-electromechanical system [MEMS] devices).

Integrated circuits are comprised of electronic circuits fabricated on substrates made of semiconducting materials, typically silicon or germanium. At a high level, manufacturing entails the definition of individual components (e.g., resistors, capacitors, and transistors) through the localized manipulation of material properties followed by the formation of a network of interconnects to connect those components together. This is done within a cleanroom environment using high-precision processes, such as thin film deposition, photolithography, doping, alloying, annealing, etching, and planarization, to develop the intricate architectures that make up the designed system.

A single machine may contain hundreds or even thousands of chips, and thus high volume, cost effective integrated circuit manufacturing is pertinent to meet current and future supply demands. Integrated circuit manufacturing is potentially one of the most critical manufacturing applications of Six Sigma and lean manufacturing processes. Defects on the nanometer scale have a profound impact on the ability of an integrated circuit to meet consumer needs or even be sellable at all. They can cause failures of all or a portion of the chip, either immediately or prematurely in the field, which can impact customer satisfaction or even safety. Process targeting and controls further affect the relationship between power consumption and speed capabilities, potentially resulting in products that fail to meet customer specifications despite being otherwise functional. For these reasons, processes and circuit parameters are meticulously tracked and controlled for quality throughout the integrated circuit manufacturing process.

This chapter explores the use of statistical process controls as they relate to the health and performance of an integrated circuit manufacturing environment. It begins with a high-level description of integrated circuits and fundamental concepts of large-scale integrated circuit manufacturing. Relevant statistical fundamentals are then introduced, with a discussion of process control charts and standard methods used in industry to quantify the impact of varying conditions on product quality. The authors will show how utilizing both lean manufacturing and Six Sigma concepts can aid in implementing a robust process control system that enables both quality monitoring and lean manufacturing opportunities.

Integrated Circuit Fundamentals

An integrated circuit typically consists of logic, memory (e.g., static random access memory [SRAM] or a local cache), and input/output contacts. Integrated circuit logic, at the most fundamental level, is made of transistors such as the metal oxide semiconductor field effect transistor (MOSFET). The MOSFET is an active circuit device, meaning that it can be manipulated to supply power to other devices. The basic structure of a planar n-type MOSFET (a negative metal oxide semiconductor [NMOS] transistor) is shown in Figure 1. Other chemical elements are selectively added to the silicon substrate, doping or alloying with it, to establish regions with distinct electrical properties derived from the properties of the doping elements. In the NMOS transistor example shown, the source and drain regions have been made n-type, meaning that they have an excess of free electrons, whereas the body region has been made p-type, having a shortage of free electrons and instead a surplus of holes (i.e., electron vacancies) in the crystalline lattice. Electric fields spontaneously form between these different regions, restricting the flow of electric current between them unless a sufficient potential is applied to overcome this energy barrier. A MOSFET is controlled through the manipulation of these energy barriers. By applying a positive voltage to the gate electrode, free electrons within the p-type substrate are attracted to the surface, effectively inverting it into a narrow n-type channel if the voltage is sufficiently high. This establishes a conductive path between the source and drain electrodes, turning on the MOSFET like an electrical switch. A p-type

MOSFET (i.e., a p-channel metal oxide semiconductor [PMOS] transistor) is built in a similar fashion, except with the n-type and p-type regions reversed.

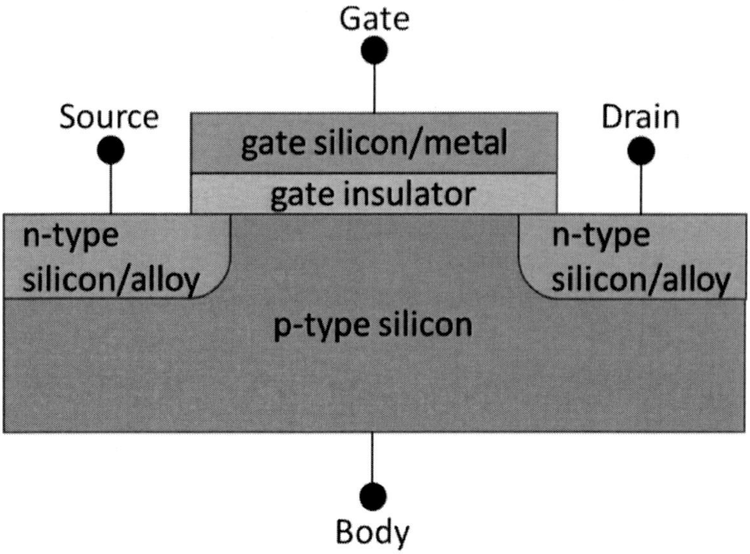

Figure 1. Basic structure of a planar n-type silicon MOSFET (NMOS device).

MOSFETs are often joined together to form logic gates (e.g., AND, OR, and NOT gates) which are themselves often combined to form structures such as registers, adders, and counters. Figure 2 shows a schematic for a complementary metal oxide semiconductor inverter (CMOS) logical NOT gate, along with its circuit symbol. The inverter is assembled through the combination of an NMOS and PMOS device. When the input voltage, Vin, is sufficiently high to turn on the NMOS transistor (i.e., at a digital 1 state), the PMOS transistor remains off, and the output voltage, Vout, is connected to ground (i.e., at a digital 0 state) through the NMOS source-drain path. Conversely, when Vin is at a digital 0 state, only the PMOS transistor is turned on and the Vout is connected to the positive supply voltage (Vdd) at a digital 1 state. Thus, a digital input of 1 results in a digital output of 0 and a digital input of 0 results in a digital output of 1 for the NOT gate. Other logic gates can be formed in a similar manner. These then become the building blocks for more complex logic such as the one-bit adder shown in Figure 3, which can be replicated to add larger numbers by routing each carry-out to the carry-in of the next higher bit. Microprocessors are essentially a combination of these types of logical features in which digital data are read from memory (e.g.,

SRAM or a local cache), processed, and written according to the instructions provided by the operating system.

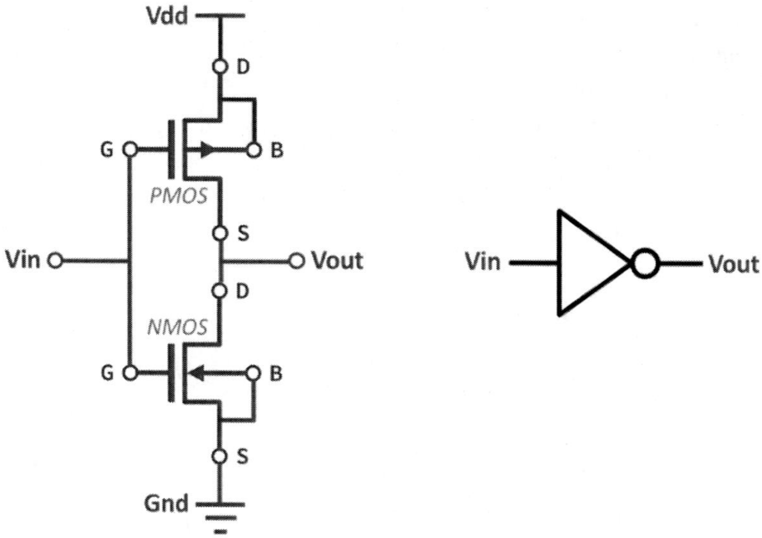

Figure 2. Schematic and symbol for a CMOS inverter, also referred to as a NOT gate.

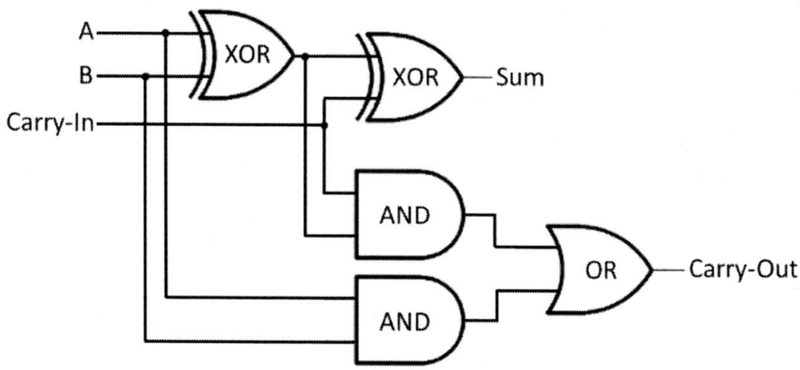

Figure 3. Schematic for a one-bit full adder with carry-in and carry-out.

A modern microprocessor consists of billions of transistors, and Intel has projected that number to reach the trillion level by 2030 [2]. It would be impossible to manufacture such a system without integrated circuit technology. Integrated circuit manufacturing revolves around a series of pattern transfers from a mask to the wafer (i.e., photolithography steps), to produce circuit components in mass quantity. The process begins with a silicon wafer, at present, typically 300 mm in diameter, manufactured at a dedicated foundry from an ingot of silicon to have a specific substrate doping and a minimal number of impurities or crystalline defects. The wafers shown in Figure 4 each contain over 200 completed integrated circuits, ready to be separated into individual chips (also called dice) and packaged in a protective housing that allows it to interface with the outside world (e.g., installed on a circuit board).

Figure 4. Processed silicon wafers prior to singulation (i.e., dicing) to extract the individual die for packaging.

Integrated Circuit Manufacturing

To manufacture integrated circuits, a highly complex and precise manufacturing process is required. In the front end of the process, MOSFETs and other circuit components are defined in the silicon through a series of doping steps, as well as through film depositions, etching, and polishing procedures to create the transistor gates. Photolithography, a process based on light exposure through a mask pattern onto a photo-sensitive film on the wafer, is used to define the patterns of localized regions for processing at each stage. Cleanliness and precision are especially critical in the front end of the process because the features are sized on the nanometer-scale and contaminants can both alter electrical properties and affect pattern transfers. The silicon circuit devices manufactured in the front end of the manufacturing process are electrically connected through a stack of interconnected layers during the back end of the manufacturing process. This may entail a dozen or more metallic films, each patterned by one or more dedicated photolithography steps to define the wire routing. Each of these lines of metal is separated by an insulating layer through which holes are patterned to create passageways between metal lines referred to as vias. Film deposition techniques such as electroplating, and plasma sputtering are commonly used to deposit these metallic films.

At various intervals throughout the overall process, metrology and inspection steps are incorporated to ensure that cleanliness requirements are being met and that process targets are on track. Inline (IL) sampling is important to ensure that any problems are caught quickly since the overall process typically requires several months to complete from start to finish, and therefore early opportunities to detect and mitigate equipment problems, human errors, etc., would be lost if only end-of-line (EOL) test data were to be used to ensure the quality of the integrated circuit.

Process controls and lean manufacturing methodologies are essential to ensure product quality, implement process changes to increase the total number of working die, or adjust their performance targets, and incorporate cost reduction opportunities such as extending maintenance intervals or qualifying a new vendor. These methodologies are dependent upon the collection of data, both IL and EOL, which must be measured accurately and be sufficiently meaningful in terms of metrics and sample rate. As previously described, IL data measurements are collected at one or more stages during the manufacturing process to maintain process targets and monitor equipment health, allowing most problems to be caught relatively quickly. Some examples of IL data include production sampling (e.g., gate leakage current, critical dimensions, or defect counts), scheduled equipment monitors (e.g., particle levels, film thicknesses, or dopant profiles), and tool parameter data (e.g., power supply current, chamber pressure, or hours since a particular maintenance activity). Since the electronic components of the integrated circuits are not fully formed at this stage, IL testing often utilizes test structures defined within unused areas in the scribe lines between the individual dice. Conversely, EOL data contain the results of measurements and functional testing obtained by probing the final integrated circuit. At EOL, the electronic circuits are fully formed, and thus EOL data are used not only to confirm process targets and defect levels for the final stages of the process flow, but also to differentiate between good and bad devices. Customer requirements often define boundaries between good and bad (i.e., defective or underperforming) devices; for example, different customers prefer different processing speed-versus-power tradeoffs.

The wafer-level yield, as a percentage, is calculated using the ratio of the sellable integrated circuits within a wafer (good die) divided by the total number of integrated circuits processed within a wafer. Lot-level yields may also be computed using wafer-level averages.

$$\%yield = \frac{number\ of\ good\ integrated\ circuits}{total\ number\ of\ integrated\ circuits}$$

$$\%integrated\ circuits\ per\ wafer = \frac{number\ of\ good\ integrated\ circuits\ on\ a\ wafer}{total\ number\ of\ integrated\ circuits\ on\ a\ wafer}$$

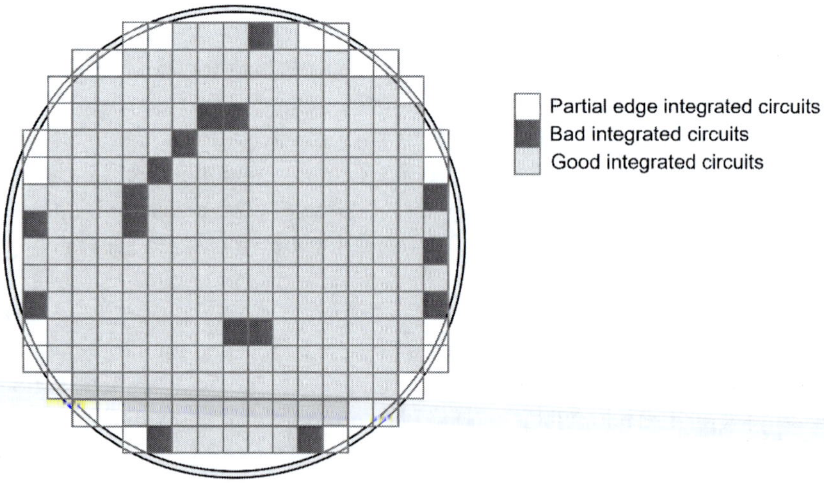

Figure 5. An example wafer map indicating good and defective integrated circuits based on defect locations.

Following testing at EOL, the fully manufactured wafers are diced into individual chips. Those chips that passed the testing process at EOL are selected for the final packaging process, which is often done at a separate manufacturing facility in which specialized equipment is used to enclose and connect the integrated circuit inside a ceramic package. Again, testing is performed to eliminate devices that failed to survive the packaging process, resulting in an overall yield metric. During process development for each integrated circuit technology generation, as well as after implementation, both IL and EOL data are critical to analyze whether elements modified within experiments, such as changes in process recipes, equipment, or commodities, improve or degrade yield.

When manufacturing at the nanometer scale, even small variations can create defects that cause the devices to fail to perform to specification. Sources of variation can be classified as either common cause (random and expected) or special cause (systematic and unexpected). Common cause variation is inherent within any process. Each manufacturing tool has its own set of capabilities and limitations that affect processing precision and uniformity. Incoming raw materials have tolerance specifications (e.g., doping and defect levels in raw silicon, contaminant levels within process chemicals, etc.), and variability may be further increased by the use of multiple vendors, which is often done to minimize supply chain risks. Various sources of vibration, heat, and electromagnetic fields in the manufacturing environment also introduce randomness into the process. Special cause variation, on the other hand, can be traced to a root cause, such as equipment wear or human error. Discriminating special cause variation from common cause variation allows for targeted quality-improvement efforts, such as re-targeting certain elements of the process away from a defect cliff, incorporating additional monitors or metrics, and changing or clarifying human-involved procedures. As integrated circuit process technologies have evolved, research and experience have continued to enhance our knowledge of the underlying physics that has helped determine many sources of random variation and render them controllable (i.e., no longer random).

In a manufacturing environment, continuous improvement requires ingenuity and vigilance in detecting and investigating sources of special cause variation. Process and quality engineers work together to optimize the factory's health through daily sustaining activities in which problems are detected and addressed. These activities employ the use of IL and EOL monitors, as well as process controls that provide a means to detect unfavorable trends and notify the appropriate stakeholders in a timely manner. As new challenges arise and root causes are determined, preventative solutions are implemented, such as additional monitoring metrics or updated maintenance procedures. Opportunities for improvement in yield, throughput, or cost may also be revealed through a controlled design of experiments

(DOE). For example, experiments may be run in which different dopant profiles or film thicknesses are tested, a delay time step may be reduced or eliminated, a maintenance procedure may be shortened, or a new vendor may be qualified. Whether proactive or reactive, these activities require the availability and analysis of data to ensure that risk is minimized whenever adjustments are made to the process or faulty equipment is repaired and returned to production.

Statistics Fundamentals

Statistical assessments are necessary to accurately account for both common cause and special cause variations that occur during the integrated circuit manufacturing process. Data using IL and EOL monitors are sampled at each manufacturing step throughout the fabrication line to model the statistical distribution of the entire population. A probability distribution relates the value of a variable to its probability of occurring. The probability distribution can take the form of either discrete (finite-outcome) or continuous (infinite-outcome) distributions.

Hypergeometric, binomial, multinomial, and Poisson distributions are a few examples of discrete probability distributions in which variables have a finite number of discrete or integer values. The binomial and Poisson distributions are used frequently in manufacturing applications [3]. For example, in a binomial distribution, each trial can have one of two discrete values (e.g., a single IL or EOL monitor passes or fails) and the Poisson distribution can be derived as a limiting form of the binomial distribution and used to model the number of defective integrated circuits per wafer [3].

The most common occurrence of a continuous distribution, where the set of possible values is infinite, is a normal distribution in which data follow a bell curve symmetrically centered around the mean, μ, as shown in Figure 6. Many IL monitors, such as critical dimensions in lithography and film thickness, are assumed to follow a normal distribution. The probability density function for a normally distributed random variable, x, is given by May and Spanos [4] as:

$$f(x) = \frac{1}{\sigma\sqrt{2\pi}} \exp\left[-\frac{1}{2}\left(\frac{x-\mu}{\sigma}\right)^2\right]$$

Figure 6 shows a normal distribution in which 68.26% of the data falls within one standard deviation, ±1σ; 95.46% falls within two standard deviations, ±2σ; and 99.73% falls within three standard deviations, ±3σ, of the process mean, μ.

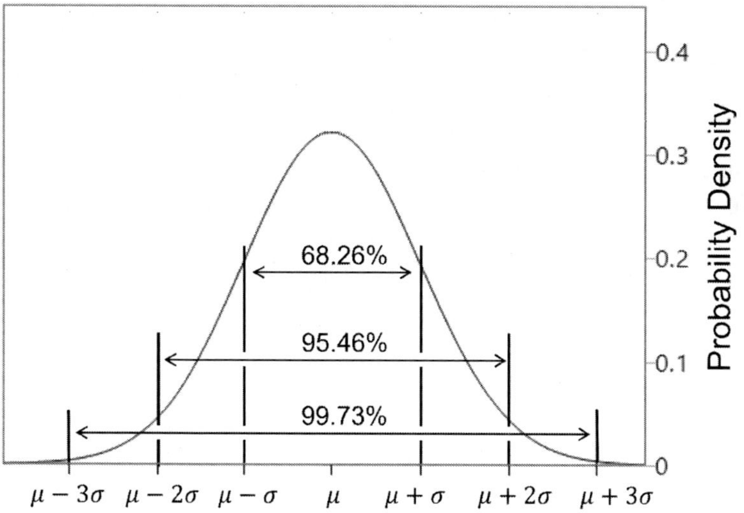

Figure 6. A normal distribution function displaying the empirical rule in which the data are evenly distributed about the mean, μ, and standard deviation, σ.

Since sampling capabilities typically only account for a small sample size in comparison to the large inventory manufactured, in some cases a variation on the normal distribution function may be necessary to model the manufacturing behavior. Exponential distribution is a continuous distribution that measures the time until a specific event occurs. For example, the decay of a power supply current can follow an exponential distribution thus enabling scheduled maintenance prior to a failure event.

Six Sigma

Six Sigma is a set of tools used to improve process quality by reducing defects and manufacturing variability. Six Sigma had its origins in the mid-1980s at Motorola where it was developed for product and process quality improvements [5]. Since its inception, Six Sigma has become an industry standard. The goal of Six Sigma is to use data to reduce defects and variability to improve quality. Sigma in Six Sigma represents the statistical variability in the process. When a process is operating at the industry standard with a 3-sigma (σ) tolerance, this is the production of 2,700 defects per million products, or a success rate of 99.73% [5]. In Six Sigma, the target is to reduce manufacturing defects to less than 3.4 defects per million products or a success rate of 99.9997% [6].

One Six-Sigma tool that can be implemented to reduce defects is the Define, Measure, Analyze, Improve, Control (DMAIC) process, shown in Figure 7. The DMAIC process is a strategy aimed at continued improvement within an existing process. In the first phase of DMAIC, the problem is clearly defined. In the second phase, data are collected (measured), which are then analyzed in the third phase to determine the root cause of defects. In the fourth phase, solutions to improve the process are implemented, and in the last phase, process controls are implemented to sustain the improvements.

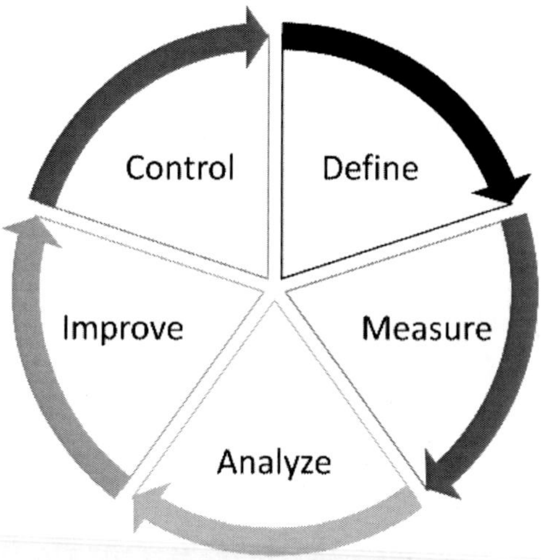

Figure 7. Six Sigma continuous improvement DMAIC tool.

Another tool used in Six Sigma is Statistical Process Control (SPC). SPC was developed by Dr. Walter Shewhart in the 1920s [3]. Typically, SPC is used to monitor normal and non-normal statistical distributions during production. The SPC control chart is the graphical representation of how a process changes over time. It includes an upper control limit (UCL) and a lower control limit (LCL) centered around the process mean. Typical control limits (i.e., boundaries) are within ±3σ from the mean, μ, as opposed to 6σ to account for inherent random variations within the process, as shown in Figure 8. Warning limits, ±1σ or ±2σ, may also be used.

Control charts provide information on outliers, drifts, and shifts within the process. The process data monitored are typically assumed to follow a normal distribution or can be transformed into a normal distribution in which 68.26% of the data lies within 1σ, 95.46% lies within 2σ, and 99.73% falls within 3σ of the process average, as shown in Figure 8. Control limits are independent of customer expectations and specification limits. Specification limits are used to account for the performance needed to meet customer and functional expectations for a given product. Generally, products that require tighter tolerances, such as integrated circuits, are more expensive to produce than those that do not require tight tolerances.

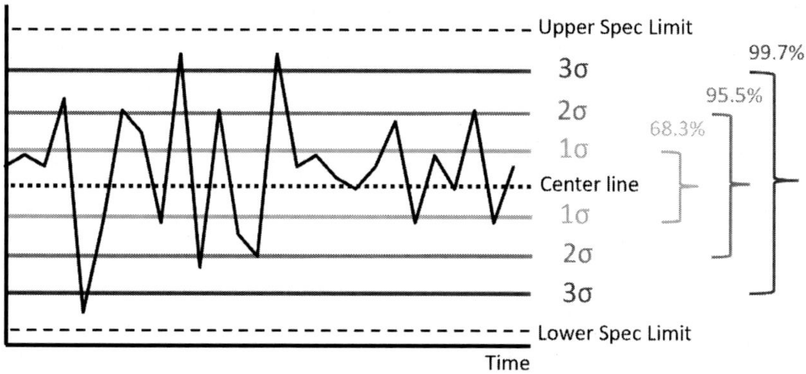

Figure 8. Illustration of a control chart with center line, upper and lower control limits, 3σ.

Control chart type is dependent on whether discrete (attribute) or continuous (variable) data are being sampled, as well as the subgroup size (Table 1) [7]. Continuous datasets can be measured, such as film thickness or process temperature, while discrete datasets are counted by attribute, such as pass/fail. Continuous data can be plotted using the individual (I) and moving range (MR) charts, X-Bar and range (R) charts, or X-Bar and sigma (s) charts. Time series data sets are plotted for I charts and the difference between successive points are calculated for MR charts. X-Bar charts can be derived from I charts by plotting the average of data points for each subgroup (e.g., measurements from four wafers from a manufacturing lot). Range charts are derived from the maximum and minimum of each subgroup. Discrete datasets are used to monitor when a deviation from stability occurs (e.g., number of good/bad computer chips on a wafer) and can be monitored with defect density (u), fraction defective (p), number of defects (c), and number of defective units (np) control charts. U charts plot the number of defects per unit, while p charts plot the percentage or fraction of defective items. C charts plot the number of defects, while np charts plot the number of defective items. Constant subgroups (i.e., the same number of samples per group) are needed for c and np charts, while u and p charts can have variable subgroup sizes.

Table 1. Table of control chart types for continuous (variable) and discrete (attribute) data

Continuous/Variable Data	Distribution	Chart Type	Subgroup Size
	Normal	I and MR charts	1
		X-Bar and R charts	< 10
		X-Bar and s charts	≥ 10
Discrete/Attribute Data	Poisson	c chart	Constant
		u chart	Variable
	Binomial	np chart	Constant
		p chart	Variable

A process is in control when only common cause variation is present. When a process is stable the mean μ and standard deviation σ are constant over time. Therefore, current process behavior will be a good predictor of future process behavior.

Control charts can be evaluated using different rules, depending on the process, to detect non-random patterns such as shifts, drifts, and outliers. One of the more commonly applied set of rules for control charts are the Western Electric rules [8]. Examples of rules of thumb for out-of-control (OOC) data and data requiring evaluation in a control chart are as follows [3, 8]:

- OOC:
  - Any data point that falls outside of 3σ control limits.
  - Two out of three consecutive data points that are outside of 2σ warning limits on the same side of the centerline, but within 3σ control limits.
  - Four out of five consecutive data points that are outside of 2σ warning limits on the same side of the centerline.

- Nine consecutive data points that are on the same side of the centerline.
- Requires Evaluation:
  - Data are in control, but there are drifts away from or towards the control limits or shifts about the centerline.

A manufactured product is a cumulative result of many parameters, each of which has its own sources of variation. Process variability can be quantified and managed at each stage using statistical process capability metrics that describe the ability of a process to repeatably produce specification conforming products. Prior to evaluating these metrics, the process should be statistically stable, with only common cause variation present. Once stability has been established, the process engineer can use specification limits to quantify the process capability, which is typically done using the indices Cp and Cpk. The former, Cp, informs the engineer of how well the data fit within the defined tolerance limits and how narrow the distribution of data are. The latter, Cpk, indicates how off-center the distribution of data is with respect to the specification limits. These parameters are calculated as follows:

$$Cp = \frac{USL-LSL}{6\sigma} \qquad (1)$$

$$Cpk = \frac{\mu-LSL}{3\sigma}, \frac{USL-\mu}{3\sigma} \quad (2)$$

If these parameters are both less than 1, then the process is considered poor, or not capable, and the risk of falling outside control limits is significant. If both parameters are marginally greater than 1, then the process is considered barely capable. Ideally, if both parameters are greater than 1.3, the process is capable and likely to remain within control limits provided that a source of special cause variation does not occur.

For example, many of the circuit structures have critical dimensions, such as line width for a metal interconnect layer. If the distribution of measurements after etching is found to overlap significantly with the upper specification limit, this means that many of the wafers have line widths that are larger than allowed. In this instance, both Cp and Cpk will likely be below the acceptable threshold. To resolve this, the process engineers would need to improve the ability of the process to meet the critical dimension limits (e.g., by moving to a different lithography tool or changing the etch time), or the design engineers would need to investigate whether the current tolerances are necessary and are appropriate given the process limitations, or both.

Lean Manufacturing

The goal of lean manufacturing is to reduce waste. The philosophy of lean manufacturing is derived from the lauded Toyota Production System (TPS), developed by Toyota Motor Corporation to improve efficiency in manufacturing and logistics [9, 10]. The TPS approach focuses on the identification and elimination of sources of waste (i.e., muda). Whether waste is generated through direct expenditures, scrapped product, manufacturing delays, or man-hours, it results in higher costs and reduced profits. The eight types of waste are described as follows [9]:

1. *Over-Production:* manufacturing products in excess of customer demand; an example of this is a computer chip manufacturer that produced more chips than currently needed.
2. *Waiting:* allowing inventory or wafers that are a work in progress to sit idle between processing stations or at EOL.
3. *Transportation:* movement of inventory or wafers that are a work in progress between different processing stations or facilities that do not create value or directly support production.
4. *Over-Processing:* adding unnecessary complexity to manufacturing processes, such as implementing more steps than necessary to successfully pattern the features required on the wafer in a particular process step.
5. *Excess Stock/Inventory:* having more inventory of products or wafers (finished and in progress), raw materials, consumables, spare parts, etc., than necessary to produce the number of computer chips in demand.
6. *Motion:* movement of humans or equipment that does not create value; this can be due to an inefficient semiconductor fabrication (fab) facility layout.
7. *Defects:* failure to meet performance requirements, resulting in rework or scrap, or both.
8. *Unproductivity:* under-utilized employees, in terms of both time and innovation.

Lean manufacturing entails following a just-in-time (JIT) approach in which products are manufactured only as needed, avoiding unnecessary raw material consumption and inventory storage. The opposite of JIT is over-production, an expensive source of waste that not only results in excess inventory at EOL, which must be stored in a climate-controlled environment, but also slows down the overall manufacturing line, reducing throughput, and consequently increasing the need for equipment and floor space within the fab.

Kanban, a Japanese word meaning signboard, is a lean manufacturing principle developed by Taiichi Ono at Toyota [10]. It is a scheduling system implemented to limit the buildup of excess inventory or works in progress (WIP) in the production line. Kanban originated as a visual restocking system for inventory, but in many industries has evolved into electronic tracking systems that signal suppliers to produce and deliver new stock when material is consumed. The pull for new material comes from customer demand when it is needed. Electronic tracking systems allow integrated circuit manufacturers to effectively manage resource planning in addition to tracking how long WIP wafers and raw materials sit waiting between process steps.

In lean manufacturing, value refers to the inherent worth of a product reflected in what a customer is willing to pay for it. Any action that does not produce value, whether by a human or machine, can be thought of as waste. These actions are referred to as non-value-added steps. While not every non-value-added step can be eliminated (e.g., maintenance, equipment health monitors), ways to reduce their impact should be investigated. Within a process, there are three types of operations:

- Value adding.
- Non-value-adding, but necessary.
- Non-value-adding and not necessary.

Operations that are both non-value-adding and not necessary, such as waiting, are fully wasteful and should be eliminated when possible. On the other hand, some operations are non-value-adding yet necessary, such as inspection and cleaning steps, and are required to sustain the business.

Value stream mapping (i.e., material and information flow mapping), is a lean manufacturing method used to visualize and reduce waste and improve efficiency in a manufacturing process. A value stream map can show both material flow and information flow within the process and can include calculations of process or cycle time, lead time, and change over time. This can help to reveal bottlenecks in the supply chain, analyze critical points for push and pull in demand, and identify waste within the process flow and fab. The goal is to develop continuous flow and maximize efficiency. In this way, lean manufacturing can help fabs understand where wafers and other raw materials spend the most time waiting between process steps, how much time it takes to set up a machine to run a modified process or experiment, and how to manage down time for scheduled preventative maintenance.

The 5 Whys is another lean manufacturing method. This method involves asking the question "Why?" repeatedly when a problem is encountered to go beyond the obvious symptoms and get to the root cause of an issue. For instance, if a repeating defect is encountered on a wafer, one could consider why the defect repeats systematically. The answer could be that similar structures exist in these locations on the wafer. If one were to ask why those structures exist in periodic locations and not randomly, the answer might be that defect pattern is consistent with the repeating pattern of integrated circuits on the wafer. If one were to ask why the defects would exist in the same location in every integrated circuit, regardless of the process tools utilized, the answer might be that only one photomask per lithography step is available to create the integrated circuit patterns. From this commonality, one might determine that the root cause of the repeated defects is a particle or defect on the photolithography mask. This mask is repeatedly exposed to light to create repeated patterns across the wafer and may become dirty or degraded over time due to a variety of factors such as particles, residues, chrome migration, or oxidation.

Lean Maintenance

Equipment engineers are responsible for ensuring that the manufacturing equipment under their purview is maintained to an acceptable standard. In the case of integrated circuit manufacturing, this entails verifying that process targets are being met, particle levels that can lead to defects are as close to zero as possible, no sources of contamination (e.g., vacuum leaks, coolant leaks, or cleaning wipes) are present, and no damage is imparted to the fragile silicon wafers by the wafer-handling robotics.

As previously discussed, scheduled monitors are frequently run to confirm process parameters and particle levels; however, all equipment requires maintenance, whether scheduled (proactive/preventative) or unscheduled (reactive). Scheduled maintenance entails the performance of documented procedures at specific intervals to prevent known problems from occurring. Equipment manufacturers provide recommendations as to the frequency with which components should be serviced or replaced, and these schedules are adjusted as new problems are encountered or as opportunities to extend component lifetimes are proven (typically through a DOE). Unscheduled maintenance, on the other hand, occurs when equipment becomes inoperative due to either a fault condition or the detection of a problem through IL or EOL data. This often causes larger challenges for the factory, as production wafers may have been placed at risk, equipment down-time is typically much longer, inventory may begin to accumulate as a result of the reduced throughput, and if the downtime is extensive, output forecasting models may become inaccurate. Finding an optimal balance between production and maintenance is a key challenge for process engineers. Through methodical analysis of workflows and equipment data, however, equilibrium can be gradually shifted in favor of increased production time, decreased down-time due to maintenance, and reduced consumable expenditures.

Lean manufacturing principles indicate that waste associated with unnecessary human or equipment motion should be eliminated where possible, and this concept is especially applicable to maintenance procedures. Even under ideal circumstances, the activities associated with maintenance are non-value-added with respect to the manufactured product, though they are necessary. To maximize equipment availability, scheduled maintenance procedures should be prepared ahead of time to avoid incurring additional down-time due to preventable delays from problems such as:

- Insufficient availability of technicians,
- Inadequate training on the procedure or unclear documentation,
- Missing or disorganized tools,
- Insufficient inventory of spare parts or waiting for parts delivery to the job location,
- Poor communication across shift changes or break schedules, and
- An unclear production re-certification strategy or insufficient quantity of test wafers.

On the other hand, it is more difficult to prepare for unscheduled maintenance events. They do not follow an engineered schedule, and the components that need to be replaced are unknown until troubleshooting has been performed. Opportunities to convert from unscheduled to scheduled maintenance (and to extend the times between scheduled maintenance events), however, may be found through predictive maintenance methodologies. Predictive maintenance makes use of sensors, data, and analytics to monitor equipment health in real time with the goals of anticipating component failures before they can impact product quality and minimizing equipment down-time through proactive preparation.

Integrated circuit manufacturing tools typically report a vast wealth of data, including parameters such as:

- Vacuum pressures at one or more locations,
- Power supply parameters, including voltage and current targets and feedback values,
- Temperatures of equipment components, coolant, and in-process wafers,
- Flow rates of gases and liquid chemicals,
- Calibration values or offsets, and
- Time or utilization counters, or both, for the overall machine or certain components.

Relationships between critical equipment parameters and product quality can be established through data mining and product testing or imaging, with many correlations or limits already well understood based on historical experience. Other non-critical parameters do not directly impact quality but are highly useful for predictive maintenance. For example, if a power supply is commanded to maintain a specific output voltage, a shift or ramp in the electric current drawn to maintain that voltage may be of interest. Provided that the tool is still meeting its target criteria with respect to the product, process, and quality, engineers may choose to keep it running with the intent of closely monitoring the situation (e.g., by increasing the frequency of scheduled monitors). In the meantime, they may begin preparing for a likely power supply failure (e.g., by ordering replacement parts and preparing a written procedure). Based on risk assessment, the decision can be made to either run to failure or to proactively replace the power supply at a convenient opportunity. In the example in Figure 9, thermal imaging is used to monitor the condition of a power station. The presence of hot spots or non-uniform temperature distribution does not necessarily indicate a problem, as certain circuits or regions may be more heavily loaded than others; equipment engineers are responsible for understanding the spectrum of normal behavior.

Deviation from the typical range of temperatures may indicate a pending equipment failure, and early intervention can prevent the failure from propagating and damaging additional equipment, or resulting in a long period of down-time, or both.

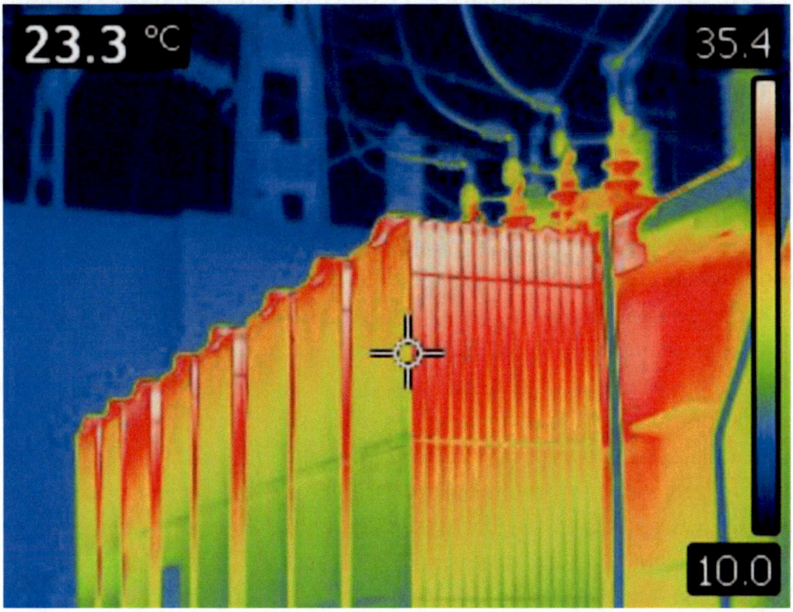

Figure 9. Thermal image of a power station showing areas of higher and lower temperature. Deviation from the normal range may indicate an upcoming equipment failure.

Often, relationships among the various equipment and quality parameters have complex multi-variate relationships. For example, integrated circuit manufacturing tools are capable of running multiple process operations and the duration or sequence of each individual recipe is often a factor in predicting component lifetimes because some recipes cause more stress to the equipment than others. The capabilities of predictive maintenance are fully realized when a high level of equipment knowledge is combined with data and analysis capabilities to build a failure prediction model from which automated alerts can be dispatched and decisions can be made quickly and effectively. Data may be structured, such as voltages or particle counts, or unstructured, such as wafer defect maps or log files, and consequently data storage and integration present a challenge. A successful model results in an enhanced understanding of the equipment and enables significant improvements to both product quality and production availability.

Maintenance activities, whether scheduled or unscheduled, benefit from planning and organization prior to removing the equipment from production. Ideally, all replacement parts and hand tools are staged at the job site ahead of time, trained technicians are available to perform the work, and the procedures are clearly documented (including the pre-staging procedure and post-maintenance production certification requirements). Further optimization may be achieved through a detailed work-flow analysis such as a Kaizen event. Kaizen, a Japanese term meaning "change for the better," refers to a focused effort to achieve a defined objective. Regarding equipment maintenance, a waste Kaizen entails a 3 to 5 day process in which a diverse group of stakeholders work together to identify and eliminate waste sources within a selected procedure. Team members include individuals trained in lean manufacturing and maintenance and Six-Sigma methodologies to guide the process, engineers knowledgeable about the equipment and its potential quality implications, and technicians who have performed the procedure numerous times and experienced first-hand the challenges and opportunities for improvement. As the procedure is methodically performed, motions of both human and hardware are observed, bottlenecks and redundancies are identified, and sources of potential defects or mistakes are considered. Proposed changes may include things such as re-ordering or eliminating tasks, new or modified checklists, labeling components at risk of being switched (such as wires or tubing), or improved organization of tools. Multiple iterations may take place as the changes are implemented and the benefits validated. Personnel are trained in the improved procedure, and if successful, an increase in equipment availability (and associated cost savings) is realized.

Thought Experiment: Is Integrated Circuit Manufacturing too Lean?

The global integrated circuit manufacturing deficit during the COVID-19 pandemic was exacerbated by supply chain shortages. In the beginning of the pandemic, when global shutdowns were occurring, automakers predicted there would be a decline in automotive demand and cancelled integrated circuit orders to avoid having excess integrated circuit inventory on hand. These predictions for decreased demand for automobiles, however, were inaccurate, and by the time the automakers realized that demand for automotives had not declined, integrated circuit manufacturers were already under pressure, struggling to meet necessary production quantities due to changes in consumer lifestyles influenced by other aspects of the pandemic.

During the pandemic, a greater proportion of the world than ever before shifted toward online accessibility including classrooms, workplaces, courtrooms, medicine, and grocery delivery [4]. As people stayed at home to avoid contracting or spreading COVID-19, they turned to computers, smartphones, tablets, and other electronic devices to connect to the world. Demand for online video connectivity and entertainment resulted in an increased demand for updated devices. Thus, there was an increased demand for laptops, tablets, and other electronic devices with cutting-edge microprocessors. This led to an unprecedented demand for integrated circuits by consumers even before automakers realized that demand for new cars, complete with embedded integrated circuits, had not diminished like they predicted.

The shortage of integrated circuits in the automobile industry and elsewhere, became a crisis. By 2021 there was projected to be only an estimated 17% capacity increase in 200-nanometer computer chip production between 2020 and 2024 [11]. The industry added more 200-nanometer fabs and as of September 2022, capacity was projected to exceed 7 million wafers per month by 2025 [12], five years after the pandemic began. Thus, there would be no quick resolution to the integrated circuit crisis.

The occurrence of this crisis continues to prompt many questions about what could have been done to avoid it. Is lean manufacturing responsible for this crisis? Are integrated circuit manufacturing industries operating too lean? Are there limits to how lean manufacturing should be? Are there better and newer ways to predict consumer demand?

Conclusion

Lean manufacturing and Six Sigma are powerful tools used in the manufacture of integrated circuits. Integrated circuit manufacturing is potentially one of the most critical manufacturing applications of the Six-Sigma process with defects on the nanometer scale having a profound impact on the ability of products to meet consumer needs or even be sellable at all. Processes and integrated circuit parameters are tracked and controlled for quality at a number of different levels both IL and EOL. This chapter has been a brief overview of some of the tools used in integrated circuit manufacturing to meet the growing demands of a more and more digital world. With Moore's law, there is a drive for continued improvement as the architecture of integrated circuits get smaller and smaller, processes get more and more complex, new manufacturing techniques such as extreme ultraviolet lithography are introduced, new tools are developed and required to meet shrinking node sizes (i.e., the integrated circuit process design rule), and new sources of defects and wastes are created.

References

[1] Lojek, Bo. 2007. History *of Semiconductor Engineering*. Berlin: Springer.

[2] Jiminez, Jorge. 2022. *"Intel says there will be one trillion transisors on chips by 2030."* Last Updated December 6, 2022, Accessed September 1, 2023. Available from https://www.pcgamer.com/intel-says-there-will-be-one-trillion-transistors-on-chips-by-2030/.

[3] May, G. S., and C. J. Spanos. 2006. *Fundamentals of semiconductor manufacturing and process control*. Hoboken, NJ: Wiley for IEEE.

[4] Moore, Samuel K. 2023. "How and When the Chip Shortage Will End, in 4 Charts." *IEEE Spectrum,* Accessed September 1, 2023. Available from https://spectrum.ieee.org/chip-shortage.

[5] Pyzdek, T., Keller, P. *The Six Sigma handbook: a complete guide for green belts, black belts, and managers at all levels 3rd.* McGraw-Hill Companies, New York, NY.

[6] Kwak, Young Hoon, and Frank T. Anbari. 2006. "Benefits, obstacles, and future of six sigma approach." *Technovation* 26 (5):708-715. doi: 10.1016/j.technovation.2004.10.003.

[7] Wortman, Bill. 2001. *The Six Sigma Black Belt Solutions Manual*. West Terra Haute, IN: Quality Council of Indiana.

[8] Western Electric. 1956. *Statistical Quality Control Handbook*. Indianapolis, IN: Western Electric Corp.

[9] Liker, Jeffrey K. 2004. *Toyota Way: 14 Management Principles from the World's Greatest Manufacturer*. 1st edition ed, *McGraw-Hill's Access Engineering*. New York: McGraw-Hill.

[10] Ōno, Taiichi, Norman Bodek, and Group Toyota. 1988. *Toyota Production System: Beyond Large-scale Production*. 1st ed. Cambridge, Mass: Productivity Press.

[11] SEMI. 2021. "Global 200mm Fab Capacity on Pace to Record Growth to Meet Surging Demand and Address Chip Shortage, SEMI Reports." Last Updated May 25, 2021, Accessed February 16, 2023. Available from https://www.prnewswire.com/news-releases/.

[12] Dieseldorff, Christian G., and Chich-Wen Liu. 2023. "200mm Fab Outlook to 2026: Worldwide 200mm Fab Activities for Semiconductors, Power Electronics, and Sensors Driven by Growth in Demand for Mobile, IoT, and Automotive Products."

Power Electronic News, Last Updated September 20, 2023, Accessed September 30, 2023. Available from https://www.powerelectronicsnews.com/global-200mm-fab-capacity-to-reach-record-levels-by-2026-according-to-semi/.

Biographical Sketches

Catrice M. Kees, PhD

Dr. Catrice Kees is a driving force in the realms of technology and semiconductor development, boasting a Ph.D. in Materials Science & Engineering from Rutgers University and a B.A. in Physics from Carleton College. Her impactful journey includes substantial contributions at Intel Corporation, specializing in the Thin Films module, where she played a key role in advancing the next generation of semiconductor products across multiple tech nodes. Her proficiency in technical project management, data analysis, and process engineering led her to Exponent, where she provided continuous improvement and process enhancement consulting, optimizing quality and efficiency for government and industry partners. While achieving professional milestones, Dr. Kees maintains a flourishing personal life in Maryland with her husband, three daughters, and two sons, embodying the fusion of academic excellence, technical expertise, and a fulfilling family life.

Melissa L Mendias, PhD, PE, CFEI

Dr. Melissa Mendias is an experienced electronics and systems engineer who spent nearly ten years working in a high-volume semiconductor manufacturing environment in both process and yield engineering. She works at Exponent as an engineering consultant where she has established expertise in automotive electronics including advanced driver assistance systems (ADAS), model based systems engineering (MBSE), and failure analysis studies of electrical systems for a variety of applications. Dr. Mendias received her Ph.D. in Electrical Engineering from Michigan Technological University where her research involved technology development for CMOS-integrated MEMS sensors with an emphasis on accelerometers. She is a licensed professional engineer in the state of Arizona and is also a certified fire and explosion investigator.

Rebecca Routson, PhD

Dr. Routson has wide-ranging experience including manufacturing, optimization, statistical and data analysis, and both simulation based and experimental biomechanics. She currently works at Exponent in the mechanical engineering practice. Prior to joining Exponent, Dr. Routson's work in semiconductor manufacturing technology development included both yield analysis and lithography, spanning multiple technology nodes and contributing to the next generation of semiconductor technology. Previously, Dr. Routson taught manufacturing processes, process control, and lean manufacturing at Colorado School of Mines and the capstone design sequence in the mechanical engineering department at Portland State University. She received her Ph.D. in mechanical engineering from the University of Texas at Austin.

Chapter 7

Quantum Computation: From Hardware Challenges to Software Engineering Tools and Technologies

Gavin D. Scott[*]
Matthew A. Pooley
and Paloma L. Ocola
Exponent, Inc., New York, NY

Abstract

Quantum computation and quantum information processing presents an alternative computational paradigm for solving certain challenging problems. While quantum computing will not serve as a replacement for modern computing systems, it may be used to address selected complex problems with solutions that are intractable, even for the most sophisticated supercomputers. This chapter discusses the requisite building blocks for quantum information processing including qubits, superposition, entanglement, and decoherence, and it addresses a number of current physical implementations of qubits. It also describes the essential steps for computing with quantum systems, and how quantum logic gates are used in the gate model of universal quantum computation. This chapter further addresses the challenges associated with mapping problems to quantum computing hardware and mapping between hardware control and software. To that end, software platforms for allowing computer scientists and engineers to leverage quantum computing effectively without requiring detailed quantum mechanical

[*] Corresponding Author's Email: gscott@exponent.com.

In: Computer Engineering Applications …
Editor: Brian D'Andrade
ISBN: 979-8-89113-488-1

knowledge, and without explicitly defining quantum processes, are being developed with a view to opening up quantum computing to a wider set of usage cases towards everyday applications.

Keywords: quantum computing, quantum information processing, qubits, quantum software, software stack, quantum programming languages

Introduction

Motivating Factors

Quantum computation and quantum information processing is a multi-faceted field of research and technology that has persisted at least since the term "quantum computer" was first coined in a 1980 article by Paul Benioff [1]. Its origins and the motivation that continues to propel the pursuit of a quantum computer emerge from the convergence of several issues. One relevant matter is the impending horizon of Moore's law and the implications it will have for the future success of traditional computing systems.

In 1975, Gordon Moore, the co-founder of both Fairchild Semiconductor and Intel, made the now famous observation that the number of transistors on a silicon chip doubled approximately every 2 years, while the feature size of the transistors (the distance between source and drain)[1] decreased at about the same rate. Known commonly as Moore's law, this trend has been generally observed over the last several decades. The observation simultaneously implies that the computational power of computers also increases at a proportional rate. The inevitable horizon of Moore's law, however, will come when the size of the transistors shrinks to a fundamental limit of nature—the length scale of individual atoms. This presents a fundamental limitation not only to the capabilities of modern semiconductor fabrication processing, but also to the computational power that may be gained by utilizing so many bits.

As the size of bits is reduced to the size of atoms, their physical properties are governed by a different set of rules. Rather than exhibiting properties that are expressed by ensemble averages, a quantum mechanical treatment is required to properly characterize the functionality of such a bit. To that end, quantum computation has also benefited from the desire of scientists and

[1] Gordon Moore's initial 1965 prediction was that the doubling rate would occur every year. In 1975 his observation was revised to every 2 years.

engineers to explore the nature of information that may be represented by components of nature at a fundamental limit. The capabilities and understanding have been propelled by the technological progress scientists have made in addressing and manipulating physical systems on a size scale that is suitable for observing and controlling quantum mechanical features.

The various physical representations that may constitute the bits of a quantum computer are often extremely small, but it is not their size alone that makes them interesting. That is, quantum computers will not merely circumvent the limitations of Moore's law; rather the allure of quantum computation is that it presents an alternative mode of computation in which some of the inherent limitations of classical computation are no longer an insurmountable obstacle. In this respect, another issue serving to motivate interest and propel the field of quantum computation and quantum information processing forward is the promise that the unique attributes of quantum computing may help solve problems that even significantly faster classical computers will be unable to tackle.

Advantages of Computation with a Quantum System

When attempting to classically simulate the interaction of N particles in a quantum system, Richard Feynman found that he was unable to develop a general solution that did not require exponentially increasing resources. He famously pointed out that some problems cannot be solved efficiently using a classical computer [2]. The traveling salesperson problem is one well-known example. Given a list of locations (cities, for instance), a salesperson would like to find the shortest possible route to visit each city exactly once and return to the city of origin. This is a problem that is simple enough to understand, and of real practical value (consider the number of stops a delivery driver makes in one outing), yet it is actually an intractable, exponentially hard problem. In this context, *hard* means that the number of resources, or computational power, needed to solve the problem grows exponentially as the problem gets bigger. In technical terms, it means that the problem has no known exact solution in polynomial time.[2] What one quickly finds is that the number of

2 A problem that can be solved in polynomial time requires a number of steps for a given input that is $O(n^k)$ for an integer k, where n is the complexity of the input.

possible routes to take as a function of the number of locations grows exponentially.[3]

With a route containing 15 different cities, there are already 10^{11} possible routes (i.e., 100 billion). To a broad approximation, a computer operating in the gigahertz range may be able to check the time of every route in about 100 seconds. But for 22 different cities, this same computer operating at the same rate would require 1600 years to check every route. For 28 cities, this computer would require a length of time longer than the age of the universe. A computer may be instructed to take the most simplistic approach wherein the problem is solved sequentially through all possible routes. To speed up this process one could reasonably put several computers in parallel, but the advantage presents merely a multiplicative factor. If a computer required 1600 years to find the shortest route for 22 cities, then two computers working in parallel could do it in 800 years, at best, and 100 computers would still require 16 years, which is an improvement, yet still much too long to be of any use.

The discovery that the boundary between problems that can and cannot be solved may be different between classical and quantum computational approaches led to a proliferation of interest in quantum computing beyond the academic world. It is now understood there are problems that cannot be solved efficiently on a classical computer (i.e., cannot be solved in a feasible amount of time), but that may be solved on a quantum computer—or, at least, with a quantum mechanical mode of computation. Solving such a problem would be emblematic of "quantum supremacy" [3], demonstrating from both the engineering and mathematical perspectives that a programmable quantum computer is operable to solve a problem that no classical computing system can solve in a reasonable amount of time. Notably, there are also problems that may be solved on either classical or quantum computers, but for which a quantum computer may solve more efficiently. Today there are many known existing material problems that may be advantageously addressed with quantum computing, touching upon a wide breadth of sectors including financial, pharmaceutical, information theory, and communication.

Quantum computing has been the subject of study for decades, at least in an academic setting, with researchers pursuing avenues of interest ranging from information theory to details of hardware technologies and computational models suitable for such hardware. In this respect, there have been, and continue to be, many subtopics of interest under the quantum

---

[3] A problem that can be solved in exponential time requires a number of steps for a given input that is $O(k^n)$ for an integer k, where n is the complexity of the input.

computing umbrella. Studies have focused on several aspects of quantum computing for many years, including the mathematical approaches and topics pertaining to information theory, as well as the physical systems that may be used to construct the basic underlying architecture and its topology. In other words, much of the focus on the theory side was centered around the topics of what a quantum computer may be used to calculate and the mathematical approach of such calculations, and on the experimental side, the physical components that may be used to represent the quantum information upon which such processing takes place. More comprehensive efforts in recent years have involved putting together systems with both the physical architecture and the ability to solve a certain problem. Much of this technology, however, remains at the level of logical operations, manually optimized, and customized for a particular problem, and thus not presently useful for any general computing purposes.

While these remain vibrant areas of research, the desire to put this into practice and to make quantum computing a reality—in one form or another—has spurred a growing interest in related areas of science and technology for the means of putting it to use (i.e., areas of technology required to bring the better-known components of quantum information processing from the laboratory to reality). This requires mapping what may initially be purely mathematical problems to hardware. And then, approaches must be developed for interfacing between hardware and software. This may entail, for instance, a language to instruct a computing system as to the type and sequence of physical operations to be executed.

As discussed by Simon Gay, the earliest formalized quantum programming language was by proposed by Emanuel Knill in 1996 in *Conventions for Quantum Psuedocode* [4, 5]. Since that time, research and development efforts have shaped the design of programming languages specifically intended for quantum computing, including aspects related to their syntax, semantics, and compilers [6]. As discussed further below, a multitude of software tools have been developed to address this problem. Indeed, research and development has been directed to nearly every component of the entire software stack necessary to create a functioning quantum computing device. Regardless of the specific hardware utilized to interact with quantum phenomena, an accessible general purpose quantum computer requires at least a means for: (i) encoding an input that defines the parameters and initial state for use within a given computation; (ii) programming a sequence of computational operations that implement a given algorithm upon the input; and (iii) outputting the final state that represents the solution obtained from performing the algorithm upon the input state. Before discussing software tools and other mechanisms for defining quantum inputs, programming quantum operations, and mapping quantum solutions to readable outputs, it is useful to first discuss some underlying aspects of quantum mechanics upon which quantum computing depends.

Basics of Quantum Information and Computation

The following section addresses some of the basic building blocks of quantum computation, how they differ from their classical counterparts, and how some aspects have natural classical analogues, while other aspects of quantum computation have no such comparable classical analogue and are inherently non-intuitive.

Building Blocks

In a classical digital computing system, including the computer used to write this text, information (i.e., data) is encoded into indivisible units represented as bits. These may take on only a binary set of values, 0 or 1. In certain contexts, it may be useful, and perfectly acceptable, for these values to be interpreted as True or False, On or Off. In modern devices, these bits are physically manifested as current flowing through transistors. If the gate voltage is off, then current is blocked from flowing, representing a 0 state. If the gate voltage is on, then the current can flow between the contacts, which can represent a 1 state.

Computer processing of the information these bits represent is dictated by a set of rules (i.e., a program) that is built largely around the use of logic gates that dictate the manner in which encoded information is transformed. Here, as in common usage among electrical engineers, logic gates in an electrical circuit typically refer to an electronic component, or set of components, that computes a Boolean logic function. For instance, if the value is 0, then change it to 1; if the value is 1, then change it to 0. This would be a type of logic NOT gate. The functionality of logic gates is delineated by their associated truth tables. Figure 1 shows examples of common classical logic gates and their accompanying truth tables, as well as their typical representation in a circuit diagram, along with a brief description of their respective functionality.

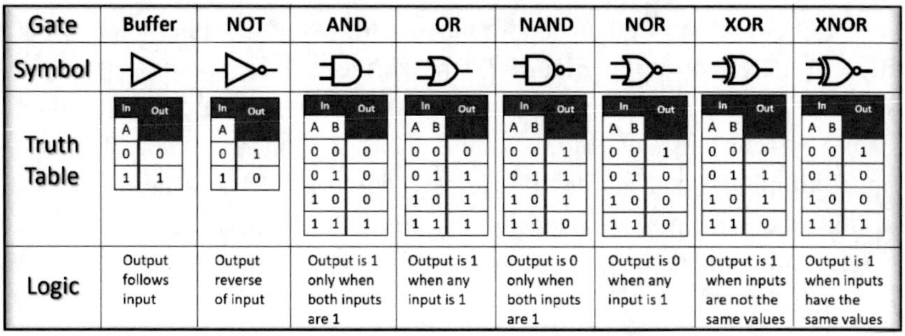

Gate	Buffer	NOT	AND	OR	NAND	NOR	XOR	XNOR
Symbol								
Truth Table	In: A; Out 0 0 1 1	In: A; Out 0 1 1 0	In: A B; Out 0 0 0 0 1 0 1 0 0 1 1 1	In: A B; Out 0 0 0 0 1 1 1 0 1 1 1 1	In: A B; Out 0 0 1 0 1 1 1 0 1 1 1 0	In: A B; Out 0 0 1 0 1 0 1 0 0 1 1 0	In: A B; Out 0 0 0 0 1 1 1 0 1 1 1 0	In: A B; Out 0 0 1 0 1 0 1 0 0 1 1 1
Logic	Output follows input	Output reverse of input	Output is 1 only when both inputs are 1	Output is 1 when any input is 1	Output is 0 only when both inputs are 1	Output is 0 when any input is 1	Output is 1 when inputs are not the same values	Output is 1 when inputs have the same values

Figure 1. Classical single- and two-bit logic gates.

A qubit is a quantum generalization of a bit—a quantum mechanical two-level system. Like a classical bit, a measurement of a qubit will result in one of two distinct states, known as basis states, which must be mutually orthogonal. That is, they must be non-overlapping and perfectly distinguishable; however rather than necessarily existing in one state or the other, a qubit can exist in a linear combination of both of these states at the same time. This property is known as superposition. To put it more formally, a qubit is a vector in a two-dimensional (2D) complex vector (Hilbert) space, which exists as a linear superposition of its basis states, expressed as

$$|\psi\rangle = a|0\rangle + b|1\rangle,$$

where a and b are probability amplitudes, which can be complex numbers. Furthermore, a and b are constrained by the following equation, which simply assures us that the total probability of all possible outcomes must be 1,

$$|a|^2 + |b|^2 = 1,$$

however, a measurement upon the state forces the qubit into one of its basis states. Thus, like a classical bit, the result of a measurement of this qubit can only give two possible answers, 0 or 1.

A more general mathematical expression of a quantum state is the density matrix $\rho = |\psi\rangle\langle\psi|$, which for the single qubit state as described above is

$$\rho = (a|0\rangle + b|1\rangle) \otimes (a^*\langle 0| + b^*\langle 1|) = \begin{bmatrix} a \\ b \end{bmatrix} \otimes \begin{bmatrix} a^* & b^* \end{bmatrix} = \begin{bmatrix} aa^* & ab^* \\ ba^* & bb^* \end{bmatrix}.$$

This is a useful representation when considering system sizes larger than a single qubit, as well as how operators act upon the state.

A qubit can be visualized as a unit vector on a unit sphere, known as the Bloch sphere, shown in Figure 2. The surface of the sphere represents the space of all possible qubit states, and thus, all possible superpositions of the qubit's two basis states. In this way one can see that the states of a classical bit are simply special cases of the qubit where $|0\rangle$ or $|1\rangle$ is assured. The surface of the sphere is parameterized by the angles θ and φ, and the vector of any single qubit state can correspondingly be written as $\cos(\theta/2)\,|0\rangle + e^{i\varphi}\sin(\theta/2)\,|1\rangle$.

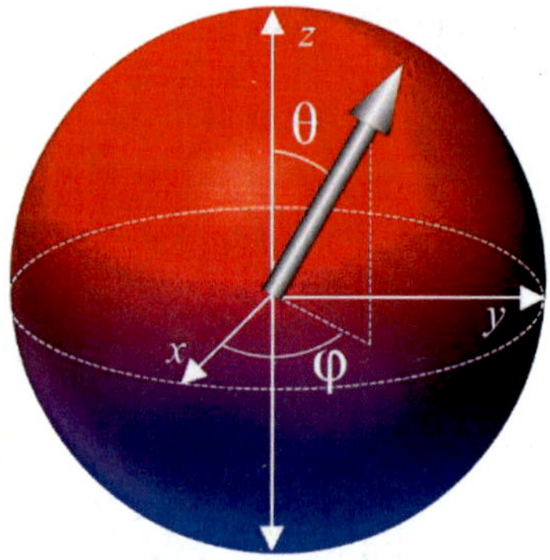

$$|\psi\rangle = a|0\rangle + b|1\rangle$$

Figure 2. The surface of the Bloch sphere provides a geometrical visualization of the state space of a quantum mechanical two-level system, wherein the state vector $|\psi\rangle$ responds to a linear superposition of the mutually orthogonal basis state vectors $|0\rangle$ and $|1\rangle$, aligned along the north and south poles of the sphere, respectively.

The Bloch sphere may be generalized to depict the state vector of an entangled system of multiple qubits. In other words, a version of the Bloch sphere may be used to show the state vector of a multi-qubit register, and its associated rotations in accordance with quantum gate operations.

There are a series of operations that can be done on a single qubit, which are easily visualized on the Bloch sphere. For example, rotating about an axis by 90° is called a $\pi/2$ rotation, and by 180° is called a π rotation. If one were to start with a state beginning in $|0\rangle$ and apply a $\pi/2$ rotation around the x-axis, the resulting state would be on the equator of the Bloch sphere and therefore an equal superposition of $|0\rangle$ and $|1\rangle$. The specific angle φ in the x-y plane of the resulting state is known as the *phase* of the superposition. More generally, phase describes the relationship between each basis state that comprises the resulting quantum state. For this example, one can see that phase φ enters the mathematical expression for a state created on the equator of this Bloch sphere as $|0\rangle + e^{i\varphi}|1\rangle$. Any arbitrary single-qubit state can be prepared on the sphere using a series of rotations. The ability to create a desired state is quantified using *fidelity*, which is mathematically expressed as the overlap between the prepared state $|\psi\rangle$ and the desired state $|\psi'\rangle$: $|\langle\psi'|\psi\rangle|^2$. The concept of fidelity is applied to states of more than one qubit as well, with the same general mathematical definition.

Entanglement of Multiple Qubits

In the same manner that a single classical bit is of little use on its own, any useful quantum computation will necessitate more than one qubit; that is, a register of qubits will be required. Indeed, it is when multiple qubits interact with one another, forming multi-qubit states, that the computational power inherent to quantum computing becomes apparent (i.e., in the form of information density).

A register of two classical bits together can exist in one of four possible states: 00, 01, 10, or 11. The quantum register of two qubits can be described by a composite state composed of the (tensor) product of those two qubits. While this composite state of two qubits can similarly exist in each of those same four states as their classical counterpart, it can simultaneously exist in a superposition of all four states. This is formally written as,

$$|\psi\rangle = \alpha_{00}|00\rangle + \alpha_{01}|01\rangle + \alpha_{10}|10\rangle + \alpha_{11}|11\rangle,$$

whereas the individual qubit had two computational basis states, and the 2-qubit register has four computational basis states. The 3-qubit register can be in one of eight possible states, but it can also exist in a superposition of its eight basis states.

$$|\psi\rangle = \alpha_{000}|000\rangle + \alpha_{001}|001\rangle + \alpha_{010}|010\rangle + \alpha_{100}|100\rangle + \alpha_{011}|011\rangle + \alpha_{101}|101\rangle + \alpha_{110}|110\rangle + \alpha_{111}|111\rangle,$$

which may be generalized as,

$$\sum_{ij\cdots N\in\{0,1\}} \alpha_{ij\cdots N}|ij\cdots N\rangle.$$

When extrapolating, one finds that an n-qubit register can exist in a superposition of 2^n possible states. A superposition is something very different from a statistical mixture. A statistical mixture, for example, is when the system is in one particular state of an n-state system, but one simply does not know definitively which state it is in. In this context, probabilities would enter the equation because of insufficient information. The ability of a qubit register to exist in a combination of all possible states at the same time, at least in an ideal scenario, reflects its enormous computational power. This is related to a classical computer that will have to process each possible state independently, sequentially, one at a time, even if it is capable of doing so at a rate of a few billion times per second. A quantum computer can act upon the superposition state. This means that a quantum computer can execute certain operations with the superposition of many possible states at once. While this explanation oversimplifies the mechanism of the quantum computation, it gives an intuition as to the origin of some of the speedups that can be found using quantum computers due to the exponential scaling of the available state-space. For example, an ideal 30-qubit state could represent more than a trillion states that may be operated on at once, containing an amount of computation power greater than the most powerful supercomputer.

A practical difficulty arises because the larger the superposition state, the more fragile the state becomes. A register of qubits that exists in a particular superposition state will remain in that state for only a finite amount of time due to unwanted interactions between the quantum system and the environment, after which it loses coherence and the information it contained is lost. This process that destroys the superposition as it causes the phase information to be lost is called decoherence. Once it falls out of this delicate superposition, the quantum register is forced to take on one of the 2^n possible classical values, just like a single qubit, when measured, takes on a 0 or 1 value. Put another way, decoherence takes a quantum superposition and turns it into a statistical mixture.

One way to deal with decoherence is to develop what is known as quantum error correction, which is a way of recognizing when errors occur and correcting for them in some way. Given that no real quantum computing system is expected to be capable of operating entirely free of errors, it is only with an effective error correcting scheme that the rate of logical errors may be suppressed to a sufficiently low threshold such that fault-tolerant quantum computing may be realized. There are well-developed methods in classical computation to correct errors, generally relying on having many exact copies of a bit and detecting a bit-flip error through some form of majority rule. These types of error correcting methods cannot be one-to-one implemented in a quantum system, however, due to the no-cloning theorem in quantum mechanics, which specifies that an identical copy of an arbitrary quantum state cannot be created without destroying the original state. Therefore, specially designed quantum error correcting schemes have been developed in recent years and continue to be the focus of ongoing research in the field. In implementing quantum error correction, some form of redundancy is also usually required. This is typically implemented by using a group of physical qubits to define one logical qubit, where the two states used to define thc logical $|0\rangle_L$ and $|1\rangle_L$ are two orthogonal multi-qubit states, and wherein the multi-qubit states used to encode the quantum information are particularly chosen to be topologically protected or stabilizable through multi-qubit measurements not in the qubit basis. Another method typically included in this redundancy is the use of additional ancillary qubits entangled with the ones used for computation, where they are only used to flag errors through measuring (and thus destroying) their quantum state while keeping the computational qubit's state intact. This may mean that in order to achieve fault-tolerant quantum computation, a calculation that initially needed 10 qubits now needs 30 or 50 qubits.

In addition to superposition and decoherence, the premise of entanglement is another inherent quantum property relevant to the data used for quantum information processing that is often non-intuitive.

As noted above, two independent qubit states, $|\psi_1\rangle$ and $|\psi_2\rangle$, can be taken together and viewed as one composite state, written as the tensor product of the two respective wavefunctions. Conversely, if any composite state of two qubits can be written as the product of two qubits, then those qubits are what is known as *separable*. If the composite state cannot be described as the product of two states, then by definition those two qubits are *entangled*, and the composite wavefunction describes an entangled state. An entangled state of two particles, for example, indicates an inter-dependance of the particles on one another. A remarkable characteristic of entangled particles is that this inter-dependence will persist across any distance, in principle.

The state $|00\rangle + |11\rangle$ is an example of a quantum state that cannot be described in terms of the state of each of its components (qubits) separately. In other words, we cannot find a_1, a_2, b_1, b_2 such that

$(a_1|0\rangle + b_1|1\rangle)\otimes(a_2|0\rangle + b_2|1\rangle) = |00\rangle + |11\rangle$, since this would require

$(a_1|0\rangle + b_1|1\rangle) \otimes (a_2|0\rangle + b_2|1\rangle) = a_1a_2|00\rangle + a_1b_2|01\rangle + b_1a_2|10\rangle + b_1b_2|11\rangle$, wherein $a_1b_2 = 0$ and $b_1a_2 = 0$, but this would imply that either $a_1a_2 = 0$, or $b_1b_2 = 0$.

States that cannot be decomposed in this way are called entangled states. These states represent situations that have no classical counterpart.

So, whereas a classical system may be entirely described by the sum of its parts if the individual parts are themselves completely defined, an entangled quantum state is essentially more definite than the sum of its parts. In attempting to describe a part of the whole, necessarily some information will be lost. For instance, given the entangled joint system AB, tracing out B to obtain the state of A (i.e., applying a partial trace over B to the density matrix representation of the initial state), the resulting state is a statistical combination of the basis states with no preserved information about the entanglement in either the phase or amplitude. A partial trace is a matrix operation that reduces the vector space solely onto the basis vectors of the A subsystem. Thus, even with complete knowledge of the joint system AB, the remaining information, when trying to describe just A, may be highly uncertain.

Computing with Multiple Qubits

The computation may be performed with a register of qubits into which information may be encoded. There are a few different models of quantum computation, but the most prevalent one is the gate model (also known the circuit model) of quantum computing.

There are three essential steps of the gate model, shown in Figure 3. To begin, the system of qubits is prepared into a well-defined initial state $|\psi_i\rangle$, for instance in the state $|0 \cdots 00\rangle$. Next, the initial state $|\psi_i\rangle$ is manipulated via a sequence of unitary transformations leading to the final state $|\psi_f\rangle$. Again, unitary transformations simply mean we must take care to maintain that the sum of all probabilities always adds to 1. Such transformations may constitute quantum logic gates for the quantum system, for the same purpose that Boolean logic gates operate upon classical bits of data, as discussed above in reference to Figure 1. Finally, a measurement is performed upon the state $|\psi_f\rangle$.

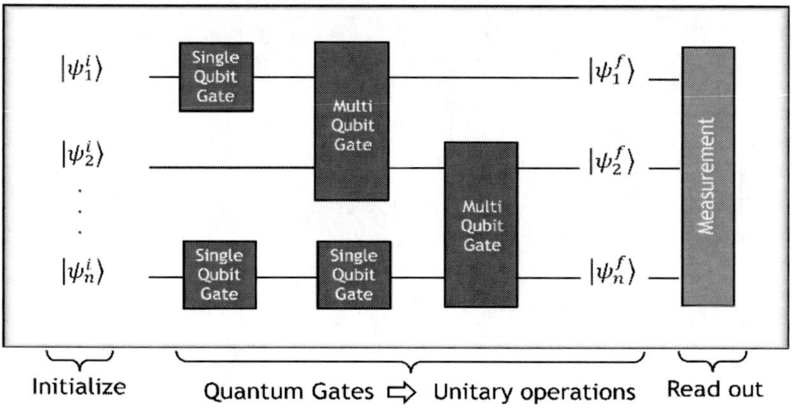

Figure 3. Three essential steps required for a computation in the gate model include initializations of the superposition state, transformation with a sequence of quantum logic gates, and read out of the final state.

All quantum gate operations are represented as matrices. They effectively represent physical rotations of the qubit around the Bloch sphere. The action of the quantum gate is found by multiplying the vector representing the quantum state by the matrix representing the gate. Figure 4 shows a list of common single-qubit gates and Figure 5 shows a couple of common two-qubit gates.

Gate	Identity	X / NOT	Y	Z	Phase	Hadamard
Symbol	I	X / ⊕	Y	Z	P	H
Matrix	$=\begin{pmatrix}1 & 0\\0 & 1\end{pmatrix}$	$=\begin{pmatrix}0 & 1\\1 & 0\end{pmatrix}$	$=\begin{pmatrix}0 & -i\\i & 0\end{pmatrix}$	$=\begin{pmatrix}1 & 0\\0 & -1\end{pmatrix}$	$=\begin{pmatrix}1 & 0\\0 & e^{i\theta}\end{pmatrix}$	$=\frac{1}{\sqrt{2}}\begin{pmatrix}1 & 1\\1 & -1\end{pmatrix}$
Truth Table	In / Out: $\|0\rangle$ → $\|0\rangle$; $\|1\rangle$ → $\|1\rangle$	In / Out: $\|0\rangle$ → $\|1\rangle$; $\|1\rangle$ → $\|0\rangle$	In / Out: $\|0\rangle$ → $i\|1\rangle$; $\|1\rangle$ → $-i\|0\rangle$	In / Out: $\|0\rangle$ → $\|0\rangle$; $\|1\rangle$ → $-\|1\rangle$	In / Out: $\|0\rangle$ → $\|0\rangle$; $\|1\rangle$ → $e^{i\theta}\|1\rangle$	In / Out: $\|0\rangle$ → $\frac{\|0\rangle+\|1\rangle}{\sqrt{2}}$; $\|1\rangle$ → $\frac{\|0\rangle-\|1\rangle}{\sqrt{2}}$
Bloch Sphere Rotation	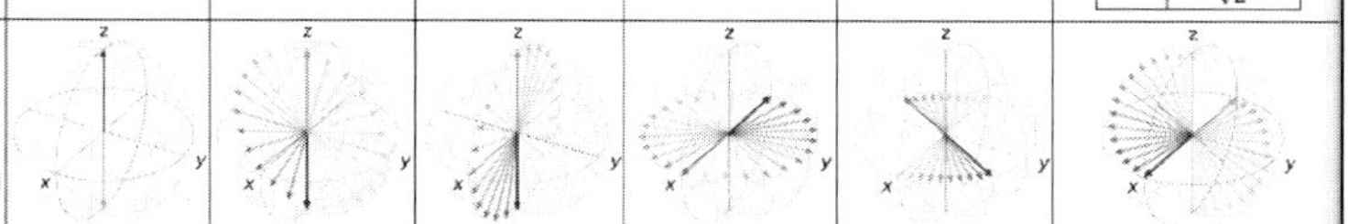					
Logic	No rotation to qubit state	Rotates qubit state 180° about x-axis	Rotates qubit state 180° about y-axis	Rotates qubit state 180° about z-axis	Rotates qubit state θ° about z-axis	Rotates qubit state 180° about an axis diagonal in the xz-plane

Figure 4. Quantum single-bit logic gates.

Gate	Controlled NOT (CNOT)	Controlled Phase (Cphase)
Symbol	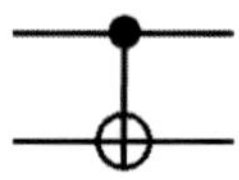	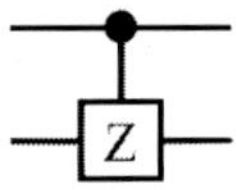
Matrix	$= \begin{pmatrix} 1 & 0 & 0 & 0 \\ 0 & 1 & 0 & 0 \\ 0 & 0 & 1 & 1 \\ 0 & 0 & 1 & 0 \end{pmatrix}$	$= \begin{pmatrix} 1 & 0 & 0 & 0 \\ 0 & 1 & 0 & 0 \\ 0 & 0 & 1 & 0 \\ 0 & 0 & 0 & -1 \end{pmatrix}$
Truth Table	In | Out $\lvert 00\rangle$ | $\lvert 00\rangle$ $\lvert 01\rangle$ | $\lvert 01\rangle$ $\lvert 10\rangle$ | $\lvert 11\rangle$ $\lvert 11\rangle$ | $\lvert 10\rangle$	In | Out $\lvert 00\rangle$ | $\lvert 00\rangle$ $\lvert 01\rangle$ | $\lvert 01\rangle$ $\lvert 10\rangle$ | $\lvert 10\rangle$ $\lvert 11\rangle$ | $-\lvert 11\rangle$
Logic	Applies X-gate to target (2nd) qubit state – i.e., rotates 180° about x-axis – if control (1st) qubit state is $\lvert 1\rangle$	Applies Z-gate to target (2nd) qubit state – i.e., rotates 180° about z-axis – if control (1st) qubit state is $\lvert 1\rangle$

Figure 5. Quantum two-bit logic gates.

A limited number of quantum gate types are required for universal quantum computation. That is, if you have access to at least a certain set of gates, you can do any possible computation. A quantum state, representing a superposition of qubits, which is processed by a gate, evolves according to the Schrödinger equation for finite length of time. In this manner, one gate can act upon the entire set states in one clock cycle. Since the number of basis states grows as 2^n, the gate can thus act upon 2^n basis states in one clock cycle.

Fidelity of individual qubit states was introduced above (i.e., initializing one or more qubits into a particular state), but more generally, fidelity is a figure of merit that serves as a mathematically useful means of measuring the "distance" between two probability distributions [7] or the overlap of two quantum states. The concept of fidelity is also applicable to quantum gates and is a measure of a quantum gate's ability to perform operations on qubits free from error. A high fidelity is essential for creating qubit gates that are operable to process information with a sufficiently low error rate, such that when a series of quantum gates are applied to complete a quantum circuit, the output of the circuit is considered meaningful. The goal is that the fidelity tends toward 1. Maintaining such high fidelities in some systems, however, may require periodic recalibrations [8], and ultimately, the minimum quantum gate fidelity required for meaningful quantum information processing applications will depend strongly on a number of factors including the quantum error correction scheme employed.

Ideal quantum computation in the gate model is reversible for operations performed with a fidelity of 1. One could put the answer of a computation into an algorithm and operate backwards to extract the initial state since logic gates are unitary transformations that preserve the total probability of the state's outcomes. Additionally, the no-cloning theorem states that identical copies of quantum information cannot be created without destroying the original state. In other words, the information contained in a quantum state cannot be copied and then distributed from a node to represent the same information at different nodes, except perhaps in an approximate form. Consider that in order to make a copy of a state, the information contained in said state would need to read out, and doing so would necessarily collapse the state's wavefunction thereby destroying the superposition.

Algorithms have been developed that may offer an advantage or speedup over classical approaches. That is, representing a system of information in a quantum state and subjecting it to a defined sequence of logical operations, the solution may be achieved in number of steps that are less than the number required if the information were represented by a classical system using traditional Boolean logic gates.

Grover's algorithm, developed by Lov Grover at Bell Laboratories in 1996 [9], searches an unsorted database. Take the example of searching for a phone number in a telephone book. A classical computer would solve this problem of finding the name that corresponds to a given phone number by checking each name and phone number pair sequentially, one at a time. If the number of names in your phone book is N, then on average a computer would have to search through half of the names ($N/2$) before hitting upon the right answer.

Grover's algorithm involves starting with an initial state comprising a superposition of all possible solutions in your database. One then uses what is referred to as an Oracle function to act upon this superposition of all answers. An Oracle function is a kind of black box or subroutine of gates that makes a decision or solves a problem and outputs an answer in one execution of its logic. In the case of Grover's algorithm, the Oracle function tags the correct answer with a negative sign and performs what is known as amplitude amplification. It reduces the probability amplitude of all the wrong answers (i.e., answers that were *not* tagged), and increases the amplitude of the correct, tagged solution. Repeating this routine increases the likelihood of finding the correct solution. The subroutine must be repeated a number of times proportional to $\sqrt{N}$ to find the solution. This is a substantial speedup compared to $N/2$ if N is a very large number. For example, if an algorithm were implemented to search a database of one trillion items, the theoretical speedup offered by Grover's algorithm could be the difference between months of work on a classical computer versus seconds on a quantum computer.

Yet, Grover's algorithm provides at most a quadratic speedup and not an exponential speedup. Shor's algorithm also developed at Bell Laboratories, does in fact deliver a truly exponential speedup—in the case of an ideal implementation—with the use of a quantum Fourier transform algorithm [10]. Shor's algorithm is designed to determine the prime factors of a number in an amount of time that is exponentially fast than the best classical solution. Here, the length of time is assumed to be proportional to the number of computing steps required to perform a calculation. Interest in this algorithm was driven in part by its applicability to data encryption. Common forms of encryption rely upon knowing the prime factors of a very large number. A prime factor is a number that is only divisible by itself and 1. It is trivial to multiply two such numbers together; however, when starting with a very large number, finding its prime factors is empirically hard.

Currently there are a large variety of quantum algorithms (e.g., algorithms for solving systems of linear equations and network flow problems) that have been developed with a host of applications—besides data encryption and database searching [11]. Many of these appear to pertain to abstract mathematical problems, but the theoretical conception of several such algorithms has been shown to be applicable to problems related to topics including machine learning, economic modeling, materials simulation and discovery, image processing, and climate modeling. These topics all include the need to solve problems that quickly become intractable with classical computers due to the exponential growth of resources required.

For example, machine-learning tasks frequently involve problems of handling, manipulating, and classifying large datasets comprising large numbers of vectors in high-dimensional tensor product spaces. Classical algorithms for solving such problems typically take a length of time polynomial in the number of vectors and the dimension of the space. Quantum algorithms for solving systems of linear equations offer a clear advantage over classical approaches.

Algorithms discussed in the sections above may offer a speedup in terms of the number of computational steps required to solve a given problem. Before any such algorithm can be implemented, however, qubits must first be fabricated that are capable of satisfying the stringent physical requirements that would make them suitable for quantum information processing applications, as discussed below. Furthermore, as discussed in the following subsection, a computer that is capable of solving more than one problem must include the capability of receiving instructions for implementing an algorithm.

Physical Qubit Implementations

There have been numerous proposals for what may be used to physically represent the quantum mechanical two-level system that is a qubit. Today there are several means by which scientists and engineers have attempted to fabricate one or more qubits. For as many types that have been realized in the laboratory environment, there have been even more proposed but never fabricated. Laboratory-fabricated qubits include those based on the polarization of single photons, spin or charge of electrostatically defined quantum dots (QD) in semiconductor materials, trapped atoms, and properties of a superconducting circuit (SC), which all have been the subject of extensive research and experimental undertakings. These studies have focused on ensuring the viability of the underlying qubit structure, and in doing so, answering essential questions such as: Can two quantum mechanical levels be accessed and easily delineated? Can a single qubit be manipulated (e.g., via qubit rotations)? Can a qubit be initialized and read out with sufficiently high fidelity? Can a qubit state be sufficiently insulated from its environment such that it may be protected from decoherence? Can a qubit be coupled with other effectively identical qubits to create an entangled state? Can all of these actions be performed on a time scale that allows for useful quantum information processing applications?

Among the multitude of different qubit manifestations that have received substantial attention and been the subject of numerous experimental investigations, a selected few are described below. Each of these is imbued with a variety of physical characteristics specific to the representation leading to certain advantages and disadvantages that may make them more or less alluring as a template upon which to build future quantum computing devices.

Qubit Type 1: Neutral Atoms

A somewhat intuitive example is using two energy levels within an atom to represent the two states of a qubit since the orthogonality of atomic orbitals and states within are well-studied. One specific implementation uses electrically-neutral atoms. A cloud of a single type of atom can be isolated from the environment using a vacuum chamber, where all other matter is extracted from inside the chamber and the atom of choice is specifically injected. Once inside, the atoms can be cooled and localized using magnetic fields and laser beams. From this cloud, individual atoms can be singled out and used as individual qubits. In one variation of this approach, an optical lattice of trapped neutral atoms can be formed by the interference of counter-propagating laser beams, thereby creating a spatially periodic pattern with one atom sitting at each lattice-site. Another approach can be selectively trapping single atoms at the center of tightly-focused beams of light known as optical tweezers [12]. Two hyperfine energy levels of the atom are typically chosen as the qubit basis states. Rotations of the qubit can be applied by addressing the individual neutral atoms with microwaves and specifically polarized laser beams, where a rotation is typically achieved by programming a timed pulse of either. The state of the atomic qubit can be determined by laser-excitation and the collection of scattered photons from the atom.

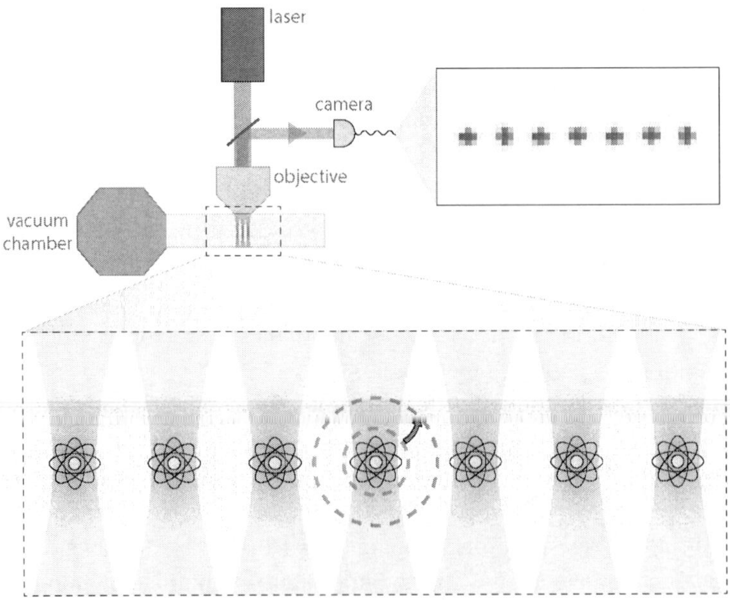

Figure 6. Illustration of an exemplary qubit implementation for neutral atoms using optical tweezers. The atoms are cooled, trapped, and imaged using laser light. Two atomic states, typically hyperfine levels in the ground state, are used to encode the qubit. Qubit rotations between the two states can also be achieved with laser light or microwaves.

Individual trapped atoms in ultra-high vacuums are well-isolated from the environment, can exhibit long quantum information storage times, and have some of the largest quantum system sizes reaching 1,000 individual trapped qubits [13]. Neutral atom platforms, however, are limited in single- and two-qubit gate fidelities as compared to other existing systems in their current implementation [14, 15].

Qubit Type 2: Ion Traps

An alternative approach is trapping electrically-charged atomic ions, wherein a qubit is represented by two stable electronic levels within each ion. Lasers are used to initially cool and ionize atoms in an ultra-high vacuum setting, while an ion is trapped through a combination of direct current (DC) and radiofrequency (RF) electric fields [16, 17]. More specifically, DC voltages are used to produce static fields that are utilized to confine an ion in a particular direction, and RF voltages are used to create the trapping potential well. The earliest version of this concept was the quadrupole ion trap, also known as the Paul trap, which created a potential minimum in up to three dimensions to confine the atoms in space. The conception and demonstration of this premise earned Wolfgang Paul and Hans Georg Dehmelt the 1989 Nobel Prize in physics. Microfabrication techniques and new methodologies have enabled the realization of so-called trap-on-chip devices—ion trap systems with smaller feature sizes and enhanced reproducibility compared to their bulkier and less practical predecessors.

While trapped ions have access to high-fidelity, single- and two-qubit gates as well as long quantum information storage times, constraints on the scalability of trapped ion qubits have limited the advancement of these devices as viable qubits for realistic quantum computing applications in their current implementation.

Qubit Type 3: Quantum Dots

Semiconductor QDs represent another manifestation of physical qubits, corresponding to variety of different QD qubits based on different materials and physical formation mechanisms. In one form, a semiconductor qubit may be created with naturally confined quantum dots based on donor or acceptor spins in silicon. For example, an implanted phosphorus atom (^{31}P) in silicon possesses a weakly bound electron and exhibits characteristics analogous to a hydrogen atom. A prominent version of QD qubits discussed in greater detail below is that of electrostatically-defined QDs formed in semiconducting materials.

Semiconductor heterostructures, comprising multiple layers of different semiconductor materials grown by molecular beam epitaxy or chemical vapor deposition, such as gallium arsenide/aluminum gallium arsenide (GaAs/AlGaAs) and silicon/silicon-germanium (Si/SiGe), enable the formation of a 2-D electron gas (2DEG) comprising a plane of electrons confined at a specific distance below the top surface at the interface between two particular material layers. The 2DEG can be shaped and divided via the application of voltages to capacitively-coupled gate electrodes lithographically patterned on the surface, which are capable of further confining small islands of the 2DEG, each of which corresponds to a QD into which individual electrons can be added or removed.

In one manifestation, the basis states of a two-level system can be encoded in the electron's charge degree of freedom. For instance, "a single electron trapped in a pair of adjacent quantum dots can encode a charge-based qubit. The two basis states correspond to the electron sitting either on the left or on the right quantum dot" [18]. A simple depiction of this is shown in Figure 7.

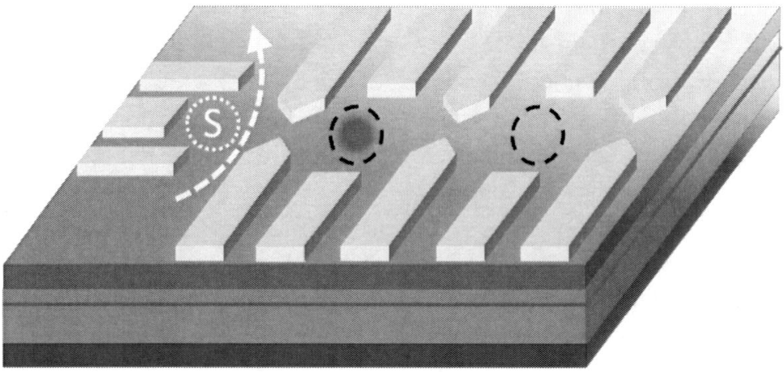

Figure 7. A double QD system formed by the collection of metallic electrodes atop the stack of semiconductor material, which are used to define two small regions in the underlying 2DEG. Here, the presence of a charge carrier in the left or right QD may be used to encode the two basis states of a qubit. In the figure, a charge is present in the left dot and absent in the right dot. The measurement of current moving along the dashed white line is used to monitor the charge state of the double QD system with the use of an adjacent charge sensor.

Alternatively, the basis states of a two-level system can be encoded in the electron's spin degree of freedom. For example, a single electron trapped in a single QD may be spin up or spin down. The application of a magnetic field leads to what is known as Zeeman splitting of the up and down spin electron energy levels. In this case, the two basis states correspond to the single electron having an up spin, and residing in the higher energy level, or having a down spin and residing in the lower energy level.

Quantum mechanical tunneling of electrons into, out of, and between dots is conditional upon the quantum properties (e.g., Pauli exclusion principle), and this conditional tunneling has led, in part, to the exploration of several different spin-based qubit encoding schemes. One of the more successful approaches has been singlet-triplet qubits, in which the basis states of the two-level system are encoded by a two-electron spin state of a double QD system [18].

The singlet state corresponds to two spin-½ electrons of opposite spin occupying the same energy level. The triplet state corresponds to one of three possible configurations: two spin-½ electrons of the same spin (both spin up or both spin down) occupying two different energy levels; or two spin-½ electrons of opposite spin occupying different energy levels. In Figure 7, two qubits are configured such that together they are capable of occupying either a singlet state or the latter triplet state. This subspace of qubit states is used in part because these states are insensitive to uniform (i.e., global) magnetic-field fluctuations [19].

Spin-based qubits with three or four electron spin states, multi-dot spin qubits, and spin-charge qubits are yet other types of QD qubit encoding schemes that have been tested [20]. The primary read out method for all QD qubit encoding types is via spin to charge conversion. Single electron transistors integrated into the qubit system may operate as charge sensors for detecting signals corresponding to the displacement of one or more charges, either between dots or between a dot and an electron reservoir.

Each QD encoding scheme requires its own mechanism for coherent rotations of state about the Bloch sphere and for entanglement. Rotations of the state about the Bloch sphere are achieved via several mechanisms such as the application of a magnetic-field gradient between the dots, often from coplanar strip lines near the QDs, or the application of fast gate voltage pulses for generating pulsed DC electric fields, or the use microwave pulses.

Since confinement of the QDs is achieved via application of gate voltages, often requiring several gates for each QD, the sheer number of control wires required to operate a chip consisting of tens or hundreds of QD qubits presents a practical (although not insurmountable) challenge to advancing this particular qubit implementation due to the introduction of electrical noise and thermal fluctuations.

Improvements to some of the key metrics of semiconductor QD qubits have been observed in devices comprising analogous structures and function but fabricated with different material environments. For example, QD qubits in Si/SiGe exhibit longer dephasing times than GaAs/AlGaAs, and silicon/silicon dioxide (Si/SiO_2) structures have been used to successfully demonstrate a high degree of two-qubit gate fidelity, toward the possibility of fault tolerance [20, 21]. Improvements of qubit state coherence times and fidelity of state rotations will be beneficial to moving this platform forward.

Qubit Type 4: Photons

Single particles of light (i.e., photons) can also be used as a qubit. The typical qubit states chosen are two orthogonal polarization states such as horizontal and vertical polarization, or left and right circular polarization. This physical implementation benefits from the availability of this type of qubit since photons of a single wavelength are easily producible using a laser. The production of entangled photon pairs can also be achieved using a well-known nonlinear process called spontaneous parametric down conversion, where a single photon of high energy can be converted into two photons of lower energy. The process is typically achieved through shining a laser of short wavelength on a specific crystalline material to produce two photons of longer wavelength, but this has an overall low efficiency. The two resulting photons are entangled with each other, and depending on the type of material used, they can either exit the process with the same or opposite polarizations.

Single-qubit rotations can be achieved using linear optical elements such as waveplates, which are a thin plate of dielectric material that can rotate the polarization of light in a defined manner. Other quantum operations can be achieved through the use of beamsplitters, which have two input ports and two output ports and are used to overlap photons and perform parity measurements. Two-qubit operations, however, are difficult to achieve on photonic qubits given the natural inability for photons to interact with each other. Therefore, a nonlinear photonic medium must be used to achieve this interaction. Active research is being performed to create more efficient photonic interactions.

The proposed mode of operation for photonic quantum computing is primarily measurement based due to the difficulty of performing two-qubit gates on a photon pair, which is an operation that would likely need to be repeated many times in a typical computation in the gate model. In a measurement-based quantum computation paradigm, the desired computation is achieved through a series of measurements performed on an initial entangled state (called a resource state) that must only be generated once, as opposed to a programmable series of single- and two-qubit gate operations performed on an initial state that is not entangled.

The current limitations for this quantum computing platform are the inherent losses associated with each optical element used. The more quantum operations necessary for achieving the solution to an algorithm, the less likely it is to have the necessary number of qubits at the end of the calculation. This, along with the low efficiency of generating entangled photon pairs, creating initial entangled resource states, and achieving photonic interactions, constitute the primary targets of ongoing research, with effort being placed on creating low-loss optics, more efficient platforms for photonic interaction, designing on-chip optics equipped with more functionality in a smaller area, and investigating more efficient generation of entangled photons.

Qubit Type 5: Superconducting Circuits

SC qubits have been utilized to fabricate systems of many interacting qubits. Most types of qubits that are among those in realistic contention for broad adoption are based on some microscopic degree of freedom, like the spin of an electron or the excited state of an atom. In contrast, SC qubits are based on a macroscopic quantum property.

SC qubits are resonant circuits constructed primarily of superconducting material; and assuming that these circuits are operated at temperatures below the critical temperature of their constituent superconducting material, they are non-dissipative. The simplest version of such a circuit would consist of an inductor and a capacitor forming a quantum harmonic oscillator with a parabolic potential. This potential energy well has many energy levels, but the two lowest energy levels may be utilized as the $|0\rangle$ and $|1\rangle$ qubit states. A basic requirement for such qubits is that the energy levels are not uniformly spaced. This is known as anharmonicity. Without this property, a photon that excites the system from the $|0\rangle$ to $|1\rangle$ state could also excite the system to another higher state, referred to as a higher harmonic. In order to create this anharmonicity and address only the transition from the $|0\rangle$ to the $|1\rangle$ state, some non-linear element must be introduced. The requisite anharmonicity is introduced with one or more Josephson Junctions, each of which corresponds to a circuit component comprising a thin layer of insulating material between two superconducting layers, in which electrons quantum mechanically tunnel through the insulating material.

Superconducting qubits come in a few distinct varieties, primarily in three basic formats—charge, flux, and phase—each of which has a particular circuit structure. Charge, flux, and phase each correspond to a physical parameter of the respective system that is used as a knob for tuning the circuit's potential energy to manipulate the system between the two basis levels of the anharmonic oscillator. For example, in the case of an SC charge qubit, the voltage-controlled presence or absence of excess Cooper pairs (electrons that pair together in the superconducting state of matter) in a defined segment of each superconducting circuit is used to manipulate the energy level of the system. In this manner, the computational basis states of the system correspond to the charge states of the circuit. Alternatively, the computational basis states of the flux-qubit correspond to the direction of circulating currents that can flow either clockwise or counter-clockwise and may be manipulated with the application of magnetic fields. Lastly, for the phase-qubit, the difference in the complex phase across the opposing superconducting electrodes of a Josephson Junction is manipulated by controlling the current through the circuit and is used to define the two basis states of the system.

Some of the most significant practical gains in commercial applications have been realized with approaches based on systems employing SC qubits [22]. For example, companies such as Google and IBM have developed their own SC qubit platforms [23, 24] often in collaboration with academic research groups. The top image of Figure 8 shows a microchip from the research group of John Martinis at the University of California, Santa Barbara, which includes four superconducting qubits, each of which is coupled to what was described as a central "memory resonator." Variations on such qubits were used as part of the milestone demonstration of quantum supremacy, which was performed on Google's Sycamore chip with 53 SC qubits (*see* bottom image of Figure 8)—a platform on which there continues to be significant scientific advances [25-27].

Figure 8. Top: Photograph of a microchip containing a resonator coupled to four surrounding SC qubits;[4] bottom: Google's Sycamore chip.[5]

All qubit manifestations have advantages and disadvantages, accounting for factors such as ease of fabrication, scalability, and decoherence time. SC qubits are not known to be particularly advantageous in terms of decoherence times and susceptibility to environmental noise. Further, unlike qubits formed from neutral atoms, ions, and photons, SC qubits have the disadvantage that they cannot be fabricated with properties that are perfectly identical to one another. Nonetheless, they have garnered additional attention and use by virtue of some of their particular advantages. For instance, qubits of this variety are compatible with modern microfabrication processing technologies [28]. That

[4] LYagovy, iStock / Getty Images Plus.

[5] Google Sycamore Chip 002" by Google (https://www.youtube.com/channel/UCK8sQmJBp8GCxrOtXWBpyEA) is licensed under CC BY 3.0. To view a copy of this license, visit https://creativecommons.org/licenses/by/3.0/?ref=openverse.

is, they may be fabricated in large quantities with relative ease using widely available materials and well-known processing techniques. The circuit-based representation also allows for the engineering of several important qubit properties. In other words, through the skilled design of SC qubits with specifically selected circuit topologies and circuit component values, a number of important qubit properties may be controlled, including resonant frequency, anharmonicity, and noise tolerance, thereby enhancing favorable attributes and mitigating negative effects.

Software Architecture

Much of the focus on quantum computing over the decades prior to 2010 was directed to the physical implementation of manually optimized qubits, or on the theoretical side, primarily concerned with the mathematics that reveal possibilities of how, and for what purpose, this mode of computation may one day be applied. As organizations, companies, and research groups race to develop hardware, areas of research relating to quantum software development have also seen a great deal of progress in the last few years [6].

A universal quantum computer operating according to the gate model should be capable of solving more than one problem, and thus must include the capability of receiving instructions for implementing an algorithm. Such instructions would come in the form of software which is needed to connect to the hardware. Modern computer architectures are commonly defined in terms of their assorted levels of abstraction, which together constitute a "stack," extending from the user interface, programming language, and compilers all the way down to the lowest-level logic gate operations on the physical hardware itself [8]. Much like the mature architecture of classical computers, in which a programmer defines the application without interacting with lower stack levels within the operating system that drives the transistors, the design of quantum computing software must enable the programming, the compilation, and the execution of quantum programs on physical hardware and on simulators such that implementing algorithm instructions is abstracted away from direct manipulation of qubits [29]. To this end, quantum programming software will necessarily comprise a software stack given that multiple software components will be required to act in order to execute the desired algorithms on the target system.

At the highest level of the stack sits what is commonly referred to as a quantum programming language comprising the human-readable source code a person may write to provide the computer instructions for what to do with the sequence of logic and subroutines that are to be used for executing the desired algorithms [30]. A compiler is required to convert the human-readable source code into the type of quantum assembly language that can provide a quantum computer with specific instructions indicating the sequence of physical quantum gate operations to perform the appropriate logic, and the qubits upon which these gates will act. Quantum computing-based schedulers and optimizers are required to enable efficient use of resources between processes, reducing latency, and ensuring effective routing and data flow. Assemblers, compilers, and optimizer tools provided as part of these frameworks enable the mapping of an assembly representation to a hardware-specific gate set as well as mapping logical to physical connectivity. Furthermore, quantum error correction code is required to efficiently integrate the quantum algorithms together with imperfect hardware to enable fault tolerant operation. Additionally, a quantum computer will likely consist of both quantum and classical computing components, in which classical computers handle inputs/outputs—e.g., keyboards/peripherals, displays, and the like—and coordinate the qubit hardware, and quantum computing components are leveraged where appropriate to complete suitable categories of tasks that are solvable using an implementable quantum algorithm.

Such computing stacks have been considered by a number of publications [6, 8, 29-32]. For example, in the context of a heterogenous computing architecture that incorporates classical computing components in a quantum computing system, Fu et al. presents "a complete system stack describing the different layers when building a quantum computer" [31]. An adaptation of the simplified overview of Fu's quantum computer system stack is shown in Figure 9.

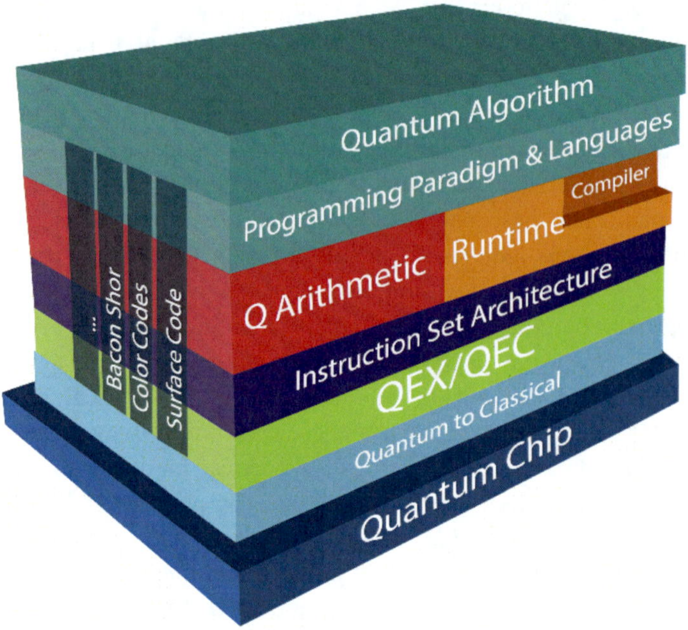

Figure 9. Adaptation of Figure 3 from Fu, et al. [31] showing an illustrative rendering of a high-level view of the quantum system stack.

The top layers of the stack described by Fu et al. [31] correspond to the algorithms for which the specific software, including languages and compilers, must be developed to ultimately exploit the bottom layer, comprising the actual qubits. The quantum compiler will perform quantum gate decomposition, reversible circuit design, and circuit mapping and functions to translate logical quantum operations to a series of physical instructions (e.g., initialization, measurements, and gate operations) [31] which belong to the Quantum Instruction Set Architecture (QISA), in accord with the choice of an error correction encoding scheme (represented by the third dimension in the figure). The quantum execution (QEX) block will then execute the physical quantum instructions that are generated by the preceding infrastructure, and it will do so in accord with the quantum error correction (QEC) layer, which is responsible for detecting and correcting errors. The quantum-classical interface, which is responsible for conversions between the analog qubit layer and the digital layers in the system stack above it, will apply the appropriate electrical signals to the quantum chip at the bottom of the stack in Figure 9 [31].

The challenges associated with addressing the various components of the stack were surveyed in the work of Gill et al. [6], in which a taxonomy of quantum computing research topics was put forward together with a detailed overview of QC hardware development, as well as quantum software tools and technologies that capture the current state-of-the-art in the respective areas. Considerations pertaining to multiple attributes of quantum software applications were discussed including quantum-based compilers, schedulers, and optimizers for both logical and physical levels, error correction firmware, and programming languages. Notably, Gill et al. [6] addressed the significance of challenges relating to the design of quantum programming languages, including their syntax, semantics, commuting operations, data types, and programming paradigms, as detailed in the comparative analysis of a previous work. More specifically, Sofge et al. [33] surveyed the history, methods, and proposed tools for quantum computing programming languages. In particular, they discuss delineating advancements between imperative programming languages in which a step-by-step procedure is specified to define how a program should be executed to achieve results, and functional (i.e., declarative) languages, in which conditions and desired results are specified that trigger the program to perform transformations that execute mappings from inputs to outputs. The quantum software tools and technologies in existence today are based predominantly on imperative programming languages; however, several different such languages are currently in use among them.

Häner, et al. [32] presented a software architecture for compiling quantum programs from a high-level language program to hardware-specific instructions. The compilation is described as a layered process for translating a quantum program written in an embedded domain-specific language (eDSL) down to hardware instructions. The use of the eDSL is intended "to maximally leverage existing classical infrastructure" [32]. The approach, however, is described as being generally applicable since the necessary layers of abstraction and the optimizing transformation are detailed for generating the successful compilation of any quantum algorithm for generic quantum hardware.

First a host language compiler/interpreter resolves the control statements of the classical code, performs initial optimizations, and dispatches quantum statements to library functions. A "High Level Compiler" further processes the code using information on the high-level structure of the program. For instance, library calls in this stage are replaced by their implementation where available. A "Low Level Compiler" further translates the code into quantum gate sequences, the structure of which is dependent upon both the hardware and the error correction approach. Häner et al. [32] then describes additional layers of the software stack disclosed therein, including layout generators and optimizers that map qubit variables to the underlying hardware. Figure 7 of Häner et al. [32] is reproduced below as Figure 10. For quantum error correction schemes involving both logical and physical qubits, Häner et al. [32] considers distinct layers of the stack that may be employed for mapping these respective qubit types. The last step of this process involves the mapping of physical gate operations to hardware control of the specific device (e.g., the application of a specific microwave pulse).

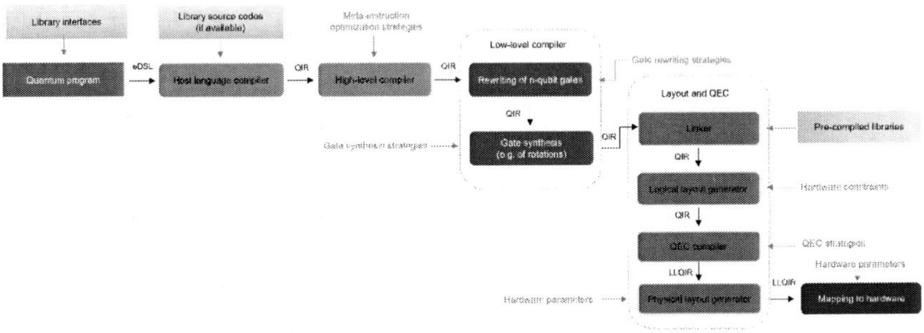

Figure 10. Adaptation of Figure 7 from Häner et al. [32] showing a flow diagram of the toolchain extending from the eDSL down to the physical mapping of hardware instructions.

Software Tools and Technologies

In order to advance a broader understanding of quantum computing and increase accessibility among computer engineers, and those generally outside the largely academic pursuit, there has been a greater development of open-source quantum computing tools that may allow users to design their own quantum algorithms. Indeed, there has been a proliferation of open-source software projects and tools for quantum computing processors and quantum simulators. In the context of existing software tools, quantum simulators are programs that run on classical computers and are able to mimic certain quantum properties of real particles without requiring the underlying qubits or associated hardware, thereby allowing one to test quantum programs in an environment that predicts how quantum systems of many qubits will react to specific operations. More specifically, a quantum simulator is a classical computer that provides the expected output from a quantum computer for a given input, but does so by classically solving the problem using conventional computing—i.e., a quantum simulator is limited to problems that can be practically solved using conventional computing, and the purpose of such simulators is to allow testing or experimentation in defining quantum operations and handling subsequent outputs to prepare for solving more complex, similar, problems on a quantum computer.

Online sources have compiled and curated lists of quantum computing development tools that are accessible to the general public, such as the 35 open source computing tools for 2022 listed by *The Quantum Insider* [34]. Published studies have systematically surveyed an array of available tools and software platforms [35]. For example, Gill et al. [6] presented a survey of quantum software tools and technologies, and further noted the rapid development of quantum-based software tools, explaining that there are now a multitude of quantum software tools, packages, and platforms available from a variety of sources. Gill et al. [6] presented a comparative analysis of 55 different quantum software tools or techniques, noting such parameters as the presence of a quantum computing library of functions or classes, toolkits, 3-D visualization capabilities, accessibility, and several other parameters, including the underpinning programming languages used in the respective tools.

Embedded domain-specific quantum programming languages and tools for quantum program expression include the languages and tools provided under the banner of large companies in the field of information technology, such as Google, Microsoft, and IBM, as well as start-up companies like Rigetti and IonQ, many of which enable assembly-level quantum programming alongside existing Pythonic code [29]. Individually, each of these implementations provides a self-contained software stack that may be directed for use in conjunction with the unique hardware implementation or simulator backend offered by the vendor.

The work of LaRose [36] runs through four examples of quantum computing platforms that are publicly accessible (according to LaRose, such a "quantum computing platform" corresponds to a quantum programming language together with other tools including compilers and simulators). With respect to each platform, LaRose [36] discusses "requirements and installation, documentation and tutorials, quantum programming language syntax, quantum assembly/instruction language, quantum hardware, and simulator capabilities," in essence, providing the information one would find useful in getting started as a user of each platform.

Figure 11 depicts a block diagram showing the pathways considered by LaRose to establish a connection between a computer and a publicly accessible quantum computer. Beginning from the computer (bottom center), light blue nodes identify software platforms that can be installed on a user's personal computer. Blue-green nodes indicate simulators that run locally. Dashed lines indicate remote application programming interface/cloud connections to resources shown in yellow-green. Quantum simulators and quantum computers made accessible by these cloud resources are highlighted in purple and orange, respectively. Red boxes indicate additional requirements.

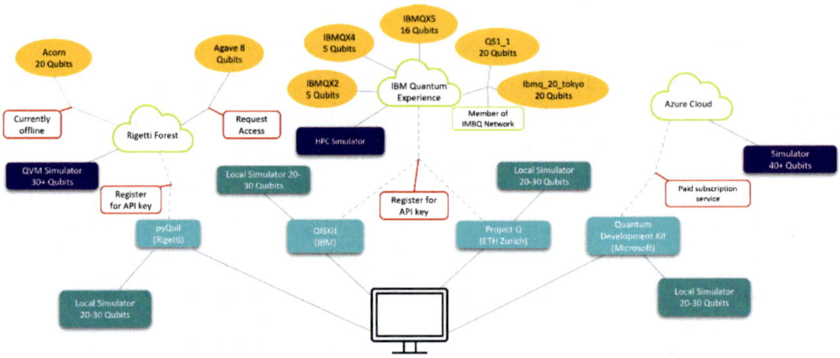

Figure 11. Adaptation of Figure 1 from LaRose [36] which depicts a block diagram showing the pathways considered by LaRose to establish a connection between a computer and a publicly accessible quantum computer.

The platforms tested by LaRose [36] included the following:

1. Rigetti Forest, a quantum software platform that enables a user to program with the open-source quantum programming language pyQuil to control local simulators or remote computing resources through a cloud-based quantum computing service provided by Rigetti Computing;
2. The IBM Quantum Experience, a cloud-computing-based platform that permits a user to interact with IBM's multi-qubit systems (each in the form of a set of superconducting qubits fabricated on a chip contained in a dilution refrigerator) via an interactive user interface that enables one to compose quantum assembly code (OpenQASM), with the use of IBM's Quantum Information Software Kit, known as

Qiskit, to help users code programs for controlling the remote quantum processors or local quantum simulators.

3. ProjectQ, an open-source quantum software platform that was developed by scientists at ETC Zurich. It allows users to implement quantum programs in Python, which ProjectQ is configured to translate, thereby enabling control of local simulators or of IBM's remote computing resources associated with the IBM Quantum Experience.
4. Microsoft's Quantum Development Kit (QDK), which allows users to program in a language called Q# that integrates with Visual Studio and Visual Studio Code, and enables users to control quantum circuit simulators locally or via its cloud-based Azure system.

Although the interface, operation, and applicable software and hardware ecosystem for each tool is generally targeted towards a specific implementation of quantum computing, there are common aspects of the approaches taken by these disparate tools. More specifically, much like common software languages enable a programmer to create and execute instructions without intimate knowledge of the underlying classical computing architecture or hardware, these quantum development tools enable a programmer to implement quantum operations without needing to directly program the control systems for the underlying qubit hardware. Put another way, these quantum development tools allow a sequence of quantum operations to be defined in a human-readable scripting language, and the programmer does not need to understand or configure the hardware used to implement the sequence.

As an example, consider a qubit system where microwave electrical pulses are used to modify the state of superconducting qubits. One approach to implementing a quantum computing program would be to program the pulse sequences and associated timing to drive the qubits as required, such that they interact with each other as needed to implement the corresponding sequence of quantum operations; however, this approach requires the programmer to first determine the desired quantum operations and then manually program corresponding pulses into the classical control system that generates microwave pulses. Through the use of a quantum development tool, the programmer can define their quantum system and operations using a scripting language that is abstracted away from the specific qubit system and its control hardware, and the tool then converts the quantum program into appropriate classical control signals to enable implementation and associated readout.

Thus, while not necessarily universal to all the tools addressed above, the general purpose of these tools is to: (i) enable the definition of quantum states, such as may be used in initial conditions of a quantum operation; (ii) enable the creation of a sequence of quantum operations, or gates, through which this state will be transitioned; and (iii) interpret the classical output signals in a way that enables the user to understand the result of the sequence.

Future Trends and Outlook

Above we discussed the quantum computing paradigm, how it contrasts with conventional computing, its theoretical advantages for solving what are presently intractable problems, and how this has motivated the study of quantum computing across a variety of fields. This chapter included a summary of the building blocks of quantum information that would be required for quantum computing, the inherently quantum mechanical phenomena that must be considered, a selection of physical qubit implementations that have been pursued, as well as a variety of software tools and technologies for exploring quantum computing approaches and applications.

The development of a quantum computer that may be employed in conventional settings for solving real-world problems will require further advancements on several different fronts, extending from the underlying hardware to the software, and everything in between. But in addition to the necessity for new and continuing discoveries and fundamental insights, further progress may be accelerated by focusing on a reduced set of approaches. For example, there is currently a multitude of various quantum programming languages and platforms, which can lead to challenges in managing multiple programming environments and bottlenecks in the associated compilation tool-chains [29]. Similarly, currently several different physical qubit implementations have been extensively pursued, at least in a laboratory environment. This leads to scientific and engineering efforts—and budgets—that are spread relatively thin across these numerous technologies. As the field develops and the need for this phase of scientific exploration diminishes, the concentration of resources around a subset of approaches may help propel progress and achieve new breakthroughs.

Further progress in the field of quantum computation may also be propelled by developing the tools that will allow for new groups of scientists and engineers to engage in this field. In particular, when newly developed tools do not require an understanding of quantum mechanics (e.g., as a result of designs that are configured to automate key processes), significant advancements will be possible thanks to the potential involvement of software and computer engineers, who henceforth will be equipped to participate in the field. For example, as discussed above, current quantum software stacks and associated tools are directed towards allowing a programmer to define sequences of quantum operations, or gates, to be performed on a given initial quantum state such that this initial quantum state represents the input to an algorithm, the quantum operations perform the algorithm, and the resulting output quantum state represents the solution. One limitation of this current approach is that the programmer requires knowledge of quantum mechanics to design and map a problem into an input state, which must be solvable through a sequence of quantum operations. Future developments in quantum software architecture may mitigate this by introducing a degree of automation into the application of quantum algorithms, such that a programmer defines the problem being addressed, and the aspects that benefit from quantum computing are automatically parsed through appropriate quantum algorithms as required. As an analogy, modern multi-core or multi-thread classical computers often include automatic mechanisms to determine what parts of computing tasks are solved utilizing parallel computing, resulting in reduced solution times without the programmer needing to explicitly instruct the hardware how to utilize sequential or parallel computing.

With developments such as those described above, engineers will be able to implement the tools once they are designed and made available, for programming, modeling, optimizing, implementing, testing, benchmarking, and debugging the systems that will be at the heart of quantum software and computer engineering [6, 37].

References

[1] Benioff, Paul. 1980. "The computer as a physical system: A microscopic quantum mechanical Hamiltonian model of computers as represented by Turing machines." *J Stat Phys* 22 (5):563-591. doi: 10.1007/BF01011339.

[2] Feynman, Richard P. 1982. "Simulating physics with computers." *Int J Theoret Phys* 21 (6):467-488. doi: 10.1007/BF02650179.

[3] Preskill, John. 2012. "Quantum computing and the entanglement frontier." *arXiv preprint arXiv:1203.5813*.

[4] Gay, Simon J. 2006. "Quantum programming languages: survey and bibliography." *Math Struct Comput Sci* 16 (4):581-600. doi: 10.1017/S0960129506005378.

[5] Knill, Emanuel. 1996. *"Conventions for quantum pseudocode."* Los Alamos, NM: Los Alamos National Laboratory.

[6] Gill, Sukhpal Singh, Adarsh Kumar, Harvinder Singh, Manmeet Singh, Kamalpreet Kaur, Muhammad Usman, and Rajkumar Buyya. 2022. "Quantum computing: A taxonomy, systematic review and future directions." *Softw: Pract Exp* 52 (1):66-114. doi: https://doi.org/10.1002/spe.3039.

[7] Nielsen, Michael A., and Isaac L. Chuang. 2010. *Quantum Computation and Quantum Information: 10th Anniversary Edition*. Cambridge: Cambridge University Press.

[8] Alexeev, Yuri, Dave Bacon, Kenneth R. Brown, Robert Calderbank, Lincoln D. Carr, Frederic T. Chong, Brian DeMarco, Dirk Englund, Edward Farhi, Bill Fefferman, Alexey V. Gorshkov, Andrew Houck, Jungsang Kim, Shelby Kimmel, Michael Lange, Seth Lloyd, Mikhail D. Lukin, Dmitri Maslov, Peter Maunz, Christopher Monroe, John Preskill, Martin Roetteler, Martin J. Savage, and Jeff Thompson. 2021. "Quantum Computer Systems for Scientific Discovery." *PRX Quantum* 2 (1):017001. doi: 10.1103/PRXQuantum.2.017001.

[9] Grover, Lov K. 1996. A fast quantum mechanical algorithm for database search. In *Proceedings of the twenty-eighth annual ACM symposium on Theory of Computing*. Philadelphia, Pennsylvania, USA: Association for Computing Machinery.

[10] Shor, P. W. "Algorithms for quantum computation: discrete logarithms and factoring," in *Proceedings of the 35th Annual Symposium on Foundations of Computer Science*, 1994, 124-134.

[11] Jordan, Stephen. 2022. *"Quantum Algorithm Zoo: Algebraic and Number Theoretic Algorithms."* Last Updated June 26, 2022, Accessed September 1, 2023. Available from https://quantumalgorithmzoo.org/.

[12] Barredo, Daniel, Vincent Lienhard, Sylvain de Léséleuc, Thierry Lahaye, and Antoine Browaeys. 2018. "Synthetic three-dimensional atomic structures assembled atom by atom." *Nature* 561 (7721):79-82. doi: 10.1038/s41586-018-0450-2.

[13] Huft, P., Y. Song, T. M. Graham, K. Jooya, S. Deshpande, C. Fang, M. Kats, and M. Saffman. 2022. "Simple, passive design for large optical trap arrays for single atoms." *Phys Rev A* 105 (6):063111. doi: 10.1103/PhysRevA.105.063111.

[14] Evered, Simon, Dolev Bluvstein, Marcin Kalinowski, Sepehr Ebadi, Tom Manovitz, Hengyun Zhou, Sophie Li, Alexandra Geim, Tout Wang, Nishad Maskara, Harry Levine, Giulia Semeghini, Markus Greiner, Vladan Vuletic, and Mikhail Lukin 2023. "High-fidelity parallel entangling gates on a neutral atom quantum computer." *arXiv preprint arXiv:2304.05420*.

[15] Wu, Yue, Shimon Kolkowitz, Shruti Puri, and Jeff D. Thompson. 2022. "Erasure conversion for fault-tolerant quantum computing in alkaline earth Rydberg atom arrays." *Nat Comm* 13 (1):4657. doi: 10.1038/s41467-022-32094-6.

[16] Monroe, C., and J. Kim. 2013. "Scaling the ion trap quantum processor." *Science* 339 (6124):1164-9. doi: 10.1126/science.1231298.

[17] Romaszko, Zak David, Seokjun Hong, Martin Siegele, Reuben Kahan Puddy, Foni Raphaël Lebrun-Gallagher, Sebastian Weidt, and Winfried Karl Hensinger. 2020. "Engineering of microfabricated ion traps and integration of advanced on-chip features." *Nat Rev Phys* 2 (6):285-299. doi: 10.1038/s42254-020-0182-8.

[18] Chatterjee, Anasua, Paul Stevenson, Silvano De Franceschi, Andrea Morello, Nathalie P. de Leon, and Ferdinand Kuemmeth. 2021. "Semiconductor qubits in practice." *Nature Rev Phys* 3 (3):157-177. doi: 10.1038/s42254-021-00283-9.

[19] Shulman, M. D., O. E. Dial, S. P. Harvey, H. Bluhm, V. Umansky, and A. Yacoby. 2012. "Demonstration of Entanglement of Electrostatically Coupled Singlet-Triplet Qubits." *Science* 336 (6078):202-205. doi: doi:10.1126/science.1217692.

[20] Laucht, Arne, Frank Hohls, Niels Ubbelohde, M. Fernando Gonzalez-Zalba, David J. Reilly, Søren Stobbe, Tim Schröder, Pasquale Scarlino, Jonne V. Koski, Andrew Dzurak, Chih-Hwan Yang, Jun Yoneda, Ferdinand Kuemmeth, Hendrik Bluhm, Jarryd Pla, Charles Hill, Joe Salfi, Akira Oiwa, Juha T. Muhonen, Ewold Verhagen, M. D. LaHaye, Hyun Ho Kim, Adam W. Tsen, Dimitrie Culcer, Attila Geresdi, Jan A. Mol, Varun Mohan, Prashant K. Jain, and Jonathan Baugh. 2021. "Roadmap on quantum nanotechnologies." *Nanotechnology* 32 (16):162003. doi: 10.1088/1361-6528/abb333.

[21] Xue, X., T. F Watson, J. Helsen, D. R Ward, D. E Savage, M. G Lagally, Susan Coppersmith, Marii Eriksson, Stephanie Wehner, and L. M. K. Vandersypen. 2019. "Benchmarking Gate Fidelities in a Si / SiGe Two-Qubit Device." *Physical Review X* 9 doi: 10.1103/PhysRevX.9.021011.

[22] Krinner, S., S. Storz, P. Kurpiers, P. Magnard, J. Heinsoo, R. Keller, J. Lütolf, C. Eichler, and A. Wallraff. 2019. "Engineering cryogenic setups for 100-qubit scale superconducting circuit systems." *EPJ Quantum Technology* 6 (1):2. doi: 10.1140/epjqt/s40507-019-0072-0.

[23] Castelvecchi, D. 2023. "News: Google's quantum computer hits key milestone by reducing errors." *Nature,* Last Updated February 22, 2023, Accessed September 1, 2023. Available from https://www.scientificamerican.com/article/googles-quantum-computer-hits-key-milestone-by-reducing-errors/.

[24] IBM. 2022. "IBM Unveils 400 Quibit-Plus Quantum Processor and Next-Generation IBM Quantum System Two." Last Updated November 9, 2022, Accessed September 1, 2023. Available from https://newsroom.ibm.com/2022-11-09-IBM-Unveils-400-Qubit-Plus-Quantum-Processor-and-Next-Generation-IBM-Quantum-System-Two.

[25] Arute, Frank, Kunal Arya, Ryan Babbush, Dave Bacon, Joseph C. Bardin, Rami Barends, Rupak Biswas, Sergio Boixo, Fernando G. S. L. Brandao, David A. Buell, Brian Burkett, Yu Chen, Zijun Chen, Ben Chiaro, Roberto Collins, William Courtney, Andrew Dunsworth, Edward Farhi, Brooks Foxen, Austin Fowler, Craig Gidney, Marissa Giustina, Rob Graff, Keith Guerin, Steve Habegger, Matthew P. Harrigan, Michael J. Hartmann, Alan Ho, Markus Hoffmann, Trent Huang, Travis S. Humble, Sergei V. Isakov, Evan Jeffrey, Zhang Jiang, Dvir Kafri, Kostyantyn Kechedzhi, Julian Kelly, Paul V. Klimov, Sergey Knysh, Alexander Korotkov, Fedor Kostritsa, David Landhuis, Mike Lindmark, Erik Lucero, Dmitry Lyakh, Salvatore Mandrà, Jarrod R. McClean, Matthew McEwen, Anthony Megrant, Xiao Mi, Kristel Michielsen, Masoud Mohseni, Josh Mutus, Ofer Naaman, Matthew Neeley, Charles Neill, Murphy Yuezhen Niu, Eric Ostby, Andre Petukhov, John C. Platt, Chris Quintana, Eleanor G. Rieffel, Pedram Roushan, Nicholas C. Rubin, Daniel Sank, Kevin J. Satzinger, Vadim Smelyanskiy, Kevin J. Sung, Matthew D.

Trevithick, Amit Vainsencher, Benjamin Villalonga, Theodore White, Z. Jamie Yao, Ping Yeh, Adam Zalcman, Hartmut Neven, and John M. Martinis. 2019. "Quantum supremacy using a programmable superconducting processor." *Nature* 574 (7779):505-510. doi: 10.1038/s41586-019-1666-5.

[26] Mi, X., M. Sonner, M. Y. Niu, K. W. Lee, B. Foxen, R. Acharya, I. Aleiner, T. I. Andersen, F. Arute, K. Arya, A. Asfaw, J. Atalaya, J. C. Bardin, J. Basso, A. Bengtsson, G. Bortoli, A. Bourassa, L. Brill, M. Broughton, B. B. Buckley, D. A. Buell, B. Burkett, N. Bushnell, Z. Chen, B. Chiaro, R. Collins, P. Conner, W. Courtney, A. L. Crook, D. M. Debroy, S. Demura, A. Dunsworth, D. Eppens, C. Erickson, L. Faoro, E. Farhi, R. Fatemi, L. Flores, E. Forati, A. G. Fowler, W. Giang, C. Gidney, D. Gilboa, M. Giustina, A. G. Dau, J. A. Gross, S. Habegger, M. P. Harrigan, M. Hoffmann, S. Hong, T. Huang, A. Huff, W. J. Huggins, L. B. Ioffe, S. V. Isakov, J. Iveland, E. Jeffrey, Z. Jiang, C. Jones, D. Kafri, K. Kechedzhi, T. Khattar, S. Kim, A. Y. Kitaev, P. V. Klimov, A. R. Klots, A. N. Korotkov, F. Kostritsa, J. M. Kreikebaum, D. Landhuis, P. Laptev, K.-M. Lau, J. Lee, L. Laws, W. Liu, A. Locharla, O. Martin, J. R. McClean, M. McEwen, B. Meurer Costa, K. C. Miao, M. Mohseni, S. Montazeri, A. Morvan, E. Mount, W. Mruczkiewicz, O. Naaman, M. Neeley, C. Neill, M. Newman, T. E. O'Brien, A. Opremcak, A. Petukhov, R. Potter, C. Quintana, N. C. Rubin, N. Saei, D. Sank, K. Sankaragomathi, K. J. Satzinger, C. Schuster, M. J. Shearn, V. Shvarts, D. Strain, Y. Su, M. Szalay, G. Vidal, B. Villalonga, C. Vollgraff-Heidweiller, T. White, Z. Yao, P. Yeh, J. Yoo, A. Zalcman, Y. Zhang, N. Zhu, H. Neven, D. Bacon, J. Hilton, E. Lucero, R. Babbush, S. Boixo, A. Megrant, Y. Chen, J. Kelly, V. Smelyanskiy, D. A. Abanin, and P. Roushan. 2022. "Noise-resilient edge modes on a chain of superconducting qubits." *Science* 378 (6621):785-790. doi: 10.1126/science.abq5769.

[27] Google AI Quantum Collaborators, Frank Arute, Kunal Arya, Ryan Babbush, Dave Bacon, Joseph C. Bardin, Rami Barends, Sergio Boixo, Michael Broughton, Bob B. Buckley, David A. Buell, Brian Burkett, Nicholas Bushnell, Yu Chen, Zijun Chen, Benjamin Chiaro, Roberto Collins, William Courtney, Sean Demura, Andrew Dunsworth, Edward Farhi, Austin Fowler, Brooks Foxen, Craig Gidney, Marissa Giustina, Rob Graff, Steve Habegger, Matthew P. Harrigan, Alan Ho, Sabrina Hong, Trent Huang, William J. Huggins, Lev Ioffe, Sergei V. Isakov, Evan Jeffrey, Zhang Jiang, Cody Jones, Dvir Kafri, Kostyantyn Kechedzhi, Julian Kelly, Seon Kim, Paul V. Klimov, Alexander Korotkov, Fedor Kostritsa, David Landhuis, Pavel Laptev, Mike Lindmark, Erik Lucero, Orion Martin, John M. Martinis, Jarrod R. McClean, Matt McEwen, Anthony Megrant, Xiao Mi, Masoud Mohseni, Wojciech Mruczkiewicz, Josh Mutus, Ofer Naaman, Matthew Neeley, Charles Neill, Hartmut Neven, Murphy Yuezhen Niu, Thomas E. O'Brien, Eric Ostby, Andre Petukhov, Harald Putterman, Chris Quintana, Pedram Roushan, Nicholas C. Rubin, Daniel Sank, Kevin J. Satzinger, Vadim Smelyanskiy, Doug Strain, Kevin J. Sung, Marco Szalay, Tyler Y. Takeshita, Amit Vainsencher, Theodore White, Nathan Wiebe, Z. Jamie Yao, Ping Yeh, and Adam Zalcman. 2020. "Hartree-Fock on a superconducting qubit quantum computer." *Science* 369 (6507):1084-1089. doi: 10.1126/science.abb9811.

[28] Wang, Yuhui. 2020. "Analysis on the Mechanism of Superconducting Quantum Computer." *J Phys Conf Ser* 1634 (1):012040. doi: 10.1088/1742-6596/1634/1/012040.
[29] McCaskey, A. J., E. F. Dumitrescu, D. Liakh, M. Chen, W. Feng, and T. S. Humble. 2018. "A language and hardware independent approach to quantum–classical computing." *SoftwareX* 7:245-254. doi: 10.1016/j.softx.2018.07.007.
[30] La Rose, R. 2019. "Overview and comparison of gate level quantum software platforms." *Quantum Science and Technology* 3 (130) doi: https://doi.org/10.22331/q-2019-03-25-130.
[31] Fu, X., L. Riesebos, L. Lao, C. G. Almudever, F. Sebastiano, R. Versluis, E. Charbon, and K. Bertels. 2016. A heterogeneous quantum computer architecture. In *Proceedings of the ACM International Conference on Computing Frontiers*. Como, Italy: Association for Computing Machinery.
[32] Häner, Thomas, Damian S. Steiger, Krysta Svore, and Matthias Troyer. 2018. "A software methodology for compiling quantum programs." *Quantum Sci Technol* 3 (2):020501. doi: 10.1088/2058-9565/aaa5cc.
[33] Sofge, D. A. "A Survey of Quantum Programming Languages: History, Methods, and Tools," in *Proceedings of the Second International Conference on Quantum, Nano and Micro Technologies (ICQNM 2008)*, 2008, 66-71.
[34] Dargan, James. 2022. "Top 35 Open Source Quantum Computing Tools [2022]." Last Updated May 27, 2022, Accessed September 1, 2023. Available from https://thequantuminsider.com/2022/05/27/quantum-computing-tools/.
[35] Upama, P. B., M. J. H. Faruk, M. Nazim, M. Masum, H. Shahriar, G. Uddin, S. Barzanjeh, S. I. Ahamed, and A. Rahman. "Evolution of Quantum Computing: A Systematic Survey on the Use of Quantum Computing Tools," in *Proceedings of the 2022 IEEE 46th Annual Computers, Software, and Applications Conference (COMPSAC)*, 2022, 520-529.
[36] LaRose, Ryan. 2019. "Overview and comparison of gate level quantum software platforms." *Quantum Sci Technol* 3 (130):130.
[37] Piattini, Mario, Guido Peterssen, and Ricardo Pérez-Castillo. 2020. "Quantum Computing: A New Software Engineering Golden Age." *SIGSOFT Softw Eng Notes* 45 (3):12–14. doi: 10.1145/3402127.3402131.

Biographical Sketches

Gavin D. Scott, PhD

Dr. Scott is a physicist with over 20 years of experience in scientific research on topics including complex electronic, magnetic, and optical interactions, control systems, and quantum mechanical phenomena. At Exponent, Dr. Scott currently applies his expertise to providing scientific technical consultation for clients on matters ranging from litigation support involving intellectual property disputes to root-cause failure analysis and technical assessments in relation to suitable industry standards. He has performed analyses of computer software and computer hardware components, as well as mobile devices, integrated circuits (ICs) and semiconductor components, light emitting diodes (LEDs) solar cells, smart home devices, industrial control systems, optical sensing components, network security systems, LiDAR, and medical devices. Previously, Dr. Scott was a research scientist at Bell Laboratories in Murray Hill, NJ where he was a principal investigator for a low temperature experimental research effort studying highly correlated electron states in magnetic nanostructures. He additionally advised management on quantum computing methodologies and quantum information processing applications aligned with business strategies. He received his B.S. from UC Santa Barbara and his M.S. and Ph.D. from UCLA before his research at Rice University where he was the recipient of the W. M. Keck Postdoctoral Fellowship. Dr. Scott now resides in Connecticut with his family.

Matthew A. Pooley, PhD

Dr. Pooley is a physicist with a background in semiconductor physics, quantum optics, and software development. He obtained his Ph.D. in Physics from the University of Cambridge, U.K., where he designed, fabricated, and characterized optoelectronic devices for use within optical quantum computers. This research focused on self-assembled quantum dots within optical cavities in electrical diode structures, which can emit individual photons for use as qubits or act as an interface between photonic qubit and solid-state qubits based on the spin of individual electrons. Dr. Pooley's research culminated in demonstrating an optical CNOT gate with quantum light, which is a potential building block for future optical quantum computers. After his Ph.D., Dr. Pooley worked as a software developer for a commercial finite element analysis package, adding tools to assist in modeling optoelectronic devices. He is currently a scientific consultant working for Exponent, where he provides a range of professional technical services to clients, often involving his expertise in semiconductor physics, optics, and software.

Paloma Ocola, PhD

Dr. Ocola has worked in the fields of quantum computation, hybrid quantum systems, and atomic physics throughout her scientific career. She has performed research at the University of Chicago for her undergraduate studies and Harvard University for her Ph.D., primarily focusing on the experimental implementation of atomic quantum platforms. Her work has been in employing and controlling complex systems of equipment, including optics, microwave electronics, and photonic devices, and integrating software control with atomic physics experiments. While she has been motivated by the realization of quantum phenomena in the lab, she has now moved to New York City where she now enjoys using her technical expertise in solving the real-world challenges of every day technologies.

Chapter 8

Battery Management Systems: From Consumer Electronics to Electric Vehicles

Michelle L. Kuykendal*, PhD
Melissa L. Mendias, PhD
and Rita Garrido Menacho, PhD
Exponent, Inc., Phoenix, AZ, USA

Abstract

Advancements in energy storage technologies are some of the key factors enabling the success of modern electronic systems. Lithium-ion batteries in particular have been adopted as the storage means of choice for most rechargeable mobile products, like laptops and cell phones, because of their relatively high storage density, voltage potential, and long lifespan. With high storage density, however, comes an elevated risk of a safety incident, and care must be taken to ensure that the battery cells do not experience a short-circuit since this can lead to a rapid, uncontrolled discharge. The highly publicized series of battery fires that occurred with the Samsung Note 7 and various hoverboard brands made clear the need for safety improvements. These came in the form of strict manufacturing requirements and the incorporation of a battery monitoring system with sensors and logic to monitor battery health, and ultimately disable them if required.

Keywords: battery, lithium-ion, vehicle, electronics

---

* Corresponding Authors' Email: mkuykendal@exponent.com, mmendias@exponent.com, rgarridomenacho@exponent.com.

In: Computer Engineering Applications …
Editor: Brian D'Andrade
ISBN: 979-8-89113-488-1

Introduction to Lithium-ion Batteries and Their Failure Modes

Lithium-ion cells, like all batteries, consist of a cathode (positive electrode) and anode (negative electrode), which are separated by an insulating material. In the case of a lithium-ion cell, the anode is most commonly a carbon-based material and the cathode is an oxide containing lithium and one or more additional metals. Sheets of anode and cathode material are stacked together, with a porous insulating layer (i.e., the separator) between them. These are then tightly rolled into a circle or flat oval-shaped structure to fit into the intended package. The structure is immersed in a lithium-containing electrolyte, from which the free lithium ions can pass through the separator layer to attach to either the anode or cathode during charge and discharge cycles, respectively, as illustrated in Figure 1. The resulting cell can have a nominal potential of around 3.6 Volts (V) or 3.7 V, and can be charged to a maximum voltage of approximately 4.2 V; however variations exist in specific battery chemistry, which enable cells to operate at nominal voltages, such as 3.8 V or 3.85 V, with a maximum fully-charged voltage of 4.35 V or 4.4 V. Multiple-cell battery packs with higher nominal voltages are achieved by connecting multiple battery cells (or blocks of cells connected in parallel) in series so their voltages add. Some energy intensive applications like cell phones, which necessitate compact packages with a long run time and high computational power, have shifted to the higher 4.4 V battery cell designs.

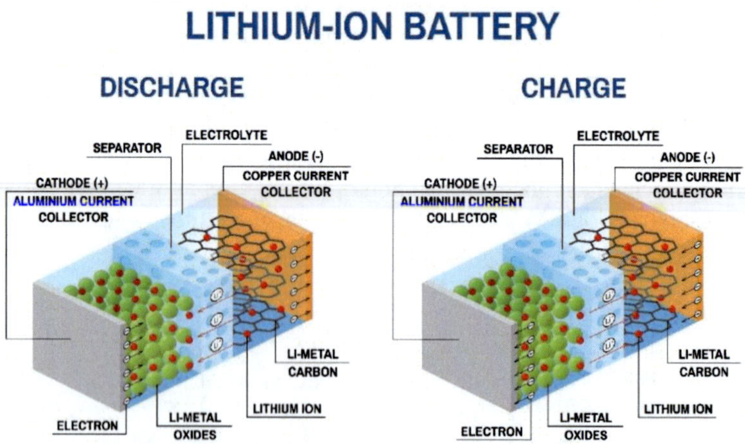

Figure 1. Internal structure of a lithium-ion cell showing the transport of lithium ions from anode to cathode when discharging and conversely when charging (Getty Images).

Failure modes of lithium-ion cells include both energetic and non-energetic types. In the ideal scenario, cells age gracefully until they can no longer retain a significant charge, at which point they are considered to have failed by non-energetic means. Energetic failures primarily concern thermal runaway events, which can occur as a result of a short-circuit (either internal or external) or internal material degradation or contamination. A short-circuit may be caused in a variety of ways:

- Mechanical damage (e.g., drop, impact, or rupture of the cell)
- External electrical defect (e.g., electromigration on the circuit board or a loose connection)
- Internal cell degradation (e.g., lithium plating at the anode due to high charging current or charging at low temperatures)
- Separator breach (e.g., dendrite growth due to cell over-discharge)
- Manufacturing defect (e.g., contamination, excessive force, or improper positioning of electrode tabs)

Internal cell degradation may also occur as a result of charging or discharging outside the battery manufacturer's specified temperature, voltage, or current range. Lithium-ion cells are typically rated to operate between approximately -20ºC to 60ºC, although many are rated up to only 45ºC [1]. Performance may be optimal near the higher end of this range as a result of increased electrochemical reaction rates, allowing more energy to be transferred in a shorter time period. Cell aging mechanisms, however, are also accelerated at higher temperatures, and usage or even storage at elevated temperatures can significantly reduce a battery's lifespan. Another mechanism of increased rate of degradation includes charging or discharging at high currents, even at moderate temperatures, since the combined effects can produce internal heat generation with localized hot spots due to manufacturing variations or damage from customer use or abuse. In addition to performance degradation, high temperatures can generate gases, which in turn lead to swelling (e.g., in flexible enclosure pouch cells) or venting (e.g., in rigid enclosure cylindrical cells), and increase the risk of a thermal runaway event. Conversely, low-temperature operation is associated with slower reaction rates and reduced particle mobility, reducing battery performance and thermal contraction of the electrode materials. As a result, free lithium is less able to diffuse through the cell or embed into the electrodes, and undesirable accumulation can occur that may ultimately grow into a film or dendrite and create an internal short-circuit.

Battery Management Systems–Mitigation Capabilities

When a battery management system (BMS) is used effectively within a lithium-ion battery pack, it acts to keep all cells within the pack at a known safe state, although a BMS cannot monitor for internal cell defect or latent manufacturing flaws that may be exacerbated by use and charge/discharge cycling. Risk factors to the cells include short-circuit, over-current, over- or under-voltage, and over- or under-temperature. To prevent these conditions from occurring, one or more of the following features may be incorporated into a BMS design:

- Short-circuit and over-current protection
- Charge current/voltage limitation
- Discharge current/voltage limitation
- Cell and environmental temperature monitoring
- Pre-charge control (for temperature considerations or highly discharged cells, although recharging over-discharged cells is not recommended)
- Cell balancing (multi-cell packs only)

The features incorporated into a BMS are dependent upon the application and number of cells within the battery pack. Smaller, inexpensive electronic devices such as toys, flashlights, and other consumer electronics often use just a single cell such as the 18650 cylindrical cell shown in Figure 2(a), the pouch cell shown in Figure 2(b), or the prismatic cell shown in Figure 2(c).

The BMS for a single-cell device may be as simple as an attached circuit board with a fuse on one of the cell terminals intended to permanently disable the device in the event of an over-current, although newer designs typically integrate far more capability than only a permanent method of disconnection. There are different design considerations even for single cell applications, especially when the battery is expected to be replaceable or not. As an example, the wearables industry has seen a significant increase in products reaching the market because of lithium-ion technology. The high energy density of these batteries enables devices to be small enough to wear in a watch or on a clothing band while still remaining operational over many hours of use. Because of the close proximity of lithium-ion batteries to human skin in wearables applications, the incorporation of battery protection electronics is even more critical for safety. Often, the single cell application of wearables includes custom battery cell designs for inclusion in compact spaces, which could be of unusual shape, like in the case of a lithium-ion powered smart eyeglasses in which the battery may be designed into the glasses arm.

Conversely, a battery pack for an electric scooter or automobile may comprise hundreds or even thousands of individual cells arranged into specific parallel and series configurations to achieve a target voltage, output current, and capacity (Figure 3).

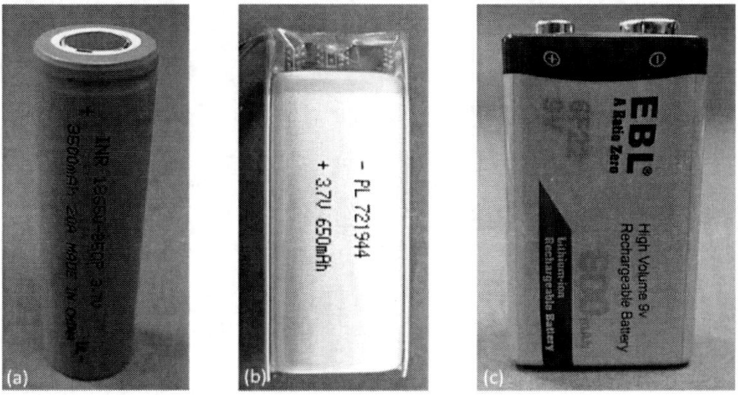

Figure 2. Three types of lithium-ion cells: (a) cylindrical, (b) pouch, and (c) prismatic.

BMS circuits for these types of systems are typically more complex because the overall voltages are higher, increasing the level of safety risk associated with a larger number of cells. Furthermore, slight variations in cell manufacture can result in the cells becoming unbalanced, in which cell voltages are mismatched over time. Most BMS circuits include, at a minimum, a disabling fuse, as well as a set of field-effect transistors (FET) that act to disable charging or discharging when the pack voltage reaches the upper or lower limit, respectively, or when the current exceeds a given threshold. Additionally, microprocessors are often incorporated into the BMS with control logic to further regulate the switching conditions of the FETs based on, for example, ambient or cell temperatures, or the time required to reach a fully charged state. The cell may further contain a redundant means of protection in the form of a thermal fuse, positive temperature coefficient (PTC) device, or other type of passive device. An example block diagram for a multi-cell BMS is shown below in Figure 4.

Figure 3. Photograph of a multi-cell battery pack, showing multiple battery groups connected in series to achieve a higher overall voltage (Getty Images).

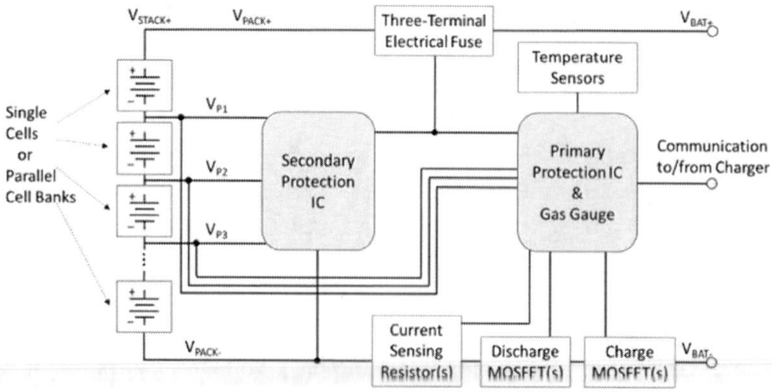

Figure 4. Block diagram of a typical multi-cell BMS circuit. Note that circuit protection components and FETs may be placed on either the positive or negative battery current paths.

In the case of a multi-cell battery pack, the overall pack voltage is calculated from the sum of multiple cells, or parallel cell blocks, which are connected in series, and the overall pack current is a function of the number of cells connected in parallel. Additional voltage sensing connections are commonly made between the BMS and each node in order to monitor all cell voltages and provide cell balancing capability. Over time, factors such as manufacturing variations and thermal gradients can alter the performance of the individual cells, and the pack voltage may not continue to be distributed evenly among them. Should the imbalance become significant, a thermal runaway event could occur when a cell/block becomes overcharged even though the pack voltage remains within specification. Cell balancing entails either dissipating energy from the higher-voltage cells or redistributing charge from higher-voltage cells to lower-voltage cells.

Beyond regulating charging and discharging conditions, a more advanced BMS will also commonly include logic to monitor or calculate the status and health of the battery pack. Features to this effect may include:

- State of charge calculation
- State of health calculation
- Battery type verification
- Fault flagging
- Data logging
- Communications hardware (wired or wireless)

The battery state of charge (SOC) is defined as the fraction of the battery manufacturer's rated capacity (the maximum charge quantity) that is presently being stored by the battery. Over time, cell aging reduces the charge storage capability. Aging occurs spontaneously due predominantly to the continual growth of passivation layers (i.e., the solid electrolyte interphase) which increase cell impedance and deplete available lithium [2, 3]. The rate at which aging occurs, however, is heavily influenced by factors such as the number and depth of charge and discharge cycles, the amount of time spent at overly high or low SOCs, and the amount of time spent at an elevated temperature. In general, a battery is considered at end of life when its state of health (SOH) has fallen below 70–80% of its original rated capacity. Many BMS circuits will communicate the battery's SOH and estimated remaining service life based on the manufacturer's testing and modeling of cell aging processes and the conditions to which the battery has been exposed. A communications medium, either wired or wireless (e.g., Bluetooth, WiFi), is used to transmit this information to a system controller or user display. Details such as battery type and configuration, flag/error status, and required charging parameters may also be transmitted to a smart battery charger.

The incorporation of lithium-ion battery technology and its associated circuitry into everyday consumer products has propelled the rapid advancement in energy storage technology. Since lithium-ion batteries offer the advantage of high energy density per battery volume that surpasses most other energy storage technologies, an increasing number of manufacturers and designers have entered the marketplace. More manufacturers, more designers, more products, and more consumers all work simultaneously to increase the rate at which the technology advances, while also reducing battery cost. The same holds true for battery protection circuitry. While early battery technology incorporated electronic protections by individual component designs, single chip integrated circuits (IC) that contain differing levels of battery protections have become common place. For example, a search of the Texas Instruments 2023 catalog returns a list of 62 different ICs that are available for battery protection, which include features for single cell designs up to 16 series cell designs [4].

Design and Manufacturing Considerations

The BMS is a safety system, and consequently adherence to best practices in design and manufacture is especially important. Failure to consider the full spectrum of tolerances and failure modes can render the BMS ineffective, creating a risk of electrical short, or thermal runaway event, or both. In the design space, factors that affect safety and reliability include:

- Placement and protection of battery connections
- Conductor size, routing, and spacing
- Circuit protection (fuses, PTCs, etc.)
- Component placement and specifications
- Temperature sensing (environment and cells) and other thermal considerations
- Single points of failure
- Redundancy
- Electrostatic discharge protection

Like all circuit boards, BMS hardware and printed circuit boards (PCB) require clean, precise manufacturing and assembly in order to ensure high quality throughout the service life of the system. Particulates should be minimized and any other sources of contamination (e.g., flux residue, solder paste, fingerprint oils) should be prevented or cleaned. Following manufacture, application of a conformal coating or potting material can help to prevent exposure to humidity and environmental contaminants, which could ultimately degrade PCB traces, or cause a short-circuit to develop via material deposition or electromigration, or both.

Solder connections, particularly those of the battery terminals, are of critical importance. Unlike most PCBs with a single power and ground supply, a BMS PCB may include a dozen or more battery connections, depending on the number of cells in the pack. Each connection can be at a different potential, and the placement and routing of these individual power source connections must be designed with cell protection in mind. Cold solder joints or metal corrosion increase the risk of a broken connection, and the potential hazards of loose wires should be considered and mitigated (e.g., with glue or epoxy). Mounting the PCB directly to the battery pack may alleviate the need for battery wires.

Circuit components, while generally considered reliable provided they are operated within their manufacturer's specifications, nevertheless may experience a failure due to unexpected circumstances such as exposure to electrical transient voltages or currents, temperature extremes, or defects generated during the manufacturing or assembly processes. Failures may take the form of either a short-circuit or open-circuit, and the risks of both should be considered during the design process, with particular focus on components that could potentially result in a short-circuit between two batteries or between a battery and ground. Mitigation may be as simple as replacing a single component with two components in series, such as replacing a resistor with two series resistors, each at half the original value, thus changing a single point of failure into a dual point of failure (i.e., two components must simultaneously fail, which is an event of much lower probability). The charge and discharge FETs are often made redundant as well, such that two separate FETs are simultaneously activated by each set of control logic and thus the design ensures that the BMS continues to operate as intended in the event that one of the FETs fails as a short-circuit. Considerations should then be paid to ensure that the control logic does not become a single point of failure in driving both sets of FETs.

Even when best practices in design and manufacturing are followed, faults can and do occur, both internal to the lithium-ion cells and within the cell protection circuitry. It is essential not only to make use of current-limiting circuit protection devices, but also to ensure that they will activate quickly and at the proper time. These commonly include electrical fuses, thermal fuses, PTC thermistors, negative thermal coefficient (NTC) thermistors, or a combination of these. BMS designers often utilize multiple levels of circuit protection, some of which only disable the battery pack temporarily (e.g., when a cell phone is left in a hot car and use would necessitate discharging the battery cell above the manufacturer's temperature specifications), while others render it permanently inoperable (e.g., due to an excessively high discharge current). PTCs and NTCs are temperature-sensitive resistors that act to raise or lower their resistance, respectively, under elevated temperatures. These are referred to as resettable fuses since they recover their nominal resistance values upon a return to a normal range of temperatures. They may be used to restrict power flow to or from an affected area, or used as temperature sensors whose values are interpreted by a microcontroller to apply battery enabling or disabling logic. Electrical fuses and thermal fuses are non-resettable and are used as a last resort when the battery current has exceeded an outer control limit. Currents measured above this limit suggest that a fault has occurred, in which case the battery should be immediately disabled to prevent the fault from propagating.

The design and incorporation of critical circuit protection components into a BMS is only one consideration to maintain a safe operating environment for a lithium-ion battery. The component and PCB manufacturing process must be well controlled through the use of standardized operations and procedures, the implementation of process monitoring and auditing, and the assurance of clean practices through training and oversight. Even a good PCB design can suffer from poor quality control.

Electric Vehicles and the Future

As battery technologies continue to evolve and mature, applications ranging from consumer electronics to the power grid are making the shift to using battery cells as their mode of energy storage. Within the transportation sector, the market for electric vehicles (EV) has seen rapid growth incentivized by the federal government and mandated by various federal agencies such as the National Highway Traffic Safety Administration [5]. The U.S. Department of Energy's Alternative Fuels Research Center indicates that this rapid shift to EVs is occurring because "all forms of electric vehicles can help improve fuel economy, lower fuel costs, and reduce emissions" [6]. As noted by the U.S. Environmental Protection Agency, the transportation sector was the leading contributor to greenhouse gases in 2021 [7]. Greenhouse gases trap heat, leading to increases in temperature and climate change. Elevated levels of pollution and visible changes in weather patterns in the past few decades have exacerbated the need for action in transportation, and pushed the continued efforts to go electric to the forefront.

The main component of an EV powertrain is the battery pack, as shown in Figure 5. The base component of the battery pack is the cell. All EVs and most plug-in hybrid EVs are composed of lithium-ion cells. These cells are then electrically connected in series and parallel to create modules. Each module is usually monitored by a slave BMS. The modules in turn are connected in series using high current and high voltage bus bars to create the battery. The battery along with its safety protection devices such as the master BMS, fuses, contactors, temperature sensors, and gas sensors comprise the battery pack.

Figure 5. EV powertrain highlighting the battery pack and vehicle motors (Getty Images).

The complexity of an EV BMS far surpasses that of consumer electronics due to the number of cells that need to be monitored. Additionally, when a BMS fault is detected in consumer electronics like laptops, cell phones, or tablets, the device is rebooted or at worst taken temporarily offline. For an EV, the latter is not an option as it could lead to hazardous situations for the user, surrounding property, or battery pack if an unexpected uncontrolled shutdown occurs. For example, due to the large currents and voltages at play in an EV, an unexpected BMS shutdown could lead to an excess momentary current flow, which in turn can damage key protection devices such as the main contactors, not only permanently disabling the battery pack, but also leaving it in a state such that safe maintenance is no longer trivial. As such, various steps are taken to ensure the safe operation of the battery pack via the BMS. These include sophisticated ICs and sensors, protective redundancies, failsafe modes, well-trained SOC and SOH battery models, etc.

The main functions of an EV BMS include the following:

- SOC and SOH Monitoring: These are key metrics to determine current and future performance of a battery as described in the beginning of this chapter. SOC is closely related to the battery's capacity, while SOH is related to cell aging and the level of degradation.
- Battery Pack Electrical Protection: The BMS is constantly monitoring for overcurrent, over-voltage, and under-voltage conditions to be able to mitigate or prevent anomalous conditions. Unlike most consumer electronics, an EV BMS will also monitor for isolation resistance to ensure the safety of the vehicle's occupants from an electric shock. According to Federal Motor Vehicle Safety Standard 305, the battery pack chassis "shall not fail to maintain an electrical isolation of no less than 500 ohms/volt between the propulsion battery system and the vehicle's electricity-conducting structure" [8].
- Charge and Discharge Control: Through monitoring of the various sensors within the battery pack (e.g., temperature, current, voltage, isolation, etc.), the BMS ensures safe charge and discharge of the battery pack by verifying that adequate currents, defined by the cell manufacturer, are flowing into and out of the cells by using appropriate charge and discharge profiles set by the on-board charger.
- Cell Balancing: The voltage of all cells within a battery pack should exist within a tight range (e.g., tens of mV) for optimal battery pack performance. If a cell drops below this range, all cells connected in parallel to this cell will rapidly transfer their energy to the faulty cell. This may result in large current spikes, localized heating, and in the worst case, a thermal event. As such, cell balancing circuits are designed such that if a cell drops below a pre-programmed voltage threshold, the energy is redistributed or dissipated so all cells are at an equal level. Passive cell balancing uses dedicated resistors to

controllably discharge the other cells within the parallel-connected group and thus mitigate a sudden in-rush of current and a potential cell failure of the faulty cell. Active cell balancing employs advanced circuitry to balance the energy between cells without the need to dissipate it through a resistor. These circuits have limitations, however, on their balancing capabilities and thus if a cell drops in voltage to a level for which the balancing circuit cannot compensate, the battery pack is permanently disabled and can no longer be charged.

- Thermal Management: EV battery packs require active cooling due to the large amount of heat generated during operation. The most common mode of active cooling is liquid cooling through the use of coolant. Most liquid-cooled EV battery packs are designed with coolant plates placed underneath the battery modules. Additionally, temperature sensors (i.e., thermistors) measure the temperature of the battery pack at key locations and feed this information back to the BMS. The BMS in turn controls the coolant flow through the coolant plates and thus regulates the temperature of the battery pack. Some EV battery pack designs will also include heaters. Heaters are generally used in cold regions to prevent the operation of the cells outside the manufacturer's specifications. Maintaining the coolant at a set optimal temperature for the cells allows safe and optimized performance of the battery pack.
- Fault Diagnosis and Assessment: If the BMS detects a fault, it generates a diagnostic trouble code (DTC) that is saved in memory. The driver is made aware of the presence of a DTC via a light illuminating on the dashboard of the vehicle. Consequently, depending on the severity of the fault, the vehicle might also transition into a failsafe or limp-home mode. The battery might also become disabled, and charging prevented depending on the nature of the DTC.
- Communication and Networking: The BMS can communicate with different electronic control units of the vehicle through a controller area network bus. For example, while the vehicle is driven, the BMS communicates with the motor control unit to determine the motor torque needed based on inputs from the driver and battery pack sensors, thus allowing smooth and safe vehicle operation. As mentioned above, the BMS also interfaces with the onboard charger

to monitor and control battery pack charging when it is connected to an external charger.

Looking to the future, EV manufacturers are working on designs that incorporate wireless BMS technologies into their vehicles. A wireless communication scheme allows for the removal of physical wiring connecting the BMS to various other control units. This cuts costs for the consumer and increases the vehicle's range by reducing the weight of the battery pack; however, the loss of wireless communication may simultaneously introduce a new risk.

Another method of cutting costs to the consumer and thus incentivizing the adoption of EVs is to incorporate less expensive cell chemistries. Lithium iron phosphate (LFP) cells have become an increasingly popular choice; they are more affordable, are safer with a lower risk of experiencing a thermal event, and have a longer lifespan compared to their nickel cobalt aluminum oxide and lithium nickel manganese cobalt (NMC) oxide counterparts [9]. Accordingly, the BMS must be redesigned to match the cell chemistry. LFP cells have a different charge profile than NMC cells. Specifically, the SOC is not readily distinguishable as a function of voltage, so sophisticated SOC estimation algorithms must be introduced into the BMS for accurate battery lifetime and performance predictions.

Overall, the goal of automobile manufacturers, the government in general, and federal agencies to tackle climate change is to accelerate the transition to EVs through incentives and lower costs. To do so safely, the battery must be adequately monitored by its BMS to reduce and mitigate field failures, the worst of which is a thermal runaway condition. As true in this and other growing and expanding fields, risk mitigation solutions are dynamic, constantly changing and evolving as new technologies are discovered and optimized. As changes are made to battery pack infrastructure, BMS complexity continues to grow to provide safe and optimal operation of the battery pack.

As EVs are more widely deployed in the marketplace, data collected through the growing number of miles on the road are providing insights into expected charging and discharging behavior, and algorithms are being developed and advanced to optimize the way in which battery SOC and battery SOH is maintained. Many of the advancements in EV battery technology are attributed to the growing number of sensors utilized throughout the battery pack, providing more granular insight into individual cell health and overall pack health. The future of EV battery pack monitoring may include humidity monitoring and moisture ingress sensors to provide a view into the maintenance of the seal on the battery pack; localized pressure sensing for detection of swelling at the cell level; and gas sensors for specific known gases that may be generated during a cell outgassing event. Additionally, the expanding number of traditional sensors that are more readily utilized in EVs, including voltage, current, and temperature, provides further improvement in precise knowledge of the battery pack. With the increasing deployment of EVs on the road, across both traditional automotive manufacturers and newer entrants into the marketplace, EV battery pack technologies will continue to rapidly advance.

References

[1] Ma, Shuai, Modi Jiang, Peng Tao, Chengyi Song, Jianbo Wu, Jun Wang, Tao Deng, and Wen Shang. 2018. "Temperature effect and thermal impact in lithium-ion batteries: A review." *Prog Natural Sci: Mat Int* 28 (6):653-666. doi: 10.1016/j.pnsc.2018.11.002.

[2] Adenusi, Henry, Gregory A. Chass, Stefano Passerini, Kun V. Tian, and Guanhua Chen. 2023. "Lithium batteries and the solid electrolyte interphase (SEI)—progress and outlook." *Adv Energy Mat* 13 (10):2203307. doi: https://doi.org/10.1002/aenm.202203307.

[3] Keil, Peter, Simon F. Schuster, Jörn Wilhelm, Julian Travi, Andreas Hauser, Ralph C. Karl, and Andreas Jossen. 2016. "Calendar Aging of Lithium-Ion Batteries." *J Electrochem Soc* 163 (9):A1872. doi: 10.1149/2.0411609jes.

[4] Texas Instruments. 2023. "Battery protectors." Texas Instruments, Accessed September 2, 2023. Available from https://www.ti.com/power-management/battery-management/protectors/products.html.

[5] Davenport, Coral, and Neal E. Boudette. 2023. "Biden Plans an Electric Vehicle Revolution. Now, the Hard Part." *The New York Times*, April 13, 2023. https://www.nytimes.com/2023/04/13/climate/electric-vehicles-biden-epa.html.

[6] Alternative Fuels Research Center. 2023. "Electric Vehicle Benefits and Considerations." U.S. Department of Energy, Accessed September 1, 2023. Available from https://afdc.energy.gov/fuels/electricity_benefits.html.

[7] U.S. Environmental Protection Agency (U.S. EPA). 2023. "Sources of Greenhouse Gas Emissions." U.S. EPA, Last Updated August 25, 2023, Accessed September 1, 2023. Available from https://www.epa.gov/ghgemissions/sources-greenhouse-gas-emissions.

[8] National Highway Traffic Safety Administration. 2022. Laboratory Test Procedure for FMVSS 305, Electric Powered Vehicles: Electrolyte Spillage and Electrical Shock Prevention. Washington, DC: U.S. Department of Transportation.

[9] Walvekar, Harsha, Hector Beltran, Shashank Sripad, and Michael Pecht. 2022. "Implications of the electric vehicle manufacturers' decision to mass adopt lithium-iron phosphate batteries." *IEEE Access* 10:63834-63843. doi: 10.1109/ACCESS.2022.3182726.

Biographical Sketches

Michelle Kuykendal, PhD, PE, CFEI, CVFI

Dr. Kuykendal's expertise is in electrical and electronic systems, including advanced driver assistance systems (ADAS), automotive electronics, consumer electronics, electric vehicles (EVs) and other battery powered devices. She specializes in evaluating the safety of electrical system designs including failure analysis and root cause investigations. Dr. Kuykendal has expertise in the evaluation of ADAS technologies including efficacy under diverse environmental conditions, variability in design implementation and sensor utilization, and performance across a wide variety of scenarios. Her evaluations are supported by rigorous design analyses in addition to extensive performance and simulated-failure testing.

Dr. Kuykendal's work focuses on the analysis of complex control systems, large-scale and small-scale lithium-ion batteries coupled with their charging and protection circuitry, device construction quality, and complete system functionality and performance. Dr. Kuykendal works extensively on evaluating the safety of consumer and automotive electronics by performing component and system-level design reviews coupled with electrical testing and on-site inspections. She regularly performs failure analyses and fire investigations relating to home, automotive, and industrial claims.

Dr. Kuykendal received her Ph.D. in Bioengineering from the Georgia Institute of Technology School of Electrical and Computer Engineering in which she developed high-throughput closed-loop analysis techniques for evaluating the efficacy of electrical stimulation on neural tissue. Her work encompassed hardware design, software development, real-time video analysis of neural activation, and closed-loop system control. She is a licensed Professional Engineer in the State of Arizona.

Melissa L Mendias, PhD, PE, CFEI

Dr. Melissa Mendias is an experienced electronics and systems engineer who spent nearly ten years working in a high-volume semiconductor manufacturing environment in both process and yield engineering. She works at Exponent as an engineering consultant where she has established expertise in automotive electronics including advanced driver assistance systems (ADAS), model based systems engineering (MBSE), and failure analysis studies of electrical systems for a variety of applications. Dr. Mendias received her Ph.D. in Electrical Engineering from Michigan Technological University where her research involved technology development for CMOS-integrated MEMS sensors with an emphasis on accelerometers. She is a licensed professional engineer in the state of Arizona and is also a certified fire and explosion investigator. mmendias@exponent.com

Rita Garrido Menacho, PhD

Dr. Rita Garrido Menacho is a condensed matter physicist with specialties in semiconductor/superconductor nanofabrication, surface characterization, and nanoscale electrical testing. She works at Exponent as an engineering and scientific consultant with a focus on failure analysis of consumer electronics, automotive electronic systems, and battery systems. Dr. Garrido Menacho's expertise includes lithium-ion battery pack quality and design evaluations as well as product design safety reviews through electrical, thermal, and mechanical testing. Dr. Garrido Menacho is also experienced in investigations involving automotive electronic system failures and recall-related matters. rgarridomenacho@exponent.com

Chapter 9

Advanced Driver Assistance Systems Sensor Technology

Michelle L. Kuykendal[1,*]
Melissa L. Mendias[1]
Sean Scally[2]
and Liyu Wang[3]
[1]Exponent, Inc., Phoenix, AZ, USA
[2]Exponent, Inc., Natick, MA, USA
[3]Exponent Inc., Menlo Park, CA, USA

Abstract

Advanced driver assistance systems (ADAS) typically use a variety, or combination, of forward facing radar, cameras, LiDAR, and ultrasonic sensors, with the objective to detect, warn, and intermittently react to objects perceived to be in the path of the vehicle that could present a risk for collision. These systems scan and monitor the roadway, processing the rapid influx of sensor information through software algorithms to evaluate the likelihood of a collision. The ability of an ADAS to accurately and reliably perceive the risk of a collision depends heavily on its sensor technologies and their specifications and limitations.

Keywords: advanced driver assistance systems (ADAS), automated driving systems (ADS), sensor, radar

---

* Corresponding Authors' Email: mkuykendal@exponent.com, mmendias@exponent.com.

In: Computer Engineering Applications …
Editor: Brian D'Andrade
ISBN: 979-8-89113-488-1

Introduction

Advanced driver assistance systems (ADAS) have seen an increased rate of deployment on new vehicle models in the last decade. While there is no unified definition of an ADAS, it generally refers to a suite of support features that provide warnings to the driver or some degree of vehicle control to assist the driver with the driving task.

SAE International Levels of Automation

SAE International (SAE), a global standards development and professional association, published a Recommended Practice (J3016) that provides a taxonomy of various ADAS and automated driving system (ADS) technologies [1]. Six levels of driving automation are defined based on the respective roles of the system and the driver in the control hierarchy. An ADAS, which supports the driver with the driving task, falls under levels 0–2. An ADS, which may under certain circumstances take over the complete driving task, refers to levels 3–5. The levels of driving automation are outlined in Figure 1.

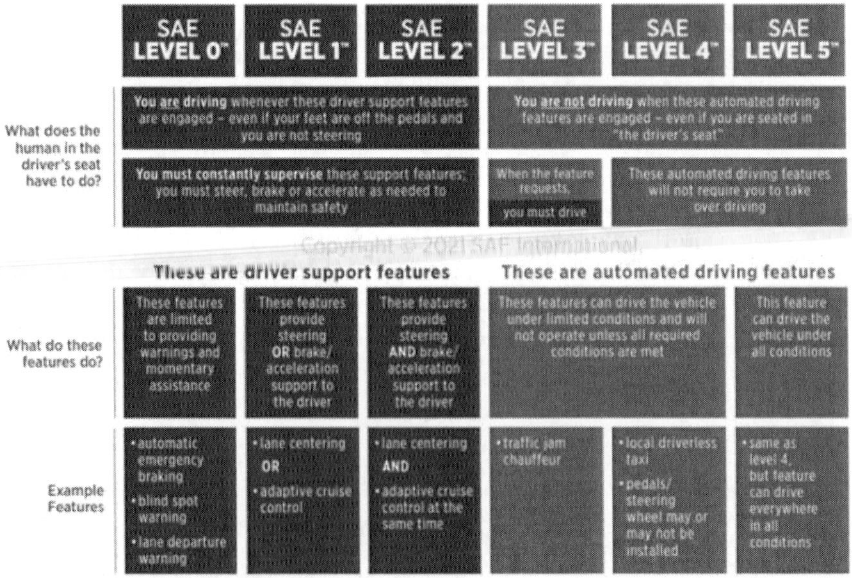

Figure 1. SAE J3016 Levels of Driving Automation [1].

Applications

While ADAS features can, under certain circumstances, assist the driver with the dynamic driving task (DDT), it is important to remember that the responsibility of the driver to monitor the driving environment and execute an appropriate response in an ADAS-equipped vehicle is no different from that of a driver in a vehicle without ADAS technology.

The names used to describe ADAS features vary greatly among automakers. Several consumer safety organizations have called for the adoption of standardized naming conventions for ADAS features [2]. A selection of these features is outlined in Table 1.

Table 1. Selection of ADAS features described by the American Automobile Association, Consumer Reports, J. D. Power, the National Safety Council, PAVE, and SAE (Version 07-2022)

Feature		Description
Collision Warning	Blind Spot Warning	Detects vehicles in the blind spot while driving and notifies the driver to their presence. Some systems provide an additional warning if the driver activates the turn signal.
	Forward Collision Warning	Detects a potential collision with a vehicle ahead and alerts the driver. Some systems also provide alerts for pedestrians or other objects.
	Lane Departure Warning	Monitors the vehicle's position within the driving lane and alerts the driver as the vehicle approaches or crosses lane markers.
	Parking Collision Warning	Detects objects close to the vehicle during parking maneuvers and notifies the driver.
	Rear Cross Traffic Warning	Detects vehicles approaching from the side at the rear of the vehicle while it is in reverse gear and alerts the driver. Some systems also warn for pedestrians or other objects.
Collision Intervention	Automatic Emergency Braking	Detects potential collisions with a vehicle ahead, provides forward collision warning, and automatically brakes to avoid a collision or lessen the severity of impact. Some systems also detect pedestrians or other objects.
	Automatic Emergency Steering	Detects potential collisions with a vehicle ahead and automatically steers to avoid or lessen the severity of impact. Some systems also detect pedestrians or other objects.
	Lane Keeping Assistance	Provides steering support to assist the driver in keeping the vehicle in the lane. The system reacts only when the vehicle approaches or crosses a lane line or road edge.

Table 1. (Continued)

Feature		Description
	Reverse Automatic Emergency Braking	Detects potential collisions while in reverse gear and automatically brakes to avoid or lessen the severity of impact. Some systems also detect pedestrians or other objects.
Driving Control **Assistance**	Adaptive Cruise Control	Cruise control that also assists with acceleration and braking to maintain a driver-selected gap to the vehicle in front. Some systems can come to a stop and continue, while others cannot.
	Lane Centering Assistance	Provides steering support to assist the driver in continuously maintaining the vehicle at or near the center of the lane.
	Active Driving Assistance	Simultaneous use of lane centering assistance and adaptive cruise control features. The driver must constantly supervise this support feature and maintain responsibility for driving.

Benefits

Forward collision warning (FCW) was introduced on passenger vehicles in the United States by Mercedes-Benz with the S-Class and CL-class for model year (MY) 2001 [3]. The feature was available as part of the optional Distronic system, which was marketed as "the world's first adaptive cruise control" [4], and is capable of issuing FCW alerts at certain speeds when adaptive cruise control (ACC) is enabled. Honda was the first to introduce automated emergency braking (AEB) on passenger vehicles in the United States with its collision mitigation braking system, part of an optional technology package on the MY 2006 Acura RL [5]. Mercedes-Benz followed shortly thereafter, releasing their Pre-Safe brake system as standard equipment on the CL-Class in the latter half of 2006.

When discussing ADAS features, an appreciation of their varying ability to assist with the DDT must be considered. Forward collision mitigation features like FCW and AEB provide intermittent support to the driver and are assessed based on their ability to warn and mitigate rear-end crashes and ultimately reduce serious or fatal injuries in this particular crash scenario. If these features are shown to be causal in a statistically significant reduction in crashes, injuries, or fatalities, they may be considered to have a tangible safety benefit. Other ADAS features, such as lane departure warning (LDW) or lane keeping assist (LKA) also provide intermittent support to the driver and are assessed based on their ability to warn and mitigate lane departures. Finally, lane centering assist (LCA) and ACC, assist the driver with dynamic control of the vehicle and are often considered convenience features. That is, they may reduce driver effort, but are not necessarily intended to reduce crashes. Thus, a reduction in crashes or injuries may not be the most appropriate measure of effectiveness for certain features.

The effectiveness and associated benefits of various ADAS features have been on a continuum. Prior to the introduction of these ADAS features to the United States market, several predictive studies attempted to estimate their effectiveness. A 1996 National Highway Traffic Safety Administration (NHTSA) working group report from the Intelligent Transportation Systems (ITS) Program Office estimated the impact of crash avoidance systems on three major crash types: rear-end crashes, single-vehicle road departures, and lane change/merge crashes. It concluded that rear-end crash warning systems could have significant benefits, but noted several limitations of the analysis, including that the study "did not take into account the effects of nuisance alarms and driver compensation which may degrade the effectiveness of any crash avoidance systems" [6].

ADAS technologies including FCW, AEB, LDW, LCA, and lane keeping assistance continue to achieve greater vehicle market penetration each year. Quantitative real-world studies of system efficacy will inherently lag behind their market deployment due to challenges associated with driver acceptance, secondary risks, and evaluating real-world performance.

Measuring the Performance of ADAS Features

Automotive safety regulatory bodies and consumer safety organizations have established various protocols to assess the performance of ADAS features in many common crash scenarios. Testing ADAS features in a reliable and repeatable fashion provides meaningful data that regulators may use to inform policy. In May 2023, NHTSA signaled its intention to update the Federal Motor Vehicle Safety Standard (FMVSS) to require the equipage of AEB, and update the test protocols used for the assessment of AEB in the New Car Assessment Program (NCAP) [7]. In this subsection, AEB testing is used as an example to show how ADAS performance is evaluated.

NHTSA has been conducting AEB confirmation tests through independent evaluations in several driving scenarios with two protocols, namely, the Crash Imminent Brake (CIB) System Confirmation Test [8] and the Dynamic Brake Support (DBS) System Confirmation Test [9]. A CIB system is one that is capable of automatically applying the brakes in situations where the system has deemed a collision is imminent. A DBS system, on the other hand, does not automatically engage the brakes when a collision is imminent, but instead will increase the braking effort if a driver's response is deemed to be insufficient to avoid the collision.

NHTSA's CIB and DBS test protocols define three test scenarios in which a subject vehicle (SV) encounters a principal other vehicle (POV) and one test scenario in which an SV encounters a steel trench plate (STP).

Test 1 – Subject Vehicle Encounters Stopped Principal Other Vehicle

This test evaluates the ability of the system to respond to a stopped lead vehicle in the forward path. For this test, the POV is parked straight in the center of the travel lane. The SV is driven in the center of the same lane directly at the rear of the POV. This test is depicted in Figure 2.

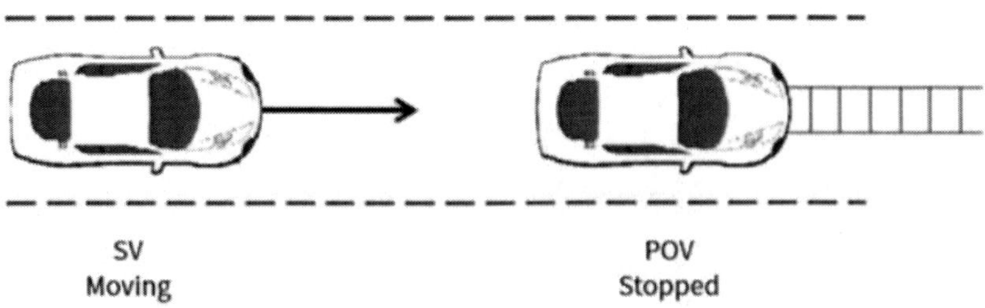

Figure 2. Depiction of Test 1 for NHTSA CIB and DBS System Confirmation Tests.

Test 2 – Subject Vehicle Encounters Slower Principal Other Vehicle

This test evaluates the ability of the system to respond to a slower-moving lead vehicle travelling at a constant speed in the immediate forward path. For this test, the POV is driven at a constant speed in the center of the travel lane. The SV is driven at a constant speed in the same travel lane directly at the rear of the POV. The closing speed (SV speed – POV speed) is varied in subsequent tests. This test is depicted in Figure 3.

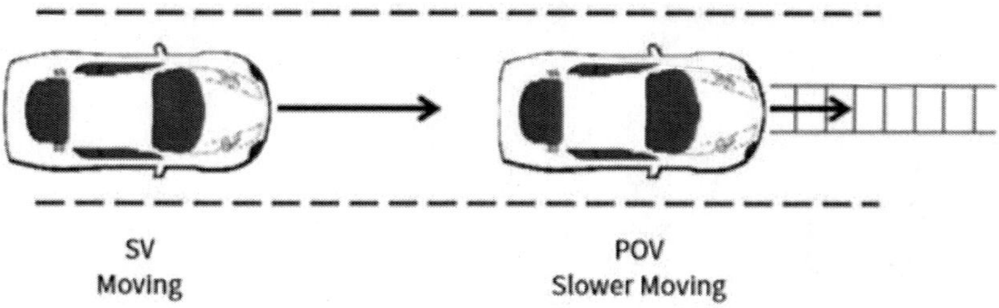

Figure 3. Depiction of Test 2 for NHTSA CIB and DBS System Confirmation Tests.

Test 3 – Subject Vehicle Encounters Decelerating Principal Other Vehicle

This test evaluates the ability of the system to respond to a lead vehicle slowing with a constant deceleration in the immediate forward path. For this test, both the POV and SV are driven at a constant speed in the center of the travel lane with a defined headway. The POV is then slowed at a defined rate (e.g., 0.3–0.5 g-deceleration). This test is depicted in Figure 4.

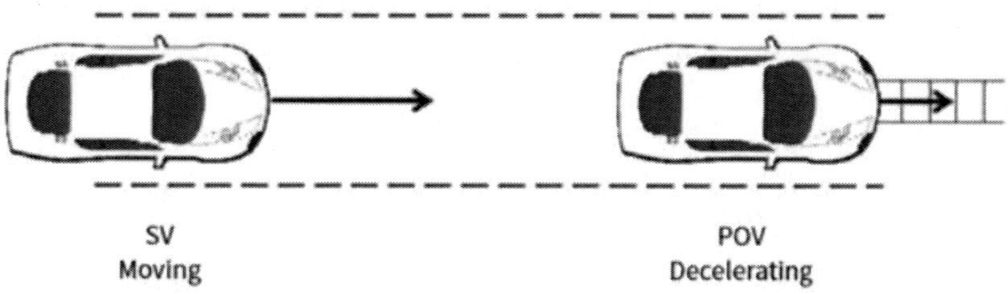

Figure 4. Depiction of Test 3 for NHTSA CIB and DBS System Confirmation Tests.

Test 4 – Subject Vehicle Encounters Steel Trench Plate

This test evaluates the ability of the system to suppress activations when presented with a scenario that may cause a false positive. For this test, the procedure is similar to that of Test 1, however an STP is placed in the center of the travel lane in lieu of a POV. The STP is large and metallic, and significantly reflects a radar signal, thus potentially confusing the FCW/AEB. Test 4 ascertains whether the system under test can discern the STP from a real threat and suppress any activations. The SV is driven at a constant speed directly towards and over the STP. This test is depicted in Figure 5.

Figure 5. Depiction of Test 4 for NHTSA CIB and DBS System Confirmation Tests.

ADAS-Enabling Sensors

Features like FCW and AEB do not replace the driver; instead they can support the driver who is ultimately responsible for vehicle control at all times. The systems that are intended to assist the driver, however, must still have the ability to detect and respond to various moving and stationary features in the path of the vehicle. Pedestrians, bicycles, other vehicles, street signs, and lane markings are just a few examples of objects that may affect a vehicle's trajectory. ADAS capabilities are enabled through a combination of sensors and logic, integrated via a communications network and microprocessors on which decision-making algorithms are executed. Sensors provide the vehicle with information about its operating conditions and surroundings. They measure quantities such as light intensity, radio waves, and inertial forces. Different types of sensors provide different types of information with different features (e.g., sensitivity and resolution) and limitations (e.g., road and weather conditions). Certain algorithms may require long-range distance measurements, whereas others may depend upon accurate identification of nearby objects. ADAS platforms typically integrate multiple types of sensors in order to deliver optimal results across their various algorithms, which may include radar, light detection and ranging (LiDAR), camera, and ultrasonic sensors, for example. Table 2 lists radar, LiDAR, and ultrasonic sensor characteristics and applications for various ADAS.

Algorithms for FCW, AEB, and ACC not only require the ability to detect objects in the path of the vehicle over a relatively long distance, but also require accurate measurements of their relative position and speed. This is commonly done using forward-facing radio detection and ranging (i.e., radar). Radar utilizes waves in the radiofrequency or microwave portion of the electromagnetic spectrum, which are transmitted in the directions of interest.

For automotive systems, this is often the forward direction, but may include other directions as well (e.g., for use in reverse automatic emergency braking and rear cross-traffic monitoring). A portion of the transmitted energy is reflected off the surfaces of objects in the path of the vehicle and is then detected by a receiving antenna. Figure 6 (a) shows an example of an automotive radar sensor component. The system contains a set of transmitting and receiving antennas (Figure 6(b)), as well as microcontroller-based circuitry to drive the output waveform and process incoming signals (Figure 6(c)).

Radar sensors are characterized as long-range (approximately 10–250+ meters), mid-range (1–100 meters), and short-range (0.15–30 meters), with the range determined by the amount of power transmitted (Figure 7). Forward-facing radar sensors used for collision avoidance and ACC are typically mounted in the grille or front bumper of the vehicle and configured for long-range detection. Radar sensors present in other locations are more likely to be configured for short-range or mid-range detection, depending on the intended application.

Analogous to radar, light detection and ranging (LiDAR) sensors utilize optical frequencies within the electromagnetic spectrum in place of radar's radiofrequency electromagnetic waves. More precisely, laser beam pulses in the near-infrared spectrum are transmitted thousands (or tens of thousands) of times per second, and the time delay between each transmitted pulse and its reflected counterpart is used to determine the distance to the interfering obstacle. While radio waves experience less attenuation and are better suited for longer distances, the shorter-wavelength light waves can resolve smaller features and are therefore able to generate higher resolution image maps. Light waves, however, are more strongly impacted by scattering surfaces such as water droplets (e.g., rain, snow, or fog) and particles (e.g., dust or smog), and therefore LiDAR sensors are subject to noise effects in adverse weather conditions. Figure 8(a) shows an example of an automotive LiDAR sensor. Inside the protective enclosure, the system is mounted on a central rotary bearing which allows it to spin a full 360° to scan the vehicle's surroundings (Figure 8(b)). Beneath the main circuit board, two arrays of smaller boards arranged in a parallel configuration contain sets of optical transmitter-receiver pairs (Figure 8(c)). Mirrors are used to guide the light to and from the lenses on the opposite side of the sensor.

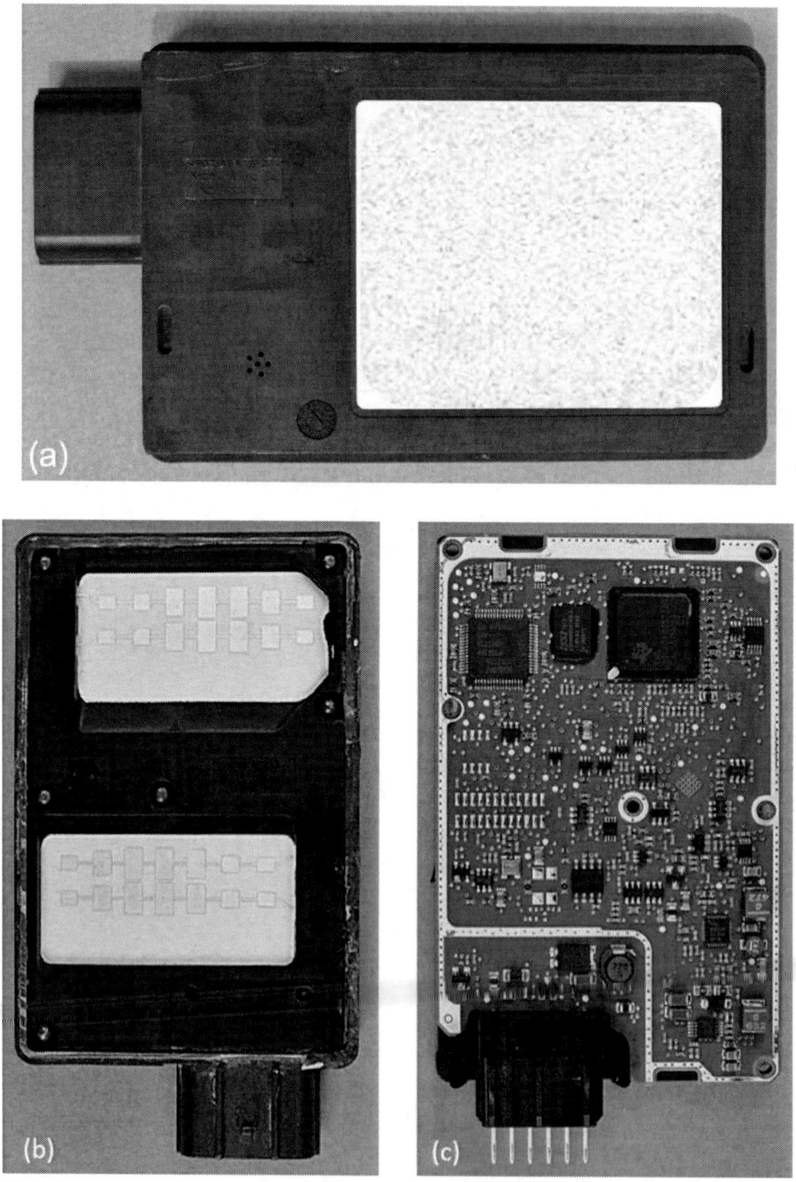

Figure 6. Exemplar automotive radar sensor and internal circuitry. Separate antennas provide transmission and reception of radio wave signals which provide data about the proximity of surrounding objects.

Radar Type	Long-Range Radars	Medium-Range Radars	Short-Range Radars
Range (m)	10–250	1–100	0.15–30
Azimuthal field of view (deg.)	±15°	±40°	±80°
Elevation field of view (deg.)	±5°	±5°	±10°
Applications	Automotive cruise control	Lane-change assist, cross-traffic alert, blind-spot detection, rear-collision warning	Park assist, obstacle detection, precrash

Classification can be made based on the operating frequency into 24–29 GHz and 76–81-GHz bands [12].

Figure 7. Classification of automotive radars based on range measurement capability [10].

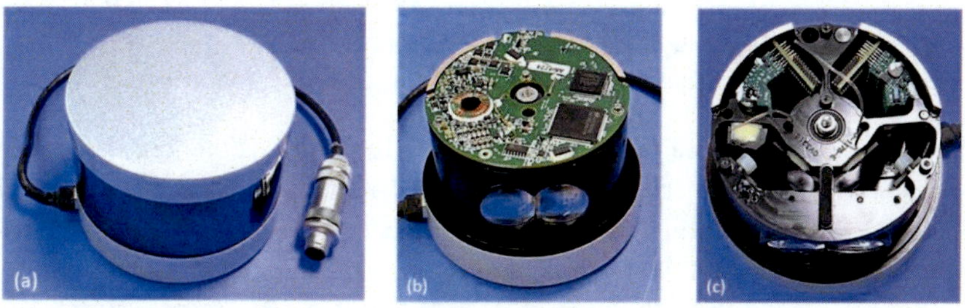

Figure 8. Exemplar automotive LiDAR sensor and internal circuitry. Opposing arrays of transmit-receive pairs emit and detect optical signals as the sensor rotates 360° about a central axis.

LiDAR sensors are often mounted on top of the vehicle and utilize rotating mirrors or prisms to project the laser beam in various directions. A series of stationary LiDAR sensors may also be used; these point in a fixed direction and cover a field of view typically between 90° and 120°. LiDAR sensors are considerably more expensive than radar and other types of sensors since they comprise a laser source, complex optic,s and signal processing logic, but they are becoming more affordable as technology and competition drive advancements.

ADAS-enabled vehicles may employ one or more cameras to provide the driver with enhanced visibility to the vehicle's surroundings and also serve as a data source for object identification algorithms that assist in functions such as collision prevention, lane monitoring, and navigation. Camera sensors are less expensive than LiDAR sensors and have the added benefit of being able to distinguish colors, which makes them valuable for identifying features within a detected shape. Their main drawback is that they generate a flat image as compared to LiDAR's three-dimensional map, thus making distance measurements challenging from a single sensor. Furthermore, they are less reliable under low-light conditions. An example of a forward-facing automotive camera system is shown in Figure 9.

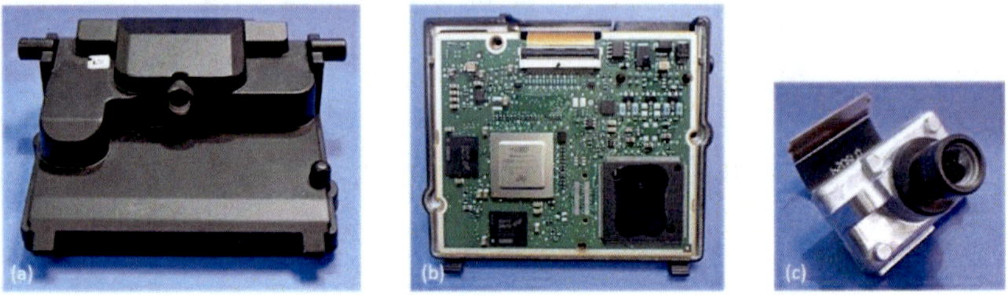

Figure 9. Windshield-mounted automotive camera system consisting of an internally mounted camera connected to a multi-core high-speed data processing network.

Forward-facing cameras are often used to identify potential hazards in a vehicle's path such as pedestrians, animals, bicycles, and other vehicles. Accurate identification of approaching objects is critical to anticipate their expected, or potential, behaviors, and camera data are often paired with that from radar or other sensors to assist in decision-making processes. Cameras may be utilized for functions that require the ability to distinguish contrasting features, such as lane markings on pavement or text on street signs. When paired with rear- and side-facing cameras, such as in parking assist features, the driver may be provided with a full view of the surrounding environment for assistance in parking, blind spot monitoring, rear cross traffic monitoring, and rearward emergency braking.

Short-distance applications such as parking assist and self-parking often utilize data provided through a series of ultrasonic sensors mounted within the front and rear bumper covers of the vehicle. These sensors transmit and receive pulsed ultrasonic waves, typically in the 40–70 kilohertz (kHz) range, that are reflected from nearby objects, some of which may be a collision risk. An automotive ultrasonic sensor is shown in Figure 10(a). The transducer is located within a remote attachment, which is connected to a potted circuit board through a twisted pair of wires (Figure 10(b)).

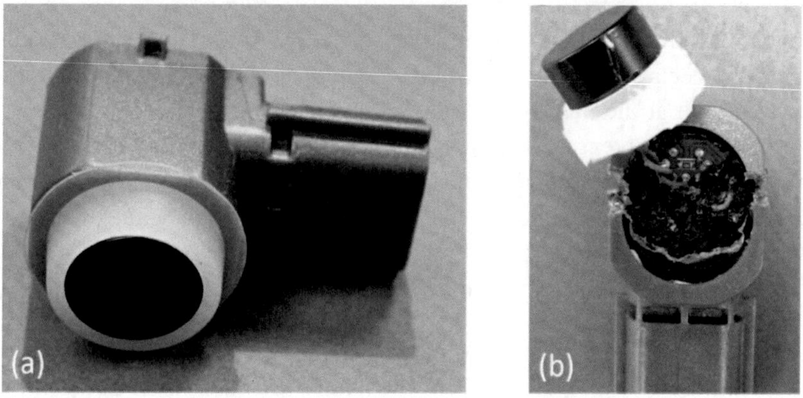

Figure 10. Exemplar automotive ultrasonic sensor. The transducer is remotely attached to the circuit board via a twisted pair of wires.

Ultrasonic waves are acoustic and their performance is dependent on the speed of sound in the air, which is approximately 344 meters per second at 20°C, but is subject to change with differences in temperature (approximately 0.17% per Celsius degree) and air composition. High humidity increases the rate of signal attenuation; decreasing the sensing range, external noise in the target frequency range, and strong air currents and turbulence can also impact signal detection. Ultrasonic sensors may utilize temperature compensation via either an internal temperature sensor or a reference ultrasonic device aligned to a fixed structure.

Table 2. Comparison of ADAS perception sensors

Variable	Sensor Type		
	Radar	LiDAR	Ultrasonic
Wavelength	12.5 mm, 3.9 mm	905 nm, 1550 nm	20–500 kHz
Distance	Short to Long Range	Short to Medium Range	Short Range
Resolution	Low-Medium	High	Low
Weather Sensitivity	Relatively insensitive to weather conditions	Signal attenuation in rain, snow, and fog	Sensitive to temperature, air flow; Attenuation in high humidity
Applications	Detection of objects in a fixed direction	3-D mapping of vehicle's surroundings	Short-distance detection of objects

Data obtained from the various ADAS sensors (radar, LiDAR, etc.) are often supplemented by measurements from inertial sensors, a class of devices consisting of accelerometers and gyroscopes that are used for quantifying linear and rotational accelerations, respectively. Automotive inertial sensors include electro-mechanical devices comprised of a mass-spring-damper system built at the micro- or nano-scale using fabrication techniques similar to those of the integrated circuit. The mass structure is often made of silicon or a metallic film, suspended above a silicon substrate, which is free to move in one or more axes. Changes in the structure's position with respect to the substrate are measured through changes in capacitance, piezoresistance, or other properties. Sensors are targeted for different applications based on axis mode (e.g., linear or rotational), orientation (e.g., lateral or vertical), and sensitivity (e.g., size of the structure or suspension flexibility), with high-g accelerometers commonly used for crash detection and low-g accelerometers commonly used for functions such as active suspension and active braking systems.

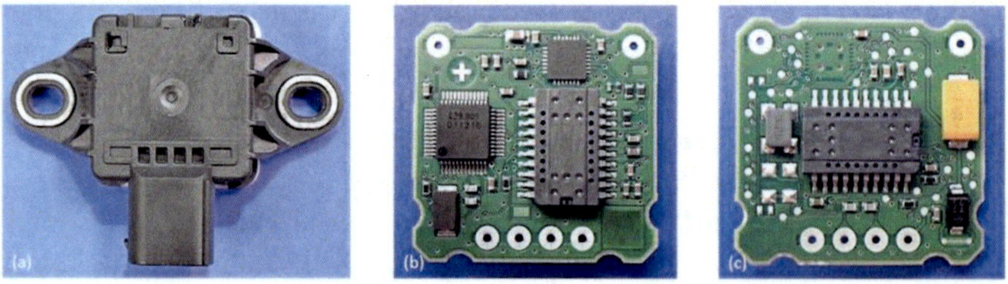

Figure 11. Exemplar automotive IMU device and internal circuitry. Two integrated circuit devices (one on each side of the circuit board) combine accelerometer and gyroscope data to provide navigational assistance and increase sensor precision.

An inertial measurement unit (IMU) is a device that integrates multiple inertial sensors into a single system. A magnetometer that measures the earth's magnetic field may also be incorporated to establish an absolute heading and provide corrections to inertial sensor data. IMUs are often used as a means of sensor fusion within the overall ADAS system, allowing for data from multiple sources to be combined in a coherent manner. Since inertial sensors are not subject to the same ambient effects as perception sensors, IMUs can help verify and adjust their data (e.g., tilt offsets or vibration cancellation). Navigation algorithms depend upon IMU data to refine global navigation satellite system position data, enabling a more precise determination of the vehicle's location, orientation, and velocity, especially in locations where satellite signals are unavailable or inconsistent (e.g., in a tunnel or near tall buildings). Finally, IMUs may be used as a fail-safe in the event that the perception sensors become inoperable, continuing to track the vehicle's position, orientation, and velocity for a short period in a process referred to as dead reckoning. Figure 11 shows an example of an automotive IMU. Its circuit board has two different sensor integrated circuits, oriented perpendicular to each other, designed to measure data along different axes. Temperature sensing and signal processing capabilities are also incorporated into the device.

Sensing Limitations – Considerations Given an Incomplete Picture of the World

Each type of sensor used for ADAS has inherent limitations. Sensors provide a partial view of the physical environment. Radar sensors provide key information to enable ADAS features including FCW and AEB. As an example, this section outlines some of the sensing limitations of automotive radar, and offers some commentary on how these are accounted for in forward-facing collision mitigation systems. When assessing radar sensors for automotive applications, several parameters are usually considered for specific applications, including:

- *Detection range.* This is important for the performance of a single sensor, and also for multiple sensors while long, medium, and short-range radar sensors are required in a certain configuration.
- *Azimuth field of view.* This is important for the angular coverage of the horizontal direction perpendicular to the line of sight.
- *Elevation field of view.* This is important for angular converge of the vertical direction perpendicular to the line of the sight.
- *Range accuracy.* This is important for assessing the accuracy of detection range as mentioned above.
- *Angle accuracy.* This is important for assessing the accuracy of the field of view angles as mentioned above.
- *Velocity accuracy.* This is important for assessing the velocity estimation.
- *Power consumption.* This is important for assessing the power consumed by the sensor.

Distance Measurement

Radar measures the distance of forward objects based on the waveform of the radio signals. When transmitted in a pulsed form, time of flight (also called transit time) can be measured between sending and receiving returned signals, which is used to estimate distance to a forward object. When transmitted in a continuous format, distances are extracted from frequency shifts encountered either due to frequency-modulated waves or the Doppler effect.

Speed Measurement

In general, radar measures the speed of a moving object by having a memory of the measured distance of the object. When the time duration is known, it is sufficient to calculate the speed. This general method applies to both the direction along the line of sight from the radar to the object and the perpendicular direction. In contrast, most modern radar systems use the Doppler effect to measure speed. These Doppler radar systems enable quick speed measurement without the need for memory because they utilize a signal that is coherent or phase synchronized. This method can be applied only to the direction along the line of sight from the radar to the object since the frequency shift from the Doppler effect contains no information about the movement in the direction perpendicular to the line of sight.

Radar Cross Section

The radar cross section (RCS) is the signature of a radar detectable object. RCS is defined as the area intercepting an amount of power, which if radiated isotropically produces the same received power in the radar. It is determined by a number of factors including size, surface angles, shape, and material of the object. Table 3 shows ranges of RCS for representative objects encountered in automotive driving.

In addition to detecting objects during driving, RCS is also used for software verification and testing in the design and development of ADAS. For example, real-time estimation mechanisms of RCS have been proposed for ADAS simulation, aimed to enable math-based virtual development and testing of ADAS [11, 12]. Human mannequins with an RCS similar to that in a real human have been used to assess the accuracy of automotive sensors [13].

Table 3. Example of radar cross sections of typical objects encountered by automotive radar

Object	RCS in square meters
Automobile/Small truck	100–200
Bicycle	2
Human	1
Birds	0.001–0.01

Radar Characteristics in ADAS Test Protocols

Until the adoption of the harmonized global vehicle target (GVT), NHTSA used the strikable surrogate vehicle (SSV) [14] for its AEB test procedures [8, 9]. The SSV has a body structure like the rear end of a 2011 Ford Fiesta, making its physical appearance representative of high-volume passenger vehicles on the road at the time it was developed (Figure 12).

One of the requirements for the SSV is that it should appear realistic (i.e., be interpreted the same as an actual vehicle) to automotive radar. To meet that requirement, several design considerations were put into place, including:

- Bumper corners were rounded.
- The simulated rear window was made from Kevlar (a radar-transparent material) rather than carbon fiber (highly radar-reflective).
- A radar-absorbing mat was secured to the inside of the SSV's rear bulkhead behind the simulated rear window.

Updates to AEB test protocols in NHTSA's New Car Assessment Program stipulate the assessment of test vehicles in response to the GVT. The GVT meets the specifications for surrogate test vehicles stipulated in the International Organization for Standardization's (ISO) 19206-3:2021 Standard, which defines requirements for passenger vehicle 3-D targets for assessment of active safety functions [15]. The ISO 19206-3:2021 standard's Annex C specifies radar-specific recognition properties and measurements. Specifically, seven RCSs are considered, as shown in Figure 13.

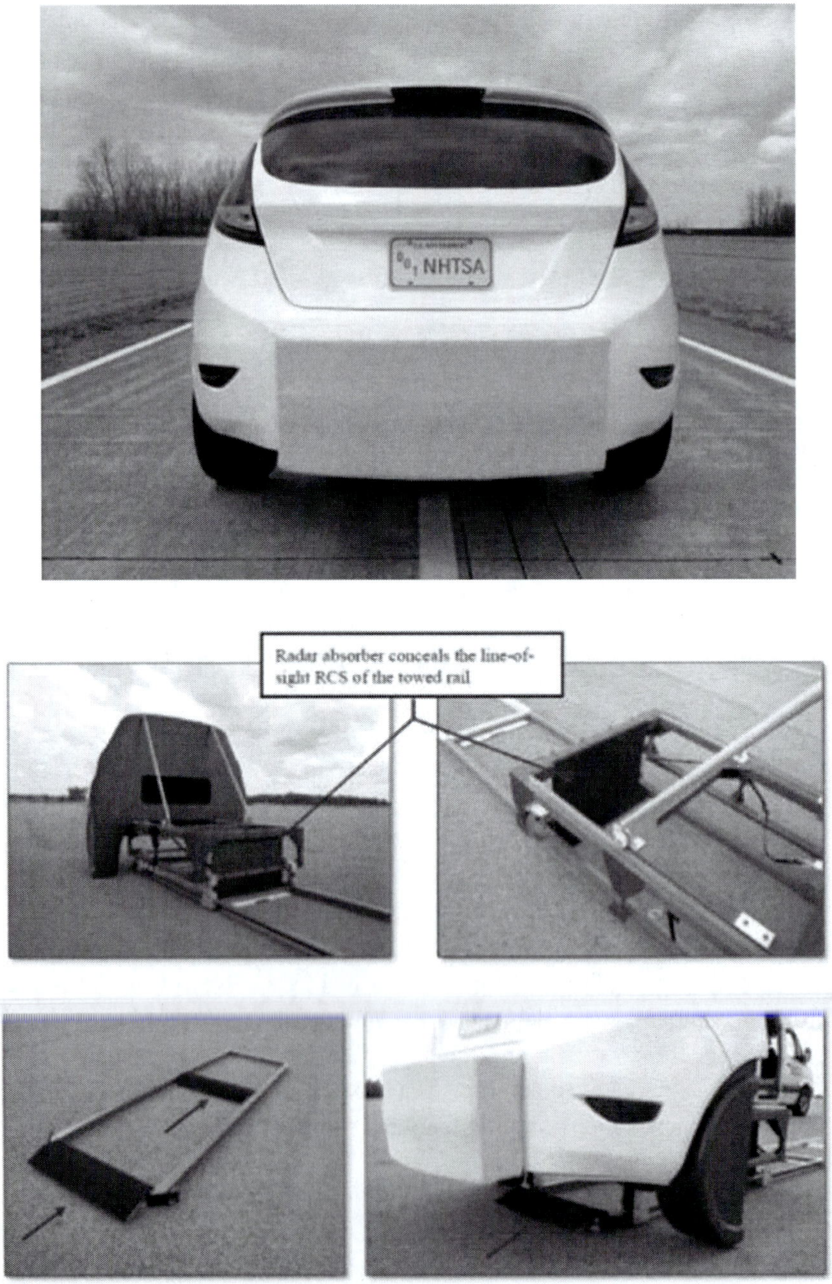

Figure 12. SSV used by NHTSA for AEB test procedures including construction details and features [14].

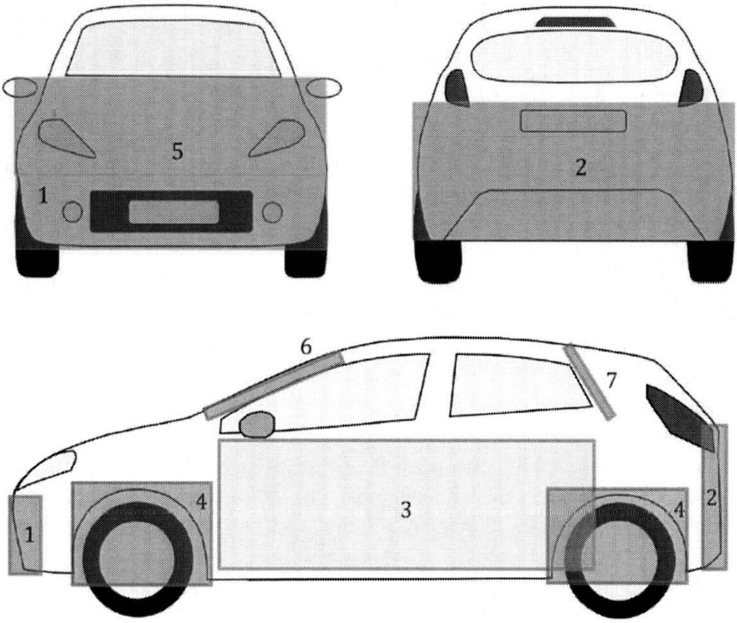

Figure 13. Distribution of RCS in the GVT. 1. Front bumper; 2. Rear bumper; 3. Side panels; 4. Wheel casings; 5. Front; 6. A-pillar; 7. C-pillar. Adapted from ISO 19206-3:2021 [15].

Radar in Automated Driving Systems

Relative to ADAS-equipped vehicles (SAE level 0–2), ADS equipped vehicles (SAE level 3 or higher) may carry a larger number of radar devices. It was proposed that a typical radar-perception configuration for autonomous driving should contain a minimum of seven radars, which include four short-range radars to have 360° coverage; two mid-range forward-looking and rearward-looking radars; and one forward-looking, long-range radar [16]. In many ADS test vehicles, there are 10 or more radar devices.

Future Sensor Technology Development

The future of sensors for automotive applications remains to be seen as they are continuously under development and the supporting technologies are expected to continue to evolve, propelled by increased market demand.

Concurrently, the expected cost for these sensors will also decrease even as the technologies advance, making more sensors, and more sophisticated sensors, accessible at a lower price point. Additionally, the utilization of sensor fusion methodologies, in which multiple sensor types are combined in an ADAS feature, some of a particular sensor's limitations may be mitigated through use of a complementary, but different sensor.

References

[1] SAE International. 2021. "Taxonomy and Definitions for Terms Related to Driving Automation Systems for On-Road Motor Vehicles J3016_202104." Warrendale, PA: SAE International.

[2] American Automobile Association, Consumer Reports, J. D. Power, National Safety Council, PAVE, and SAE International. 2022. "Clearing the Confusion: Common Naming for Advanced Driver Assistance Systems." Last Updated July 25, 2022, Accessed August 2023. Available from https://newsroom.aaa.com/wp-content/uploads/2023/02/Clearing-the-Confusion-One-Pager-New-Version-7-25-22.pdf.

[3] Cicchino, Jessica B. 2017. "Effectiveness of forward collision warning and autonomous emergency braking systems in reducing front-to-rear crash rates." *Accident Analysis & Prevention* 99:142-152.

[4] Mercedes-Benz. 2001. "S-Class Brochure."

[5] Acura. 2005. "2006 Acura RL Press Kit." Last Updated August 17, 2005, Accessed August 2003. Available from https://acuranews.com/en-US/releases/.

[6] NHTSA Benefits Working Group. 1996. "Preliminary Assessment of Crash Avoidance Systems Benefits." Washington, DC: NHTSA.

[7] National Highway Traffic Safety Administration (NHTSA). 2023. "Proposed Rule - Federal Motor Vehicle Safety Standards: Automatic Energy Braking Systems for Light Vehicles. Document ID NHTSA-2023-0021-0007. 49 CFR Parts 571 and 596." Washington, DC: NHTSA.

[8] National Highway Traffic Safety Administration (NHTSA). 2015. "NHTSA-2015-0006-0025 - Crash Imminent Brake System Performance Evaluation." Washington, DC: NHTSA.

[9] National Highway Traffic Safety Administration (NHTSA). 2015. "NHTSA-2015-0006-0026 - Crash Imminent Brake System Performance Evaluation Confirmation Test." Washington, DC: NHTSA.

[10] Patole, Sujeet M., Murat Torlak, Dan Wang, and Murtaza Ali. 2017. "Automotive radars: A review of signal processing techniques." *IEEE Signal Processing Magazine* 34(2):22-35.

[11] Li, Xin, and Weiwen Deng. 2017. "Real-Time Estimation of Radar Cross Section for ADAS Simulation." Warrendale, PA: SAE International.

[12] Owaki, T., and T. Machida. "Real-time data-driven estimation of radar cross-section of vehicles," in *Proceedings of the 2020 IEEE/SICE International Symposium on System Integration (SII)*, 2020, 737-742.

[13] Marchetti, Emidio, Rui Du, Ben Willetts, Fatemeh Norouzian, Edward G. Hoare, Thuy Yung Tran, Nigel Clarke, Mikhail Cherniakov, and Marina Gashinova. 2018. "Radar cross-section of pedestrians in the low-THz band." *IET Radar, Sonar & Navigation* 12(10):1104-1113.

[14] National Highway Traffic Safety Administration (NHTSA). 2014. "NHTSA-2012-0057-0037 - Automatic Emergency Braking System (AEB) Research Report." Washington, DC: NHTSA.

[15] International Organization for Standardization (ISO). 2021. "ISO 19206-3:2021. Road vehicles—Test devices for target vehicles, vulnerable road users and other objects, for assessment of active safety functions—Part 3: Requirements for passenger vehicle 3D targets " Geneva, Switzerland: ISO.

[16] Sun, Shunqiao, Athina P. Petropulu, and H. Vincent Poor. 2020. "MIMO Radar for Advanced Driver-Assistance Systems and Autonomous Driving: Advantages and Challenges." *IEEE Signal Processing Magazine* 37(4):98-117. doi: 10.1109/MSP.2020.2978507.

Biographical Sketches

Michelle Kuykendal, PhD, PE, CFEI, CVFI

Dr. Kuykendal's expertise is in electrical and electronic systems, including advanced driver assistance systems (ADAS), automotive electronics, consumer electronics, electric vehicles (EVs) and other battery powered devices. She specializes in evaluating the safety of electrical system designs including failure analysis and root cause investigations. Dr. Kuykendal has expertise in the evaluation of ADAS technologies including efficacy under diverse environmental conditions, variability in design implementation and sensor utilization, and performance across a wide variety of scenarios. Her evaluations are supported by rigorous design analyses in addition to extensive performance and simulated-failure testing.

Dr. Kuykendal's work focuses on the analysis of complex control systems, large-scale and small-scale lithium-ion batteries coupled with their charging and protection circuitry, device construction quality, and complete system functionality and performance. Dr. Kuykendal works extensively on evaluating the safety of consumer and automotive electronics by performing component and system-level design reviews coupled with electrical testing and on-site inspections. She regularly performs failure analyses and fire investigations relating to home, automotive, and industrial claims.

Dr. Kuykendal received her Ph.D. in Bioengineering from the Georgia Institute of Technology School of Electrical and Computer Engineering in which she developed high-throughput closed-loop analysis techniques for evaluating the efficacy of electrical stimulation on neural tissue. Her work encompassed hardware design, software development, real-time video analysis of neural activation, and closed-loop system control. She is a licensed Professional Engineer in the State of Arizona.

Melissa L Mendias, PhD, PE, CFEI

Dr. Melissa Mendias is an experienced electronics and systems engineer who spent nearly ten years working in a high-volume semiconductor manufacturing environment in both process and yield engineering. She works at Exponent as an engineering consultant where she has established expertise in automotive electronics including advanced driver assistance systems (ADAS), model based systems engineering (MBSE), and failure analysis studies of electrical systems for a variety of applications. Dr. Mendias received her Ph.D. in Electrical Engineering from Michigan Technological University where her research involved technology development for CMOS-integrated MEMS sensors with an emphasis on accelerometers. She is a licensed professional engineer in the state of Arizona and is also a certified fire and explosion investigator.

Sean Scally, M.Sc.

Mr. Scally's education and professional background cover a range of vehicle engineering topics associated with emerging technologies in passenger and commercial vehicles including testing and evaluating ADAS systems and how drivers interact with them. Mr. Scally holds a M.Sc. in Mechanical Engineering from Delft University of Technology in the Netherlands. In collaboration with Volvo Group Trucks Technology he has studied the performance of forward collision mitigation systems in commercial vehicles. With Exponent, Mr. Scally has investigated and evaluated the design and performance of various ADAS features and enabling technology for passenger cars and commercial vehicles.

Liyu Wang, PhD, PE, CSWA

Liyu Wang specializes in design, control and testing of electromechanical systems, as well as time-series data analysis. As a licensed professional engineer, he provides technical and scientific consultancy to clients on some of the most challenging industry problems. As a certified developer in machine learning, he developed fault diagnosis algorithms for intelligent car manufacturing by integrating physics engines, semantic web technologies, signal processing, and artificial intelligence. As a certified mechanical designer and trained robotics scientist, he designed and developed a number of robotic systems ranging from vertical climbing robots, reconfigurable end-effectors, legged robots, to an automated repairing system. He is the author of a book in robotics and 25+ peer reviewed papers. He received postdoctoral training from the University of California at Berkeley, a doctoral degree in mechanical engineering from ETH Zurich, and master's degree in engineering from the University of Oxford.

Chapter 10

Medical Robotics and Computing

Yulia Malkova[1,*]
Anirudh Sharma[2]
and Nadia Barakat[3]
[1]Exponent, Inc, New York, NY, USA
[2]Exponent, Inc., Bowie, MD, USA
[3]Exponent, Inc., Natick, MA, USA

Abstract

Minimally invasive medical robotics is rapidly gaining popularity as a cutting-edge field that revolutionizes surgical procedures and expedites patient recovery. This chapter examines advancements in medical robotics, focusing on commercially successful medical robotic devices that have gained Food and Drug Administration (FDA) clearance. It encompasses various categories of robots and their designs, covers medical device manufacturers' obligations, and outlines the prerequisites for FDA approval, contingent on the device's classification. Given that medical robotics is currently in an evolving stage, it is imperative to address the obstacles it confronts and contemplate the future trajectory of this field. Furthermore, the significance of computational modeling and simulation in design, validation, and verification of such devices and clinical trials is underscored.

Keywords: medical device, medical robotic systems, autonomous robotics, telesurgery, minimally invasive surgeries, robotic surgery, computer modeling and simulation, design verification, clinical trial design

* Corresponding Author's Email: ymalkova@exponent.com.

In: Computer Engineering Applications …
Editor: Brian D'Andrade
ISBN: 979-8-89113-488-1

Introduction

Over the past few decades, medical robotics has seen substantial growth, encompassing assistive devices and sophisticated surgical systems. This dynamic field continues to evolve, significantly influencing the trajectory of healthcare. Notably, there's a rising demand for robotic surgeries, driven by their clear advantages over traditional methods. Surgical robotic systems empower surgeons, allowing access to challenging anatomical areas and delivering unparalleled precision. This chapter investigates various types of surgical robots, emphasizing their control by surgeons through dedicated consoles.

In the realm of advancing medical technology, computer modeling plays a pivotal role in developing and evaluating new medical devices and therapies. With the remarkable growth in computational power, these models simulate intricate biological processes within the human body, offering predictive insights into potential therapies, medical devices, and physiological responses. The integration of computer modeling into the medical device development process is indispensable, yielding cost efficiencies, facilitating virtual testing for safety assurance, and providing essential data to meet regulatory requirements.

Minimally invasive robotic surgery

Definition of Minimally Invasive Surgery

Minimally invasive surgery is a medical procedure performed with small incisions or through natural openings in the body, such as nostrils or the mouth, instead of large incisions for traditional open surgery. The minimally invasive procedures typically include laparoscopic, endoscopic, robotic, and other similar techniques. The main approach of minimally invasive procedures is to minimize damage to the surrounding tissues and reduce post-surgical complications, meaning shorter hospital stays and faster recovery. In addition, typical minimally invasive surgery is often less painful and results in smaller scars and a lower risk of infections compared to traditional open (i.e., non-minimally invasive) surgery. Minimally invasive procedures encompass a broad spectrum of medical techniques spanning various specialties. These include laparoscopic surgical procedures in general surgery, arthroscopy for joint inspection and treatment, coronary angioplasty for opening narrowed or blocked arteries, robotic-assisted surgery (RAS), laser eye surgery, radiofrequency ablation, and minimally invasive thoracic and urologic surgical procedures.

Specialized equipment is a prerequisite for minimally invasive surgery due to the high accuracy and precision required, necessitating specialized training for both surgeons and nurses. Proficiency in handling such advanced technology is crucial to achieve successful outcomes. Surgeons and their teams are mandated to undergo extensive training. Additionally, it is essential to acknowledge that not all procedures can be adapted to a minimally invasive approach.

Minimally invasive surgical techniques are in a constant state of progress, continually enhancing the capabilities and precision of surgical tools. A clear trend is emerging towards increasing the autonomy of these procedures, effectively reducing the potential for human error. Without a doubt, minimally invasive surgeries have revolutionized the medical field, expanding the scope of treatable conditions and driving innovations in various other medical domains.

Development of Robotic Surgery

Robotics has experienced remarkable advancements, particularly in the medical field. Doctors now have access to various medical robotic devices that perform minimally invasive surgeries, which benefit patients by aiding rehabilitation, among other factors. This rapid progress in medical robotics can be attributed to significant hardware advancements, which have consequently fueled enhancements in computational modeling, software development, and image processing.

During the 1980s, advancements in both hardware and software played a significant role in shaping the impact of human-controlled medical robotics. The National Aeronautics and Space Administration (NASA) had a substantial impact in advancing human-operated robotic surgery. Collaborating with the Ames Research Center, they developed the concept of telepresence surgery (i.e., telesurgery) via the virtual environment. Recognizing the immense potential, Scott Fisher and Joe Rosen from the Department of Plastic Surgery at Stanford University's Stanford Research Group, collaborating with Phil Green of the Stanford Research Institute, explored applying virtual reality to surgical procedures. Their system allows surgeons to manipulate dexterous arms and conduct surgeries on patients remotely [1].

Imaging is essential for enabling robotic surgery. The advancement in magnetic resonance imaging (MRI) and X-ray imaging technology, such as computer tomography (CT), has been pivotal in propelling the development of image-guided robotic surgery. The first recorded instance of applying CT to robotic surgery dates back to 1985, when a robot maneuvered a tube with an inserted needle inside a human brain under a CT scanner [2]. Furthermore, substantial enhancements in optoelectronic tracking systems have resulted in significant strides in motion tracking, seamlessly integrated with robotic surgical systems [3].

Last but certainly not least, robust software development stands out as a significant factor in medical robotics, with appropriate real-time operating systems (RTOS) playing a crucial role. Medical robotics is approaching a state of autonomy due to the development of artificial intelligence (AI) and machine learning (ML), where human supervision may no longer be required. In the context of AI integration in surgical procedures, a common scenario involves a robot (such as a microbot or needle) following a specific path that is defined either by a surgeon or an AI mechanism. The U.S. Food and Drug Administration (FDA) processes an unprecedented volume of product submission applications, many of which involve AI or ML. While in 2020, FDA granted authorization for cardiac ultrasound software that incorporates AI, the regulatory framework for AI/ML-based Software as a Medical Device (SaMD) is still in progress.

Importance and Benefits of Minimally Invasive Robotics Surgery

Based on numerous research studies, robotic procedures demonstrate superiority over traditional laparoscopic procedures. Robotic surgery is typically linked to reduced human errors and less ergonomic strain on the surgeon. Multiple surveys indicated that robotic surgery leads to significantly lower levels of physical discomfort for the surgeon during a procedure compared to both traditional open and laparoscopic surgery [4].

When comparing medical robots to conventional surgical instruments, there are several distinct advantages:

- Robots can offer extended and consistent performance without experiencing fatigue.

- Robots can be programmed to prioritize the needs of the patient.
- Robots have the capability to gather patient data to achieve optimal surgical outcomes and assist in postoperative recovery.
- Robots demonstrate precision and minimize errors compared to traditional surgical procedures.
- Robots have the capability for remote surgery.

Without a doubt, medical robotics is reshaping the healthcare industry, presenting greater opportunities for conducting surgeries with enhanced efficiency and precision.

The Robotic Surgical System

Robotic Surgical System Components

RAS devices are computer-assisted surgical systems that allow surgeons to utilize computer and software technology to perform a range of minimally invasive procedures. It is crucial to highlight that RAS devices are not autonomous; they function as assisting tools and cannot conduct surgery without direct human control, thus functioning as surgical assistants.

The two main types of surgical assistant devices are the surgeon extender and auxiliary surgical support. The surgeon extender, a surgeon-operated robotic device, allows the surgeon to manipulate surgical instruments remotely, often in virtual reality. Employing auxiliary surgical support, the surgeon operates in tandem with the RAS system, benefiting from secondary support such as the system's ability to hold medical instruments [5]. Compatibility with the surgical theater stands as a primary prerequisite for RAS devices.

An RAS surgical extender device consists of a console, a bedside cart, and a separate cart.

- The console is the control center for the surgeon; it is set to see the surgical area. In certain literature, the console is also referred to as the *master*, through which the motions of the surgeon's hands are transmitted back to the robot, which is called the *slave*.

- The bedside cart includes multiple hinged arms (usually three to four) with a high-resolution camera, enabling the review of the surgical area and instruments.
- The separate cart holds hardware and software components for support.

Every piece of equipment must be kept sterile, particularly robot components that touch the patient during surgery. Currently, the most common approach involves using presterilized bags to cover the robot.

Typical examples of RAS devices include scalpels, forceps, graspers, dissectors, scissors, retractors, and suction irrigators.

The current development of surgical extender devices is focused on size and weight minimization of robotic manipulators. Yet, positioning a smaller extender within the patient's body becomes increasingly difficult. To overcome this challenge, a standard solution is to add a passive arm, which has a restricted subset of functions due to reduced degrees of freedom. Hence, such a robotic system is a combination of active and passive mechanisms [5].

Robotic Instrument Manipulation and Control

The choice of control and medical manipulation techniques varies based on the specific robotic system. The human-machine interface (HMI) refers to the technology involved in the interaction between the surgeon and the medical robot. Common HMI choices include teleoperation, or the incorporation of haptic feedback technology, or both. A primary challenge in such systems is to offer valuable and pertinent information to surgeons without overwhelming them with excessive details. The accuracy of information provided by the medical robot is critical to ensure that the surgeon's decisions are not influenced by erroneous data, which could potentially harm the patient [5].

Telesurgery/Teleoperation

The idea of telesurgery was first introduced in 1972, suggested to provide remote surgical care to orbiting astronauts. Telesurgery, often called teleoperation, represents a form of medical robotic surgery enabling surgeons to perform procedures from a distant location. These systems possess the capability to receive and translate real-time surgical data. This functionality presents the chance to deliver life-saving procedures of excellent quality in remote and challenging locations. To ensure seamless operation, however, it requires a consistent internet connection for the telesurgery system and robust feedback such as high-quality video and minimal latency.

da Vinci Medical Robot

One of the most widely recognized and commercially successful examples is the da Vinci medical robot shown in Figure 1. The formal development of the da Vinci robot commenced in 1995 when Intuitive received authorized privileges from SRI International, International Business Machines, and the Massachusetts Institute of Technology (MIT). The initial prototype underwent testing in 1997, and by 1999, the system architecture for the da Vinci system was finalized. Following successful trials, the da Vinci system obtained FDA approval in 2000 [6].

The da Vinci is a master-slave type of robot with three to four robotic arms—one arm is designated for real-time imaging, while the remaining arms serve as tools for the surgeon, including the scalpel, scissors, and bovies, all under the surgeon's control.

The surgeon operates the da Vinci system remotely using the da Vinci console. This console includes a high-definition display that provides the surgeon with a visual feed of the surgical area. Additionally, it features hand controls and pedals. By using hand controls, the surgeon can manipulate the robotic arm, mirroring the surgeon's movements. The pedals serve an additional role, allowing the surgeon to manage functions such as refining camera angles for better views or toggling specific instruments on or off.

Within the operating room, an operating table is positioned alongside a robotic tower. This tower acts as a support for robotic arms. An adjacent video tower delivers high-definition video feeds to medical personnel for the purpose of closely monitoring the procedure. It is crucial to emphasize that the surgeon's placement within the operating room is in accordance with FDA regulations.

The da Vinci system offers a wide range of applications, including gastrointestinal surgeries, transoral robotic surgeries, hysterectomies, myomectomies, prostatectomies, and numerous other types of minimally invasive procedures.

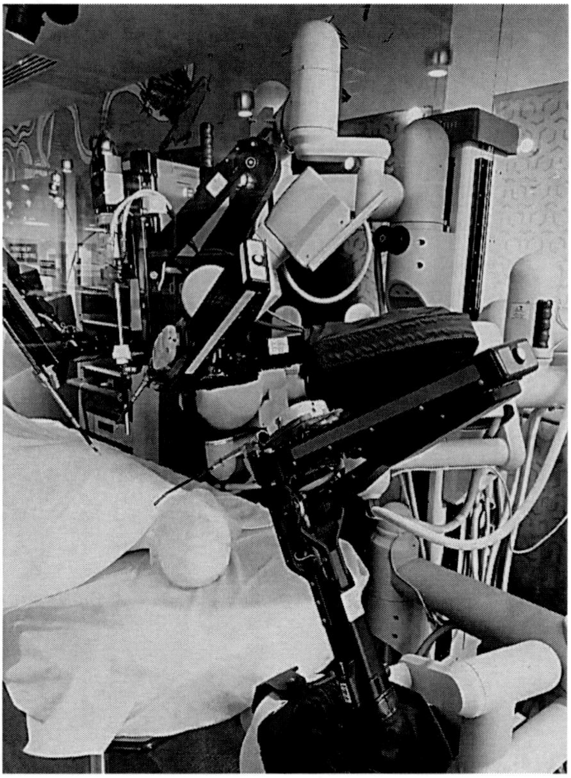

Figure 1. da Vinci robotic system.

Haptic Feedback Surgery Needle Control Systems

Haptic feedback can be categorized separately in medical robotic systems or integrated into a telesurgery system. Haptic feedback involves conveying various sensations, such as vibration, to provide sensory information to the user.

In medical robotics, the integration of haptic feedback is intended to enhance surgical precision by offering surgeons greater control during procedures, thus providing greater accuracy for medical procedures.

Haptic control integration is particularly beneficial for needle control systems where precise needle placement is crucial, for example, in percutaneous procedures.

Haptic feedback is commonly linked to force feedback, which involves the system estimating the forces applied to a patient during a procedure. This estimation often requires the integration of force sensors into the hardware of robotic devices. However, the implementation of this type of feedback for medical robotic systems faces challenges, primarily due to the constraints posed by the surgical environment, making it difficult to establish a robust control system [7].

MSR-5000 REVO-I Surgical Robot System

The REVO-I system is an example of integrating telesurgery with haptic feedback. The MSR-5000 REVO-I surgical robot system, developed in 2015 by the Meere Company in South Korea, resembles the da Vinci system. The MSR-5000 is comprised of an operating table, console, and four arms. The surgeon is offered haptic feedback through the master control unit of the MSR-5000 console [7]. Haptic feedback offers substantial information during tissue manipulation, thus increasing operation precision.

Autonomous Robotic Medical Systems

Amid the surge in AI and the pursuit of autonomous (i.e., self-driving) vehicles, the emergence of autonomous medical devices cannot be overlooked. Just like any autonomous technology, these devices are in their preliminary developmental phases, where the main focus is on ensuring patient safety and the reliability of the robotic systems. Presently, FDA is actively engaged in addressing these concerns and formulating new regulations to ensure the safety of patients.

Smart Tissue Autonomous Robot

The Smart Tissue Autonomous Robot (STAR) is a commercially successful illustration of a medical robotic system with AI integration. STAR was developed by Cambridge Medical Robotics in the United Kingdom, and has received FDA approval. This innovative robot is designed for minimally invasive surgeries. Equipped with a sophisticated vision system and sensors, the STAR system offers real-time feedback control. The presence of a surgeon overseeing the process ensures system accuracy, allowing corrections when necessary. The STAR system integrates trained ML models, enabling it to learn from interactions with the surgeon and evolve over time.

The STAR system presents a diverse array of applications, including laparoscopic surgeries, colorectal surgeries, gynecological surgeries, urological surgeries, and cardiovascular surgeries.

Safety Considerations

FDA Regulations

FDA is responsible for ensuring the safety of various products, including food, drugs, medical devices, among others. In order to get FDA approval for a minimally invasive robotic device, it is first important to understand its class. Each class is associated with the risk of the device, as follows:

- Class I (low-risk devices)
- Class II (moderate risk devices)
- Class III (high-risk devices)

FDA has designated specific pathways for the approval of medical devices—Premarket Notification 510(k), Premarket Approval Application (PMA), and *de novo* classification. The 510(k) application is appropriate in situations where a new medical device is similar to a device previously-approved by FDA. Therefore, the manufacturer can use the 510(k) submission to demonstrate the safety and comparable functionality of the new device based on the approved medical device.

Previously, we discussed minimally invasive robots categorized under telesurgery, which can perform laparoscopic, urological, and gynecological surgeries. These medical robotic systems fall within the Class II classification, specifically labeled "Endoscope and accessories." Since the da Vinci robot obtained FDA clearance in 2000, devices resembling the da Vinci system can pursue a 510(k) application for approval [8].

To obtain FDA approval for a novel medical device that lacks a legally approved predecessor in the Class I or Class II device categories, one can pursue the *de novo* regulatory pathway. It is essential to emphasize that even when a manufacturer opts for the de novo process, they are still obligated to submit a 510(k) application to demonstrate that the new device is not equivalent to any existing devices in the market. Devices categorized under the higher-risk Class III, such as implantable devices, necessitate premarket approval (PMA). This involves demonstrating the safety of a new device for patients, often through the conduct of clinical trials.

Manufacturer Responsibilities

Medical robotic devices are safe and effective to perform certain procedures when used properly, and when surgeons and medical staff undergo proper training.

Primary manufacturer obligations include:

- Developing the medical robotics system to align with safety and performance norms prevalent in the industry.
- Executing risk assessments to mitigate potential risks linked to the medical device.
- Undertaking clinical trials to provide FDA with substantiating evidence regarding the device's safety and functionality.
- Collaborating with FDA by submitting regulatory applications in accordance with the medical device's classification.
- Providing clear and comprehensive instructions for users and technicians.
- Delivering training to healthcare professionals.

Robotic Training and Certification for the Surgeon

Traditional surgical skills are insufficient when it comes to performing minimally invasive robotic surgery. Given the technical complexity of robotic systems, a novel approach to training medical personnel is necessary.

One of the initial training stages involves familiarizing medical personnel with the robotic system itself. This step is crucial to comprehend the system's functionalities and become proficient at its operation. Following this, a more comprehensive user interface training ensues, encompassing a deep understanding of controls and the feedback mechanisms of the robotic system.

Subsequently, surgeons are required to undergo training in manipulating robotic arms through a console. Typically, medical robot manufacturers arrange simulator or virtual reality training sessions. These sessions provide direct feedback to trainees, facilitating skill evaluation.

Last but certainly not least, effective communication within the surgical team, including between nurses and the surgeon, is vital for seamless operation [9].

Advancements and Future Directions for Robotic Surgery

Challenges and Limitations

The primary difficulties associated with minimally invasive robotic systems arise from obfuscated sensory feedback to the surgeon. The control console restricts the surgeon's sensory perception and situational awareness. Consequently, there is a crucial need to enhance and integrate more feedback mechanisms into robotic systems, with haptic feedback as one proposed solution to address this issue. The manufacturer of a medical robot must also give attention to ergonomics to facilitate the interaction between the surgeon and the device [10].

Furthermore, a notable issue arises because minimally invasive surgeries often occur within confined spaces. Surgery in confined spaces has limited room for maneuverability and severely limits the range of movement. Consequently, the design and functionality of these robotic systems must be carefully planned to accommodate this challenge.

The Future of Minimally Invasive Robotic Surgery

Over the last thirty years, a distinct pattern has emerged in the continuous advancement of medical robotics. The field of medical robotics is undergoing rapid evolution, generating substantial interest from both the scientific community and the medical industry. With the ongoing progress of AI, medical robotic systems hold the potential to assist surgeons in their tasks. The currently accessible medical robotic systems in the market can potentially undergo cost reductions and increased availability, expanding patient access to such devices. Moreover, innovations in novel robotics systems are proceeding at a rapid pace, some of which incorporate soft robotics technology into their designs. The integration of computer modeling and simulation into the medical device development process improves the efficiency and safety of these devices. This, in turn, speeds up the development timeline and helps address regulatory challenges. Computer modeling is discussed further in the following sections.

The Role of Imaging in Surgery

Imaging plays a crucial role in various aspects of surgery. In general, this role can be broadly divided into the following categories:

1. *Diagnosis and pre-operative planning:* Medical imaging techniques such as ultrasound, X-rays, CT, and MRI scans provide detailed information about the anatomy and condition of the patient's body before surgery. Surgeons use imaging data to assess the location and extent of abnormalities and contraindications, establish operating trajectories, and determine the optimal surgical approach.
2. *Intra-operative guidance and navigation:* During surgery, real-time imaging can aid surgeons in navigating complex anatomical structures and pinpointing the precise location of operating sites and surrounding structures. Techniques like fluoroscopy and intraoperative CT/MRI scans provide visual guidance, enhancing the accuracy and safety of surgical maneuvers.
3. *Post-operative follow-up and monitoring:* Imaging conducted after surgery tracks the healing process, monitors tissue regeneration, and ensures the absence of complications. It provides essential information for postoperative care and potential interventions. For example, for patients implanted with prostheses or those who have undergone cancer surgery, serial image assessment provides an important monitoring tool for outcome management.

Computer Modeling of Medical Devices and Treatments

With rapid advances in computational speed, increased storage, and improved mathematical algorithms, the adoption of computer modeling and simulation (CM&S) for design and verification of medical devices, drugs, and patient treatment planning is being increasingly adopted in clinical settings [11]. CM&S is also being increasingly adopted by regulatory agencies like FDA in guiding premarket assessment and approval and policy development and implementation. This trend is a natural progression since CM&S complements experimental preclinical and clinical data and optimizes the use of resources by simulating different failure scenarios to ensure device or drug safety. Without the predictive capability of CM&S, empirical testing would be too expensive or time consuming. This is especially true for devices and drugs where physics, first-principles, or pharmacokinetic-based models can be used (rather than statistical models) for the design and verification of devices, drugs, and processes.

In this regard, regulatory agencies like FDA have given the integration of CM&S in premarket approval and policy development top priority, thus encouraging stakeholders to supplement their submissions with CM&S [11].

Design, Verification, and Clinical Validation of Medical Devices

The Centers for Devices and Radiological Health within FDA has drafted a document on design controls for medical devices to provide guidelines to manufacturers that help them balance device design goals for the intended clinical application with meeting regulatory safety requirements (e.g., FDA quality system requirements) [12]. These design controls extend from device inception to the end of the device's lifecycle. The process involves discussions between engineering and clinical teams in each stage, as follows:

1. *Device Design:* Requirements for design inputs, outputs, and safety constraints are specified, often first simulated by a computational model where possible.
2. *Device Verification:* A quality assurance step that confirms the design output at each stage meets initial specifications (i.e., aligns with the design inputs) the team specified at the onset. This may also include failure testing and sensitivity analysis where the power of computational modeling is often leveraged, as well as hardware-in-loop testing that allows real-time evaluation of device data in a simulated environment. One of the outcomes of this analysis can be that certain design parameters are prioritized to meet optimal function and safety.
3. *Design Validation:* In this step, the final function and safety of the device is clinically established either through a clinical trial or through rigorous laboratory testing, which, as part of the process, validates (or invalidates) simulation data.
4. *Design Review:* The final function and safety of the device is assessed by all teams involved in the design process.

The above process allows inclusion of various checks and balances and facilitates better documentation of design controls that can be helpful during premarket assessment.

CM&S can aid in streamlining this process for medical devices with well-established physics that can be modeled and with a sensitivity analysis that can ascertain the most important variables governing device function [11]. A representative area where such device development has been useful is thermal therapies like thermal ablation and hyperthermia, where coupled electromagnetic and heat transfer physics can be solved in complex three-dimensional (3-D) anatomical models using finite element methods [13-15]. Such models allow the incorporation of dynamic characteristics like time- and temperature-dependent blood flow and tissue damage, which mimic clinical realities. These are modeled through ordinary differential equations for lumped approximations and partial differential equations where spatiotemporal modeling of the treatment is desired. Additionally, models developed through well-established physics and known principles can be verified potentially through analytical solutions and validated in preclinical settings using simple geometric tissue phantom models [13-15].

These CM&S verification and validation methods allow failure mode and effects analysis testing, safety assessment, and cross-examination by engineering and clinical teams simultaneously before scaling to clinical applications. Additionally, with methods like hardware-in-loop testing, often the clinical performance of a prototype medical device can be tested with simulations [11].

Clinical Trial Design and Virtual Patient Selection

The goal of any therapy is to improve patient survival. Clinical trials are designed to statistically test the efficacy of a drug or intervention against a disease and improve survival by enrolling patients in various treatment (single-agent or combination therapies) and control groups. The safety profile and the maximum tolerable dose (MTD) are ascertained through dose-escalation studies in early phase I and II trials, and the MTD is scaled to larger populations in phase III trials to statistically test the therapeutic efficacy. However, the approval rates for various therapies for diseases like cancer remain small, resulting in loss of patient benefit from the large amounts of resources expended during a clinical trial (e.g., experimental work, research funding, etc.) [16, 17]. This low success rate, at least in part, can be attributed to non-optimal trial designs in terms of patient population, treatment, and control groups [16, 17]. It is worth noting that the optimal therapy for each patient (e.g., dose, schedule) may be slightly different because of both genomic and phenotypic heterogeneity, even within a given disease (e.g., cancer). As such, the therapeutic dosage and schedule may need to be fine-tuned to each patient in a cohort being treated for the same disease. Patient-specific precision medicine, therefore, is the ideal goal. Computational modeling can aid in both optimal trial design and patient-specific tuning of the therapies.

With advances in high throughput genomic profiling and molecular phenotyping of diseases such as cancer, multiomics, and big data statistics can aid in drawing correlations between patient-specific disease biomarkers as pharmacological targets and treatment response from small molecule therapy or immunotherapeutics. When these correlative computational methods are combined with physiologically-based pharmacokinetic modeling of drug pharmacokinetics in humans and in preclinical models (scaled to humans), and deterministic (i.e., ordinary differential equation or partial differential equation) models of disease (e.g., tumor growth and resistance), inferences can be drawn on mechanistic pathways of drug targeting that are useful in drug screening, rational drug design, and discovery of novel therapeutics [18, 19]. These inferences at the cellular and tissue/tumor level can then be correlated to patient- and population-level data in terms of responders versus non-responders, toxicity profiles, and survival kinetics. ML-based methods that identify patterns in large multi-dimensional datasets can be useful in ascertaining such correlations and predicting treatment responses to novel drugs. Additionally, these data at the cellular, tissue, and patient level are used in computational/systems biology to assemble complex networked disease models where proteins, genes, cytokines, and the immune environment are modeled as interacting elements in a networked system [17, 19, 20].

Deterministic disease models such as tumor progression and cancer resistance to immunotherapy have been modeled successfully using ordinary differential equations and used to translate outcomes at a cellular level to the patient level and further to a population level. These models can further be used to test the robustness of the trial design such as sample size, treatment groups, and randomization [17].

Additionally, with increasing computational power and storage, and the development of AI-based image segmentation tools, highly accurate 3-D anatomical models of tissues, organs, and whole humans can be generated from large radiological image datasets (e.g., MRI, CT) [21, 22]. The advantage of such models is that physical therapies like radiation and thermal therapies, which involve complex multiphysics, can be simulated in such virtual patients for the assessment of safety and efficacy [23, 24]. Since the virtual patients are based on radiological images taken from patients, the models provide an avenue to develop and optimize patient-specific therapies.

References

[1] Faust, Russel A. 2007. *Robotics in Surgery: History, Current and Future Applications*. New York: Nova Sciences Publishers, Inc.

[2] Cleary, K., and C. Nguyen. 2001. "State of the art in surgical robotics: clinical applications and technology challenges." *Comput Aided Surg* 6(6):312-328.

[3] Camarillo, David B., Thomas M. Krummel, and Kenneth J. Salisbury Jr. 2004. "Robotic technology in surgery: past, present, and future." *Am J Surg* 188(4):2-15.

[4] Wee, Ian Jun Yan, Li-Jen Kuo, and James Chi-Yong Ngu. 2020. "A systematic review of the true benefit of robotic surgery: Ergonomics." *Int J Med Robot* 16(4):e2113.

[5] Taylor, Russell H., Arianna Menciassi, Gabor Fichtinger, Paolo Fiorini, and Paolo Dario. 2016. "Medical Robotics and Computer-Integrated Surgery." In *Springer Handbook of Robotics*, edited by Bruno Siciliano and Oussama Khatib, 1657-1684. Heidelberg: Springer Berlin.

[6] Ballantyne, Garth H., and Fred Moll. 2003. "The da Vinci telerobotic surgical system: the virtual operative field and telepresence surgery." *Surgical Clinics* 83(6):1293-1304.

[7] Cepolina, Francesco, and Roberto P. Razzoli. 2022. "An introductory review of robotically assisted surgical systems." *Int J Med Robot* 18(4):e2409.

[8] U.S. Food and Drug Administration (FDA). 2015. Discussion Paper. Robotically-Assisted Surgical Devices. Rockville, MD: FDA.

[9] Silvennoinen, M., J-P. Mecklin, P. Saariluoma, and T. Antikainen. 2009. "Expertise and skill in minimally invasive surgery." *Scand J Surg* 98(4):209-213.

[10] Simaan, Nabil, Rashid M. Yasin, and Long Wang. 2018. "Medical technologies and challenges of robot-assisted minimally invasive intervention and diagnostics." *Ann Rev Control Robot Auton Syst* 1:465-490.

[11] U.S. Food and Drug Administration (FDA). 2021. Assessing the Credibility of Computational Modeling and Simulation in Medical Device Submissions. Draft Guidance for Industry and Food and Drug Administration Staff. Rockville, MD: Centers for Devices and Radiological Health.

[12] U.S. Food and Drug Administration (FDA). 1997. Design Control Guidance For Medical Device Manufacturers. Rockville, MD: Centers for Device and Radiological Health.

[13] Fuentes, David, Rex Cardan, R. Jason Stafford, Joshua Yung, Gerald D. Dodd III, and Yusheng Feng. 2010. "High-fidelity computer models for prospective treatment

planning of radiofrequency ablation with in vitro experimental correlation." *J Vasc Interv Radiol* 21(11):1725-1732.

[14] Yeniaras, E., D. T. Fuentes, S. J. Fahrenholtz, J. S. Weinberg, F. Maier, J. D. Hazle, and R. J. Stafford. 2014. "Design and initial evaluation of a treatment planning software system for MRI-guided laser ablation in the brain." *Int J Comput Assist Radiol Surg* 9(4):659-667.

[15] Sharma, Anirudh, Erik Cressman, Anilchandra Attaluri, Dara L. Kraitchman, and Robert Ivkov. 2022. "Current challenges in image-guided magnetic hyperthermia therapy for liver cancer." *Nanomaterials* 12(16):2768.

[16] Hwang, Thomas J., Daniel Carpenter, Julie C. Lauffenburger, Bo Wang, Jessica M. Franklin, and Aaron S. Kesselheim. 2016. "Failure of investigational drugs in late-stage clinical development and publication of trial results." *JAMA Int Med* 176(12):1826-1833.

[17] Creemers, Jeroen H. A., Ankur Ankan, Kit C. B. Roes, Gijs Schröder, Niven Mehra, Carl G. Figdor, I. Jolanda M. de Vries, and Johannes Textor. 2023. "In silico cancer immunotherapy trials uncover the consequences of therapy-specific response patterns for clinical trial design and outcome." *Nat Commun* 14(1):2348.

[18] Zhuang, Xiaomei, and Lu Chuang. 2016. "PBPK modeling and simulation in drug research and development." *Acta Pharmaceutica Sinica B* 6(5):430-440.

[19] McDonald, Thomas O., Yu-Chen Cheng, Christopher Graser, Phillip B. Nicol, Daniel Temko, and Franziska Michor. 2023. "Computational approaches to modelling and optimizing cancer treatment." *Nat Rev Bioengin*:1-17.

[20] Li, Allen, and Raymond C. Bergan. 2020. "Clinical trial design: Past, present, and future in the context of big data and precision medicine." *Cancer* 126(22):4838-4846.

[21] Christ, Andreas, Wolfgang Kainz, Eckhart G. Hahn, Katharina Honegger, Marcel Zefferer, Esra Neufeld, Wolfgang Rascher, Rolf Janka, Werner Bautz, Ji Chen, Berthold Kiefer, Peter Schmitt, Hans-Peter Hollenbach, Jianxiang Shen, Michael Oberle, Dominik Szczerba, Anthony Kam, Joshua W Guag, and Niels Kuster. 2009. "The virtual family--development of surface-based anatomical models of two adults and two children for dosimetric simulations." *Phys Med Biol* 55(2):N23.

[22] Iacono, Maria Ida, Esra Neufeld, Esther Akinnagbe, Kelsey Bower, Johanna Wolf, Ioannis Vogiatzis Oikonomidis, Deepika Sharma, Bryn Lloyd, Bertram J. Wilm, Michael Wyss, Klaas P. Pruessmann, Andras Jakab, Nikos Makris, Ethan D. Cohen, Niels Kuster, Wolfgang Kainz, and Leonardo M. Angelone. 2015. "MIDA: a multimodal imaging-based detailed anatomical model of the human head and neck." *PloS One* 10(4):e0124126.

[23] Arabi, Hossein, and Habib Zaidi. 2020. "Applications of artificial intelligence and deep learning in molecular imaging and radiotherapy." *Eur J Hybrid Imaging* 4(1):17.

[24] Moche, Michael, Harald Busse, Jurgen J. Futterer, Camila A. Hinestrosa, Daniel Seider, Philipp Brandmaier, Marina Kolesnik, Sjoerd Jenniskens, Roberto Blanco Sequeiros, Gaber Komar, Mika Pollari, Martin Eibisberger, Horst Rupert Portugaller, Philip Voglreiter, Ronan Flanagan, Panchatcharam Mariappan, and Martin Reinhardt. 2020. "Clinical evaluation of in silico planning and real-time

simulation of hepatic radiofrequency ablation (ClinicIMPPACT Trial)." *Eur Radiol* 30(2):934-942.

Biographical Sketches

Yulia Malkova, PhD

With a foundation in robotics, scientific modeling, and thermal/cold plasma applications, Dr. Malkova possesses a broad range of expertise in electrical engineering and applied physics. This knowledge base extends to areas such as power circuits, control theory, device prototyping, and the development of medical devices. Dr. Malkova's academic journey includes a Bachelor of Science in Physics with a focus on Nuclear and Particle Physics from the National Research Nuclear University (MEPhI), Russia in 2013. She further pursued a Master of Science in Physics specializing in Thermonuclear Synthesis Physics from the same institution in 2015. She further achieved a Ph.D. in Electrical Engineering from Drexel University in 2022.

Anirudh Sharma

Dr. Anirudh Sharma is an experienced electrical engineer with over 10 years of expertise at the interface of electrical engineering, materials science, and translational biomedical sciences. Through his PhD, postdoctoral research and published work, he has demonstrated a strong expertise in experimental and computational electromagnetics and nanomagnetics, design, verification and validation of biomedical feedback control devices, thermal therapies for cancer, nanoparticle-based cancer therapies, electromagnetic RF technologies for organ cryopreservation and electromagnetic interference (EMI/EMC) in medical devices and implants. As a Postdoctoral Fellow in the Department of Radiation Oncology at the Johns Hopkins University School of Medicine, Dr. Sharma designed MRI and CT image-guided and computational modeling-based treatment planning workflows that predicted the treatment efficacy of magnetic hyperthermia therapies in canine glioblastoma patients. He experimentally designed, verified, and validated temperature feedback control devices to optimize the thermal treatments in canine patients suffering from glioblastoma. As part of his doctoral research at the University of Minnesota, Dr. Sharma specialized in magnetic nanoparticle design, synthesis, coating and characterization for biomedical and photonic applications. Through this research, he addressed important engineering questions pertaining to the design and properties of nanoparticles, including shape, size, composition, magnetic properties for sensing, surface functionalization, nanoparticle aggregation and integration of this technology with various imaging techniques and platforms. Dr. Sharma has co-chaired various symposia at international conferences focused on biodetection, therapy and biomedical applications of magnetic materials.

Nadia Barakat, PhD

Dr. Barakat is driven by a professional commitment to employ extensive knowledge of engineering principles to improve medical outcomes and make a meaningful contribution to medical imaging. Having held positions at prestigious institutions like Boston Children's Hospital and Shriner's Hospital for Children, she focused her NIH-funded research on establishing Diffusion Tensor Imaging (DTI) as a neurodiagnostic tool in examining the pediatric spinal cord. Her work in this domain was awarded the Derek Hardwood-Nash Award for best paper in pediatric neuroradiology by the American Society of Neuroradiology. Dr. Barakat holds a Bachelor of Science in Electrical Engineering, a Master of Science in Bioengineering, and a Ph.D. in Engineering, from Temple University in Philadelphia, PA.

Index

M

N

O

P

Q

R